WHAT LINCOLN BELIEVED

What Lincoln Believed

The Values and Convictions of America's Greatest President

Michael Lind

DOUBLEDAY

New York   London   Toronto   Sydney   Auckland

PUBLISHED BY DOUBLEDAY
A division of Random House, Inc.
1745 Broadway, New York, New York 10019

DOUBLEDAY and the portrayal of an anchor with a dolphin are
trademarks of Doubleday, a division of Random House, Inc.

Book design by Richard Oriolo

Library of Congress Cataloging-in-Publication Data
Lind, Michael, 1962–
What Lincoln believed : the values and convictions of America's
greatest president / Michael Lind.— 1st ed.
p. cm.
Includes bibliographical references (p.) and index.
1. Lincoln, Abraham, 1809–1865—Political and social views.
2. Lincoln, Abraham, 1809–1865—Philosophy. 3. Social
values—United States. 4. Presidents—United States—Biography.
5. United States—Politics and government—1861–1865. I. Title.

E457.2.L846 2003
973.7'092—dc22
[B]   2004041333

ISBN 0-385-50739-9

PRINTED IN THE UNITED STATES OF AMERICA

June 2005

FIRST EDITION

10 9 8 7 6 5 4 3 2 1

ACKNOWLEDGMENTS

In preparing this study, I have benefited from the patient labor of generations of scholars, only a few of whom could be acknowledged in the notes. I would like to express my gratitude for their efforts.

I am indebted to Adam Bellow, my editor at Doubleday, and to my agent, Kristine Dahl of International Creative Management. In addition, I would like to express my gratitude to Ted Halstead, President of the New America Foundation, and to John C. Whitehead, for his generous support of the Whitehead Senior Fellowship at the New America Foundation.

Contents

———∞∞∞———

ABRAHAM LINCOLN:
THE MYTH AND THE MAN

IN 1863 THE democratic republic as a form of government was rare—
and in danger of extinction.

In Europe, the dominant region of the world, monarchs and aristocrats
were securely in command. The nations of Central and Eastern Europe and
the Balkans were divided among the empires of three dynasties: the Habs-
burgs, the Romanovs, and the Ottomans. Germans who did not live in
Hapsburg lands were ruled by petty dukes and princes in a handful of large
kingdoms, of which the most important, Prussia, was the domain of the
Hohenzollern family. Italy was carved into small and weak states subject to
Habsburg or French domination. Iberia and Scandinavia, too, had their
kings and aristocrats. France was a dictatorship ruled by Louis Napoleon,
who like his uncle had posed as a champion of republican government before declaring himself emperor.

Britain was the most liberal great power in Europe, but it was far from democratic. The monarchy and the House of Lords were hereditary. The House of Commons was elected by a tiny elite of commoners. The Reform Act of 1832 increased the percentage of the adult population in Britain permitted to vote from 1.8 percent to 2.7 percent. Subsequent reform legislation in 1867 and 1884 increased the electorate to 6.4 percent and 12.1 percent, respectively.[1] British colonists in Canada, Australia, and New Zealand were subject to imperial authority, while in India and other parts of the empire nonwhite subjects lacked not only the suffrage but basic civil rights. Although Britain had abolished slavery in its domains in the 1830s and had moved to suppress the transatlantic African slave trade, British authorities and colonists had substituted other kinds of forced labor scarcely better than slavery, such as contract or "coolie" labor.

Outside of Europe and the European empires, the prospects for liberal democracy were even bleaker. From North Africa to the Persian Gulf, the dissolving Ottoman Empire provided a tattered canopy over local rulers and spheres of influence obtained by Britain and France. In the Chinese empire, weakened by British and French aggression and local rebellions, the only tradition of governance was one of despotism tempered by bureaucracy. Black Africa, a patchwork of kingdoms and tribes, would soon be incorporated into a handful of European colonial empires.

In this world of empires, monarchs, and hereditary nobles, republics were scarce. In Europe the Swiss republic and the tiny Republic of San Marino were oddities. In Africa the only republics were those of Dutch-descended Boer farmers and the struggling Republic of Liberia, founded by the United States as a home for former slaves. The largest state in Latin America, Brazil, was an empire ruled by a Portuguese monarch. The Spanish monarchy continued to govern Cuba, Puerto Rico, and other island possessions. The former mainland colonies of Spain, from Mexico to Argentina, were republican in form. But since they had gained their independence, most of these Latin American states had oscillated between dictatorship and anarchy. In 1863 much of Mexico, the home of a series of failed republics, was under the control of a Hapsburg princeling named Maximilian, who had been installed as "Emperor of Mexico" by the French emperor Louis Napoleon.

Two waves of liberal and democratic revolutions—the first beginning with the French Revolution in 1789, and the second taking the form of the revolutions of 1848 in Europe—had failed to replace aristocratic monarchy with democratic republicanism as the dominant form of government in Europe and the world. Attempts to establish democratic republics in Germany, Italy, and Hungary had been smashed by the forces of monarchy, and the French republic had been extinguished by Louis Napoleon's dictatorship. Not only many advocates of republicanism but also many proponents of liberal, parliamentary monarchy had been executed, jailed, or exiled by the authoritarian royal governments of continental Europe. Many liberal German political activists and intellectuals, known as Forty-Eighters, had fled their homeland for refuge in the United States. The two most famous European proponents of liberalism and republicanism in 1863 were both in exile: the Italian statesman and theorist Giuseppe Mazzini and the French poet and politician Victor Hugo.

In the realm of political thought as in the realm of practical politics, the tide was running against liberal republicanism in 1863. A generation of young idealists in Europe had been disillusioned by the shattering of republican hopes on the hard realities of monarchy and militarism. In France many embittered intellectuals chose art for its own sake as an alternative to a depressing reality, while others, equally indignant, concluded that idealism was a trap in art as well as in politics and developed harsh forms of realism in literature and painting and sculpture. To many thinkers in Europe and the world, democracy seemed unworkable and the idea of the rights of man an illusion of naïve eighteenth-century utopians. Popular government inevitably collapsed into anarchy, to be followed by the restoration of authority by a strongman. Hierarchy, not democracy, was the normal condition of humanity, many disenchanted thinkers of the mid-nineteenth century believed. The historian Priscilla Robertson describes the depth of the hostility to liberal democracy in Europe in the mid-nineteenth century: "Albert, the workingman, was called by his first name all the time he was a member of the French government; Baron Doblhoff in Vienna was suspected because he gave parties where the nobility could meet the middle classes socially for the first time; the King of Prussia could label an assembly of professors 'the gutter'; Macaulay could stand up in the House of Commons to say that universal suffrage would destroy civilization and everything that made civilization worthwhile. . . ."[2]

In the past, autocracy and aristocracy had been justified by religion. By the middle of the nineteenth century, political thinkers were turning to another source of legitimacy: biology. Even before Darwin published his theory of natural selection in *On the Origin of Species* (1860), a growing number of influential theorists, of whom the most important was Joseph Arthur de Gobineau, had rejected the Enlightenment ideals of human equality and innate individual rights in favor of the supposed reality of racial inequality. Whether God or nature had created humanity, some races were destined to rule others—and within races and nations, some individuals were naturally superior and fated to lead. In the words of the British conservative Benjamin Disraeli, "All is race." To the growing number of Western thinkers who adopted versions of racial determinism, talk of the rights of man and democracy was sentimental nonsense, discredited both by the failure of democratic governments and the teachings of natural science.

In 1863 only one functioning democratic republic on the scale of a nation-state existed on earth: the United States of America. Beginning in 1861, the United States had been consumed in civil war. The Northern states, acting through the federal government, had fought to prevent the secession of the Southern states, which were controlled by a small minority of rich slave-owning landholders who feared the loss of their power and privileges to an unsympathetic Northern majority. Some of the leading statesmen of the Southern confederacy, echoing contemporary European pessimism about human rights and democracy, had declared that human rights were limited to Caucasians and that democratic government was not an ideal valid for all humanity but an inheritance of Anglo-Saxons alone. America's Founding Fathers had been mistaken about these matters, they argued, and the new Confederate States of America would be founded not on eighteenth-century illusions but on nineteenth-century theories about race and inequality.

It was in this context that Abraham Lincoln, the President of the United States, delivered brief remarks at the dedication of the military cemetery at Gettysburg, Pennsylvania, on November 19, 1863, where at great cost Federal forces had earlier defeated an invasion by the Confederate army: "Fourscore and seven years ago our fathers brought forth on this continent a new nation conceived in liberty and dedicated to the proposition that all men are created equal. Now we are engaged in a great civil war testing whether that nation, or any nation so conceived and so dedicated, can long endure. We are met on a great battlefield of that war. We have come to dedicate a portion of that field as a final resting-place for those who here gave their lives that that nation might live. It is altogether fitting and proper that we should do this. But, in a larger sense, we cannot dedicate, we cannot consecrate, we cannot hallow this ground. The brave men, living and dead, who struggled here have consecrated it far above our power to add or detract. The world will little note nor long remember what we say here, but it can never forget what they did here. It is for us the living rather to be dedicated here to the unfinished work which they who fought here have thus far so nobly advanced. It is rather for us to be here dedicated to the great task remaining before us—that from these honored dead we take increased devotion to that cause for which they gave the last full measure of devotion—that we here highly resolve that these dead shall not have died in vain, that this nation under God shall have a new birth of freedom, and that government of the people, by the people, for the people shall not perish from the earth."[3]

According to Lincoln in the Gettysburg Address, the American Civil War had a global as well as a local significance. Its local significance was the preservation of a United States within whose borders slavery would be abolished—the "new birth of freedom" which by 1863 had become an explicit war aim of the Lincoln administration. The global significance of the Civil War, by contrast, involved the future of democracy, not the future of slavery. In a world in which republican government had failed again and again since the eighteenth century, Abraham Lincoln called on his countrymen to prove that a "government of the people, by the people, for the people" could be a strong and enduring government—not a brief episode between eras of firm authoritarian rule. Lincoln rejected the idea that democracy was a unique product of American conditions or an inheritance of the Anglo-Saxon "race" alone. Other countries, too, were capable of becoming democratic republics, "so conceived and so dedicated" to the ideals of legal and political equality. But if the United States disintegrated because some of its citizens who lost an election took up arms rather than accept the result, then democrats everywhere would be disheartened, and the advocates of monarchy and dictatorship would point to the failure of the United States as further evidence that republican government could not "endure." If the United States crumbled into anarchy, then even if a few genuine republics survived here and there, "government of the people, by the people, for the people" as a significant form of government might well "perish from the earth."

FOR ABRAHAM LINCOLN, the goals of the Union forces in the American Civil War were not limited to reuniting the country or to eliminating slavery in the United States. In addition to achieving these immediate goals, the victory of the Union would vindicate democratic republicanism as a practical form of government. This was a theme that Lincoln addressed repeatedly, in public and private. On the basis of his own statements, it would be natural to remember him as the Great Democrat.

But succeeding generations of Americans and others have remembered Lincoln differently. Lincoln has been invoked as an icon by groups as diverse as advocates of equality for homosexual citizens and apologists for the Confederacy for whom he symbolizes tyranny. Three images of Lincoln have been dominant in popular memory: the Savior of the Union, the Great Commoner, and the Great Emancipator.[4]

All of these images existed in his lifetime. During the campaign of 1860, the Republican Party emphasized the "Great Commoner" theme of Lincoln's lowly frontier origins. His promulgation of the Emancipation Proclamation in 1863 transformed a president who had delayed wartime moves against slavery into the Great Emancipator, and the surrender of the South, shortly before his assassination in 1865, had confirmed his role as Savior of the Union. All three images have coexisted. But at different times, one image has been more influential than another in American culture and politics.

The image of Lincoln as Savior of the Union dominated American public discourse by the early twentieth century. In the late nineteenth century, a partial reconciliation of white Northerners and white Southerners was based on the formula that while the North had been right about the Union and slavery, the white South had been right about race. Most white Southerners conceded that it was for the best that the integrity of the United States had been preserved and that slavery had been abolished; most white Northerners agreed with white Southerners that the attempt to promote racial equality in the South during Reconstruction had been a terrible mistake. It was widely believed that Lincoln, if he had lived, would have been more lenient toward the defeated Confederates and less devoted to what was considered the misguided doctrine of racial equality than the Radical Republicans of the Reconstruction Era.

A haze of nostalgia obscured the deep divisions between the sections and the issues over which the Civil War had been fought. Viewed through the mist of sentiment, Lincoln was less a polarizing politician than a benevolent hero who could be claimed by Northerners and Southerners alike. Lincoln's early political career as a Whig was all but forgotten as he shed his partisan associations. The Savior of the Union had to be above mere political parties and debates over issues like tariffs and taxes. H. L. Mencken described this version of Lincoln as "the chief butt of American credulity and sentimentality . . . a plaster saint . . . a sort of amalgam of John Wesley and the Holy Ghost."[5] Lincoln became a hero for most Americans at the price of the reduction of his thought to a mystical Unionism.

By the mid-twentieth century, the conjunction of mysticism and nationalism seemed sinister in light of the world's experience with modern dictatorships. In his influential book *Patriotic Gore* (1962), the literary critic Edmund Wilson was the first to see, in Lincoln's warning against Caesarism in his 1838 address to the Young Men's Lyceum in Springfield, an unconscious prediction of his own future career: "[Towering genius] thirsts and burns for distinction; and, if possible, it will have it, whether at the expense of emancipating slaves or enslaving freemen." Wilson compared Lincoln to modern state-building autocrats: "Lincoln and Bismarck and Lenin were all men of unusual intellect and formidable tenacity of character. . . . They were all, in their several ways, idealists, who put their ideals before everything else."[6] Wilson, a disillusioned former liberal, considered all political ideologies to be mere camouflages for attempts to seize power. He dismissed abolitionists as "fanatics" and wrote that opposition to slavery "supplied the militant Union North with the rabble-rousing moral issue which is necessary in every modern war to make the conflict appear as a melodrama."[7]

Wilson inaugurated a tradition in which this 1838 address was viewed as an unconscious revelation by the young Lincoln of his own desire to be a powerful ruler. Following Wilson's lead, historians including George P. Forgie and Dwight Anderson wrote "psychobiographies" of Lincoln that portrayed him as a figure consumed by ambition and—in some versions—willing to provoke or prolong civil war in order to assure his greatness.[8] In this variant of the theme of Lincoln as the Savior of the Union, his devotion to the Union became something sinister, if not psychotic.

THE IMAGE OF Lincoln as a mystical Unionist was already being eclipsed, in the 1930s, by his image as the Great Commoner. Lincoln had warned: "It is a great piece of folly to attempt to make anything out of my early life. It can all be condensed into a simple sentence . . . 'the short and simple annals of the poor.' "⁹ (Lincoln's allusion was to the eighteenth-century English poet Thomas Gray's "Elegy Written in a Country Church-yard.") Nevertheless, generations of American schoolchildren grew up on tales of Lincoln's childhood in pioneer communities in Kentucky, Indiana, and Illinois. Until the early twentieth century the story of Lincoln's rise from the log cabin to the White House reinforced the mythology of laissez-faire individualism, along with the rags-to-riches tales published by Horatio Alger. What changed in the 1930s was the appropriation of Lincoln as a symbol by the egalitarian Left.

A key event in this appropriation was the publication between 1926 and 1939 of Carl Sandburg's Pulitzer Prize–winning biography of Lincoln in six volumes. Sandburg, a Midwestern populist sympathetic to Soviet communism, helped to remake Lincoln, the patron saint of a Republican Party dominated by industrialists, financiers, and small-town businessmen, into a folksy symbol of farmers and the working class. Like Sandburg, Aaron Copland, a composer sympathetic to communism, wrote a cantata entitled "Lincoln Portrait" that was adopted by the international Left. One group of American leftists who volunteered to fight in the Spanish civil war in the 1930s called themselves the Abraham Lincoln Brigade. Walt Whitman, like Lincoln, was adopted as an icon of the radical Left around the world; the racial prejudice against blacks that Whitman shared with Lincoln was ignored by Marxists for whom class, rather than race, was the most important social division.

The liberal Left, no less than the radical Left, sought to enlist the prestige of the Great Commoner. Franklin Roosevelt's Democratic coalition, which dominated U.S. politics between the 1930s and the 1970s, was an unstable alliance of three major groups—conservative and populist Southerners and Westerners, largely Catholic European immigrant workers in the industrial states, and middle-class progressives from the Northeast and Midwest and West Coast. The alliance between Southern conservatives and working-class European immigrants in the North against their common enemy,

Northern capitalists, went back to the early nineteenth century. The progressive Northern Protestant Democrats were the newest members of the Democratic coalition. Many of them came from the progressive wing of the Republican Party and had followed Theodore Roosevelt and Robert La Follette into the Progressive Party before finally acquiring a new political home in the Democratic Party of Franklin Roosevelt.

The Democratic Party until the mid-twentieth century was not a progressive party. It had long been the party of agrarianism, free trade, white supremacy, and states' rights. Even the populists, who sometimes sounded like radicals of the Left in their denunciations of corporations, were nostalgic Jeffersonians trying to restore a lost world of small-scale farmers and craftsmen. The great populist William Jennings Bryan, the Democratic candidate for president three times, was a Protestant fundamentalist whose last public act shortly before his death was serving as the prosecution in the infamous Scopes "Monkey Trial" of 1925, in which a Tennessee high school teacher was found guilty of violating a state law banning the teaching of Darwin's theory of evolution.

The progressives who joined the Democratic Party in the 1920s and 1930s therefore had a problem. They needed what Van Wyck Brooks, in the context of American culture as a whole, called "a usable past." Many of the progressive converts favored civil rights for black Americans, and yet they were in the party historically identified with slavery and the harshest forms of segregation. They favored an activist federal government, and yet they were in the party of free market ideology, limited government, and states' rights.

The progressives—now called liberals—in Franklin Roosevelt's Democratic Party rewrote history. They were egalitarians, so they defined the Democratic tradition as the egalitarian tradition in American history. Some liberal Democratic thinkers and politicians sought to make a liberal icon of Thomas Jefferson, whom most progressives from Republican backgrounds, like Theodore Roosevelt and Herbert Croly, disliked. Liberals emphasized Jefferson's egalitarian rhetoric and minimized his pseudoscientific racism and his states' rights ideology. This attempt by liberal Democratic mythmakers to draft Jefferson to campaign for Franklin Roosevelt was too much for conservative "Jeffersonian" Democrats, who claimed plausibly that they, not progressive New Dealers, were the spiritual heirs of the lord of Monticello. Ceding Jefferson to the Right, other liberals found a "usable past" in the career of Andrew Jackson. In his influential popular history *The Age of Jackson,* the young Arthur Schlesinger, Jr., an ardent New Deal Democrat, turned Andrew Jackson, the reactionary Jeffersonian slave owner who ethnically cleansed the South of the Cherokee Indians, into a precursor of Franklin Roosevelt and made Jackson's war against the Second Bank of the United States a precedent for New Deal–style regulation of a rampant plutocracy.[10]

In addition to enlisting Jackson, the New Deal liberals sought to enlist Lincoln as a political ancestor as well. But the North was full of Republicans who considered Lincoln to be theirs in the same way that conservative Southern Democrats claimed Jefferson as their own. What the New Deal liberal historians and intellectuals did was breathtaking in its audacity. They tried to detach Lincoln from the Republican Party, and sought to erase all memory of the larger Hamiltonian tradition that had been carried on, in successive eras, by the Federalist, Whig, and Republican parties.

Franklin Roosevelt himself helped orchestrate the campaign to associate his presidency with Lincoln's. In 1940 he hired Sherwood Anderson, author of the popular play *Abe Lincoln in Illinois,* as a White House speechwriter. Roosevelt invoked Lincoln to justify recovery programs and his campaign to enlarge the Supreme Court. The struggle for the New Deal was "a conflict as fundamental as Lincoln's . . ."[11] He compared isolationist opponents of his foreign policy to Clement Vallandigham, the Ohio congressman whose criticism provoked the Lincoln administration to deport him to the Confederacy: "Well, Vallandigham, as you know, was an appeaser," Roosevelt said.[12] After Roosevelt's meeting with Churchill in the Atlantic, the *New York Times* on October 19, 1940, ran this headline: PRESIDENT BIDS NATION AWAKE TO PERIL / ROOSEVELT IS GRIM / QUOTES LINCOLN TO SHOW

A PARALLEL BETWEEN THOSE DAYS AND THESE.[13] Lincoln's most famous biographer, Carl Sandburg, an ardent supporter of the New Deal, helped by writing articles with titles like "Lincoln—Roosevelt."[14]

The New Deal intellectuals succeeded in creating a new version of the American past. By the second half of the twentieth century, most educated people thought of Abraham Lincoln as an orphan in politics who left no political heirs. When Lincoln, first as a Republican candidate and then as the first Republican president, was asked about his views, he repeatedly identified himself as a Henry Clay Whig. Henry Clay had helped organize the Whig Party in opposition to Jackson, the hero of the New Deal Democrats, so the liberal historians who sought to create a usable past for the Democratic Left detached Lincoln from his hero and role model. Cut off from his political predecessors, Lincoln was also separated from the Republican presidents who succeeded him, such as William McKinley and Herbert Hoover. Hoover's own response to the Left's appropriation of Lincoln was the remark: "I was under the impression he was a Republican."[15] Generations of Americans were taught by partisan liberal Democratic historians that every Republican president between Lincoln and FDR was a mediocrity and a pawn of unethical corporations and unscrupulous tycoons, with the possible exception of the progressive Theodore Roosevelt, who, according to his cousin Franklin, was "a better Democrat than the Democratic candidate" who opposed him in 1904.[16]

Lincoln was posthumously deprived not only of his political tradition, but of most of his career in politics. His life was reduced, by the liberal historians and intellectuals who dominated America's view of its past, to two episodes—his idyllic rural youth and his campaign against slavery and secession, beginning with the Lincoln-Douglas debates and concluding with his wartime presidency. Lincoln was born in a log cabin, grew up to split rails as a young man, debated Douglas over slavery, saved the Union, freed the slaves, and was murdered by John Wilkes Booth, whereupon Herbert Hoover led the country into the Great Depression and Franklin Roosevelt led the country out of it just in time to save the world from Hitler.

Ironically, the image of Lincoln as an egalitarian liberal or leftist was taken up in the 1950s by conservative intellectuals who accepted the equation of Lincoln and FDR—and rejected both. Willmoore Kendall, one of the members of the new conservative movement that coalesced around William F. Buckley, Jr.'s *National Review* in the 1950s and 1960s, popularized a theory that had long been held by apologists for the Confederacy. In this view, the egalitarian ideals of 1776, symbolized by the Declaration of Independence, had been rejected by the more conservative Founders who drafted the federal Constitution in 1787. Lincoln, while pretending to preserve the U.S. Constitution, had actually abolished the old Constitution, based on individual liberty and states' rights, and replaced it with a new, centralizing, egalitarian regime. Lincoln's replacement of the libertarian Constitution of 1787 with a new regime based on the egalitarianism of 1776 inevitably produced the large and intrusive government of Franklin Roosevelt and his successors. Kendall wrote that "the developing struggle between contemporary American conservatism and the Liberal Revolution is, correctly understood, a struggle between those who are determined to 'make good' Abraham Lincoln's new act of founding on the one hand, and those who demand, with greater clarity each passing day, that the new act of founding [by Lincoln] be set aside in favor of the principles of the original founders."[17]

One of Kendall's young colleagues at the conservative magazine *National Review* in the 1950s, the journalist Garry Wills, popularized Kendall's dubious theory in his book *Lincoln at Gettysburg: The Words that Remade America* (1993). Wills recycled Kendall's thesis that in the Gettysburg Address, Lincoln had substituted equality for liberty in America's civil religion, perpetrating, in the words of Wills, a "giant, if benign, swindle" and a "clever assault upon the constitutional past."[18] After Wills revived Kendall's charge that Lincoln was a covert egalitarian revolutionary, this misconception was endorsed by George P. Fletcher, a professor at Columbia University Law School, in *Our Secret Constitution: How Lincoln Redefined American Democracy* (2001). "The themes articulated at Gettysburg captured the American yearning for a postbellum order based on principles radically different from the ideas that founded the Republic in the Constitution that took force in 1789."[19] Fletcher, like Kendall and Wills and a long line of neo-Confederate conservatives and libertarians, argued that Lincoln substituted the egalitarian values of the 1776 Declaration of Independence for the libertarian values of the Constitution of 1787: "The Secret Constitution and its principles of organic nationhood, equality, and popular democracy have progressively won the upper hand against the 1787 values of voluntary association, freedom, and republican elitism."[20] Kendall, Wills, and Fletcher all agreed that Lincoln had somehow perpetrated a constitutional coup d'etat, although they differed in their evaluation of the alleged egalitarian revolution; Kendall disapproved of it from the Right, Wills and Fletcher approved from their standpoints on the political Left. In hindsight it is clear that these writers belonged to the same broad tradition as Sandburg, Copland, and Franklin Roosevelt's speechwriters—a tradition in which Lincoln, the Great Commoner, was praised or damned as a patron saint of the egalitarian policies of New Deal liberalism.

WHILE THE EGALITARIANISM of the New Deal was legitimated by the image of Lincoln as the Great Commoner, the civil rights revolution produced a new emphasis on Lincoln as the Great Emancipator. This image had long been cherished by many proponents of racial equality, black and white alike. But the identification of Lincoln with civil rights had been a minor theme in mainstream American culture for generations following Lincoln's death.

In 1939, when Howard University, the black college in Washington, D.C., wanted the soprano Marian Anderson to perform at Constitution Hall, the site's owners, the Daughters of the American Revolution (DAR), denied the request because Anderson was black. First Lady Eleanor Roosevelt promptly resigned from the DAR and arranged for Anderson to sing before seventy-five thousand people on Easter Sunday, April 9, 1939, on the steps of the Lincoln Memorial. On August 28, 1963, almost a century after Lincoln delivered the Gettysburg Address, Martin Luther King, Jr., delivered his stirring "I Have a Dream" speech from the same location: "Five score years ago, a great American, in whose symbolic shadow we stand, signed the Emancipation Proclamation."[21] Between them, Anderson and King converted the Lincoln Memorial into a symbol of civil rights for black Americans.

Those who made Lincoln an icon of the black civil rights movement tended to treat Lincoln's arguments against the enslavement of black Americans as though they were arguments in favor of black equality. A debate about Lincoln's actual views about race and segregation erupted in 1968 with the publication in *Ebony* of the black journalist and historian Lerone Bennett's epochal article, "Was Abe Lincoln a Racist?" In 2000 Bennett expanded his polemic into a book, *Forced into Glory: Abraham Lincoln's White Dream.*[22] Although Bennett's book was widely criticized for its prosecutorial tone, his scholarship was irrefutable. With familiar documents as well as obscure sources, Bennett documented a Lincoln whose attitudes were no less racist for being widely shared among the white Americans of his time. As Bennett pointed out, in his career in Illinois and in national politics, Lincoln not only had supported racial segregation but had also sought to ban black migration to Illinois and—long before the Civil War—took part in the movement to encourage all blacks to leave the United States for a foreign colony.

Between the publication of Bennett's essay in 1968 and his book in 2000, many white American historians refused to confront the fact of Lincoln's racism candidly. Instead, they downplayed his opposition to black social and political equality and to the migration of free as well as enslaved blacks to the North and West while emphasizing his principled opposition to slavery.

THE IMAGES OF Lincoln as the Savior of the Union, the Great Commoner, and the Great Emancipator are not lies; they are myths. Each conception of Lincoln's significance is based in part on fact. But around each kernel of fact has grown a crust of falsehood.

There was nothing mystical, for example, about Lincoln's Unionism. In his first inaugural address he pointed out that states that wanted to secede could do so, with the consent of the rest of the nation rather than unilaterally. "This country, with its institutions, belongs to the people who inhabit it. Whenever they shall grow weary of the existing Government, they can exercise their constitutional right to amend it or their revolutionary right to dismember it or overthrow it."[23] Edmund Wilson was wrong. Lincoln was no Bismarck. And no Lenin. A lawyer in the White House, Lincoln believed that unilateral secession of American states by violence was nothing less than armed insurrection, which the president's duty to enforce federal laws required him to suppress. In his beliefs and actions, Lincoln represented the mainstream of American constitutional jurisprudence. Nothing Lincoln said or did prevents a state from attempting to leave the Union by peaceful and legal means, after obtaining the permission of the remaining states by an amendment of the federal Constitution.

The claim that Lincoln was a fanatic who deliberately used the slavery issue to provoke the Civil War, in order to assume despotic powers, is a fantasy of libertarians and neo-Confederate conservatives. Far from seeking to provoke the South into secession, Lincoln, both before and during the Civil War, proposed compromise measures that would have preserved slavery where it existed while preventing its extension to other states. If Lincoln's initial plans had succeeded, the Civil War would have ended quickly with compensation to slave owners and with slavery intact until the early twentieth century at least. It was the South's rejections of a series of proposed compromises and the rising costs of the struggle that radicalized Lincoln along with many other conciliatory Northerners and turned a war for reunion into a war against slavery.

Far from showing Lincoln's unconscious tendencies toward Caesarism, as Wilson and his school have maintained, Lincoln's Lyceum Address of 1838 merely rehearses the conventional political philosophy of Lincoln's Whig Party. Having begun as the opposition to the popular and powerful president Andrew Jackson, the Whigs were born, as it were, with a suspicion of executive power. As the party of the educated and economic elites, the Whigs were also opposed to the populism of the dominant Democratic Party. It was natural for a Whig like Lincoln to dread an alliance of the mob and a strongman, and to find justification for that fear in the fate of the Roman republic.

The image of Lincoln as the Great Commoner is equally misleading. Just as Lincoln was no mystical nationalist of the Bismarck school, so he was not a social democrat or populist of the Left. Lincoln praised democracy as a form of government in which ordinary people could rise—but they had to rise by their own efforts, in the tradition of the "self-made man" (a phrase coined by Lincoln's political hero Henry Clay). Lincoln, like generations of Chamber of Commerce Republicans who succeeded him, approved of equality of opportunity, not equality of result. Lincoln favored government help for industry and agriculture—canals and railroads, high tariffs to protect manufacturing, the conversion of federal land into family farms. But he opposed government economic support for ex-slaves, saying that they should take to heart the slogan "Root, hog, or die."[24] Like most of his fellow Whigs and Republicans, Lincoln probably would have regarded most twentieth-century welfare state measures as dangerously socialistic. One can only imagine what Lincoln, the wealthy railroad lawyer and champion of private enterprise, would have thought of his adoption as a symbol by American communists fighting on behalf of Stalin in the Spanish civil war. During his campaign for the presidency in 1860 he declared: "I take it that it is best for all to leave each man free to acquire property as fast as he can. Some will get wealthy. I don't believe in a law to prevent a man from getting rich; it would do more harm than good."[25] His populist image notwithstanding, his two White House secretaries, in their semiofficial biography, wrote that Lincoln "preferred through life the better sort to the majority."[26]

Lincoln would have been astonished to learn, from Willmoore Kendall, Garry Wills, and George P. Fletcher, that by delivering the Gettysburg Address and suppressing "the Rebellion" he had converted the United States from a libertarian to an egalitarian state. The very idea that 1776 and 1787 stood for separate and incompatible ideals would have struck Lincoln as bizarre. Lincoln saw himself as a preserver of the antebellum American regime and sought to keep the constitutional fabric intact with only minimal alterations, such as the Thirteenth Amendment that abolished slavery, the only amendment he envisioned before his death. To attribute the measures of radical Republicans after his death to a supposed Lincolnian revolution is illegitimate given the major differences that existed between Lincoln and the radical wing of his party. Like other Republicans in the Hamiltonian tradition, he saw the great expansion of both the civilian and military capabilities of the federal government during his presidency as fulfillment of a potential that had existed since the federal Constitution was adopted. If not for the opposition of Southerners in Congress and the White House, many of the government programs that Congress enacted during the Lincoln years, such as national banking, high tariffs, and massive railroad subsidies, would have been enacted decades earlier by the Federalists or the Whigs.

If Lincoln was not an egalitarian revolutionary, neither was he the political ancestor of the twentieth-century civil rights movement. Lincoln was always a "Free-Soiler" rather than an abolitionist. Most members of the Free-Soil movement opposed the extension of slavery to the Western territories because it wanted them reserved for white Americans and European immigrants. Free-Soilers like Lincoln tended to be white-racial nationalists who combined moral and political opposition to slavery with the desire for a homogeneous white population. Lincoln, a colonizationist as well as a Free-Soiler, hoped that blacks would exercise their natural rights somewhere other than in the United States—in Africa, the Caribbean, or Central America. If the colonization plan that Lincoln proposed to Congress had succeeded, then Marian Anderson and Martin Luther King, Jr., might never have been born because their ancestors would have been voluntarily "deported," to use a word Lincoln sometimes employed.

Lincoln supported the abolition of slavery by means of the Thirteenth Amendment before he died. But if Lincoln had lived, it is unlikely that there would have been a period of radical Reconstruction of the South, and without radical Reconstruction it is unlikely that citizenship would have been nationalized by the Fourteenth Amendment or the right to vote guaranteed by the Fifteenth Amendment. Lincoln, a lifelong segregationist and opponent of black social equality, probably would have been satisfied with the provision of minimal legal and property rights to ex-slaves, with black suffrage left as a question for the states to decide. Lincoln, to be sure, was not the only white American who opposed both slavery and racial integration without any consciousness of contradiction. Most white Americans between the mid-nineteenth and mid-twentieth centuries believed that nonwhites were inferior to whites. They believed further that nonwhite inferiority, while it did not justify slavery, did justify social and political segregation as well as laws banning nonwhite immigration to the United States.

The conversion of the Lincoln Memorial into an icon of antiracism by Marian Anderson and Martin Luther King, Jr., then, is misleading. Most of the white American opponents of slavery in his time, like Lincoln, had no intention of creating a color-blind, multiracial society in the United States. Among Lincoln's contemporaries, only a minority of white abolitionists and Radical Republicans such as Wendell Phillips, William Lloyd Garrison, Thaddeus Stevens, and Charles Sumner, together with black abolitionists such as Frederick Douglass, could envision an America in which citizens of all races formed a single community. They—not Abraham Lincoln—are the genuine patron saints of postracist America, and it is an injustice to their memory to give credit for antiracist reforms to Lincoln rather than to them and their successors in movements for racial and sexual equality.

Paradoxically, in their contemporary versions, both the Savior of the Union image and the Great Commoner image owe their origins to anti-Lincoln propaganda circulated by apologists for the Confederacy. The literature portraying Lincoln as a mystical nationalist, as we have seen, sprang from Edmund Wilson's essay on Lincoln in *Patriotic Gore*. The first sentence of that essay is this: "What precisely did Alexander Stephens mean when he said that for Lincoln the Union had risen to the sublimity of religious mysticism?"[27] Alexander Stephens, the vice president of the Confederate States of America, published a multivolume tome following the Civil War in which he argued that the South fought for states' rights. In that book Stephens wrote the sentence to which Wilson referred: "The Union with him in sentiment, rose to the sublimity of a religious mysticism."[28] (When first published, Wilson's essay on Lincoln was entitled "The Union as Religious Mysticism.") Near the beginning of the Civil War, in his "Cornerstone Speech," Stephens announces that the Confederate government owed its superiority to the fact that it was the first in history to be explicitly founded on "the great truth, that the Negro is not equal to the white man . . ." Stephens suggested that many defenders of the ideal of human equality were mentally ill: "One of the most striking characteristics of insanity, in many instances, is forming correct conclusions from fancied or erroneous premises; so with the anti-slavery fanatics. . . ."[29] Stephens would have been gratified to learn that, in the second half of the twentieth century, his vision of Lincoln as a deranged fanatic, disseminated by Edmund Wilson to a broad public, would become influential. Even more influential has been another argument of apologists for the Confederacy, the claim that Lincoln had substituted the ideals of the Declaration of Independence for the different ideas of the U.S. Constitution. The wide diffusion of images of Lincoln as an irrational zealot or a secretive egalitarian revolutionary by Edmund Wilson, Willmoore Kendall, Garry Wills, and others represent belated victories by the Confederates in the war of ideas.

The Popular Conceptions of Lincoln as Savior of the Union, Great Commoner, and Great Emancipator, then, have been half truths promoted to serve partisan purposes by different groups at different times. Each image of Lincoln is partly true: Lincoln did save the union; he did rise to power from humble origins and championed the rights and interests of "the laboring man" as he understood them; he did issue the Emancipation Proclamation that temporarily destroyed Southern slavery during the Civil War; and he did insist on passage of the Thirteenth Amendment to the U.S. Constitution that permanently eradicated slavery in the United States. But by emphasizing one or another of these accomplishments to the exclusion of others without reference to their context in Lincoln's life and career, later generations of Americans have substituted a saint for a politician and a symbol for a man.

Before Lincoln became a symbol onto which others projected their beliefs, he was an individual with strong beliefs of his own. To a degree that is rare among politicians, he prided himself on his ability to justify particular policies by their connection to larger ideals and a coherent body of thought. What Lincoln said about slavery he might have said about any public policy: "Whenever this question shall be settled, it must be settled on some philosophical basis. No policy that does not rest upon some philosophical public opinion can be permanently maintained."[30] From Lincoln's statements and deeds as well as from the recollections of those who knew him, it is possible to reconstruct the "philosophical basis" upon which he built his own career as a public figure.

In his approach to the basic questions of existence and the nature of reality, Lincoln belonged, like most of the American Founders, to the tradition of the Enlightenment. Although he was born into a Baptist family and matured during the Second Great Awakening of the early nineteenth century, a time of widespread Protestant revivalism, Lincoln rejected orthodox Christianity at an early age for the post-Christian deism of Enlightenment thinkers such as Thomas Jefferson and Tom Paine. In his youth he wrote a book rejecting Christianity, which he burned on the advice of friends who feared it would harm his political career. As a politician, Lincoln avoided giving offense to religious believers, and his oratory was rich with biblical allusions. But he refused to join a Christian congregation and never made conventional professions of Christian faith.

Lincoln's God was the God of the philosophers, not that of Moses and Jesus, an abstract Providence whose will could be known, if at all, only through the events of history such as the Civil War. "Reason, cold, calculating, unimpassioned reason," Lincoln once remarked, had to be the basis of the American republic. Reason, not revelation, was Lincoln's guide in life. His rationalism explains everything from his refusal to drink alcohol, which muddied the mental powers, to his enthusiasm about the then-novel theory of biological evolution. Lincoln's emphasis on reason was all the more urgent because, like others in the Enlightenment tradition, he thought that most human beings were driven by self-interest, passion, and habit. Unlike many great political leaders, he was not a great hater, and his willingness to forgive both personal and political enemies was rooted in his low opinion of human nature. It was a pessimistic Enlightenment rationalist, not a benevolent Christian, who told his fellow Northerners that they would act as the Southerners did were they in their place.

Skeptical about Christianity but fascinated by natural science, from an early age Lincoln was devoted to the project of using advanced technology to modernize the primitive rural regions in which he spent his childhood. For Lincoln, progress was symbolized by canals, steamships, railroads, and cities. In his youth he expressed his ambition to be "the De Witt Clinton of Illinois," referring to the New York governor who was given credit for building the Erie Canal. Lincoln's law partner William Herndon explained Lincoln's vision of the future Midwest: "Every river and stream . . . was to be widened, deepened, and made navigable . . . cities were to spring up everywhere, . . . people were to come swarming in by colonies, until . . . Illinois was to outstrip all others, and herself become the Empire State of the Union."[31]

From the earliest years of the republic, the question of "internal improvements" had divided Americans between two broad traditions of thought, founded respectively by Alexander Hamilton, Washington's brilliant treasury secretary, and Thomas Jefferson, Washington's equally brilliant secretary of state and the third president of the United States. Hamiltonians favored a strong central government that actively promoted the industrial modernization of the United States. While Jeffersonians believed that republicanism as a way of life required a weak, decentralized government and a mostly agricultural economy. In the 1830s, when Lincoln first entered politics in a race for the Illinois legislature, the Jeffersonian agrarian tradition was carried on by Andrew Jackson's Democratic Party while the Hamiltonian project of industrial development was associated with the Whig Party.

"I have always been an old-line Henry Clay Whig," Lincoln explained in 1861.[32] From the 1830s until the 1850s, when the party disintegrated, Lincoln was an Illinois member of the Whig Party whose major national leader was Clay. On the issues of tariffs to protect American industries from foreign competition, national banking, and federal support for infrastructure projects like canals and railroads, Lincoln was a faithful adherent of Clay's "American System," a comprehensive program for using the federal government to promote industrial capitalism in what was then a predominantly rural economy. In his views on race and slavery, Lincoln was also a disciple of Clay. "I can express all my views on the slavery question by quotations from Henry Clay," he insisted once. "Doesn't this look like we are akin?"[33] Repeatedly in his career Lincoln quoted from Clay's address to the American Colonization Society in 1827, in which Clay, during the course of arguing for the expatriation of blacks, said that slavery could not be defended without rejecting the idea of liberty everywhere: "They must blow out the moral lights around us, and extinguish that greatest torch of all which America presents to a benighted world—pointing the way to their rights, their liberties, and their happiness."[34] In 1852, before he became prominent in national politics by rejecting the claim that the phrase "all men are created equal" in the Declaration of Independence applied only to whites, Lincoln said in his public eulogy for Clay: "He did not perceive, that on a question of human right, the negroes were to be exempted from the human race."[35]

Like Clay, Lincoln rejected both slavery and the idea of a multiracial American society and promoted schemes to encourage free blacks as well as emancipated slaves to leave the United States and move to one or another foreign country. Lincoln's Secretary of the Navy Gideon Welles was familiar with Lincoln's views: "Opposed to the whole system of enslavement, but believing the Africans were mentally an inferior race, [Lincoln] believed that any attempt to make them and the whites one people would tend to the degradation of the whites without materially elevating the blacks, but that separation would promote the happiness of each."[36] An integrated, multiracial society was unimaginable to Lincoln and most of his contemporaries. A few brave and visionary white Americans in his day joined black Americans in opposing white supremacy as well as slavery. Lincoln was not among them.

Like all statesmen, Lincoln was the product of many influences. But Lincoln's description of himself as "an old-line Henry Clay Whig" cannot be surpassed. The younger Kentuckian was a disciple and successor of the older Kentuckian. Such relationships have been common in American politics. Thomas Jefferson was the brilliant architect of a political program that was promoted by his admirers and successors in the White House, including James Madison and James Monroe. President James Polk's role as political heir of Andrew "Old Hickory" Jackson was signaled by his nickname, "Young Hickory."

The closest parallel, perhaps, is found in the twentieth century. Henry Clay was to Abraham Lincoln what Franklin Delano Roosevelt was to Lyndon Johnson—a lifelong hero and role model as well as the architect of a political philosophy adopted and implemented by the younger politician. In the 1960s, as president, Johnson sought to complete Roosevelt's New Deal programs of the 1930s. Exactly a century earlier, as president, Lincoln, even while fighting to defeat Southern secession, presided over the enactment by Congress of much of Clay's American System and sought unsuccessfully to end slavery, as Clay had sought to do, by means of a combination of compensated, gradual emancipation with the colonization of blacks abroad.

Lincoln's description of himself as a Whig in the mold of Henry Clay, then, deserves to be taken seriously. Once the extraordinary magnitude of Lincoln's intellectual and political debt to Clay is acknowledged, the flaw in most studies of Lincoln becomes evident. Biographers and historians tend to break Lincoln's career in politics into two halves—a boring Whig half, from the 1830s until the 1850s, and an exciting Republican half in the 1850s and 1860s. Lincoln I is an uninteresting figure concerned with dull issues like the tariff; Lincoln II is an inspiring figure who defends human rights against racism, defeats secession, and destroys slavery.

But there was only one Lincoln, not two. Lincoln's interest in race and slavery did not begin in the 1850s, and Lincoln's Whiggish concern with economic issues continued throughout his presidency. Lincoln's views on economics and slavery, both derived from Clay, were remarkably stable. The shift in his emphasis during his political career reflects the shift in national debate from questions of political economy to the divisive question of the future of slavery. When, as President of the United States, he wrestled with the questions of national authority and presidential power, he found the answers in the Hamiltonian tradition of political thought that the Republican Party inherited from the Whig Party.

SHOULD LINCOLN, THEN, be remembered chiefly as a follower of Henry Clay, who, unlike his hero, managed to win the presidency? This would be an injustice to Lincoln, who was a great statesman and a great thinker in his own right. Lincoln was not, like Clay or Jefferson, a great synthesizer who could weld diverse policies into a coherent program. Lincoln was content to inherit his program from Clay with little modification.

Lincoln's genius lay in his ability to articulate, in succinct and memorable language, the political principles of the American republic. To this task Lincoln was uniquely suited by a rationalist temperament and a legalist style of thinking. More than any other president before or since, Lincoln served as theologian of America's civil religion. Phrases minted by Lincoln, memorized by generations of Americans and foreigners, constitute a catechism of liberal democracy.

Liberal democracy was the ideal that inspired Lincoln from the beginning of his political career to the end. And because he lived in the United States, the first sustained, large-scale republic since antiquity, Lincoln could treat democracy not merely as a theory but as a tradition to be upheld.

In the 1850s that tradition came under threat as a growing number of Southern apologists for slavery began to question the philosophy of Enlightenment liberalism that had inspired the American Founders. In the course of arguing against black equality, some radicals of the Southern Right began to argue that the Founders had been mistaken in believing in human equality in general—even as an ideal. As Lincoln perceived, this line of reasoning went beyond the old debates among Hamiltonian and Jeffersonian democrats. At its most extreme the proto-Confederate ideology was a philosophical assault on the premises of American democracy, followed in due course by the South's military assault on the institutions of American democracy. First in debate as a senatorial candidate, and then in practice as President of the United States during the Civil War, Lincoln defended both the theory and institutions of American democracy. And he believed that in doing so he was helping to keep democracy alive as an ideal not only for Americans but for people everywhere. As he said at Gettysburg, the victory of the Union in the Civil War would help ensure "that government of the people, by the people, for the people shall not perish from the earth."

When Lincoln is thought of as the Great Democrat, many of the apparent contradictions in his thought and deeds disappear. While Lincoln, like most of his white contemporaries, believed that blacks were inferior to whites, he passionately rejected the idea that whites had the right to rule blacks—either as slaves or as the subjects of white colonial empires. Lincoln wanted a white-only American republic. But he was sincere and consistent in hoping that Latin Americans, Africans, and Asians as well as Europeans would one day live under republican governments of their own. And he believed that the fate of democracy in the world depended upon its success in the United States. What Lincoln said in his eulogy for Henry Clay in 1852 could be said of him: "He loved his country partly because it was his own country, but mostly because it was a free country; and he burned with a zeal for its advancement, prosperity, and glory because he saw in such the advancement, prosperity, and glory of human liberty, human right, and human nature."[37]

"ALL-CONQUERING MIND":
THE EDUCATION
OF ABRAHAM LINCOLN

AFTER ABRAHAM LINCOLN was shot on April 14, 1865, by John Wilkes Booth and died the next day, Richard Oglesby, the governor of Illinois, pleaded with Mary that the former president be buried in Springfield. The grieving widow finally consented, but, over the objections of the governor, who wanted Lincoln's tomb to be near the governor's mansion, she ordered that he be buried in Oak Ridge, a suburban cemetery. If she did not get her way, she threatened to have him buried in Chicago.[1]

Why not Chicago? After all, it was in the vast "Wigwam" in Chicago that the Republican Convention had nominated Lincoln for president while he waited for the news in Springfield. It was on lecture stages and in offices and hotel bars in Chicago that Lincoln had spent much of his political and professional life, orating, socializing, wheeling and dealing. Often

Lincoln had sat in theaters in Chicago, listening to actors deliver his favorite lines in Shakespeare's plays or laughing at white actors in blackface imitating blacks in the minstrel shows that he enjoyed. Lincoln was at home in Chicago.

But to later generations the juxtaposition of Lincoln and Chicago has seemed incongruous. The great industrial center of the American Midwest may have been in Lincoln's state, but it was not in Lincoln's world. Later generations have been taught to think of Lincoln as a quaint rural figure, more at home in the village of New Salem, Illinois, where he spent part of his young adulthood, than in the larger city of Springfield, where he spent most of his career. Lincoln's world is an idyllic world of green trees, gurgling creeks, and meadows fenced by rails he split by hand—not an urban landscape of skyscrapers, meat processing plants, smoking factory chimneys, ornate mansions, immigrant tenements, steel bridges, and converging railroads. To avoid Chicago, and even Springfield, a dangerously substantial city where Lincoln owned a disturbingly big house in which he and his family were waited on by a series of white and black maids, the popular imagination, influenced by countless books, plays, and films, skips over most of Lincoln's life so that Lincoln goes almost directly from splitting rails in tiny New Salem to Washington, D.C. Here he saves the Union and frees the slaves, pausing only to defend the ideal of human equality in his debates with Stephen A. Douglas, his Democratic rival for a U.S. Senate seat from Illinois.

The Lincoln of popular myth is a Jeffersonian Lincoln, the embodiment of the Jeffersonian ideal of the yeoman farmer, uncorrupted by contact with cities and big business and political machines. The genuine Lincoln was the product of a pioneer farm family on what was then the Western frontier of settlement in the United States; in that respect, he fit the Jeffersonian stereotype. But his principles as a politician and public philosopher were those of the tradition founded by Jefferson's rival, Alexander Hamilton. Jeffersonians liked government to be small and close to the people; Lincoln as a matter of principle favored a strong, centralized, activist federal government that promoted industrial capitalism. Jeffersonians thought that independent farmers were nobler than factory workers; Lincoln from his twenties onward campaigned for state and government sponsorship of manufacturing industries in Illinois and the nation as a whole. Jeffersonians preferred the country to the city; Lincoln, born on the farm, became not only an urbanite but an enthusiastic "booster" of schemes to turn wilderness and farmland into cities. Lincoln's early biographers, his former law partner William Herndon, and his bodyguard Ward Hill Lamon shared his contempt for the low level of civilization found on the frontier. Herndon described it as a "stagnant putrid pool" while Lamon said it was a "dung hill" characterized by "the utter absence of all romantic and heroic elements."[2]

The villains in America's Jeffersonian mythology are the friends of Lincoln, an affluent lawyer whose clients included giant corporations, millionaires, real estate speculators, and corporate executives. Lincoln came from humble origins, but he made his career among the prosperous and powerful. In American myth, Lincoln resembled the Jeffersonian ideal of the honest, awkward maverick in public service more than one of the villains of the American morality play: the cunning party politician making secret deals in smoke-filled rooms. Lincoln, an abstemious man, did not smoke or drink, but he rose to prominence in a cloud of cigar smoke within earshot of spittoons.

The legendary Lincoln in the popular imagination is a martyred saint succeeded by scoundrels. The Civil War, a crusade for human liberty, is followed by the Gilded Age, an era of massive political corruption, class inequality, and industrial pollution. How and why the good Republicans of the Civil War turned abruptly into the bad Republicans of Western railroad scandals and gaudy mansions in Newport is never explained.

The same popular culture that for generations vilified the post–Civil War Republican North has also idealized the elegant lost world of the antebellum plantation South. The industrial North won the Civil War, but the agrarian South along with the agrarian West won the cultural war. The millionaire industrialist may be an American archetype, the city slicker may have been the norm for generations, but the rural American—the yeoman farmer, the cowboy, even the aristocratic Southern planter—has been the American ideal, to judge by Hollywood movies and popular fiction. Industrialization and urbanization represented a fall from Arcadian innocence in the American collective mind. The farmer defending his land against commercial real estate developers, the cowboy gazing sadly at the barbed wire fence mutilating the once-free range—these symbols have a deep resonance in the American imagination.

It is no wonder, then, that Americans have chosen to pretend that Abraham Lincoln was someone other than a lifelong proponent of urbanization and industrialization. The real Abraham Lincoln—the lifelong opponent of the Jeffersonian politicians of his day, the urban lawyer who wanted to replace the woods and fields with factories, cities, railroads, and canals—looks disturbingly like the serpent in America's Eden. The solution has been to bracket off his life and career from the Gilded Age that followed and to pretend that the "robber baron" industrialists betrayed Lincoln's vision of America instead of fulfilling it in places like late-nineteenth-century Chicago.

CHICAGO IS THE informal capital of the Midwest. The single most important fact about Abraham Lincoln is that he was, by adoption although not by birth, a Midwesterner. In the nineteenth century the three major regions of the United States were the Northeast, the South, and the Midwest. The key political event of the nineteenth century was the regional realignment in national politics caused by the issue of the expansion of slavery. That realignment turned the Midwest from an ally of the South in national politics into an ally of the Northeast. When the South, fearing a loss of power in national government, attempted to secede, the Northeast-Midwest alliance crushed the rebels. From the 1860s until the 1930s the alliance of the Northeast and Midwest within the Republican Party dominated American politics and policy. Lincoln owed his presidency to this alliance of the two regions. Despite his relative obscurity and lack of extensive national political experience, Lincoln was chosen as the presidential candidate of the Republican Party in 1860 chiefly because he was a prominent Republican from an important Midwestern state. But Lincoln was not simply a passive beneficiary of this regional coalition. From 1854 onward, by helping to lead the campaign against the extension of slavery, Lincoln had done as much as anyone to unite the Midwest with the Northeast in a common cause.

Lincoln's opposition to the expansion of slavery was rooted in the experiences of his family—a family of white yeoman farmers who had migrated from a South dominated by rich, slave-owning landlords to the more egalitarian Midwest. The Midwest to which they moved was a promised land for ordinary white Americans compared to the Northeast, dominated by wealthy urban families, and the plantation South. Americans in later generations would attribute the egalitarianism of the Midwest—or, as it was known in Lincoln's time, the Old Northwest—to the conditions of the frontier. But the frontier of the South expanded westward as well, along the coast of the Gulf of Mexico, bringing hierarchy rather than equality with it. In reality the egalitarianism of the Midwest was the product of conscious social engineering by the federal government. Three government policies created the Midwest of Lincoln's day and later generations—the Northwest Ordinance, Indian removal, and the reform of American land laws.

The Northwest Ordinance of 1787 was enacted by the final U.S. Congress that met under the Articles of Confederation, before a new federal government under the present federal Constitution took power in 1789. The Northwest Ordinance was a republican solution to a political dilemma—what to do with the vast territory east of the Mississippi and north of the Ohio River that the federal government had obtained from Britain at the conclusion of the American war for independence. For the inhabitants of this territory to be ruled without their consent by Washington, D.C., as the colonists had been ruled by London, would be unrepublican.

Therefore the ordinance's first provision was to divide the Northwest Territory into six states, each of which, on meeting a minimum population standard, would be admitted to the union "on an equal footing with the original states." Ultimately the Old Northwest was divided into the states of Ohio, Indiana, Illinois, Michigan, Wisconsin, and Minnesota. Because a literate citizenry was considered essential for a republic, the Northwest Ordinance's second provision was that revenue from the sale of part of each township in each state would fund public education—an early example of federal support for American education. The third provision was that "neither slavery nor involuntary servitude" would be permitted in the Old Northwest. Finally, the ordinance said that the rights of the Indians would be respected.

The first three provisions of the Northwest Ordinance were enforced, but the promise to respect Indian rights was soon ignored. The British imperial government had prevented the American colonists from coming into conflict with Indians by banning settlement west of the Appalachians. The resentment this provoked was one of the causes of the Revolutionary War. No longer restrained by London, white settlers swarmed over the Appalachians. In the wars that resulted, the settlers, with the aid of the federal and state governments, swept Indian communities aside. The Shawnee were conquered and expelled from Ohio in the 1790s. The last great battle for the Midwest between whites and Indians was the Black Hawk War of 1832, in which the young Abraham Lincoln served in the Illinois militia. The Fox and Sauk tribes had been forced into the Iowa territory and then returned to their old homes in northern Illinois. The war began when Illinois settlers murdered the emissaries of Sauk and Fox Indians, led by Black Hawk, and ended after Illinois militia massacred Sauk men, women, and children at the Bad Axe River in Wisconsin. This ethnic cleansing of Indians was the precondition for converting the Midwest into a paradise for white settlers like the Lincolns.

A third government policy that profoundly affected the future development of the Midwest was the Northwest Ordinance's provision that all government sales of land would be in "fee simple." This represented a victory for Jeffersonian populists. The Jeffersonians did not achieve their most ambitious goal, which was the provision of free land by the government to settlers who agreed to work it; that would be achieved much later by the Homestead Act of 1862, which President Abraham Lincoln would sign into law. But Jeffersonians succeeded in inserting a provision in the Northwest Ordinance that guaranteed that yeoman farmers would own their land free and clear, and not suffer from the complex forms of "fee-tail" or encumbrances which in British law were a relic of feudalism.

Already in his lifetime Abraham Lincoln was being identified as the archetypical Midwesterner—and with good reason. The history of the Lincoln family was shaped by the three trends that formed the Midwest: the conflict between settlers and Indians (the grandfather for whom Lincoln was named was killed by an Indian); the injustice caused by feudal land law (Lincoln's father was forced to give up two farms because of uncertainties about his title to them); and the creation of the new Midwestern states, including Indiana and Illinois, to which the Lincolns moved as a part of a major migration of poor white Southerners drawn by the opportunities of the Old Northwest.

THE FIRST MEMBERS of the Lincoln family arrived in Massachusetts in the 1630s, and later generations moved southward and westward to New Jersey and then Pennsylvania. By the late eighteenth century the Lincolns had intermarried with the relatives of Daniel Boone, who were part of the stream of settlers pouring into Virginia's Shenandoah Valley. New Jersey–born John Lincoln (1716–88) became known as Virginia John when he moved his family to Rockingham County, Virginia, in the Appalachian Mountains. John's son Abraham Lincoln (1744–86) started a family on a farm near that of his father. In 1782 the first Abraham Lincoln moved his family from Virginia to a farm in Kentucky.

Here, in 1786, the struggle between the Shawnee Indians and the invading white settlers drew in the Lincoln family. While Abraham and his three sons Thomas, Josiah, and Mordecai were clearing a field, a group of Native Americans, probably but not certainly Shawnees, attacked, shooting Abraham dead. As eight-year-old Thomas sat stunned at the side of his slain father, the oldest son, Mordecai, ran into the cabin, aimed a gun between the logs, and shot and killed the Indian who had killed his father.

After the death of their father Abraham, the three sons and two daughters were raised by relatives. Abraham's daughters married Kentuckians, but his three orphaned sons moved westward, eventually ending up in Indiana (Josiah) and Illinois (Mordecai, Thomas). Thomas Lincoln moved to Kentucky in 1803, where, three years later, at the age of twenty-eight, he married Nancy Hanks, like him a native of Virginia. On February 12, 1809, Nancy Hanks Lincoln gave birth to Abraham Lincoln. According to Lincoln's law partner William Herndon, Lincoln believed that his mother Nancy Hanks had been the illegitimate daughter of a Virginia planter. His evidence was the inferiority of the rest of her family; according to Herndon, Lincoln said, "The Hanks are the lowest people in the world."[3] This reported remark lends credence to the morose speculation of his cousin and childhood housemate Dennis Hanks following Lincoln's death: "When he was with us, he seemed to think a great deal of us; but I thought sometimes it was hypocritical, but I am not sure."[4]

When the future president was two years old, the family moved to a farm on Knob Creek, only to move again, when he was seven in 1816, to a new farm in Indiana just north of the Ohio River on Pigeon Creek. Here, in 1818, Lincoln's mother died. Fourteen months later Lincoln had a stepmother, Sarah Bush Johnston Lincoln, a friend of Nancy Lincoln who had lost her own husband in 1816. At the age of ten the young Abraham found himself part of a larger family created from the blending of his father's first family (Abraham and his sister Sarah) with the children of his new stepmother, Sarah, by Daniel Johnston (John, Elizabeth, and Matilda) and his cousin, Dennis Hanks. In 1830, Lincoln moved with his father's family and a number of in-laws to Illinois. As in Indiana, many of their neighbors were yeoman farmers from the upper South.

In his brief 1860 autobiography, Lincoln explained the reasons for the family's migration as "partly on account of slavery; but chiefly on account of the difficulty in land titles."[5] Thomas Lincoln, who was illiterate, found himself forced to abandon two farms when others claimed title to them. His experience was like that of many yeoman farmers on the frontier who lacked either the education or the financial resources to mount successful legal struggles against rival claimants, such as wealthy slave owners in slave states or creditors who had liens on a particular piece of property. Their situation was made worse by the persistence of complex systems of overlapping rights in land inherited from British law. An English lawyer who visited Lincoln in the White House in 1864 reported that the president, in commenting on British and American land law, "talked of the landed tenures of England, and said we had some 'queer things in the legal way' at home, of which he seemed to think 'quit rents' as queer as any. And then he told us how 'in the state of Kentucky, where he was raised, they used to be so troubled with the same mysterious relics of feudalism, and titles got into such an almighty mess with these pettifoggin' incumbrances turnin' up at evry fresh tradin' with the land, and no one knowin' how to get rid of 'em' . . ."[6]

According to Lincoln, his father moved his family from Kentucky to the free state of Indiana not only because of "the difficulty in land titles" but "partly on account of slavery." In Kentucky the Lincolns joined a separate Baptist group that broke with the South Fork Baptist Church over slavery and formed the Little Mount Baptist Church.[7] Their objections to the institution probably arose from its effect on people like them. In a slave state like Kentucky, small farmers like Thomas Lincoln often found themselves at a disadvantage in economic competition with nearby slave plantations, and they were despised by the snobbish planter elite. In a campaign biography written to promote Lincoln in 1860, the journalist J. L. Scripps explained that Thomas Lincoln "realized in his daily experience and observation how slavery oppresses the poorer classes, making their poverty and social disrepute a permanent condition through the degradation which it affixes to labor."[8]

Lincoln may have been thinking of his own family when he remarked in 1860: "Slave States are places for poor white people to remove from; not to remove to. New free states are the places for poor people to go to and better their condition."[9] Arguing in the 1850s for keeping slavery out of the West, Lincoln said: "Is it not rather our duty to make labor more respectable by preventing all black competition, especially in the territories?"[10] If the institution of slavery were allowed to spread through the West, Lincoln warned, then "Negro equality will be abundant, as every White laborer will have occasion to regret when he is elbowed from his plow or his anvil by slave niggers."[11]

IN 1831, WHILE working for a local businessman named Denton Offutt, Lincoln and a few others took a flatboat of merchandise to New Orleans. When he returned after two months, Lincoln went to work for Offutt as a clerk at his store in New Salem, an Illinois town that no longer exists.

Having moved out of his father's house, Lincoln now began his adult career. In 1832 he ran for the state legislature and lost. After an uneventful stint in the Illinois militia during the conflict with the Black Hawk Indians, Lincoln returned to New Salem and supported himself as half owner of a store and then, beginning in 1834, as a county surveyor. In the same year he was elected for the first time to the Illinois legislature. He became a lawyer after a brief course of study like the one he later recommended to a young man who asked him about a legal education: "It is only to get books and read and study them carefully. Begin with Blackstone's Commentaries, and after reading carefully through, say twice, take up Chitty's Pleadings, Greenleaf's Evidence, and Story's Equity in succession. Work, work, work, is the main thing."[12]

"Lincoln . . . was not enamored of the life of a common laborer," Ward Hill Lamon wrote in his biography of Lincoln in 1872. "He preferred to clerk, to go to war, to enter politics—anything but that dreary round of daily toil and poor pay."[13] His law partner William Herndon agreed, recalling that Lincoln "dwelt entirely in his head and in the land of thought, and while he was physically a lazy man, yet he was intellectually energetic . . ."[14]

After becoming a prosperous lawyer and politician, Lincoln was distant from his family. Lincoln did not invite any members of his family to his marriage to Mary Todd in 1842. According to one family member, Thomas and Sarah Lincoln did not even know Abraham had married until he visited them later in Coles County as part of his circuit riding.[15] He refused his dying father's request for a final visit. He did, however, name one son Thomas in 1853, two years after his father's death.

In its outward events the life of the young Abraham Lincoln was similar to that of many of his contemporaries on the nineteenth-century Midwestern frontier. And yet Abraham Lincoln is a paradoxical figure. The child of devout Baptists in one of the most religious regions of the United States, he concluded at an early age that Christianity was false and never professed orthodox Christian belief, even when doing so might have helped his political career. The product of a culture that favored brawn over brain, he disliked manual labor and was addicted to books. Lacking what he considered to be an adequate formal education, he became a politician who impressed his associates with his intellectual powers and who prided himself on his philosophical rigor. Brought up on farms, he dreamed of factories, hoped that the wilderness in which he was raised could quickly be replaced by cities and fields set in a web of canals, roads, and railway lines—and even became the only U.S. president to patent an invention (to help ships float over shoals). Born in a log cabin on the Western frontier, he became a politician who championed the interests of Eastern manufacturers and merchants. A native of a region that cherished Jeffersonian traditions of states' rights and limited government, he became the most important president in the centralizing, nationalist tradition of Jefferson's rival Alexander Hamilton.

It is difficult to think of another major American political leader who so thoroughly repudiated the traditions of his family and his native region in everything from political and economic beliefs to religion. Abraham Lincoln did not flamboyantly rebel against the traditions in which he was raised. He quietly jettisoned them. In their place he adopted a view of the world that he inherited not from his parents, or his neighbors, or his community, or his region, but from a source that had more influence on him than all of those personal influences combined. More than most people, Abraham Lincoln was a product of the books he read.

Lincoln's cousin Dennis Hanks, who grew up with him in Thomas Lincoln's household, described Lincoln's early education in an interview with Lincoln's law partner and biographer William Herndon: "About Abs Early Education: and his sisters Education let me say this—Their mother first learned [taught] their Abc's and then Ab's. She learned them this out of Websters old spelling book: it belonged to me & cost in those days 75c, it being Covered with Calf skin—or suchlike Covering. I taught Abe his first lesson in spelling—reading & writing—. I taught Abe to write with a buzzards quillen which I killed with a rifle & having made a pen—put Abes hand in mind [sic] & moving his fingers by my hand to give him the idea of how to write—. We had no geese then—for the Country was a forrest. I tried to kill an Eagle but it was too smart—wanted to learn Abe to write with that."[16] It is a pity that the bird was "too smart" to be killed by Hanks; the image of the young Lincoln being taught to write using the quill of an eagle is attractive.

The earliest account of Lincoln's formal education was provided by Lincoln himself. At the request of Jesse W. Fell, a Republican organizing Lincoln's presidential campaign, Lincoln—reportedly at a table in the Bloomington courthouse—wrote a memoir that was published in the newspapers. In Indiana, Lincoln recalled: "There were some schools, so-called, but no qualification was ever required of a teacher beyond readin', writin' and cipherin' to the rule of three."[17]

Lincoln recalled that his father's "idea of a thorough education . . . was to have me cipher through the rule of three."[18] While Thomas Lincoln indulged his bookish son, he depended on the children for labor, "his father having sometime to slash him for neglecting his work by reading."[19] Lincoln's family and neighbors agreed that reading was Lincoln's favorite pastime as a boy. According to his stepmother, "He read all the books he could lay his hands on. He read diligently—studied in the day time . . . went to bed Early—got up Early and then read." His cousin John Hanks reported that in the family cabin "he would go to the Cupboard—Snatch a piece of Corn bread—take down a book—Sit down on a chair—Cock his legs up as high as his head and read."[20] When Lincoln first lived on his own in his twenties in New Salem, he was free to read whenever he pleased. A neighbor re-called: "While Lincoln was still keeping store at [New] Salem, Ill., he formed the acquaintance of Lawyer Logan, of Springfield, who loaned him law books to read. He has often walked from Salem to Springfield and re-turn [sic], carrying these books, and would read one or two while walking before reaching home, so eager was he for knowledge."[21]

LINCOLN WAS INTRODUCED by his reading to the dominant secular tradition of early American society: the tradition of republicanism. The founders rejected the idea of directly copying this or that ancient soci-ety. Alexander Hamilton wrote: "[I]t is as ridiculous to seek for models in the simple ages of Greece and Rome, as it would be to go in quest of them among the Hottentots and Laplanders."[22] Even so, the importance of classi-cal antiquity for the politics of the early American republic can hardly be ex-aggerated.

The public philosophy of the early American republic was saturated with ideas from the Roman tradition. The very term "republic" is Roman—res publica, the public thing or common-wealth. The idea of pop-ular sovereignty was another ancient Roman doctrine revived in the Renaissance. The concept of a senate to check the excesses of a popular as-sembly, like the body's name, is Roman. Pater Patriae, "Father of His Country," the title Americans bestowed on George Washington, was the ti-tle that Cato had given to his fellow statesman of the Roman republic, Cicero. Another title for Washington, "First in War, First in Peace, First in the Hearts of His Countrymen," echoes the Roman phrase "First Citizen" *(princeps)* without any overtones of despotism (the category "prince," in the writings of Machiavelli and other republican theorists, includes elected leaders as well as kings and military dictators). Chief Justice John Marshall, in his five-volume biography of George Washington, made Washington a parallel of Cicero.[23]

Not only modern republicanism but modern liberalism and constitutionalism have Roman roots. "The rule (or empire) of laws, not of men," an axiom of transatlantic republicanism, is a phrase inspired by the Roman historian Livy. The social contract theory, in various versions such as Locke's and Rousseau's, develops the belief of Roman philosophers and jurists that originally human beings were solitary savages who banded together to form communities based on common interests. "All men are created equal" is a quotation from Roman law: *omnes hominae natura aequales sunt,* "all men are by nature equal."

The central cultural hero of the elite in the early American republic was the Roman orator and statesman Marcus Tullius Cicero (106–43 B.C.), who gave his life in the struggle to defend the institutions of the Roman republic. John Adams wrote of Cicero that "all the ages of the world have not produced a greater statesman and philosopher united in the same character."[24] From the American Revolution until the Civil War, the dominant type in American politics was the Ciceronian lawyer-statesman-orator-journalist who could argue a case before a jury, campaign for office, deliver a public oration, or write a pamphlet on an issue of the day. The oration, in the form of the political speech or the sermon, was the major literary genre in the United States between the founding era and the middle of the nineteenth century. Educated people read collections of speeches and sermons the way that their successors would read novels and collections of short stories and poems. The nineteenth-century equivalent of famous twentieth-century novelists like Hemingway, Faulkner, Fitzgerald, and Wolfe were orators like Edward Everett, Daniel Webster, Ralph Waldo Emerson, and the Unitarian minister Theodore Parker. The romantic idea that fiction is more "creative" than nonfiction was alien to a literary culture still influenced by the classical tradition of Rome, the Renaissance, and eighteenth-century Europe, in which oratory, history, and biography, along with epic, were considered the preeminent literary genres. Another Romantic idea, that the great writer is a solitary figure communicating with an individual reader through the written page, was equally unfamiliar in a culture in which orators addressed vast crowds and in which families and friends read aloud to one another. Like many of his contemporaries, Lincoln was fond of reading aloud to his family, friends, aides, and even, when he was president, his Cabinet officers.

In American colleges in the early nineteenth century, one-half of the curriculum was devoted to Greek and Latin studies; the rest was divided among moral philosophy, logic, rhetoric, belles lettres, history, and natural philosophy.[25] Proficiency in Latin was required by every college for graduation, and by many for acceptance. In his campaign memoir, Lincoln regretted his lack of opportunities to study Latin: "If a straggler supposed to understand Latin happened to sojourn in the neighborhood he was looked upon as a wizard." Lincoln's lack of a classical education prompted an amusing recollection by John Locke Scripps, who wrote Lincoln's campaign biography in 1860, *Life of Abraham Lincoln.* "When the pamphlet was printed, I sent a few copies to Mr. Lincoln, and in an accompanying note, I said to him, I was in doubt only as to one statement I had made—and that was as to whether or not he had read 'Plutarch's Lives.' I had trusted somewhat to my memory on the subject of his early reading; and while I was not certain he had enumerated this book among them he had read in his boyhood, yet as I had grown up in about such a settlement of people as he had in Indiana, and as I had read Plutarch in my boy-hood, I presumed he had had access to it also. If I was mistaken in this supposition, I said to him, it was my wish that he should at once get a copy, and read it, *that I might be able to testify as to the perfect accuracy of the entire sketch.* Mr. Lincoln did not reply to my note, but I heard of his frequent humorous allusions to it."[26] As president, Lincoln replied to Secretary of War Edwin M. Stanton's objection to a prospective appointee on the grounds that his education was inadequate: "I personally wish Jacob R. Freese, of New Jersey to be appointed a Colonel . . . and this regardless of whether he can tell the exact shade of Julius Caesar's hair."[27]

Despite his lack of Latin, Lincoln was exposed to the classical tradition through translations. Dennis Hanks recalled: "Abe was so attached to reading that we had to buy him—hire him too work—bought him, I think the Columbian Orator or American Preceptor."[28] Evidently Lincoln as a boy was "hired out" to another farmer to work for a while so he could earn the money for the book. Caleb Bingham edited both *The American Preceptor; Being a New Selection of Lessons for Reading and Speaking* (1794) and *The Columbian Orator; Containing a Variety of Original and Selected Pieces; Together with Rules Calculated to Improve Youth and Others in the Ornamental and Useful Art of Eloquence* (1797). Dennis Hanks also claimed that Lincoln's father bought him "the united States Speaker." This was probably *The American Speaker; A Selection of Popular, Parliamentary and Forensic Eloquence; Particularly Calculated for the Seminaries in the United States* (1811). The titles of both *The American Speaker* and *The Columbian Orator* alluded to Cicero's *De Oratore (The Orator),* one of the central texts in Western elite education for almost two millennia.

Cicero makes an appearance in the second sentence of the introduction to *The Columbian Orator,* which is entitled "General Instructions for Speaking—Extracted from Various Authors" and begins with "On Pronunciation": "The best judges among the ancients have represented Pronunciation, which they likewise called Action, as the principal part of an orator's province; from whence he is chiefly to expect success in the art of persuasion. When Cicero, in the person of Crassus [in *The Orator*], has largely and elegantly discoursed upon all the other parts of oratory, coming at last to speak of this, he says: 'All the former have their effect as they are pronounced.' "[29] The introduction is dominated by the precepts of Cicero and examples from his life and practice, supplemented by references to the Athenian orator Demosthenes and the Roman teachers of rhetoric

Quintilian and Hortensius.[30] Turning from the introduction to the first of a number of selections, Lincoln would have found another encomium to Cicero in the "Extract from an Oration on Eloquence, Pronounced at Harvard University on Commencement Day, 1794" by an otherwise unidentified "Perkins": "Let us now direct our attention to that other garden of eloquence, the Roman commonwealth. Here, as in Greece, a free government opened the list to such as wished to dispute the palm in oratory. Numbers advance and contend manfully for glory. But their glory is soon to fade; for Cicero appears; Cicero, another name for eloquence itself. It is needless to enlarge upon his character as an orator. Suffice it to say, that if we ransack the histories of the world to find a rival for Demosthenes, Cicero alone can be found capable of supporting a claim to that distinguished honour." But the United States could prove to be a greater "garden of eloquence" than either Athens or Rome. "May Columbia always afford more than one Demosthenes, to support the sacred cause of freedom, and to thunder terror in the ears of every transatlantic Philip. May more than Ciceronian eloquence be ever ready to plead for injured innocence, and suffering virtue."[31] The analogy between the Roman republic and the American republic is reinforced in the next two selections—an "Extract from President Washington's First Speech in Congress, 1789" followed by a "Speech of Paulus Emilius to the Roman People As He Was Taking the Command of Their Army." In *The Columbian Orator* the future statesman and lawyer could have found "An Oration on the Powers of Eloquence, Written for an Exhibition of a School in Boston, 1794": "When the enlightened statesman is discussing the interests of a country, on which are engrafted his fortune, fame and life, he *must* be eloquent. When the compassionate lawyer, without hope of reward, advocates the cause of the suffering widow, or injured orphan, he *must* be eloquent."[32]

Lincoln's contemporaries did not consider him a great orator, of the rank of Henry Clay, Daniel Webster, or Edward Everett. His former law partner Joshua Speed observed, "That while no set speech [of Mr. Lincoln] (save his Gettysburg speech) will be considered artistically complete—Yet when gems of American literature come to be selected from great Authors as many will be selected from Lincolns speeches as from any American author."[33] Lincoln's terse, logical style is quite different from the expansive, sentimental style of oratory favored by Clay and Webster, the Whig orators he admired. In part this reflects a generational shift. By the 1830s, as the elite politics of the early American republic gave way to a more democratic political system, a plainer style of public speaking, more accessible to the majority, replaced the older, more elaborate style. According to Joshua Speed, Lincoln's rhetorical style was influenced by that of John C. Calhoun, the South Carolina senator whose defenses of states' rights and slavery helped inspire Confederate ideology: "So far as I now remember of his study for composition it was to make short sentences & a compact style—Illustrative of this—he was a great admirer of the style of John C. Calhoun—I remember reading to him one of Mr. Calhouns speeches in reply to Mr. Clay in the Senate—in which Mr. Clay had quoted precedent—(I quote from memory). Mr. Calhoun replied 'that to legislate upon precedent is but to make the error of yesterday the law of today.' Lincoln that [*sic*] that was a great truth greatly uttered—."[34]

Lincoln's genius for rhetorical concision is illustrated by his phrase in the Gettysburg Address: "That government of the people, by the people, for the people shall not perish from the earth." Lincoln's phrase had two sources. One was a speech he admired and consulted in preparing for his presidential inauguration, Daniel Webster's Second Reply to Hayne, of 1830, in which Webster, in the course of defending the supremacy of the Union over the states, spoke of "the people's government, made for the people, made by the people, and answerable to the people." In a lecture on "The Effect of Slavery on the American People" by the liberal Boston Unitarian preacher Theodore Parker (in a book of Parker's sermons he borrowed from his law partner William Herndon), Lincoln found another variant of the formulation he would later make famous: "Democracy is direct self-government, over all the people, for all the people, by all the people."[35] Lincoln distilled these phrases into a simpler, definitive version—"government of the people, by the people, for the people"—and in doing so he may have been influenced by John C. Calhoun, whose philosophy he despised but whose prose he admired.

The Columbian Orator and books like it, including The American Preceptor and The American Speaker, provided a kind of inexpensive classical education in English for Americans like Lincoln who lacked the opportunity to study Latin and Greek. Lincoln's determination to earn enough money to buy the book was justified. It is not accurate to say, as many authors do, that the major influences on Lincoln's education and rhetoric were the Bible and Shakespeare. Lincoln's political values were profoundly shaped by the neo-Roman republican tradition, which influenced Lincoln both directly through texts like The Columbian Orator and indirectly through the classical influences that saturated the culture and politics of the early American republic.

THE CICERONIAN LAWYER-POLITICIANS of the early United States formed an elite, a culture of neoclassical republicanism, that coexisted uneasily with orthodox Protestant Christianity. In addition to republicanism, deism was another gift of the Romans to eighteenth-century American and French elites. Many ancient Greek and Roman philosophers had realized that the different cults of particular peoples were parochial superstitions. Instead of abandoning belief in the divine, many ancient thinkers posited the existence of what Jefferson would call "Nature's God"—an abstract being responsible not only for the physical universe but for universal laws of morality that transcended local customs. Between the seventeenth and twentieth centuries, deism appealed to many thinkers who could not believe in Christianity or other revealed religions, and yet who were unwilling to become consistent atheists or agnostics like the ancient Greek philosophers Democritus and Epicurus and the ancient Roman poet Lucretius, who believed in a universe governed only by chance and physical laws.

Deism was less controversial than atheism in societies in which the majority of people were conventional Protestant or Catholic Christians. Deist politicians could talk about "God" and "providence," using language that would be understood in one way by Christian listeners and interpreted differently by the elite minority of fellow deists. And deists in Europe and America learned from an early deist, Cicero, that belief in an abstract God of Nature should be coupled with pious observance of the outward forms of traditional religion, such as the ancient rites of the Roman people. No less than Christians, many deists sincerely believed that atheism—belief in no God rather than in Nature's God—was incompatible with morality and good citizenship. Not all deists believed in a non-Christian afterlife in which moral behavior would be rewarded and evil punished, but most assumed that people would not be moral unless they believed that moral norms were divine laws rather than human customs.

Lincoln was known to friends and enemies alike throughout his life as a deist, a fact that illustrates the influence of eighteenth-century thought on his outlook. "I am not a Christian," he told Newton Bateman, the superintendent of education in Illinois.[36] According to Lincoln's first law partner, John Todd Stuart: "He was an avowed and open infidel and sometimes bordered on atheism; . . . went further against Christian beliefs and doctrines and principles than any man I ever heard; he shocked me. I don't remember the exact line of his argument; suppose it was against the inherent defects, so-called, of the Bible, and on grounds of reason. Lincoln always denied that Jesus was the Christ of God—denied that Jesus was the son of God as understood and maintained by the Christian Church."[37] David Davis, the Illinois judge and political ally whom Lincoln appointed to the U.S. Supreme Court, explained: "He had no faith, in the Christian sense of the term—had faith in laws, principles, causes and effects."[38] In Herndon's words, "Scientifically regarded he was a realist as opposed to an idealist, a sensationalist as opposed to an intuitionist, a materialist as opposed to a spiritualist."[39]

In his youth, Lincoln read the attacks on Christianity of Tom Paine and French philosopher Constantine Volney. "Our ideas, not only of the Almightyness of the Creator, but of his wisdom and his beneficence, become enlarged in proportion as we contemplate the extent and the structure of the universe," Paine wrote in *The Age of Reason*. Not only human beings, but rational beings on other planets could infer the existence of a benevolent Creator from the observation of Nature: "The inhabitants of each of the worlds, of which our system is composed, enjoy the same opportunities of knowledge as we do." The true heretics are those who base religion on supernatural revelations rather than on natural science: "It has been, by rejecting the evidence, that the word, or works of God in the creation, affords to our senses, and the action of our reason upon that evidence, that so many wild and whimsical systems of faith, and of religion, have been fabricated and set up."[40] In Volney's book *The Ruins*, Lincoln read: "It is then in vain that nations attribute their religion to heavenly inspirations; it is in vain that their dogmas pretend to a primeval state of supernatural events. . . . Reason, strengthened by these contradictions, rejecting everything that is not in the order of nature, and admitting no historical facts but those founded on probabilities, lays open its own system, and pronounces itself with assurance."[41] Volney's *Ruins* was controversial in the early United States not only because of its deism, but because of its surmise that blacks had created great civilizations in the past. The first American edition removed favorable references to blacks; Volney published a corrected translation that included them.

Inspired by Paine, Volney, and perhaps others, in 1834, according to Herndon, Lincoln wrote "a little book on Infidelity" in which he questioned "the divinity of Christ—Special Inspiration—Revelation &c."[42] His friends, fearing it would harm his political ambitions, persuaded Lincoln to burn the only book he ever wrote. Evidently Lincoln's skepticism about the veracity of the Bible began at an early age. According to his cousin Dennis Hanks, "Lincolns mother learned him to read the Bible—study it & the stories in it and all that was moraly & affectionate it [*sic*] it, repeating it to Abe & his sister when very young. Lincoln was often & much moved by the stories." Hanks relates: "One day when Lincolns mother was weaving in a little shed Abe came in and quizzically asked his good mother who was the father of Zebedee's Children: she saw the drift and laughed, saying get out of her [*sic*] you nasty little pup, you: he saw he had got his mother and ran off laughing."[43] As a child, Hanks recalled, Lincoln would amuse the other children by standing up "on a stump or log" and "mimacing the Style & tone of the old Baptist Preachers" until his father would "come and make him quit—send him to work."[44] It is also significant that Lincoln's favorite poet was the Scottish poet Robert Burns, because Burns was notorious in Lincoln's time as the poet of those who scoffed at the prudery and hypocrisy of organized religion.

In 1834, the year in which he wrote and burned his "little Book on Infidelity," Lincoln criticized the followers of Democratic politician Peter Cartwright, a former evangelist, as "in some degree priest-ridden." More than a decade later, in 1846, when Lincoln, then running for a seat in the U.S. House of Representatives, was accused of infidelity, he issued the following statement: "A charge having got into circulation in some of the neighborhoods of this District, in substance that I am an open scoffer at Christianity, I have by the advice of some friends concluded to notice the subject in this form. That I am not a member of any Christian Church is true; but I have never denied the truth of the Scriptures; and I have never spoken with intentional disrespect of religion in general, or of any denomination of Christians in particular." Lincoln went on to admit: "It is true that in early life I was inclined to believe in what I understand is called the 'Doctrine of Necessity'—that is, that the human mind is impelled to action, or held in rest by some power, over which the mind has no control; and I have sometimes (with one, two or three, but never publicly) tried to maintain this opinion in argument. The habit of arguing thus however, I have, entirely left off for more than five years." Lincoln concluded this disingenuous statement: "I do not think I could myself, be brought to support a man for office, whom I knew to be an open enemy of, and scoffer at, religion."[45]

In private, however, Lincoln continued to scoff at Christian clerics. In 1860, according to Herndon, when he was told that most of the clergy in Springfield opposed him as president, "He commented bitterly on the attitude of the preachers and many of their followers, who, pretending to be believers in the Bible and God-fearing Christians, yet by their votes demonstrated that they cared not whether slavery was voted up or down."[46]

Lincoln's non-Christian fatalism—the "doctrine of necessity"—persisted throughout his life. He told Albert G. Hodges during the Civil War, on April 4, 1864, "I claim not to have controlled events, but confess plainly that events have controlled me."[47] In the same year Lincoln said that he had hoped "for a happy termination of this terrible war long before this; but God knows best, and has ruled otherwise."[48] In his Proclamation of Thanksgiving of October 20, 1864, he spoke of "the Great Disposer of events."[49]

From these and similar statements, some scholars have attempted to work out a theory of predestination influenced by Calvinist theology.[50] But many statesmen have attributed their political successes to divine providence, for the reason that Francis Bacon explained in his essay "Of Fortune": "All wise men, to decline the envy of their own virtues, use to ascribe them to Providence and Fortune; for so they may the better assume them; and, besides, it is greatness in a man, to be the care of the higher powers . . . And it hath been noted, that those who ascribe openly too much to their own wisdom and policy, end infortunate [sic]."[51]

While Lincoln never publicly attacked religion, he also refused throughout his life to join a religious congregation, although he attended church services with his wife and children. James Smith, pastor of the First Presbyterian Church of Springfield, knew Lincoln well. After the death of Lincoln's son Edward, Smith observed, "I found him very much depressed and downcast at the death of his son, and without the consolation of the gospel. Up to this time I had heard but little concerning his religious views, and that was to the effect that he was a deist and inclined to skepticism as to the divine origin of the scriptures, though, unlike most skeptics, he had evidently been a constant reader of the Bible."[52] Orville Hickman Browning frequently attended the Presbyterian church with the Lincolns. Apart from reading the Bible, Hickman recalled, he "never knew of his engaging in any other act of devotion. He did not invoke a blessing at table, nor did he have family prayers."[53]

Despite his lack of Christian faith, Lincoln's oratory is suffused with phrases and images from the King James Bible. Lincoln's first use of the quotation from the Gospel of Mark, "A house divided against itself cannot stand," came in the context of an 1843 debate about the organization of the Whig Party.[54] In his Second Inaugural Address, Lincoln quoted two verses from the Bible: "Woe unto the world because of offenses! for it must needs be that offenses come; but woe to that man by whom the offense cometh!" The verse is from Matthew 18:7 in the King James Version. Luke 17:1 contains another version: "Then said he unto the disciples, It is impossible but that offenses will come: but woe unto him, through whom they come!" In addition to these direct quotes, the Second Inaugural contains a number of scriptural allusions. Two verses from the Bible—"In the sweat of thy face shalt thou eat bread" (Genesis 3:19), and "Judge not, that ye be not judged" (Matthew 7:1, Luke 6:37)—are combined in Lincoln's sentence: "It may seem strange that any men should dare to ask a just God's assistance in wringing their bread from the sweat of other men's faces, but let us judge not, that we be not judged." Lincoln's phrase "to bind up the nation's wounds" comes from Psalm 147:3: "He healeth the broken in heart, and bindeth up their wounds." Near the end of the Second Inaugural, Lincoln quoted Psalm 19:9: "The judgments of the Lord are true and righteous altogether."[55] Two historians have seen the influence of St. Paul on Lincoln's phrase "The Almighty has his own purposes" (Ephesians 1:11, "according to the purpose of him who worketh all things after the counsel of his own will") and the phrase "With malice toward none, with charity toward all."[56]

Lincoln's knowledge of the Bible permitted him to make obscure allusions. When a Presbyterian preacher, seeing Lincoln addressing a crowd, cried, "Where the great ones are, there will the people be," Lincoln shouted back, "Ho! Parson a little more Scriptural; 'Where the carces [*sic*] is there will the eagles be gathered together.' "[57] The allusion was to Luke 17:37.

Lincoln's use of quotations from the Bible has often been cited as evidence of his piety. However, a Springfield neighbor who served as a babysitter for the Lincolns related, "He read the Bible quite as much for its literary style as he did for its religious or spiritual content. He read it in the relaxed, almost lazy attitude of a man enjoying a good book."[58] Lincoln told one acquaintance that "the Bible is the richest source of pertinent allusions."[59]

ACCORDING TO HERNDON: "He lived and acted from the standard of reason—that throne of logic, home of principle—the realm of Deity in man."[60] One manifestation of Lincoln's rationalism was his fascination with natural science. His law partner wrote that Lincoln did not have the patience to do more than peruse Herndon's copies of books by Darwin and other British scientists. Nevertheless, Lincoln became an enthusiastic convert to the theory of evolution. "A gentleman in Springfield gave him a book called, I believe, 'Vestiges of Creation,' which interested him so much that he read it through. The volume was published in Edinburgh, and undertook to demonstate the doctrine of development or evolution. The treatise interested him greatly, and he was deeply impressed with the notion of the so-called 'universal law'—evolution; he did not extend greatly his researches, but by continued thinking in a single channel seemed to grow into a warm advocate of the new doctrine."[61] The book to which Herndon referred was by Robert Chambers, *Vestiges of Creation* (1844). The idea that human beings and other animals had evolved from more primitive organisms was controversial but familiar, even before Charles Darwin provided natural selection as a plausible mechanism for evolution.

Technology as well as science fascinated Lincoln. Herndon explained that "his mind, apparently with an automatic movement, ran back behind facts, principles, and all things to their origin and first cause—to that point where forces act at once as effect and cause. He would stop in the street and analyze a machine. He would whittle a thing to a point, and then count the numberless inclined planes and their pitch making the point. Mastering and defining this, he would then cut that point back and get a broad transverse section of his pine-stick, and peel and define that. Clocks, omnibuses, language, paddle-wheels, and idioms never escaped his observation and analysis. . . ."[62]

Even while serving in politics, Lincoln tried to become an inventor. In his youth, when he took a boatload of merchandise for the New Salem merchant Offutt to New Orleans, his flatboat was stranded, and years later the ship he was on in the Great Lakes got stuck on a sandbar. While serving in the U.S. House of Representatives, Lincoln patented "A Device for Buoying Vessels Over Shoals" (Patent number 6,469, May 22, 1849). The device consisted of bellows that inflated beneath a ship's waterline in order to help the ship rise in shallow water. Although he paid for a wooden model of the invention, which is now in the National Museum of American History of the Smithsonian Institution, he never sold it. Lincoln apparently pondered other inventions. In 1859 he told the crowd at a Wisconsin fair that he had given much thought to "a steam plow."[63]

While Lincoln's career as an inventor was brief and unsuccessful, throughout his life he maintained his interest in novel technologies. The Lincoln of popular myth spent the Civil War pacing the halls of the White House in tragic solitude, mourning the calamity that had befallen the nation. The real Lincoln frequently and enthusiastically took part in tests of new weapons in the Washington Navy Yard or, sometimes, on the White House lawn. After spending two hours watching the test-firing of a machine gun and learning that it worked because gas was prevented from escaping, Lincoln turned to a journalist and asked, "Now have any of you heard of any machine, or invention, for preventing the escape of 'gas' from newspaper establishments?"[64] Among the models of proposed weapons that Lincoln collected in his White House office were a brass cannon that rested on a pile of land patents and a grenade that Lincoln used on his desk as a paperweight.[65] These details, incompatible with the picture of a Christlike Man of Sorrows, have been edited from Lincoln's historical image.

LINCOLN'S RATIONALIST VIEW of world history is found in a lecture he delivered to a delegation of Native American chiefs who visited the White House on March 27, 1863. The speech is seldom mentioned by historians, perhaps because Lincoln's attitude toward Native Americans seems offensive in an era sensitive to cultural differences and inclined to romanticize premodern peoples. But Lincoln was a product of the Enlightenment, and he had no doubt that civilization was an improvement on barbarism.

Using quaint language that he must have derived from popular literature and the theater, Lincoln subjected the chiefs to a scientific lecture. "We pale-faced people think that this world is a great, round ball. . . ." At this point the president directed their attention to a globe, and Professor Joseph Henry, the first Secretary of the Smithsonian Institution, gave a brief account of world geography, pointing out Washington, D.C., and their own region. Lincoln then told the Native Americans: "The pale-faced people are numerous and prosperous because they cultivate the earth, produce bread, and depend upon the products of the earth rather than wild game for subsistence." Another reason for the greater wealth and power of "the pale-faced people," Lincoln continued, was the absence of anarchic violence: "Although we are now engaged in a great war between one another, we are not, as a race, so much disposed to fight and kill one another as our red brethren." Lincoln continued: "You have asked for my advice. . . . I can only say that I can see no way in which your race is to become as numerous and populous as the white race except by living, as they do, by the cultivation of the earth." What the Native Americans thought of all this is unknown, although the record states that "The President's remarks were received with frequent marks of applause and approbation. 'Ugh,' 'Aha' sounded along the line as the interpreter proceeded, and their countenances gave evident tokens of satisfaction."[66]

In advising the Indians to abandon "the habits and customs" of their race for a "new mode of life," Lincoln did not even mention a goal long cherished by many white Americans—the conversion of the Indians to Christianity. His own post-Christian deism had no discernible content beyond a belief in "the providence of the Great Spirit, who is the great Father of us all," and as a deist he may have thought that the Great Spirit was as good a name as Yahweh or the Christian Trinity for the abstract force behind nature and history. In his address to the Indians, Lincoln completely ignored Christianity and its predecessor, Judaism, both in his account of the rise to power of Europeans and Euro-Americans solely as a function of their advanced technology and in his recommendations for the future of Native American communities. In light of the religiosity that permeated American society in his time, it is significant that when Lincoln decided to instruct the Indian chiefs, he arranged for the presence in the White House not of a preacher but of a professor.

While Lincoln was enthusiastic about science and technology, he did not believe that progress was inevitable. In a seldom-noted passage of his Second Lecture on Discoveries and Inventions, written in February 1859, Lincoln briefly set forth what can only be called a sociological theory of history that emphasizes the degree to which technological and social progress has been the outcome of a series of three lucky and unforeseeable accidents, all of which occurred between the Renaissance and the nineteenth century.

One lucky accident was the invention of printing. Although writing had been around for millennia, "for the three thousand years during which printing remained undiscovered after writing was in use, it was only a small portion of the people who could write, or read writing. . . ." Printing inspired an explosion of education and invention: "I will venture to consider it," the autodidact said somewhat pompously, "the true termination of that period called 'the dark ages.' " According to the would-be inventor, the development of patent laws was the second of the three greatest events in world history.

The third fortunate accident, Lincoln declared, was the creation of new settler societies in the Western Hemisphere: "Just now, in civilization, and the arts, the people of Asia are entirely behind those of Europe; those of the East of Europe behind those of the West of it; while we, here in America, think we discover, and invent, and improve, faster than any of them. They may think this is arrogance; but they can not deny that Russia has called on us to show her how to build steam-boats and railroads—while in the older parts of Asia, they scarcely know that such things as S.Bs & RR.s. exist. In ancient established countries, the dust of ages—a real down-right old-fogyism—seems to settle upon, and smother the intellects and energies of man. It is in this view that I have mentioned the discovery of America as an event greatly favoring and facilitating useful discoveries and inventions."[67]

But even the break with stultifying traditions experienced by pioneers in a new country might not be sufficient if the immigrant society lacked the "habit" of scientific thought. Lincoln attributed the technological superiority of Anglo-Americans not to racial characteristics but to culture: "But for the difference in habit of observation, why did yankees, almost instantly, discover gold in California, which had been trodden upon, and over-looked, by indians and Mexican greasers, for centuries?"[68] Despite his pejorative characterization of Mexicans, his analysis was remarkably free of parochial American self-regard. Americans could not take pride in their technological superiority, because they owed it to a fortunate combination of the weakness of custom in a frontier society and the influence of the novel method of scientific thought. Americans happened to be ahead of the world "just now," but other nations might learn to "discover, and invent, and improve." And Americans might fall behind if they succumbed to conservatism or "old-fogyism."

For Lincoln, then, not only democracy but industrial civilization was the result of an unpredictable series of unexpected innovations—

Gutenberg's perfection of the printing press and the early modern refinement of natural science from natural philosophy—and the historical accident of the discovery and settlement of the Americas by science-minded Europeans and their descendants. But for these flukes of history, the human race as a whole might forever have remained agrarian, illiterate, superstitious, and governed by priests and autocrats with the aid of unquestioned tradition. Lincoln's contempt for tradition as "old-fogyism" was confirmed by Herndon: "He had no faith and no respect for 'say so's,' come though they might from tradition or authority. . . . Time could hide the error in no nook or corner of space in which he would not detect and expose it."[69]

Of religious piety and military heroism, the two main components of elite ethics before the democratic era, scarcely any trace can be found in Lincoln's rationalist and progressive worldview. Lincoln was capable of eloquent tributes to American soldiers who fell in the service of the republic. Even so, to Lincoln, the self-made man of the middle class, the heroic military ethic in its traditional form seemed as absurd as the miracles he had ridiculed in the book mocking Christianity that he wrote and then prudently destroyed. To a supporter who vowed to die to prevent interference with his inauguration, Lincoln told the story of a young soldier whose sisters were embroidering a belt with the motto "Victory or death." "No, no," said the youth, "don't put it quite that strong. Put it 'Victory or get hurt pretty bad.' "[70] During the 1848 presidential campaign, when Lincoln was campaigning on behalf of the Whig candidate Zachary Taylor, a hero of the Mexican War, he compared his own military record to that of the Democratic nominee Lewis Cass, a veteran of the War of 1812. "Yes, sir, in the days of the Black Hawk war, I fought, bled and came away," Lincoln said, explaining that "I had a good many bloody struggles with the mosquitoes; and, although I never fainted from loss of blood, I can truly say I was often very hungry." Referring to the story that Cass had broken his sword in wrath in response to the news that Detroit had surrendered to the British forces, Lincoln said, "It is quite certain I did not break my sword, for I had none to break; but I bent a musket pretty badly on one occasion."[71] No conservative traditionalist could have joked in this way.

THE INFLUENCE OF eighteenth-century rationalism is evident in Lincoln's speech to the Springfield Washington Temperance Society of 1842. The members who had joined the society out of Christian fervor must have thought it an odd address. Lincoln criticized traditional temperance reformers for using "impolitic" denunciations of "drunkards" and "dramsellers" instead of "persuasion, kind, unassuming persuasion": "It was impolitic, because, it is not much in the nature of man to be driven to any thing; still less to be driven about that which is exclusively his own business; and least of all, where such driving is to be submitted to, at the expense of pecuniary interest, or burning appetite." Instead of identifying self-interest with sin, in accordance with Christian tradition, Lincoln, like Enlightenment thinkers, took self-interest for granted as the basis of human behavior. "Such is man, and so must he be understood by those who would lead him, even to his own best interest." Enlightened self-interest, not spiritual salvation, was the goal of the temperance movement, as Lincoln defined it.

The devout members of the audience must have been even more baffled by Lincoln's attempt to treat temperance not as a religious crusade, but as a fulfillment of the secular political ideas of the United States. He compared "the temperance revolution" to the American Revolution and made his earliest recorded statement of what was to become a repeated theme, culminating in the Gettysburg Address: "Of our political revolution of '76, we all are justly proud. . . . In it the world has found a solution of that long mooted problem, as to the capability of man to govern himself. In it was the germ which has vegetated, and still is to grow and expand into the universal liberty of mankind." Lincoln concluded with a peroration in which he viewed both the American Revolution and the temperance revolution as reaching their fulfillment with the triumph of rationalism: "And when the victory shall be complete—when there shall be neither a slave nor a drunkard on the earth—how proud the title of that Land, which may truly claim to be the birth-place and cradle of both those revolutions, that have ended in that victory. How nobly distinguished that People, who shall have planted, and nurtured to maturity, both the political and moral freedom of their species."[72] Lincoln's peroration echoed not Christian theology, with its emphasis on revelation, but the optimism of the Age of Reason: "Happy day, when, all appetites are controlled, all passions subdued, all matters subjected, mind, all conquering mind, shall live and move the monarch of the world. Glorious consummation! Hail fall of Fury! Reign of Reason, all hail!" Lincoln's opposition to moral fervor and perhaps his secular rationalism as well appear to have alienated some of the religious crusaders. According to Herndon, his involvement with the temperance movement "was damaging to Lincoln, and gave rise to the opposition on the part of the churches which confronted him several years afterwards when he became a candidate against the noted Peter Cartwright for Congress."[73]

Lincoln's implicit rejection of supernatural religion in favor of reason as the basis of the "moral freedom" that is the corollary of republican freedom is clear as well as in his January 27, 1838, talk to the Young Men's Lyceum of Springfield. If individual intoxication is one threat to the republic, mob violence is another. In both cases the cure is the same: "Reason, cold, calculating, unimpassioned reason, must furnish all the materials for our future support and defense."[74] Instead of requiring the support of Protestant Christianity or other supernatural doctrines, Lincoln argued that American liberty can be supported by a purely secular "political religion" of obedience to man-made law. This is not to be confused with utopian secular religions like Marxism and Comtian Postivism. Rather, Lincoln was commending the piety toward legal institutions recommended by Cicero and by the more conservative Founders such as John Adams, who were most deeply influenced by neo-Roman republicanism: "Let reverence for the laws, be breathed by every American mother, to the lisping babe, that prattles on her lap—let it be taught in schools, in seminaries, and in colleges;—let it be written in primers, spelling books, and in almanacs;—let it be preached from the pulpit, proclaimed in legislative halls, and enforced in courts of justice. And, in short, let it become the political religion of the nation; and let the old and young, the rich and the poor, the grave and the gay, of all sexes and tongues, and colors and conditions, sacrifice unceasingly upon its altars."[75] The government is not to promote Christian morality; rather, the Christian "seminaries" and "the pulpit" are to be enlisted to promote the "political religion" of secular law and republican government. In both his temperance address on Washington's birthday and in his Lyceum address he invoked the model of George Washington, like him a deist, in connection with dispassionate rationalism.

The French Enlightenment philosopher Volney, in *The Ruins,* may have influenced Lincoln's metaphor of "the political religion of the nation":

And the people raised before the pyramid a new altar, on which they placed a golden balance, a sword, and a book with this inscription:

TO EQUAL LAW, WHICH JUDGES AND PROTECTS.

And having surrounded the pyramid and the altar with a vast amphitheatre, all the people took their seats to hear the publication of the law. And millions of men, raising at once their hands to heaven, took the solemn oath to live equal, free, and just; to respect their reciprocal properties and rights; to obey the law and its regularly chosen representatives.[76]

The fact that Lincoln is known to have read and discussed Volney a few years earlier may explain the similarity between this passage and Lincoln's peroration in his Lyceum address.

Lincoln also may have found a model for his secular, rationalist approach to temperance in *The Ruins.* Chapter 6 of the French philosopher's book is entitled "On Temperance." The young Lincoln read the following rationalist catechism:

Q. What is temperance?

A. It is a regular use of our faculties, which makes us never exceed in our sensations the end of nature to preserve us; it is the moderation of the passions. . . .

Q. How is drunkenness considered in the law of nature?

A. As a most vile and pernicious vice. The drunkard, deprived of the sense and reason given us by God, profanes the donations of the divinity: he debases himself to the condition of brutes; unable even to guide his steps, he staggers and falls as if he were epileptic; he hurts and even risks killing himself; his debility in this state exposes him to the ridicule and contempt of every person that sees him; he makes in his drunkenness, prejudicial and ruinous bargains, and injures his fortune; he makes use of opprobrious language, which creates him enemies and repentance; he fills his house with trouble and sorrow, and ends by a premature death or by a cacochymical old age.

Q. Does the law of nature interdict absolutely the use of wine?

A. No; it only forbids the abuse. . . .[77]

John Hay told Herndon, "He was very abstemious—ate less than any man I know. He drank nothing but water, not from principle but because he did not like wine or spirits. Once, in rather dark days early in the war, a temperance committee came to him and said that the reason we did not win was because our army drank so much whisky as to bring the curse of the Lord upon them. He said it was rather unfair on the part of the aforesaid curse, as the other side drank more and worse whisky than ours did."[78] In his biography of Lincoln, Herndon told the story of a Kentuckian who, finding himself in a stagecoach with Lincoln, successively offered him a chew of tobacco, a cigar, and a cup of brandy. " 'See here, stranger,' he said, good-humoredly, 'you're a clever, but strange companion. I may never see you again, and I don't want to offend you, but I want to say this: My experience has taught me that a man who has no vices has d—d few virtues. Good-day.' Lincoln enjoyed this reminiscence of the journey and took great pleasure in relating it."[79]

INTOXICATION WAS ONE enemy of reason. Insanity was another. In his youth Lincoln suffered from emotional and perhaps mental disturbances provoked by romantic frustrations. William Herndon claimed that Lincoln had been in love with Ann Rutledge, the daughter of a tavern-keeper in New Salem, Illinois. When she died in 1835, according to Herndon, "He became plunged in despair, and many of his friends feared that reason would desert her throne. . . . If, when we read what the many credible persons who knew him at the time tell us, we do not conclude that he was deranged, we must admit that he walked on that sharp and narrow line which divides sanity from insanity."[80] While some historians have questioned the reality of Lincoln's alleged love for Ann Rutledge, there is no doubt that Lincoln became deeply depressed after he broke off his first engagement to Mary Todd in 1840. "To remain as I am is impossible; I must die or be better, it appears to me," Lincoln wrote on January 23, 1840, to his law partner John T. Stuart, then serving in the U.S. Congress. On the previous day a Springfield acquaintance had written: "We have been very much distressed, on Mr. Lincoln's account; hearing he had two Cat fits, and a Duck fit since we left."[81]

Madness was the subject of one of two surviving poems of Lincoln's, published anonymously in the *Quincy Whig* on May 5, 1847. In a letter, Lincoln explained the poem's genesis: "The subject of the present [poem] is an insane man. His name is Matthew Gentry. He is three years older than I, and when we were boys we went to school together. At the age of nineteen he unaccountably became furiously mad, from which condition he gradually settled down into harmless insanity. When, as I told you in my other letter I visited my old home in the fall of 1844, I found him still lingering in this wretched condition. In my poetizing mood I could not forget the impressions his case made upon me. Here is the result—

> But here's an object more of dread
>> Than ought the grave contains—
> A human form with reason fled,
>> While wretched life remains.
>
> Poor Matthew! Once of genius bright,
>> A fortune-favored child—
> Now locked for aye, in mental night,
>> A haggard mad-man wild . . .
>
> I've heard it oft, as if I dreamed,
>> Far distant, sweet, and lone—
> The funeral dirge, it ever seemed
>> Of reason dead and gone.[82]

NOTWITHSTANDING LINCOLN'S RATIONALISM, there was, according to Herndon, "more or less superstition in his nature, and, although he may not have believed implicitly in the signs of his many dreams, he was constantly endeavoring to unravel them."[83] Lincoln was fond of relating his dreams to friends and acquaintances in a tone of quizzical amusement that indicated he did not take them very seriously. After describing how Lincoln related a dream in which a president who had been assassinated was lying in state in the White House, Lamon continued: "Once the President alluded to this terrible dream with some show of playful humor. 'Hill,' said he, 'your apprehension of harm to me from some hidden enemy is downright foolishness. . . . In this dream it was not me, but some other fellow, that was killed. It seems that this ghostly assassin tried his hand on some one else.' "[84]

On the day of his assassination, Lincoln mentioned a dream in which he was sailing toward an unknown shore. Telling General Ulysses S. Grant that the dream had come to him repeatedly before turning points in the Civil War, Lincoln suggested that it presaged a victory by Sherman's army in North Carolina. Following his assassination, others made the connection between the dream and his death.

His interest in dreams notwithstanding, the evidence indicates that Lincoln's skepticism about the supernatural extended to the occult as well as revealed religion. Popular journalism and history have sometimes attributed to Lincoln superstitious beliefs that in fact were held by his wife. For example, Lincoln told several acquaintances that, shortly after his election as president in 1860, while in his home in Springfield, he saw a double reflection of himself in his mirror. Lamon claimed that Lincoln had told him the image predicted "that death would overtake him" in his second term as president. However, another acquaintance, Noah Brooks, attributed the belief to Mary, quoting Lincoln as saying: "She thought it was 'a sign' that I was to be elected to a second term of office, and that the paleness of one of the faces was an omen that I should not see life through the last term."[85]

Mary Todd Lincoln was an unstable personality whose emotional and mental problems were worsened by the death, before their eighteenth birthdays, of three of her four sons, and the murder of her husband. To the distress and embarrassment of her husband, as First Lady she exhibited the spendthrift behavior that inspired their only surviving son, Robert, to have her committed to an insane asylum in her old age. After their eleven-year-old son Willie died in 1862, Mary Lincoln began attending spiritualist séances in Washington. While Lincoln indulged his wife, the president's attitude toward spiritualism can be inferred from his request that Joseph Henry, the Secretary of the Smithsonian Institution, witness a demonstration by the medium Charles J. "Lord" Colchester; Henry concluded that Colchester was a fraud.[86] It is possible that Lincoln was humoring Mary when he took their sick son Robert to Terre Haute, Indiana, to touch a "madstone" to which curative properties were attributed. As Lamon explained, Lincoln "was no dabbler in divination—astrology, horoscopy, prophecy, ghostly lore, or witcheries of any sort."[87] The legend that his ghost haunts the White House no doubt would have amused Lincoln.

LINCOLN'S WORLDVIEW WAS an amalgam of republicanism, deism, and scientific rationalism derived from the books he read rather than from the Christian beliefs and rural folkways of his family and neighbors. Lincoln signaled his rejection of the anti-intellectual climate of the Jacksonian Southern culture into which he was born in his first campaign manifesto, written at the age of twenty-three: "For my part, I desire to see the time when education, and by its means, morality, sobriety, enterprise, and industry, shall become much more general than at present."[88] The frontier was a frightening place, according to a poem Lincoln composed when, while campaigning for Henry Clay's 1844 presidential bid, he revisited his father's farm: "When first my father settled here, 'Twas then the frontier line: / The panther's scream, filled night with fear / And bears preyed on the swine."[89]

He wanted to help build a society that would be the opposite in almost every way of the rural society in which he had grown up. Instead of wilderness there would be cities; instead of manual labor there would be machine production of goods and mechanized harvesting of farm products; instead of widespread ignorance there would be universal literacy and education; widely shared affluence would replace poverty; temperance would spread and alcoholism decline. The world that American mythology associates with Lincoln, the world of the frontier farmer, is one that he despised and wanted to leave behind. He was born on the frontier but he moved to the city, and he dreamed of railroads and factories. "Intense thought with him was the rule and not, as with most of us, the exception," his friend Joshua Speed recalled.[90] Ward Hill Lamon agreed: "Morbid, moody, meditative, thinking mostly of himself and things pertaining to himself, regarding other men as instruments furnished to his hand for the accomplishment of views which he knew were important to him, and, therefore, considered important to the public, Mr. Lincoln was a man apart from the rest of his kind, unsocial, cold, impassive—neither a 'good hater' nor a fond friend."[91]

Indoctrinated into the rationalist worldview of the eighteenth-century Enlightenment by the books he read, the young Abraham Lincoln identified with the party of progress. And in the context of the United States in the 1830s, the aspiring politician identified the party of progress with the Whig Party of Henry Clay.

THREE

⸺∞⸺

AN OLD-LINE
HENRY CLAY WHIG

ON THE MORNING of July 16, 1852, businesses were closed in Springfield, Illinois. The Reverend Charles Dresser presided over a funeral service in the Protestant Episcopal church in memory of Henry Clay, who had died seventeen days earlier in Washington, D.C. Following the service, a procession formed outside the church in this order: chief marshal, assistant marshals, clergy and orator, judges and officers of the United States circuit and district courts and members of the bar, officers of the state, officers of the county, mayor and city council, citizens, the Sons of Temperance, the Independent Order of Odd Fellows, and the Masonic Order. At 11 A.M., seventy-six guns fired to mark each year of Clay's life, and then the church bells tolled.

A forty-minute oration followed. The speaker was the Springfield lawyer and former member of the U.S. House of Representatives and the

Illinois legislature, Abraham Lincoln. Lincoln's eulogy to Henry Clay begins, like the Gettysburg Address and a number of his other speeches, with the Declaration of Independence: "On the fourth day of July, 1776, the people of a few feeble and oppressed colonies of Great Britain, inhabiting a portion of the Atlantic coast of North America, publicly declared their national independence, and made their appeal to the justice of their cause, and to the God of battles, for the maintenance of that declaration. . . . Within the first year of that declared independence . . . Henry Clay was born. The infant nation, and the infant child began the race of life together.

"Mr. Clay's predominant sentiment, from first to last, was a deep devotion to the cause of human liberty—a strong sympathy with the oppressed everywhere, and an ardent wish for their elevation. . . . He loved his country partly because it was his own country, but mostly because it was a free country. . . ." Lincoln spoke with admiration of Clay's encouragement of republicanism abroad: "Mr. Clay's efforts in behalf of the South Americans, and afterwards, in behalf of the Greeks, in the times of their respective struggles for civil liberty are among the finest on record, upon the noblest of all themes; and bear ample corroboration of what I have said was his ruling passion—a love of liberty and right, unselfishly, and for their own sakes."

Lincoln praised Clay's nationalism: "As a politician or statesman, no one was so habitually careful to avoid all sectional ground. Whatever he did, he did for the whole country. . . . Feeling, as he did, and as the truth surely is, that the world's best hope depended on the continued Union of these States, he was ever jealous of, and watchful for, whatever might have the slightest tendency to separate them." Lincoln called Clay "that truly national man." "Such a man the times demanded, and such, in the providence of God was given us."[1] Lincoln would attempt to be such a man.

HENRY CLAY DOMINATED American politics between the War of 1812 and the 1850s. Only Andrew Jackson, Daniel Webster, and John C. Calhoun rivaled his influence and celebrity. The central figure in the Whig Party that coalesced to oppose Andrew Jackson's Democrats in the 1830s and 1840s, idolized by his supporters as "Harry of the West," the Virginia-born Kentucky planter was hated by abolitionists as a hypocrite who talked of liberty while owning numerous slaves and by many of his fellow Southern slave owners as a traitor to his region. Repeatedly disappointed in his quest for the presidency, although he served in the Cabinet of several presidents, Clay dominated national politics as speaker of the House and later as a leading senator.

The seventh of nine children, Clay was born to the Reverend John and Elizabeth Hudson Clay on April 12, 1777. At the age of three he had watched the soldiers of the infamous British colonel Banastre Tarleton ransack his family home in Hanover County, Virginia, and dig up family graves in search of buried treasure.[2] After his widowed mother remarried, his step-father helped obtain a job as a clerk in a chancery office for the teenage Clay, who had a limited formal education. In 1797 Clay moved from Virginia to Kentucky, where he became a successful lawyer, married into an influential landholding family, and set himself up as a country gentleman at Ashland, a plantation worked by hundreds of slaves. Despite his affluence, Clay proudly considered himself a "self-made man," a phrase that he coined. In a House debate with John Randolph of Roanoke, a patrician from Virginia, Clay once declared, "I know my deficiencies. I was born to no patrimonial estate; from my father I inherited only infancy, ignorance, and indigence." "The gentleman might continue the alliteration, and add insolence," Randolph replied.[3]

Clay was over six feet tall and homely, with a wide mouth described by a historian in 1857: "In his old days, when the men crowded around him for a shake of his hand, and the women beset him for a kiss of his patriarchal lips it was remarked that his capacity of gratifying this latter demand was unlimited, for the ample dimensions of his kissing apparatus enabled him completely to *rest* one side of it, while the other side was upon active duty."[4] Clay's speeches are seldom impressive on paper, but his theatrical ability made him one of the leading orators in a time when political oratory was a major form of public entertainment.

Clay entered Kentucky state politics in 1803 when he was elected to the general assembly. At twenty-nine he was appointed by the Kentucky legislature to the U.S. Senate. Clay was speaker of the House during the Twelfth to Sixteenth Congresses, where he was one of the leading agitators for war with Britain. Following the War of 1812 he was appointed as one of the commissioners to American-British peace negotiations in Ghent, Belgium, in 1814. He became a hero to Latin Americans when he argued passionately for U.S. recognition of the Latin American republics that had seceded from the Spanish empire. Clay served as a U.S senator from Kentucky from the 1830s until his resignation in 1851; he died the following year.

Clay was perhaps the most important American politician never to be elected president. He sought the presidency in 1824, 1832, and 1844. In the 1824 election, no candidate won a majority of the electoral vote, and under the provisions of the U.S. Constitution the decision was made by the House of Representatives. Even though Andrew Jackson had won the most votes, John Quincy Adams was elected after Clay's supporters rallied to him. When Adams appointed Clay Secretary of State, rumors of a "corrupt bargain" began and haunted Clay for the rest of his career. Whig presidents were elected only twice, and both, with unfortunate symbolism for the party, died while in office. William Henry Harrison, elected in 1840, died a month after his inauguration in 1841 and was succeeded by Vice President John Tyler, while Zachary Taylor, elected in 1848, died in 1850 and was replaced by his vice president, Millard Fillmore.

Clay is remembered as the "Great Compromiser" who in two crises helped avert Southern secession and civil war. In 1821 he helped guide the Second Missouri Compromise through Congress. In his seventies, frail and often sick, Clay promoted the Compromise of 1850, which passed piecemeal after the omnibus package he had designed fell apart. By preventing Southern secession for a decade, the Compromise of 1850 permitted the North's advantage in population and industry to grow. The combination of ardent Unionism and the defense of the idealism of the American Revolution in the thought of Abraham Lincoln was an inheritance from Clay and other leading Whigs such as Daniel Webster.

Clay is remembered as well for the "American System"—a program inspired by Alexander Hamilton for promoting the industrialization of the United States by means of protective tariffs to help American industries, internal improvements like canals and railroads, and a sound system of national banking. But the American System was only half of Clay's program for the future of the United States. The other half was a racial policy inherited from Alexander Hamilton's rival, Thomas Jefferson. The Jeffersonian racial policy united three elements: Indian removal, to clear land for white settlement; the colonization of emancipated black slaves and free blacks abroad; and the reception of white immigrants, who would join native white Americans in settling territories emptied of Indians and blacks. Henry Clay's plan for the American nation-state combined an industrial economy created by Hamiltonian methods with a white-only society created by Jeffersonian racial policies. His disciple Abraham Lincoln adopted Clay's entire nation-building program as his own.

In the Realm of political economy, Henry Clay's American System was a response to the domination of the world economy by Britain. The major debate about economics in the nineteenth-century United States pitted Hamiltonians such as Clay and Lincoln, who wanted the United States to catch up with Britain as an industrial superpower, against Jeffersonians, based in the rural South, who were content to have the United States remain an agricultural country that would supply industrial nations with cotton and other crops and raw materials.

As the first country to exploit the Industrial Revolution, Britain achieved levels of power and wealth without precedent in history. By the middle of the nineteenth century, Britain had a per capita level of industrialization equal to the combined levels of those of France, Russia, the German states, the Austrian Empire, and Italy, and its manufacturing surpassed the combined output of France and Russia.[5] Britain had not simply grown in power; it was a great power of a new kind, the first and for a time the only industrial superpower in a world of agrarian states.

Britain had achieved its lead in manufacturing by skillful use of protectionism and subsidies to promote its industries at the expense of those of its colonies and other nations. Between the seventeenth and nineteenth centuries the English used their political control of the British Empire to destroy competing manufacturing industries in its colonies. The Wool Act of 1699 wiped out the Irish wool industry in order to promote the inferior English wool industry.[6] A year later a ban on imports of cotton calicoes from India crippled that region's cotton manufacturing industry.[7] Not content to strangle manufacturing in Ireland and India, the British government used its authority to prevent the industrialization of the American colonies. The 1699 Wool Act annihilated an emerging textile industry in America as well as the existing one in Ireland. In the 1720s London abolished British import duties on raw materials like timber and hemp from the American colonies and provided the colonists with "bounties" or export subsidies for these goods. The purpose was to encourage the colonists to specialize in raw material exports and discourage them from going into manufacturing.[8] In 1732, to eliminate an American beaver hat industry, London passed a law banning colonies from exporting hats to one another or to foreign countries in order to force the colonists to ship the beaver pelts to Britain, where the hats would be manufactured.[9]

The British parliamentarian Edmund Burke, a friend of the colonies, described the cynical strategy by which Britain sought to prevent the industrial development of its North American domain: "These colonies were evidently founded in subservience to the commerce of Great Britain. From this principle, the whole system of our laws concerning them became a system of restriction. A double monopoly was established on the part of the parent country: 1. a monopoly of their whole import, which is to be altogether from Great Britain; 2. a monopoly of all their export, which is to be no where but to Great Britain, as far as it can serve any purpose here. On the same idea it was contrived that they should send all their products to us raw, and in their first state; and that they should take every thing from us in the last stage of manufacture."[10]

Even after the United States won its independence, British manufacturers routinely sought to wipe out nascent American industries by "dumping," or selling their products in American markets at a loss for a time. In 1819 John Adams recalled: "I am old enough to remember the war of 1745, and its end; the war of 1755, and its close; the war of 1775, and its termination; the war of 1812, and its pacification. . . . The British manufacturers, immediately after the peace, disgorged upon us all their stores of merchandise and manufactures, not only without profit, but at certain loss for a time, with the express purpose of annihilating all our manufacturers, and ruining all our manufactories."[11] To further promote its goal of denying advanced technology to other nations, the British government passed laws making it a crime to export technological information, such as that found in factory and machine blueprints. The U.S. textile industry was founded by industrial espionage on the basis of plans smuggled out of Britain.[12]

By the end of the Napoleonic Wars in 1815, Britain's ruthless promotion of its own industries at the expense of those of Ireland, India, its British-American colonies, and other nations had made it the world's leader in manufacturing. Having lost its major North American colonies in the American war of independence, Britain in the early nineteenth century created a new, informal colonial empire by pressuring nominally independent countries in Latin America and Asia into signing "unequal treaties" rigged to favor British manufacturing exports over local manufacturing. Britain, in alliance with France, went to war with China during the Opium Wars (1839–42) in order to force China to accept the sale of Indian opium by British merchants and to strip China of its economic autonomy. Beginning with the Treaty of Nanking (1842), China was compelled by Britain to sign a number of unequal treaties, resulting in the appointment of a British official as the head of Chinese customs from 1863 to 1908.[13]

Many British economists and politicians argued that the goal of a British monopoly of global manufacturing capability also could be achieved by encouraging other countries to join Britain in adopting free trade. Under a regime of free trade the flood of manufactured goods from Britain's established industries would make it difficult for industrial enterprises to succeed in other countries. With their infant industries killed in the cradle by British imports, those countries would then be forced to compete with one another to supply Britain with food and raw materials. Britain would enjoy a monopoly of manufacturing and benefit from the low prices created by an oversupply of the commodities it bought. To provide an incentive for other countries to specialize in agriculture and raw materials exports, British free-traders argued that Britain should abolish its own tariffs on such items, such as its Corn Laws, which Britain repealed in 1846 (British "corn" is wheat, not American maize). The parliamentarian Richard Cobden argued that free trade would discourage other countries from industrializing, the way that the United States and Germany already had begun to do: "The factory system would, in all probability, not have taken place in America and Germany. It most certainly could not have flourished, as it has done, both in these states, and in France, Belgium, and Switzerland, through the fostering bounties which the high-priced food of the British artisan has offered to the cheaper fed manufacturer of those countries."[14] The British economist Stanley Jevons boasted: "Unfettered commerce . . . has made the several quarters of the globe our willing tributaries."[15] Adam Smith in *The Wealth of Nations* served Britain's strategic interests by arguing that the Americans should specialize in agriculture instead of using tariffs to promote American manufacturing: "Were the Americans, either by combination or by any other sort of violence, to stop the importation of European manufactures, and, by thus giving a monopoly to such of their own countrymen as could manufacture the like goods, divert any considerable part of their capital into this employment, they would retard instead of accelerating the further increase in the value of their annual produce, and would obstruct instead of promoting the progress of their country towards real wealth and greatness."[16] If Americans had paid attention to Adam Smith, the United States never would have become the world's greatest industrial economy, because it never would have become an industrial economy at all.

British free trade theorists who argued that the American people forever should leave manufacturing to Britain, and specialize instead in agriculture, found allies in the United States in the Southern slave owners who supplied the textile mills of Britain with cotton. Some Southerners recognized the need for the United States to produce at least some equipment. Jefferson wrote in 1812: "We have reduced the large and expensive machinery for most things to the compass of a private family, and every family of any size is now getting machines on a small scale for their household purposes."[17] But like Jefferson, most Southern planters opposed government efforts to encourage a large manufacturing sector in the economy of the United States for both economic and social reasons. If tariffs were used to keep out British and European manufactured goods, then agrarians would be forced either to pay tariffs on imports or to pay a higher price for American manufactured goods than they would have done in the absence of tariffs. The same objection applied to other government efforts to promote American industries, such as bounties (subsidies); these, like tariffs, would redistribute wealth from the agrarian sector to the manufacturing sector of the U.S. economy.

Because alternate ways of financing the federal government, such as taxes on income or wealth, were unthinkable, the Southern oligarchs conceded the need for a modest tariff to supply the needs of the federal government, along with sales of public lands and excise taxes. For this reason the Southern plantation elite supported a "tariff for revenue" while opposing a "tariff for protection"—and was determined to keep both the tariff and the size of the federal government small.

An aversion to being taxed, directly or indirectly, to subsidize Northern manufacturers was not the only reason that the Southern plantocracy opposed government-sponsored industrial capitalism in the United States. Neither the climate nor the population of the South was incompatible with an industrial society, as the industrialization of the South in the twentieth century proved. But in an industrializing South, the old plantation families might be shoved aside by prosperous, upwardly mobile factory owners, and the rural society of ranks—with the slave owner at the top, the slave at the bottom, and the poor white in between—would disintegrate. Fear of the social effects of industrialization may have been even more important than the economic costs in explaining why most Southerners agreed with the British economists and the British elite that the United States should forever remain a nonindustrial supplier of food and raw materials in a two-tier world economy, in which Britain and a few other industrial nations would dominate the highest tier. The alliance between British manufacturers and Southern slave owners in favor of free trade grew deeper between 1810 and 1860, when the percentage of Britain's cotton imported from the American South rose from 48 percent to more than 90 percent.[18]

The agrarianism of Jefferson and his fellow slave owners appealed to many ordinary citizens in an America that was still largely rural. In 1800, when, as a result of the Industrial Revolution, only 36 percent of the population of England was employed in agriculture, nine out of ten Americans still lived on farms or were engaged in the rural economy. But not all Americans wanted the United States to consign itself forever to the role of a supplier of raw materials and food for Britain and other industrial nations. Alexander Hamilton, the brilliant first Secretary of the Treasury of the United States, wanted the U.S. to emulate Britain by becoming a major manufacturing nation.

The rationale for government promotion of "infant industries" in the United States was set out by Hamilton in his "Report of the Secretary of the Treasury on the Subject of Manufactures" (1791). In the report, Hamilton pointed out that "the United States cannot exchange on Europe on equal terms; and the want of reciprocity would render them the victim of a system, which should induce them to confine their views to Agriculture and refrain from Manufactures."[19] The unacknowledged model for Hamilton's program of economic nationalism was the system established under the first British prime minister, Robert Walpole, in the early eighteenth century. In 1721 British commercial law was reformed to promote manufacturing by raising tariffs on foreign manufactured goods, eliminating export duties on most British manufactured goods, lowering or eliminating tariffs on raw materials used by British manufacturers, and providing subsidies to British export industries such as silk and gunpowder.[20] The same era witnessed the founding of the Bank of England (1694), the model for Hamilton's First Bank of the United States. Another model was the economic nationalism of the French minister Jean Baptiste Colbert. Hamilton learned of Colbert's economic nationalism in a book by the British author Malachi Postlethwayte, which he read while serving as Washington's chief aide during the war of independence.[21] For their part, Southern agrarians like Jefferson, influenced by the rural "country party" in eighteenth-century Britain, considered the Walpolean system to be not a rational method of promoting industrialization and commerce, but a sinister scheme to enrich financiers, factory owners, and corrupt politicians.

In the first half of the nineteenth century, Hamiltonians who opposed the "British School" of free trade favored by the Jeffersonian Southern plantation owners formed their own "American School" of "national economy" or economic nationalism. According to economic thinkers of the American School, the United States, having won its political independence from the British Empire, now needed to win its economic independence from the British economy.

Baltimore, then one of the three largest ports in the United States, was home to both Hezekiah Niles, publisher of a protectionist journal, *The National Register,* and the lawyer Daniel Raymond, who published a defense of economic nationalism, *The Elements of Political Economy,* in two volumes in 1823.[22] Another important economist of the American School was Francis Wayland, who published his best-selling treatise *The Elements of Political Economy* in 1837.

Because its location near coal and iron mines made it a natural site for steam-powered factories, Pennsylvania became the intellectual and political capital of American protectionism—a role played on the other side by New York, whose financial elite, with ties to Southern cotton exporters and British financial interests, traditionally favored free trade. The American School protectionists found an important ally in Friedrich List, a German liberal in exile in the United States between 1825 and 1830. After residing in Pennsylvania, where he allied himself with local manufacturers, List became so enthusiastic about the American School of "national economy" that he publicized economic nationalist doctrines in France and Germany, where he is remembered to this day as an important figure in the history of German economic modernization.[23]

The most important American School economist was the Pennsylvanian Henry C. Carey, the son of Mathew Carey, an Irish immigrant who helped found the Philadelphia Society for the Promotion of National Industry and a kindred Pennsylvania Society for the Protection of Domestic Industry. Karl Marx and Ralph Waldo Emerson, among others, considered Carey the most important economist the United States had produced.[24] Henry Carey began as a free trader, but inherited his father's opinions along with a publishing empire closely allied with Hezekiah Niles's *National Register* and Pennsylvania iron and coal interests. Carey's spokesman in the U.S. Congress was William "Pig-Iron" Kelley, who dedicated a book of his speeches to the economist, and when Carey died, his will revealed extensive holdings in Pennsylvania coal lands as well as shares in the Mammoth Vein Coal Company.[25] Carey's disciples—E. Pershine Smith, Horace Greeley, H. C. Baird, R. E. Thompson, and William Elder—formed a successor generation of the American School of economic nationalism in the 1870s and 1880s.[26] Another Carey ally, the industrialist Joseph P. Wharton, who made his fortune in iron and coal, founded the Wharton School at the University of Pennsylvania to spread the gospel of protectionism.

Like his Irish immigrant father, Carey came to view free trade as the economic corollary of the British imperialism that had ruined Ireland, India, and other British colonies. "By adopting the 'free trade,' or British system, we place ourselves side by side with the men who have ruined Ireland and India, and are now poisoning and enslaving the Chinese people," he wrote.[27] In 1860 Carey, who became one of Lincoln's advisers, would welcome the nomination of Abraham Lincoln, a lifelong adherent of protectionist American School economics, and declare that the Republican Party platform was "the new [economic] Declaration of Independence [from the British system]."[28]

Henry Clay, the Kentucky plantation owner, was an unlikely convert to the policies of the Pennsylvania-based industrial interests and their intellectual allies, the economic nationalists of the American School. Clay began his political career as a Jeffersonian opponent of the Hamiltonian program of national banking and internal improvements. Clay rose to national prominence as a War Hawk advocating the war with Britain, which the United States declared in 1812. The excuse for the war was the British practice of "impressing," or conscripting, American sailors, but as the French fleet engaged in the same practice, this also would have justified war with France. According to Clay, the chief reasons for war were economic and strategic. Britain's Orders in Council, which sought to impose an embargo on Napoleon's France, had crippled American exports to Europe. Clay argued that the target of British policy was not only France but also the former American colonies, which the British government wanted to prevent from growing into an industrial and military rival: "She sickens at your prosperity, and beholds, in your growth—your sails spread on every ocean, and your numerous seamen—the foundations of a power which, at no very distant day, is to make her tremble for her naval superiority."[29]

Clay's progression from War Hawk to economic nationalist was logical. Like Hamilton, who had realized the extent of American industrial weakness during the Revolution, Clay viewed domestic manufacturing enterprises as an essential element of U.S. national security and sought to "afford them protection, not so much for the sake of the manufacturers themselves, as for the general interest. We should thus have our wants supplied, when foreign resources are cut off, and we should also lay the basis of a system of taxation, to be resorted to when the revenue from imports is stopped by war."[30]

In his exposition of the American System in the House of Representatives on March 30–31, 1824, Clay linked two themes: the need for the United States to have a machine-based economy of its own, and the military as well as economic threat posed by the industrial supremacy of Britain: "But Britain is herself the most striking illustration of the immense power of machinery. . . . A statistical writer of that country, several years ago, estimated the total amount of the artificial or machine labor of the [British] nation to be equal to that of one hundred millions of able-bodied laborers. . . . In the creation of wealth, therefore, the power of Great Britain, compared to that of the United States, is as eleven to one."[31]

While Hamilton's model for the industrial and financial modernization of the United States had been found in the policies of eighteenth-century Britain and seventeenth-century France, Clay's inspiration was Napoleon's Continental System, the economic bloc centered on France and incorporating French-occupied Europe that Napoleon created, under duress, in response to Britain's blockade of Continental Europe. Clay evidently studied the details of the Continental System while he was in Europe as a U.S. peace commissioner in the talks between the United States and Britain that followed the War of 1812. Soon he was speaking of the program of American industrialization encouraged by the federal government as "the American System" (a phrase he first used to refer to a projected alliance between the republics of the Western Hemisphere).

Between the 1820s and the 1840s, Clay promoted the American System, from which he financially benefited as a grower of protected hemp for ropes. Under the leadership of Clay, the 1816 tariff was revised to protect American industries. Imports on all manufactured goods averaged 40 percent while tariffs on imported agricultural products were also increased—in some cases amounting to 60 percent.[32] Southerners and Northern supporters of free trade denounced the 1828 tariff as "the Tariff of Abominations," and South Carolina threatened to "nullify" the law by refusing to collect the duties at Charleston. When President Andrew Jackson, a Southern Jeffersonian who was also a strong Unionist, threatened to use troops to enforce the law, South Carolina backed down. The crisis led to the Compromise Bill of 1832, and the average tariff diminished to 20 percent over the decade by 1842.[33] The influence of the Southern Democrats was seen in the Tariff of 1846, which imposed average duties on the major imports of 27 percent. This regime remained in place with few changes until 1861.

Clay also promoted the use of funds from federal land sales to finance internal improvements such as canals and railroads. This goal was shared by others in the Hamiltonian tradition in the successive Federalist, National Republican, and Whig parties. After retiring from the presidency, John Quincy Adams wrote that he had sought to use federal revenues to subsidize internal improvements so that "the whole surface of the nation would have been checkered over with Rail Roads and Canals."[34] In the 1820s, nearly half a century before he shared a speaker's platform with Lincoln at Gettysburg, Edward Everett, who later became a leading Whig, said that the settlement of the frontier by pioneers was only the first stage of development. After "the hard labor of the human hands" of the "husbandman" had cleared the wilderness, the time would come for "the manufacturer, the engineer, and the mechanic" who would transform the landscape further "by machinery, by the steam-engine, and by internal improvement. . . . We must, in every direction, have turnpike roads, unobstructed rivers, canals, rail-roads, and steamboats."[35]

After manufacturing and internal improvements, the third element of the Hamiltonian triad that made up Clay's American System was national finance. In 1791, under Hamilton's guidance, the First Bank of the United States was established. The fact that it was largely privately owned by Northeastern investors created hostility toward it by Thomas Jefferson and other Southerners. In 1811 Clay, then a young Jeffersonian, approved of Congress's refusal to renew the charter of Hamilton's national bank. But he learned from the economic suffering of the United States during the Napoleonic Wars and the War of 1812, and from the model of Napoleon's Continental System. Converted to Hamiltonian economic nationalism, he supported the creation of the Second Bank of the United States in 1816, and from 1822 to 1824, between stints in Congress, he served as the Bank's general counsel. Clay led the unsuccessful battle to prevent President Jackson from destroying the Bank and redistributing many of its holdings to banking concerns allied with Jackson and his vice president, Martin Van Buren. Jackson's destruction of the Bank resulted in the catastrophic Panic of 1837.

WHILE CLAY IS often thought of as a Hamiltonian, this expresses only half the truth. There was more to Henry Clay's program for the United States than his Hamiltonian American System. The other half of Clay's unique synthesis was a grandiose program of social engineering, which he inherited from Thomas Jefferson: a plan to create an all-white America by means of the removal of all blacks from the United States.

Thomas Jefferson, author of the Declaration of Independence, was also one of the founders of racial pseudoscience and a slave owner who bought and sold hundreds of slaves during his life. Jefferson argued in his *Notes on the State of Virginia* (1781) that there was not a single case of a black who "had uttered thought above the level of plain narration." Jefferson contrasted alleged black inferiority with the accomplishments of Roman slaves, who "were of the race of whites. It is not their condition, then, but nature, which has produced the distinction." Consequently, Jefferson concluded, emancipation in America could not be followed by the amalgamation of former slaves and masters into a single population: "Among the Romans emancipation required but one effort. The slave, when made free, might mix with, without staining, the blood of his master. But with us a second is necessary, unknown to history. When freed, he is to be removed beyond the reach of mixture."[36]

Jefferson's racial program, designed to prevent the possibility of white-black intermarriage, combined the settlement of whites on lands from which Indians had been vacated with the expatriation of blacks to Africa and their replacement by white immigrants from Europe. Jefferson opposed the emigration of free blacks to new territories, telling Virginia governor and future president James Monroe in 1801: "However our present situation may restrain us within our limits, it is impossible not to look forward to distant times, when our rapid multiplication will expand beyond those limits, and cover the whole northern, if not the southern continent, with a people speaking the same language, governed in similar forms, and by similar laws; nor can we contemplate with satisfaction blot or mixture on that surface."[37] The two policies of limiting settlement in the West to whites and promoting the emigration of blacks after their emancipation from slavery, Jefferson hoped, would lead to the elimination of both slavery and the black population in the United States. Once blacks had been shipped abroad, a white-only America would be ensured by U.S. immigration rules dating back to the 1790s, which permitted only "free white persons" to immigrate to the United States and become naturalized citizens.

A year after Jefferson published his proposal for black colonization in his *Notes on Virginia,* his ally and fellow Virginia slave owner James Madison endorsed a combination of gradual emancipation and colonization. In 1816 Henry Clay presided over the meeting in Washington, D.C., that established the American Society for the Colonization of Free People of Color of the United States, better known as the American Colonization Society. He became its president in 1836, succeeding Madison.

While there were a few black colonizationists, most black Americans disagreed with Jefferson, Madison, and Clay. A month after Clay and the rest had formed the American Colonization Society, three thousand blacks gathered in Bethel Church in Philadelphia. The protestors claimed that colonization would "stigmatize the free Negro population, and it countenanced the perpetuation of human bondage and encouraged it by seeking to remove free blacks."[38] Indeed, the American Colonization Society was dominated by Southern slave owners like Clay and Madison, who feared the growth in the numbers of free blacks and the prospect of a biracial or mixed-race nation as much as they were troubled by the immorality of a slave plantation system that enriched them. In 1845 Clay said: "In whatever mode the U.S. may get rid of the Free Blacks, I believe it will be better for them and for the whites."[39] Like most of his white contemporaries, Clay thought that non-whites were innately inferior. In 1830 Clay opposed the Indian removal policy of President Andrew Jackson as likely "to bring a foul and lasting stain upon the good faith, humanity and character of the Nation."[40] But in 1825, according to then-President John Quincy Adams in his memoirs, Clay, then Secretary of State, told Secretary of War James Barbour, who sought to help the Indians, that he "believed that they were destined to extinction, and, although he would never use or countenance inhumanity towards them, he did not think them, as a race, worth preserving."[41]

Despite his racism, Clay was unwilling to argue that the "self-evident" truths of the Declaration of Independence applied to whites alone. In a presidential address to the American Colonization Society in 1848, Clay distinguished between abstract rights and rights in practice. He believed in the declaration's statement of equality as a "principle," but asked where "does the black man . . . enjoy an equality with his white neighbor in social and political rights? In none: no where. As to social rights, they are out of the question. In no city, town, or hamlet throughout the entire land is he regarded as on an equal footing with us."[42] Clay argued that colonization would benefit Africa as well as former American slaves. Earlier, in his address to the Colonization Society of Kentucky on December 17, 1829, Clay had held out the democratization and Christianization of Africa as two of the reasons to emancipate American slaves: "And may we not indulge the hope, that in a period of time, not surpassing in duration, that of our own Colonial and National existence, we shall behold a confederation of Republican States on the western shores of Africa, like our own, with their Congress and annual Legislatures thundering forth in behalf of the rights of man, and making tyrants tremble on their thrones?"[43]

In 1822, during the first wave of colonizationist activity, the country of Liberia was established as a potential colony for both emancipated slaves and free blacks from the United States. A second wave of enthusiasm for colonization began in the 1840s and swelled in the 1850s during the debate over slavery and its extension. When Kentucky held a convention to amend its constitution in 1849, Clay made his last major effort to promote emancipation and colonization by the state. Making an argument that Lincoln later borrowed in his debates with Stephen A. Douglas, Clay dismissed the argument that black intellectual inferiority, if genuine, justified enslavement, otherwise "then the wisest man in the world would have a right to make slaves of all the rest of mankind." If blacks were intellectually inferior, then that imposed on whites a duty "to instruct, to improve, and to enlighten them."[44]

Clay echoed Jefferson, who in 1809 wrote of blacks that "whatsoever be their degree of talent it is no measure of their rights. Because Sir Isaac Newton was superior to others in understanding, he was not therefore lord of the person or property of others."[45]

Clay's 1849 plan would have kept slaves in that condition for life and freed only those born after 1855 or 1860 on reaching a specified age such as twenty-five. By doing so, Clay wrote, "We shall remove from among us the contaminating influence of a servile and degraded race of different color; we shall enjoy the proud and conscious satisfaction of placing that race where they can enjoy the great blessings of liberty, and civil, political, and social equality . . . and we should demonstrate the sincerity with which we pay homage to the great cause of the liberty of the human race."[46] Clay's plan for the emancipation and colonization of Kentucky's slaves anticipated the federal colonization scheme that Lincoln would propose to Congress as president. Millard Fillmore, Clay's ally and one of the four Whig presidents, considered suggesting a federal program of colonization in his Annual Message to Congress in 1852, but decided against it.[47]

Throughout his career, Clay's campaign for colonization earned him denunciation by abolitionists and the enmity of many of his fellow Southern slave owners. In 1851, the year preceding his death, Clay confessed to a correspondent that he had abandoned his belief in "the possibility of establishing a system of gradual emancipation of the slaves of the United States." Clay continued: "I confess I despair of obtaining the object by legal enactment. I nevertheless confidently believe that slavery will ultimately be extinguished when there shall be a great increase of our population, and a great diminution in the value of labor."[48] "Despair" was the right word for Clay's final assessment of the subject. Slave owners would voluntarily emancipate their slaves only after overpopulation in the United States caused wages to fall so low that wage workers, white and black alike, would be cheaper than slaves.

ABRAHAM LINCOLN'S POLITICAL career began in 1832 when he campaigned unsuccessfully for election to the Illinois state legislature, and ended with his reelection as President of the United States in 1864. Throughout his political career Lincoln described himself as a disciple of Henry Clay, his "beau ideal of a statesman."[49] In a debate in Peoria, Illinois, on October 16, 1854, he complained: "Finally, Judge Douglas invokes against me the memory of Clay and Webster. They were great men and men of great deeds, but have I assailed them? For what is it that their lifelong enemy shall now make profit by assuming to defend them against their lifelong friend?"[50] In 1861 Lincoln declared: "I have always been an old-line Henry Clay Whig."[51] During Lincoln's presidency, one member of Congress observed that he "belongs to the old Whig party and will never belong to any other."[52]

Why did the young Abraham Lincoln become "an old-line Henry Clay Whig"? Most of his family and neighbors in Kentucky, Indiana, and the part of Illinois settled by Southern migrants were supporters of Clay's archenemy, Andrew Jackson. Indeed, Lincoln's first political job, appointment as the postmaster of New Salem, came from the Jackson administration.

In 1866 Dennis Hanks told Lincoln's biographer and former law partner William Herndon: "what year Did A Lincoln Turn whig After He Cum to Illinois a Bout 1830 for he was allways a Jacson Man tell He went to Springfield So you can tell your Self a Bout that he Never Voted for Jackson for he was two yung in Ia [Indiana] he allways Loved Hen Clays Speeches I think that was the Cause Mostly Sum of the whigs a Bout Springfield Judge Logan and others." According to Hanks, Lincoln's father bought him, among other books, "the Life of Washington and Henry Clay."[53] Washington and Clay were the two leaders whom Lincoln most frequently cited as great American statesmen in speeches throughout his career.

The biography of Clay to which Dennis Hanks referred was George Denison Prentice's *Biography of Henry Clay* (1831). In its pages the young Lincoln found a description of Clay as the ideal republican orator: "His keen eye kindles into new brightness from the irrepressible fires within him; and his whole countenance discovers [reveals] like a mirror the transit of the star-like thoughts, which beam upon lips touched with the living coal of eloquence."[54] In the book Lincoln also found a defense of Clay's entire public philosophy, ranging from broad construction of the constitutional powers of the federal government to the need for canals, railroads, and protective tariffs as an aid in America's economic rivalry with Britain. From 1831 onward, Lincoln adopted Clay's political program wholesale; he may have first encountered it as a system in Prentice's biography of Clay.

What may have made the greatest impression on the young man who would soon join Clay's Whig Party were the quoted passages in which Clay linked a particular public policy debate to the importance of America's role as the world's model republic, a trademark of Clay's rhetoric that became central to Lincoln's thought and oratory. Prentice quoted Clay on the higher meaning for republican government of the struggle between civilian and military authority which he perceived in General Andrew Jackson's occupation of Spanish Florida in 1817–18: "We are fighting a great moral battle, for the benefit, not only of our own country, but of all mankind. The eyes of the whole world are fixed in attention upon us. . . . Everywhere the black cloud of [monarchical] legitimacy is suspended over the world, save only one bright spot, which breaks out from the political hemisphere of the West, to enlighten and animate and gladden the human heart. Obscure that, by the downfall of liberty here, and all mankind are shrouded in a pall of universal darkness."[55] Clay anticipated not only the theme but the language of Lincoln's Gettysburg Address, with its famous phrase "fourscore and seven years ago": "Beware how you give a fatal sanction, in this infant period of our republick, scarcely yet two score years old, to military insubordination."[56]

More than any other influence, Clay's oratory may have shaped the political philosophy and allegiance of the young Lincoln. Later in life, preparing his speeches against slavery extension and his debates with Douglas, Lincoln relied heavily on a two-volume work, *The Life and Speeches of Henry Clay* (1854).[57] One scholar has counted forty-one quotations from or allusions to statements by Clay in Lincoln's speeches.[58]

The Kentucky connection may also have influenced Lincoln's choice of the Whig Party. The Kentucky-born Lincoln may have seen a role model in the great statesman from Kentucky who, like him, was a "self-made man." In Springfield Lincoln belonged to a circle of affluent and politically active Whigs, which included members of his wife's family, the Todds, whose Kentucky relatives were wealthy slave owners. Mary's cousin John T. Stuart recalled, "All the prominent Clay men here [in Springfield] and in other parts of the county were for him."[59] Lincoln's White House secretaries John Nicolay and John Hay, in their official biography, wrote that "the better sort of people in Sangamon County were Whigs . . . and he preferred through life the better sort to the majority."[60] Mary reportedly told neighbors in Springfield that if Lincoln died before her, "his spirit will never find me living outside the limits of a slave state."[61] During the Civil War, three of her half brothers and her half sister's husband were killed fighting for the Confederacy.

Mary Todd Lincoln's relatives in Kentucky knew Clay. After Lincoln was elected to Congress in 1847, he and his wife and two sons, on the way to Washington, spent three weeks in Lexington, Kentucky, with his in-laws, Robert S. Todd and his wife. On November 15, 1847, Lincoln was in the audience in the Lower Market-House in Lexington when Clay denounced the Polk administration's foreign policy in an address entitled "The Conduct of the Mexican War." Once he had taken his place in the House of Representatives, Lincoln, inspired by Clay, and perhaps trying to impress him, gave a speech contesting Polk's claim that the war originated when Mexican troops attacked U.S. troops on American soil in newly annexed Texas. Arguing like other Whigs that the territory in Texas south of the

Nueces River was disputed, Lincoln rhetorically taunted the president, asking him to identify the "spot" on which American blood had been shed.[62] Whatever Clay might have thought of the freshman congressman's performance, if he noticed it at all, the public back in Illinois was angered by Lincoln's seeming lack of patriotism, and the Democrats nicknamed him "Spotty" Lincoln, a label that clung to him for years. While Lincoln followed Clay's lead in opposing the Mexican War, in his 1852 eulogy for his hero, he justifies Clay's role as one of the "War Hawks" of 1812: "Meanwhile British aggressions multiplied, and grew more daring and aggravated. By Mr. Clay, more than any other man, the struggle was brought to a decision in Congress."[63]

The Lincolns visited Kentucky again when Robert Todd died in 1849 and Lincoln helped settle his estate. A relative, Lyman Beecher Todd, claimed in 1901: "I have seen him [Lincoln] when twice he visited Lexington, Kentucky,—on last occasion when he was the guest of Mr. Clay at Ashland."[64] In addition to visiting Clay on his plantation, Lincoln also may have met his hero in Washington.

During the Civil War, two of Clay's sons were Unionists while one fought for the Confederacy and died in exile in Canada. In 1862, when Clay's son John sent Lincoln one of his father's snuffboxes along with best wishes from his widowed mother, Lincoln replied, "Thanks for this memento of your great and patriotic father. Thanks also for the assurance that, in these days of dereliction, you remain true to his principles. In the concurrent sentiment of your venerable mother, so long the partner of his bosom and his honors, and lingering now, where he *was,* but for the call to rejoin him where he *is,* I recognize his voice, speaking as it ever spoke, for the Union, the Constitution, and the freedom of mankind."[65]

It may be that Clay's vision of a dynamic, industrial America was what appealed to Lincoln the most. In 1856 William D. Kelley, a Pennsylvania congressman who championed the American System, gave a speech in which he noted how many poor white Southerners emigrated from slave states to only two free states, Indiana and Illinois, "making the total of those who had left these nine planting States to go to those two agricultural and grazing States, 105,755"—or about half of the "206,638 persons who were born in the slave States living in the free States."[66] Lincoln was one of the white migrants from the South to the Midwest, and the contrast between the poverty of the South he left and the prosperity of the Midwest he entered may explain his rejection of the Jeffersonian political values of the rural South.

As the party of economic modernization, then, the Whigs may have appealed to Lincoln. The Whigs were also the party of law and order. This may have appealed to Lincoln the rationalist, who was as horrified by the anarchy and violence of Southern Jacksonian culture as he was by its illiteracy and religious fervor. All of these may have been factors in the decision of Lincoln, from a family of Jacksonian Democrats in a heavily Democratic state, to join the Whig Party of Henry Clay.

THROUGHOUT HIS CAREER in politics, first as a Whig and then as a Republican, Lincoln sought to realize both aspects of Henry Clay's program—the Hamiltonian plan for industrializing the United States by means of massive infrastructure projects and protectionist import-substitution policies, and the Jeffersonian scheme for eliminating both slavery and the black population from the United States by means of colonization.

In 1860 Lincoln's future adviser Henry C. Carey, the preeminent theorist of the American School of economic nationalism, identified the Republican presidential candidate Lincoln as "a man who has been all his life a protectionist."[67] Lincoln's record confirms the observation of Joseph J. Lewis, a supporter in 1860, that "Mr. Lincoln has been a consistent and earnest tariff man from the first hour of his entering public life."[68] "I was an old Henry-Clay-Tariff Whig," Lincoln wrote a correspondent on October 11, 1859. "In old times I made more speeches on that subject than any other. I have not since changed my views."[69]

Lincoln sought to promote Clay's American System both as a state legislator and a member of the U.S. Congress. Lincoln's campaign manifesto of

1832 announced his dedication to Clay's American System: "My politics are short and sweet, like the old woman's dance. I am in favor of a national bank . . . in favor of the internal improvements system and a high protective tariff."[70] Lincoln studied the American School economist Francis Wayland. According to Lincoln's law partner William Herndon, Lincoln "ate up, digested, and assimilated . . . Wayland's little book."[71] Indeed, for much of his career, Lincoln illustrated the definition by a contemporary in protectionist Pennsylvania of man as "an animal that makes tariff speeches."[72]

Many of Lincoln's speeches in support of high protective tariffs have not survived. The ones that have are not impressive. Notes on protectionism that he wrote in December 1847 show that his grasp of the arguments for infant-industry tariffs was that of an amateur. Like other Whig and Republican protectionists, Lincoln argued that the manufacturer and importer, not the consumer, paid the costs of the tariff.[73] While this argument was widespread, it was false; most economists agree that the costs of tariffs are passed on to consumers. Another argument, that transportation of products and raw materials was inherently wasteful, contradicted his support of government funding for internal improvements, the most important of which were transportation projects in the interests of commerce.

In his speech of June 20, 1848, in the House in favor of internal improvements, Lincoln conceded: "Such products of the country as are to be consumed where they are produced, need no roads or rivers—no means of transportation, and have no very proper connection with the subject [of internal improvements]."[74] The commercial economy, not the subsistence economy, would benefit from internal improvements. This contradicts his argument in his notes on the tariff, in which he seems to be suggesting that everything should be made everywhere and that any transportation, either of finished goods or the raw material that went into them, is wasteful. As president-elect in a speech of February 15, 1861, in Pittsburgh, Lincoln made this argument again: "If we had no iron here, then we should encourage its shipment from foreign countries; but not when we can make it as cheaply in our own country. This brings us back to our first proposition, that if any article can be produced at home with nearly the same cost as abroad, the carriage is lost labor."[75]

Lincoln's argument was wholly erroneous. If the cost of transportation in fact made local products cheaper than imports, the federal government would not need to protect American industries by enacting a protective tariff; distance alone would achieve the same result. It was precisely because the American market for manufactures could be supplied cheaply by British factories, the minor costs of transportation notwithstanding, that American School economists and policymakers insisted on a protective tariff to foster America's infant industries. And despite Lincoln's suggestion that every good would be produced everywhere, the American System's program for internal improvements assumed interregional specialization within the United States. Southern cotton would be moved not to British textile mills but to New England textile mills; but it would still be moved. And even if a Southern textile industry arose, as it did in the twentieth century, there would still be a need for commerce across as well as within state lines.

There were legitimate arguments to be made for temporarily protecting infant industries with tariffs, but Lincoln did not make them. However, he got one thing right—one major purpose of the American System was to undermine British economic and military supremacy. In arguing for a protective tariff, Lincoln identified Britain as the economic enemy and claimed that Anglophile snobs who loved imported British goods were unpatriotic enemies of the American workingman: "[T]hose whose pride, whose abundance of means, prompt them to spurn the manufactures of their own country, and to strut in British cloaks, and coats, and pantaloons, may have to pay a few cents more on the yard for the cloth that makes them. A terrible evil, surely, to the Illinois farmer, who never wore, nor never [sic] expects to wear, a single yard of British goods in his whole life."[76] Early in his career Lincoln had worn a suit of homespun jeans as a legislator, in emulation of George Washington's decision to dress in homespun for his inauguration, encouraging the spirit later manifested in "Buy American" campaigns.

AS A LOYAL Whig follower of Henry Clay, Abraham Lincoln devoted much of his time both as an Illinois state legislator and U.S. representative to promoting the Hamiltonian program of rationalizing American finance by means of central banking. In defending the modernization of the American financial system, Lincoln found himself obliged to combat misconceptions about banking that were widespread in the largely rural population of Illinois. For example, in a speech in Springfield on December 26, 1836, Lincoln mocked the primitive ideas about money held by many Jeffersonian agrarians, who believed that it was illegitimate for banks to make loans on the basis of their deposits: ". . . [T]he revenue is to be collected, and kept in iron boxes until the government wants it for disbursement; thus robbing the people of the use of it, while the government does not itself need it, and while the money is performing no nobler office than that of rusting in iron boxes."[77] Lincoln also pointed out the flaw in the demand by Jeffersonian Democrats that the government collect all of its revenues only in the form of "specie" or gold rather than paper money: "Thus it is seen, that if the whole revenue be collected in specie, it will take more than half of all the specie in the nation to do it," eliminating the basis of much of the paper money then in circulation.[78]

Unable to reestablish a national banking system along Hamiltonian lines as long as the presidency and Congress were dominated by Jeffersonian Democrats from the South and their allies in other regions, Whigs like Lincoln supported state banks such as the Illinois state bank as an alternative. On December 5, 1840, when Democrats in the legislature sought to pass a law requiring the Illinois state bank to redeem money in specie rather than in banknotes, Lincoln persuaded a majority of his fellow Whigs to stay home, to ensure that the absence of enough legislators for a quorum would prevent the vote. When ailing Democrats were brought from their sickbeds to vote in the First Methodist Church of Springfield, where the state legislature met until the new state capital was completed, Lincoln and two fellow Whig legislators sought to prevent a quorum by climbing out of a first-story window after discovering that the doors to the chamber were blocked to prevent their escape. In spite of this dramatic parliamentary maneuver, Lincoln's plan to delay the resumption of specie payments by the state bank of Illinois was defeated.[79]

WHEN HE WAS promoting national banking reforms, as when he was arguing on behalf of high tariffs, Lincoln was more the dutiful Whig Party activist than the engaged expert. Of the three elements of the American System, it was the subject of internal improvements that energized Lincoln the most.

The chief obstacle to the development of both commercial agriculture and manufacturing in Illinois was the lack of an adequate transportation network in the form of navigable rivers, canals, roads, and railroads. In 1832 the twenty-three-year-old Lincoln, planning a run for the legislature, devised a publicity stunt to illustrate both the possibilities of infrastructure development and his own commitment to the cause. A steamship named *Talisman* had made its way up the Sangamon River to Springfield, where this relatively new kind of craft must have impressed the citizens. After the cargo was unloaded, Lincoln persuaded its captain, Vincent A. Bogue, to pay him and his friend Rowan Herndon to escort the ship farther up the river, to Beardstown. Along the way Lincoln cut down branches in the way of the ship.[80] In his subsequent campaign for a seat in the Illinois legislature that year, Lincoln appealed to "independent voters" to support his plan to improve the Sangamon River, and during his bid for reelection in 1836, the only issue he discussed was internal improvements: "Whether elected or not, I go for distributing the proceeds of the sales of the public lands to the several states, to enable our state, in common with others, to dig canals and construct railroads, without borrowing money and paying interest on it."[81] The image of the young politician riding the steamship up the river, clearing nature to make way for the latest symbol of technological progress, provides a better sense of Lincoln than the image of the "rail-splitter," which he opportunistically cultivated during his 1860 presidential campaign.

Lincoln's work in his youth as a surveyor enabled him to take part in infrastructure construction because surveyors were needed to lay out proposed roads. The prospect of economic growth made land near proposed roads or canals increase in value. In addition to signing petitions asking the Illinois legislature to construct new roads, Lincoln bought one share of stock in the Beardstown and Sangamon Canal Company, which planned to connect the Illinois River to the Sangamon River at the town of Huron. Anticipating an increase in property values, Lincoln bought forty-seven acres of land near Huron. In this way Lincoln would profit both from the canal company and from the appreciation in real estate that the company's activities would produce. The canal was never built, and what Lincoln hoped would become town lots remained rural acreage.[82]

After Lincoln became a lawyer, the Illinois Central Railroad was Lincoln's most important client. He also obtained work as a lawyer from other railroad companies that had Illinois interests, including the Ohio & Mississippi Railroad, the Alton & Sangamon Railroad, and the Tonica & Petersburg Railroad.[83]

The efforts of Lincoln and his fellow Whigs in the state legislature on behalf of internal improvements in Illinois ended in failure. The rise and fall of his hopes for New Salem foreshadowed later debacles. Lincoln's efforts as the guide of the steamboat *Talisman* in 1832, far from proving that the Sangamon River could be used by steamboats, demonstrated the reverse. Reasonably enough, Lincoln made improvements in the navigability of the Sangamon part of the platform of his unsuccessful campaign for the state legislature in 1832. But the state legislature did not act on this proposal, and New Salem went into decline, losing its own post office in 1836, and it lost the coveted role of county seat to nearby Petersburg in 1839. By the time it was reduced to a ghost town in 1840, Lincoln had been living in Springfield for three years, having moved there in 1837. Springfield, which with the support of Lincoln, among others, won a long campaign to become the new state capital in 1837, was, like New Salem, on the Sangamon River, to whose use as a transportation network Lincoln had given so much thought.

The statewide internal improvement schemes that Lincoln supported were failures. In 1837 Lincoln and other Whigs in the state legislature successfully pushed for the enactment of a $12 million plan to build a transportation infrastructure for the state. In the words of Lincoln's law partner William Herndon, "every river and stream . . . was to be widened, deepened, and made navigable. A canal to connect the Illinois River and Lake Michigan was to be dug, . . . cities were to spring up everywhere, . . . Illinois was to outstrip all others, and herself become the Empire State of the Union." However, "the internal improvement system, [in] the adoption of which Lincoln had played such a prominent part, had collapsed, with the result that Illinois was left with an enormous debt and an empty treasury."[84] Similar overly ambitious schemes failed in other states, some of which, like Illinois in 1848, amended their constitutions to ban state subsidies to private enterprise.

The pattern is a familiar one in the history of technological revolutions in transportation and revolution: a new technology (the steamboat, the locomotive, the automobile, the telephone, electricity, the Internet) inspires overinvestment by the private sector and government, followed by subsequent collapse. Following the initial boom and bust, however, the innovations are widely adopted and increase the productivity of the economy. Although it must have been small consolation to the taxpayers of Illinois, who had to pay down the state debt, and to those who lost money investing in private companies and land hoping to take advantage of the state internal improvements program, a few decades later Illinois was crisscrossed by railroads and canals, and one city in the state became not only a national but a global center of commerce, manufacturing, and finance: Chicago.

The failure of the state internal improvements program in Illinois did not reduce Lincoln's commitment to the American System. Soon after being elected to the U.S. Congress in July 1847, Lincoln attended a Rivers and Harbors Convention at Chicago, where he spoke out in favor of federal funding for internal improvements and against the Democratic president, Franklin Pierce, for opposing this policy.[85] During his first and only term in the U.S. Congress, on June 20, 1848, Lincoln defended federal subsidies for internal improvements. Rebutting Jeffersonian arguments that the Constitution forbade federal aid to private enterprises, Lincoln argued that "no one, who is satisfied of the expediency of making improvements, needs be much uneasy in his conscience about its constitutionality."[86] The broad construction of constitutional grants of power to the federal government was typical of the approach of Hamiltonian Whigs like Lincoln and Clay.

THE ISSUES OF infrastructure development and the use of the public domain were entwined. As a member of the minority Whig Party in a state dominated by Jeffersonian and Jacksonian Democrats, Lincoln was compelled at times to distance himself from Whigs who reflected the priorities of commercial and industrial elites along the Atlantic seaboard. This was particularly important where the issue was the future of federal land, a subject of vital concern in the agrarian Midwest.

Controversy over the future of the federal lands within the borders of new states created out of former federal territories crystallized around three issues: preemption, graduation, and homesteading. Preemption laws sought to favor actual settlers or "squatters" over speculators and absentee owners, while a policy of graduation, by requiring the government to sell land at different prices, was intended to allow more people to purchase government land.

Preemption and graduation policies were supported by populist Jeffersonian Democrats in the Midwest and tended to be opposed by the Whig Party, which reflected the interests of wealthy elites for whom land was a speculative investment. Early in his career as an Illinois legislator, Lincoln voted regularly in favor of populist, pro-squatter measures.[87] However, in the late 1830s he began to vote against both preemption and graduation.[86] The reason was Lincoln's commitment to Henry Clay's proposal to use sales of federal land to finance infrastructure projects such as canals and railroads in Illinois. To allow settlers to buy land at low prices meant fewer revenues for internal improvements in Illinois.

After the collapse of the Illinois internal improvement scheme in the early 1840s, Lincoln seems to have reconsidered his opposition to populist land policies. In 1844 Robert Smith, a U.S. representative from Lincoln's Illinois, proposed the first national homestead legislation, which would have provided eighty acres for poor farmers who promised to work them. Voted down, the proposal was renewed in each Congress only to face the opposition of Northern Whigs, who served the interests of Northeastern speculators in Western lands, and Southern Democrats, who reflected the interests of rich slave owners rather than poor white farmers. As a member of Congress in 1848, Lincoln joined the minority of Whigs from the Old Northwest who voted in favor of considering homestead legislation.[89] Because the homestead issue divided members of both the Whig and Republican parties, however, Lincoln, as a presidential candidate in 1860, maintained a diplomatic silence, which he broke only after his election, on February 12, 1861, when he told an audience at Cincinnati: "I am in favor of cutting up the wild lands into parcels, so that every poor man may have a home."[90] Many affluent Northeastern Republicans, most of them former Whigs, remained opposed to the homestead policy. But Republican support for the Jeffersonian homestead policy was the price for the alliance between Midwestern agrarians and Northeastern commercial and industrial interests that put Lincoln in the White House, defeated Southern secession, and produced the primacy of the Republican Party in national politics between the Civil War and the Great Depression.

LINCOLN'S INVOLVEMENT IN controversies about slavery and race did not begin in the 1850s. He voted and campaigned on issues affecting both slaves and free blacks throughout his career as a legislator in Springfield and Washington. On these subjects, no less than on others, he followed the lead of "Harry of the West." "I can express all my views on the slavery question by quotations from Henry Clay," he insisted once. "Doesn't this look like we are akin?"[91]

Clay's abandonment of hope in the possibility of colonization at the end of his life, expressed in private, was unknown to Lincoln and the general public. In his public eulogy for Clay in Springfield in 1852, Lincoln concluded with a long discussion of Clay's opposition to slavery and support for black colonization. Noting that Clay was a slave owner, Lincoln said: "He ever was, on principle and in feeling, opposed to slavery. The very earliest, and one of the latest public efforts of his life, were both made in favor of gradual emancipation of the slaves in Kentucky. He did not perceive, that on a question of human right, the negroes were to be exempted from the human race." Lincoln defended Clay's opposition both to abolitionists "who would shiver into fragments the Union of these states" and "the opposite extreme," "an increasing number of men, who, for the sake of perpetuating slavery, are beginning to assail and to ridicule the white-man's charter of freedom—the declaration that 'all men are created free and equal.' So far as I have learned, the first American, of any note, to do or attempt this, was the late John C. Calhoun. . . ." Lincoln mockingly continued, "We, however, look for, and are not much shocked by, political eccentricities and heresies in South Carolina." Then he quoted "a very distinguished and influential clergyman of Virginia" rejecting the statement "All men are created equal" as a passage not to be found in the Bible but one that comes "from Saint Voltaire, and was baptized by Thomas Jefferson . . ." Having quoted this remark, Lincoln, an admirer of post-Christian Enlightenment deists like Voltaire, Jefferson, Paine, and Volney, said: "This sounds strangely in republican America." He then quoted from Clay's address to the American Colonization Society in 1827, in which Clay said that slavery could not be defended without rejecting the idea of liberty everywhere: "They must blow out the moral lights around us, and extinguish that greatest torch of all which America presents to a benighted world—pointing the way to their rights, their liberties, and their happiness." Lincoln endorsed Clay's panacea of emancipation, followed by colonization: "If as the friends of colonization hope, the present and coming generations of our countrymen shall by any means, succeed in freeing our land from the dangerous presence of slavery; and, at the same time, in restoring a captive people to their long-lost fatherland, with bright prospects for the future; and this too, so gradually, that neither races nor individuals shall have suffered by the change, it will indeed be a glorious consummation. And if, to such a consummation, the efforts of Mr. Clay shall have contributed, it will be what he most ardently wished, and none of his labors will have been more valuable to his country and his kind."[92] The claim that colonization, if successful, would have been a posthumous victory outweighing all of Clay's other achievements gives some sense of how central the expatriation of America's black population was in Lincoln's thought.

Lincoln had heard Clay's views about colonization from the great man in person. When Lincoln sat in the audience and listened to Clay give his speech against the Mexican War on November 13, 1847, he heard his hero declare: "I have ever regarded slavery as a great evil, a wrong, for the present, I fear, an irremediable wrong to its unfortunate victims. I should rejoice if not a single slave breathed the air or was within the limits of our country." However, it would be a mistake simply to end slavery in Southern states where whites were outnumbered by blacks: "Collisions and conflicts, between the two races, would be inevitable, and, after shocking scenes of rapine and carnage, the extinction or expulsion of the blacks would certainly take place." The solution, according to Clay, was gradual emancipation accompanied by colonization.[93]

Clay was the dominant influence on Lincoln's thinking about race, slavery, and colonization, but not the only one. In 1864 Lincoln told an acquaintance that Leonard Bacon, the colonizationist who wrote *Report of the Committee . . . to inquire respecting the black population of the United States* (1823), "had much to do with shaping my thinking on the subject of slavery."[94] Then there was Thomas Jefferson himself, whose plan for a white-only America had inspired the efforts of his fellow slave owners James Madison and Henry Clay, both of whom served as presidents of the American Colonization Society.

Lincoln's views about Jefferson are not clear. William Herndon told Ward Lamon in 1870: "Mr. Lincoln hated Thomas Jefferson as a man" and "as a politician."[95] In September 1860 the *Chicago Times* quoted a speech recorded in the *Macomb (Illinois) Eagle* that Lincoln was alleged to have made while campaigning for Henry Clay for president in 1844: "The character of Jefferson was repulsive. . . . Continually puling about liberty, equality, and the degrading curse of slavery, he brought his own children to the hammer, and made money of his debaucheries." Lincoln did not publicly disown the speech, but encouraged the statement that appeared in the *Illinois State Journal* on September 6: "This is a bold and deliberate forgery. . . . Mr. Lincoln never used any such language in any speech *at any time.*"[96]

In his support for a strong federal government and government-encouraged industrial capitalism, Lincoln, like Clay, followed Hamilton, not Jefferson. However, he sought to appeal to voters whose political culture was Jeffersonian, so it was politic to quote Jefferson for Hamiltonian ends. For example, in his Annual Message to Congress on December 3, 1861, Lincoln tried to neutralize the Jeffersonian objection that his plan for black colonization might require the federal government to appropriate money to acquire territory. Lincoln observed: "The power was questioned at first by Mr. Jefferson, who, however, in the purchase of Louisiana, yielded his scruples on the plea of great expediency."[97]

There was no need for such disingenuous argument, however, when Lincoln cited Jefferson in connection with race and slavery. He agreed with Jefferson along with Clay that slavery was evil and that the ideals of the American Revolution applied to all races; and agreed with them as well that blacks could realize those ideals only in a country other than the United States. Lincoln disagreed with the constitutional and economic theories of Jefferson and his school, but he was completely sincere when he cited the words of Jefferson as "the axioms of a free society." Lincoln claimed: "I have never had a feeling politically that did not spring from the sentiments embodied in the Declaration of Independence."[98] In the speech that made him a national celebrity at the Cooper Institute in New York on February 27, 1860, Lincoln quoted Thomas Jefferson: "[I]n the language of Mr. Jefferson, used many years ago, 'It is still in our power to direct the process of emancipation, and deportation, peaceably, and in such slow degrees, as that the evil will wear off insensibly; and their places be, *pari passu,* filled up by free white laborers.'"[99] Here Lincoln offers a vision of the South from which not only slavery but blacks were gone, their places taken by white workers and farmers. This was the vision that Lincoln had inherited from Jefferson by way of Henry Clay.

AT THE TIME he delivered his Lyceum address in 1838, Lincoln believed that the American republic was threatened equally by proslavery Southerners and antislavery Northerners. "[Towering genius] thirsts and burns for distinction; and if possible, it will have it, whether at the expense of emancipating slaves, or enslaving freemen."[100] This passage has been wrongly interpreted as a forerunner of Lincoln's later career. In fact the young Lincoln was arguing that abolitionists and proslavery advocates were equivalent threats to public order and the U.S. Constitution, an equation he would later make again in his 1852 eulogy for Henry Clay. During his one term in Congress, Lincoln acted as a cautious moderate on the question of slavery. On December 21, 1848, he voted with the losing Southern minority against a resolution by a New York representative, Daniel Gott, that called for a bill to ban the slave trade in the District of Columbia. Then, on January 10, 1849, Lincoln announced his intention to offer a bill providing for the gradual emancipated compensation of slaves in the District. Growing defensive after being questioned about his claim that the bill had the support of fifteen white citizens of the District, Lincoln abandoned the project. Lincoln's bill, never introduced, provided that "all persons now within said District lawfully held as slaves, or now owned by any person or persons now resident within said District, shall remain such" and that gradual, compensated emancipation would require "the consent of the free white people of said District . . ." All children born after January 1, 1850, would be free, but only after being "apprenticed" to slave owners until adulthood.[101] Lincoln's attempt to stake out a moderate position in the debate followed the example of his role model, who published his own plan for the gradual emancipation of slaves in Kentucky in the spring of 1849.

Lincoln's support for the colonization movement inspired him to take part in colonization efforts at the level of state government. In Illinois the first colonization society was organized in 1830 in Vandalia, then the state capital. John T. Stuart, the cousin of Lincoln's wife, Mary, was secretary of the chapter established in Springfield in 1833, whose president was Charles Matheny, father of James Matheny, Lincoln's friend and the best man at his wedding. When this lapsed, a Springfield chapter of the American Colonization Society, called the Sangamo Colonization Society, was organized and led by people who had close ties to Lincoln. His relatives by marriage John Todd and John Stuart served as vice presidents while the president was Charles Dresser, the Episcopal pastor who performed the wedding of Abraham Lincoln and Mary Todd. In the 1840s a statewide organization, the Illinois State Colonization Society, established a chapter in Springfield. In these successive colonization societies in Springfield, four-fifths of the officers were Whigs like Lincoln. When black citizens in Springfield and elsewhere in Illinois organized meetings and published protests against colonization, the white colonizationists paid no attention. They never asked the free blacks whom they wanted to ship out of the country whether they wanted to leave.[102]

Like Jefferson and Clay, the colonizationists in Illinois combined hostility to abolitionists with idealistic rhetoric about putting "the wandering children of bereaved Africa in the bosom of their mother land."[103] Lincoln began taking active part in the colonization movement in 1853 as an ally of the Reverend James Mitchell, a Negro Methodist minister (that is, a white minister to blacks). Mitchell had taken part in earlier campaigns to persuade the Indiana legislature to adopt its own program of colonizing blacks in Africa. In his speeches and polemics in Indiana, Mitchell had argued that blacks could never compete with racially superior Anglo-Saxons and that the United States should remain a racially homogeneous republic. In 1853 Mitchell's efforts paid off when the state of Indiana created a state board of colonization with Mitchell as the agent. Mitchell's effort to purchase Grand Cape Mount, an area near Monrovia, Liberia, as the basis for the "Indiana Colony," failed when the locals demanded a higher price, and only forty-seven black Indianans settled in Africa as part of the state program.[104] While his hopes for the Indiana program were still intact, Mitchell made a trip to Springfield in July 1853 "to promote the cause of colonization and to organize the state of Illinois in its interest as [he] had already organized Indiana." A Presbyterian pastor recommended Lincoln, who, Mitchell recalled later, "earnestly believed in and advocated colonization as a means of solving 'the race problem.' "[105] Following his contact with Mitchell, on August 30, 1853, Lincoln gave a speech on colonization at the First Presbyterian Church of Springfield.

Mitchell's activities in Illinois increased in 1855. On January 1 Governor J. A. Matteson called on the Illinois legislature to raise funds for colonization in order to "thereby separate the blacks from the whites, and send them to the land of their fathers." On January 4 a resolution in the Illinois legislature was introduced that sought information from Mitchell on such questions about colonization as the possibility of Illinois establishing its own African colony for "the accommodation of the colored people" along the lines of the Indiana colony that Mitchell was trying to establish at the same time. On the evening of January 4 Lincoln gave a speech before the Illinois State Colonization Society during its annual meeting in Springfield. Apparently Mitchell, Lincoln, Matteson, and the society were working closely together.[106] In 1857 the Illinois State Colonization Society elected Lincoln one of its eleven managers.[107]

In order to understand Lincoln's racial views, it is important to understand that the targets of the colonization movement in free states like Illinois were free blacks, not slaves. Many citizens of antebellum Illinois, in addition to hoping that free blacks could be persuaded to leave, supported legislation that discouraged free blacks from moving into the state. This was modeled on the laws of other border states. Fearing an influx of emancipated former slaves from the South, by 1807 Maryland, Delaware, Kentucky, and Ohio banned blacks from taking up permanent residence in their borders.[108]

Antiblack legislation antedated the statehood of Illinois itself. Although the Northwest Ordinance prohibited slavery in the territory from which Illinois and other states were formed, the first Illinois constitution of 1818 contained a loophole that permitted renewable one-year "contracts." To deter the immigration of free blacks, the Illinois legislature passed a series of cruel Black Laws, which denied political and civil rights to free blacks and did not permit them to enter the state unless a white Illinoisan posted a thousand-dollar bond. Unlike the 1818 constitution, the new Illinois constitution adopted in 1848 banned slavery. Disagreement between the Yankee-settled northern counties and the counties settled by Southerners in the south led to the detachment of a provision banning the immigration of free blacks to Illinois from the constitution. When put to a popular vote, however, the ban on black immigration was approved by 70 percent statewide and 84 percent of Springfield voters, making Illinois the third state, after Indiana and Oregon, that banned black immigration in its constitution.[109] Lincoln never challenged the Illinois Black Laws throughout his career in Illinois politics, and he defended them during his debates with Stephen A. Douglas over slavery extension in the 1850s.

Lincoln's participation in the colonization movement, aimed at the exclusion of free blacks, preceded his participation in the movement against slavery extension, which began only when the geography of slavery became a national issue again. Lincoln was a colonizationist before he was a Free-Soiler. Both movements had the same goal: preventing black migration to the West.

WHAT, APART FROM the example of Henry Clay, led Lincoln to devote himself to the cause of removing from the United States his free black fellow citizens of Illinois before the slavery extension battles of the 1850s? During the controversy about the extension of slavery, he emphasized the prospect of economic competition between white workers and black slaves. But the number of free blacks in Illinois was so tiny that the protection of whites from economic competition could hardly account for

Lincoln's support for keeping free blacks out of the state and colonizing the few who were already residents.

The racial bias of a Southern white was probably one factor. One Illinois citizen who had emigrated to the state from Kentucky, as Lincoln had done, explained the reason for his support of the ban on black immigration in the Illinois constitution. "We are men who have come here from southern and slaveholding states, we are men who have seen the evils of a negro population, we came here to escape them, and we wish to prevent the increase within this state of that class of population even more vicious and more degraded than even slaves—free negroes."[110] Lincoln may have been thinking of the experience of his father, a struggling poor white farmer in the slave state of Kentucky who moved to the plantation-free states of Indiana and Illinois, when he warned that if slavery expanded beyond the South, "Negro equality will be abundant, as every White laborer will have occasion to regret when he is elbowed from his plow or his anvil by slave niggers."[111]

Lincoln's younger law partner, William Herndon, converted to abolitionism at Illinois College by teachers from New England, attributed Lincoln's dislike of abolitionism—"this New England importation"—to his Southern culture: "Abstractly, and from the standpoint of conscience, he abhorred slavery. But born in Kentucky, and surrounded as he was by slaveholding influences, absorbing their prejudices and following in their line of thought, it is not strange, I repeat, that he should fail to estimate properly the righteous indignation and unrestrained zeal of a Yankee Abolitionist."[112] Lincoln, according to Herndon, could often be found "mimicking the antics of the negro minstrel . . ."[113] Throughout his life Lincoln amused white friends and acquaintances with "darky" jokes. Soon after his election to the presidency in 1860, in a conversation with some friends, Lincoln drew an analogy between his situation and that of a Kentucky farmer elected as justice of the peace: "The first case he was called upon to adjudicate was a criminal prosecution for the abuse of Negro slaves. . . . But his search for precedents proved in vain, and growing still more puzzled, he exclaimed at last, angrily, 'I will be damned if I don't feel almost sorry for being elected, when the niggers is the first thing I have to attend to.' "[114]

As a Whig and later as a Republican, Lincoln sometimes appealed to white racism as a weapon against the Democrats. In 1840 Lincoln, campaigning for the Whig candidate William Henry Harrison, denounced the Democratic presidential candidate Martin Van Buren for supporting black voting rights in New York. In Tremont, Illinois, on May 2, 1840 Lincoln attacked "the political course of Mr. Van Buren, and especially his votes in the New York Convention in allowing Free Negroes the right of suffrage . . ."[115] The *Old Soldier,* a Whig newspaper coedited by Lincoln, denounced Van Buren on July 28, 1840, under the headline MARTIN VAN BUREN FOR FREE NEGRO SUFFRAGE: *"Martin Van Buren* is in favor of allowing *FREE NEGROES and SLAVES* to swear in Courts against *WHITE MEN!!"*[116]

As this suggests, Lincoln was capable of using racist demagogy when it served his purposes. One of the worst examples of this is found in a speech he gave during the 1852 presidential campaign to the Springfield Scott Club, formed to support the Whig candidacy of General Winfield Scott. The speech was an attack on Stephen Douglas, who had given a speech in Richmond ridiculing Scott.

At one point Lincoln argued that Douglas, who had accused Scott of saying different things to Southern and Northern audiences, had misconstrued Scott: "As an example, take a sentence from an old and well known book, not much suspected for duplicity, or equivocal language, which sentence is as follows: 'And Enoch walked *with* God; and he was not, for God took him.' Try, for yourselves, how Judge Douglas' substitutes for the word 'with' will affect this sentence. Let Judge Douglas be brought to understand that he can advance the interest of a locofoco candidate for the presidency by criticising this sentence; and forthwith he will hie away to the African church in Richmond, Virginia, and make a great speech, in which he will find great difficulty in understanding the meaning of the words 'walked with God' . . . He will show that it is, and was designed to be, susceptible of two constructions, one at the North, and another at the South; that at the North the word 'with' will be read 'NOTWITHSTANDING,' 'ALTHOUGH HE DEFIES,' 'ALTHOUGH HE SPITS UPON;' and finally he will thrill, and electrify, and throw into spasms of ecstasy his African church auditors by suggesting that such monstrous duplicity could not have been conceived by Enoch or Moses, but must have been dictated by Gen. Seward!!!"

One of the stock characters of minstrel show humor, and its twentieth-century descendants such as the radio program *Amos 'n' Andy*, was the black preacher or politician who put on airs and impressed his ignorant audience with absurd disquisitions and the inaccurate use of fancy language. Whether Lincoln's Whig audience was amused by his portrayal of Douglas as a pompous preacher in an "African church" is not recorded. Lincoln concluded the same speech by envisioning the Democratic presidential candidate Franklin Pierce as a political "mulatto." Quoting a song about "a bright Mullatter" named Sally Brown, Lincoln said: "Why Pierce's only chance for presidency, is to be born into it, as a cross between New York old hunkerism, and free soilism, the latter predominating in the offspring. . . . Now, should Pierce ever be President, he will, politically speaking, not only be a mulatto; but he will be a good deal darker one than Sally Brown."[117] As late as 1852, Lincoln was associating "free soilism" with blackness—"the latter predominating in the offspring." This made no sense inasmuch as the very opposition of Free-Soilers to blacks in the West would lead him to join their movement in a few years, but Lincoln did not let logic get in the way of a good smear. He made the same equation between Free-Soilers and blacks that racist opponents of the Republican Party later made when they spoke of "Black Republicans." And Lincoln could think of no more damaging and comical insult than a comparison between a rival politician and an individual of mixed race.

During the Lincoln-Douglas debates, after Douglas taunted him for his alleged alliance with the black abolitionist Frederick Douglass, whom Lincoln met only years later, when he was president, Lincoln retaliated by snidely referring to "Judge Douglas' old friend Col. Richard M. Johnson," Van Buren's vice president, who had two children by a mulatto mistress. "[I] have never had the least apprehension that I or my friends would marry Negroes if there was no law to keep them from it [laughter] but as Judge

Douglas and his friends seem to be in great apprehension that they might, if there were no law to keep them from it, I give him the most solemn pledge that I will to the very last stand by the law of this State, which forbids the marrying of white people with Negroes."[118] During the 1860 campaign, mockery of Johnson, who was accused of marrying his mistress, was revived by pro-Lincoln Republicans, who responded to charges that they were "Black Republicans" by denouncing the "Mulatto Democracy."[119]

As all of this suggests, Lincoln, like most of his white contemporaries, was both alarmed and titillated by racial amalgamation. Lincoln proclaimed in Springfield in 1857: "There is a natural disgust in the minds of nearly all white people, to the idea of an indiscriminate amalgamation of the white and black races."[120] On the subject of "mixing blood by the white and black races," Lincoln said: "On this point we fully agree with the Judge; and when he shall show that his policy is better adapted to prevent amalgamation than ours we shall drop ours, and adopt his."[121] Lincoln invoked "God," presumably the "Nature's God" of the deists, to justify laws against racial intermarriage: "I protest, now and forever, against that counterfeit logic which presumes that because I do not want a Negro woman for a slave, I do necessarily want her for a wife. [Laughter and cheers.] My understanding is that I need not have her for either, but as God made us separate, we can leave one another alone and do one another much good thereby. . . ."[122] In his debate with Douglas on June 26, 1857, Lincoln declared, "I have said that the separation of the races is the only perfect preventive of amalgamation. I have no right to say all the members of the Republican party are in favor of this, nor to say that as a party they are in favor of it. There is nothing in their platform directly on the subject. But I can say a very large proportion of its members are for it, and that the chief plank in their platform—opposition to the spread of slavery—is most favorable to that separation." Lincoln went on to say, "Such separation, if ever effected at all, must be effected by colonization," which would "transfer the African to his native clime."[123]

There is the answer in Lincoln's own words—the purpose of colonizing emancipated slaves as well as free blacks was to prevent the blending through intermarriage of the white and black populations in the United States. His desire to prevent racial amalgamation explains Lincoln's support for the Illinois Black Laws and his support for the colonization of free blacks in Illinois as well as his subsequent opposition to the extension of slavery and support for a system of gradual, compensated emancipation that would transfer Southern blacks immediately to a foreign country without any interval of residence in the North or West. In 1857 Lincoln asked the Illinois legislature to appropriate money for the colonization of free blacks in Illinois in order to prevent the possibility of racial amalgamation.[124]

Why did Lincoln consider racial blending such a threat that he needed to take time away from his promotion of the American System to promote Henry Clay's other grand scheme, colonization? Lincoln's Secretary of the Navy, Gideon Welles, explained: "Opposed to the whole system of enslavement, but believing the Africans were mentally an inferior race, [Lincoln] believed that any attempt to make them and the whites one people would tend to the degradation of the whites without materially elevating the blacks, but that separation would promote the happiness of each."[125] While Lincoln avoided the crassly racist language used by many of his contemporaries, including many of his fellow Republicans, he left no doubt about his low opinion of black intellectual abilities. During the Lincoln-Douglas debates he suggested that God gave blacks "but little . . ."[126] One of his final acts as president was to "suggest" that the new Louisiana constitution permit "the very intelligent" blacks to vote.[127] Contemporary historians, desperate to make Lincoln a civil rights hero, argue that this showed that just before his assassination he was moving toward the abolitionist position of full civil equality for blacks.[128] In fact, the logic behind his recommendation was the same one that rationalized later "literacy tests" used to disfranchise Southern black voters; only a few blacks were assumed to be as capable as even the least educated whites.

According to the man whom Lincoln as president put in charge of federal colonization policy following years of collaboration in the Illinois colonization movement, Lincoln was "fully convinced" that "the republic was already dangerously encumbered with African blood that would not legally mix with the American. . . ." In an interview with James Mitchell published by the *St. Louis Daily Globe-Democrat* on August 26, 1894, Mitchell spoke of Lincoln's "honest conviction that that it was better for both races to separate. This was the central point of his policy, around which hung all his private views, and, as far as others would let him, his public acts."

According to Mitchell, "He regarded a mixed race as eminently anti-republican, because of the heterogeneous character it gives the population where it exists, and for similar reasons he did not favor the annexation of tropical lands encumbered with mixed races. . . ."[129] This comment by Mitchell suggests that Lincoln, like many Whigs, opposed U.S. acquisition of Mexican territory and the proposed acquisition of Cuba not only out of opposition to the likely extension of slavery but out of fear that great numbers of mestizos and mulattos, brought into the United States, eventually might merge with the white population. In his speech on "Discoveries and Inventions," Lincoln referred to Mexicans as "ignorant greasers."[130] In his debates with his Democratic rival Stephen A. Douglas in the Illinois Senate race of 1858, Lincoln warned that expansionists might follow the Mexican War with "a grab for the territory of poor Mexico, an invasion of the rich lands of South America, then the adjoining islands will follow, each one of which promises additional slave fields. And this question is to be left to the people of those countries for settlement. When we shall get Mexico, I don't know whether the Judge [Douglas] will be in favor of the Mexican people that we get with it settling that question for themselves and all others; because we know the Judge has a great horror for mongrels, [laughter] and I understand that the people of Mexico are most decidedly a race of mongrels. [Renewed laughter.] I understand that there is not more than one person there out of eight who is pure white, and I suppose from the Judge's previous declaration that when we get Mexico or any considerable portion of it, that he will be in favor of these mongrels settling the question, which would bring him somewhat into collision with his horror of an inferior race."[131] Lincoln's remarks suggest that the desire to prevent amalgamation between white Americans and Mexican mestizos and Indians may have been a factor in his opposition to the war with Mexico and the acquisition of Mexican territory. In 1862, in an official report prepared for the Lincoln administration, Congress, and the public, James Mitchell, then Lincoln's "colonization minister," declared that a "perpetual barrier" needed to be "reared between us and that land of the mixed races of this continent—Mexico."[132]

Following the 1856 presidential campaign, Mary Lincoln reassured her half sister in Kentucky that although Lincoln was now a Republican, he was not an antislavery radical: "Although Mr. L is, or was, a Fremont man, you must not include him with so many of those who belong to that party, an *abolitionist*. In principle he is far from it. All he desires is that slavery shall not be extended, let it remain where it is."[133]

IT SHOULD BE clear by now that the traditional bifurcation of Lincoln's career into two halves—an ignoble and uninteresting Whig half in which he was concerned with economic issues, and a noble and inspiring Republican half in which he devoted himself to the issues of race, slavery, and freedom—is simply inaccurate. Lincoln's politics, like Clay's, had a racial component from the beginning. In the 1830s and 1840s, while he campaigned for tariffs, canals and railroads, and a national bank, he supported colonization and Illinois's Black Laws, just as he supported tariffs, canals and railroads, and a national bank during his campaign against slavery extension in the 1850s.

Abraham Lincoln's description of himself in 1861 as "an old-line Henry Clay Whig" was accurate. In political philosophy and in practical politics, Lincoln was not an original thinker but a follower of Henry Clay. He supported both halves of Clay's unique political synthesis—the Hamiltonian half, the American System of industrial policy; and the Jeffersonian half, the program of producing a white-only America by means of the voluntary colonization of blacks in Africa or elsewhere.

Neither his political ideology nor his vision of public policy as a whole changed between the 1830s and the 1860s. What changed was his emphasis, when the national debate over the extension of slavery to the Western territories shattered the American party system and turned Abraham Lincoln from a little-known Illinois politician into the President of the United States.

⸻

FOUR

THE SLAVE POWER

IN 1850 ABRAHAM Lincoln was an obscure former one-term member of the United States House of Representatives from Illinois. Only ten years later, in 1860, he was elected President of the United States. In response, a number of Southern states seceded from the Union, formed the Confederate States of America, and fought for their independence from the government Lincoln led.

Lincoln was an ambitious and skillful politician, and he helped create the political realignment that put him in the White House. But the major credit for shaping an American political majority hostile to the South belongs to Southern extremists themselves. By alienating the Northern majority, the leaders of the South ensured that they would lose, first at the ballot box, and then on the field of battle after they attempted to destroy the United States rather than accept the results of an election.

The intransigence of the Southern political elite in the 1850s was responsible for the rise of Abraham Lincoln from obscurity to national leadership. In the course of the 1850s, Southern demands, by splitting Southern from Northern wings, destroyed three national parties: the Whig Party, the American Party, and the Democratic Party. Southern insistence that the slave system be extended or nationalized shattered the party to which Lincoln first belonged, the Whigs, a party associated with compromise over slavery. And Southern extremists helped create the new Republican Party, which Lincoln joined and led, by driving white Midwestern farmers, the South's traditional allies, into a new coalition with Whiggish business elites and idealistic abolitionists—a coalition perfectly symbolized by Lincoln, a Midwesterner and a former Whig. Finally, the angry defection of Southern Democrats from the national Democratic Party in 1860 ensured that the Republican Party, although it won a minority of the popular vote, would capture the presidency. It was the deeds and words of the Southern political elite during the 1850s that made Abraham Lincoln the leader of the Republican Party, President of the United States, and commander in chief of the armed forces that would destroy the South's bid for independence. The Southern elite itself, without intending the result, was responsible for the career of the man who would defeat it.

THE IMMEDIATE CAUSE of the Civil War was the secession of the South in response to Lincoln's election and Lincoln's determination to treat secession as an illegal and unconstitutional rebellion against the authority of the federal government. The ultimate cause of the Civil War was the institution of slavery in the South. Linking the ultimate origin of the conflict to its immediate trigger, the proximate cause was the distribution within the federal government of power—including the power to regulate, prohibit, or abolish slavery. All of the disputes about slavery in American territories and states were always at the same time disputes about political power in Washington, D.C.

From the earliest years of the American republic, white Southerners have been a minority of the U.S. population. Nevertheless, the white Southern minority managed to dominate the federal government for most of the time between 1789, when the federal Constitution went into effect, and the election of Abraham Lincoln in 1860. For two-thirds of this era the presidents were Southerners. No Northern president was ever reelected. All five two-term presidents—Washington, Jefferson, Madison, Monroe, and Jackson—were Southern slave owners. Most House Speakers and Senate presidents pro tem were Southerners as were eighteen of the thirty-one Supreme Court Justices. The party most identified with Southerners, the Republicans, which evolved into the Democratic Republicans and then the Democrats, controlled Washington, D.C., for most of this period, following the election of Jefferson as president in 1800. The first predominantly Northern party, the Federalists, had disintegrated in 1815. Many of its members regrouped as a faction of the dominant Republican party, called the National Republicans. The mostly Northern Whig Party in which Lincoln spent most of his career, the successor to the Federalists and National Republicans, controlled the presidency only during the two four-year terms of William Henry Harrison and his posthumous successor John Tyler, and Zachary Taylor and his posthumous successor Millard Fillmore.

The minority of white Americans who lived in the South obtained and maintained disproportionate power in the federal government by a number of means, formal and informal. In the U.S. House of Representatives, Southern political power was magnified by the three-fifths clause in the U.S. Constitution, which provided that slaves would be counted as three-fifths of a person for purposes of apportioning congressional districts.

In addition, the three-fifths clause gave the slave states a bonus in the presidential electoral college of between seven and twenty-five votes, with an average of seventeen.[1] Two of four critical presidential elections—in 1789 (Washington), 1800 (Jefferson), 1824 (Jackson), and 1860 (Lincoln)—had outcomes influenced by the three-fifths clause. If slaves had been eliminated as a basis of representation, John Adams would have been elected president in 1800 with 51.5 percent of the electoral college vote. Jefferson won the White House only because of the three-fifths clause.[2] In 1824 none of the candidates won an electoral college majority. Henry Clay, then Speaker of the House, threw his support to John Quincy Adams, who was installed as president by the House rather than Andrew Jackson, who won more popular votes. If Southern influence in the electoral college had not been exaggerated by the three-fifths clause, then the House would have chosen among Clay, Adams, and Jackson, and Clay might well have become president.[3]

In the Senate, the disproportionate influence of the Southern white minority was achieved by the informal custom of maintaining a balance between slave and free states. The Missouri Compromise of 1820 and the Compromise of 1850 had both involved the balance of power between slave and free states in the Senate. In 1819 there had been twenty-two states—eleven free and eleven slave. The admission of Missouri, a slave state, threatened the North, and the crisis was resolved only when Maine, formerly a territory of Massachusetts, was admitted as a free state to offset the entry of Missouri. This established the practice of admitting one slave state for every free state, so that by 1849 three slave states (Florida, Arkansas, and Texas) had been admitted along with three free states (Michigan, Wisconsin, and Iowa). Following the Mexican War of 1846 to 1848, however, the insistence of the North that slavery be banned from the former Mexican territories was resolved only by the Compromise of 1850, which admitted California as a free state but permitted the other territorial governments to choose their status. This compromise, Henry Clay's last effort, postponed sectional conflict for only four years, until the Kansas-Nebraska Act repealed the Missouri Compromise in the older Louisiana Purchase territories acquired from France in 1803, long before the Mexican War.

Southern influence over the presidency was reinforced by two informal aspects of the political party system. The first was the unspoken agreement that all national political parties would have Southern members and would defer to the demands of the Southern elite on all issues related to the South's "peculiar institution" of slavery. And the second was the alliance of the

South and Midwest, many of whose small farmers viewed Northeastern commercial and manufacturing elites as a greater threat to their interests than Southern plantation owners.

What doomed the South's exaggerated influence in the federal government was the steady rise of the percentage of the nation's population that lived in the North, as a result of high fertility rates and the influx of European immigrants. Almost all of the 4.5 million immigrants—most of them Irish, German, and British—who emigrated to the United States between 1830 and 1860 settled in the North. In 1860 the 18 million white Northerners outnumbered the 8 million white Southerners by more than two-to-one. These demographic trends convinced many Southern leaders that their privileged position in the federal government could not last. In the House of Representatives the percentage of seats held by the South declined from 46 percent after the reapportionment of 1800 to 38 percent after 1850.[4] The growing imbalance between the regions in the House made it all the more important for the South to maintain control of the presidency and the Senate, where all eight antislavery measures that were passed by the House between 1800 and 1860 were killed.[5]

The political power of the Southern planter oligarchy would shrink dramatically if the territories were all converted into free states. To maintain their political power, many Southerners insisted that if Western territories unsuitable for plantation slavery were to enter the Union as free states, the United States would have to compensate the Southern planter class by conquering and annexing Cuba and other Caribbean islands or portions of Mexico and Central America, creating new slave states. In 1859 Mississippi senator Gallatin Brown declared: "I want Cuba, and I know that sooner or later we must have it. . . . I want Tamaulipas, Potosi, and one or two other Mexican States; and I want them all for the same reason—for the planting or spreading of slavery. . . . Yes, I want these countries for the spread of slavery."[6]

But Senator John C. Calhoun of South Carolina, the most brilliant leader of the Southern conservatives, did not think that a Senate divided between slave and free states would be sufficient on its own to protect the interests of the planter oligarchy. Calhoun, who died in 1850, proposed that the federal Constitution created by the Founding Fathers be replaced by a new system, which would in effect create a binational state, giving the outnumbered white South as a distinct region a formal veto over all federal policies. The alternative to adoption of this dual government or "concurrent majority," Calhoun warned, was the secession of the South.

In the midterm congressional elections of 1858, the Republican Party gained control of the House of Representatives. Then in the presidential election of 1860, the Republican candidate, Abraham Lincoln, won the presidency. The nightmare of Calhoun and other Southern conservatives was coming true. In the federal government, the executive branch and one-half of the legislature were now dominated by leaders of a national majority who refused to give in to the demands of the minority of white Americans in the South. The Republicans claimed that they had no intention of interfering with slavery in the South itself. But perhaps they would—if not in 1860, then in 1870 or 1880. Rather than take that risk, the Southern elite sought to break up the United States and form a new, smaller country that they could control forever.

THE DEBATES IN the 1850s about the extension of slavery, then, were as much about political power in Washington, D.C., as they were about conditions in the Western territories and the new states to be formed from them.

A complex subject can be simplified by thinking of U.S. expansion as the successive annexation of three big portions of territory: the former territory of the British Crown, which, after the United States won its independence, became the Old Northwest (today's Midwest); the Louisiana Territory, purchased from France in 1803; and the Mexican Cession or Far West, obtained from Mexico in the Treaty of Guadalupe Hidalgo, which ended the U.S.-Mexican War in 1848. Together with the former Spanish Florida Territory, annexed as a U.S. territory in 1819 as a result of the Adams-Onis Treaty, and the state of Texas, a former independent republic admitted as a state in 1845, these three major territories—the Old Northwest, the Louisiana Purchase, and the Mexican Cession—rounded out the shape of the continental United States.

Each of these three huge territories was to be converted into new states, admitted on an equal basis to the existing Union. But each had a different system regulating slavery in its boundaries, established by the U.S. Congress at different dates. The Northwest Ordinance of 1787 banned slavery from being established in the states formed from the Old Northwest. The Louisiana Purchase, however, was divided into free and slave zones along the latitude of 36 degrees, 30 minutes by the Missouri Compromise of 1820. And the Compromise of 1850 established yet a third system for the Mexican Cession, providing that California would be admitted as a free state while settlers themselves would resolve the status of New Mexico and Arizona by exercising their "popular sovereignty" in drafting state constitutions.

Many white Northerners believed that slavery should have been banned from the Louisiana Purchase and the Mexican Cession as it had been banned from the Old Northwest. For reasons that are not entirely clear to historians, Southern leaders accepted the exclusion of slavery from the Old Northwest by the Northwest Ordinance, perhaps in the mistaken belief that the area would be thinly inhabited. But Southern threats of secession had forced Northerners to agree to the creation of slave states from part of the Louisiana Purchase in the Compromise of 1820 and from part of the Mexican Cession in the Compromise of 1850. The latter compromise represented a defeat for the Wilmot Proviso, sponsored by David Wilmot, a Pennsylvania Democrat, who at the beginning of the Mexican War in 1846 sought to ban slavery from all territories that might be annexed from Mexico. Popular among white Northerners, the Wilmot Proviso was passed repeatedly by the House of Representatives, only to be killed repeatedly by Southerners and their allies in the Senate.

Opponents of the extension of the slave plantation system could be for-given for viewing the sequence of the Northwest Ordinance of 1787, the Compromise of 1820, and the Compromise of 1850 as evidence of grow-ing Southern power and assertiveness in an era in which the Southern pop-ulation as a percentage of the whole was steadily declining. This sense of political as well as moral injustice turned into alarm when the slave South and its Northern allies went from extorting new compromises to overturn-ing old ones.

In 1850–51 Senator Stephen Douglas of Illinois ensured the passage of the Compromise of 1850 as a series of separate measures after the omnibus bill promoted by the ailing Henry Clay failed to pass Congress in its entirety. It is ironic, therefore, that Douglas, one of the chief architects of that sec-tional compromise, destroyed it only a few years later. In January 1854 Douglas introduced legislation that sought to organize a portion of the Louisiana Purchase territory as the Nebraska Territory. Douglas proposed to allow the territorial legislature to determine the status of slavery in the ter-ritory. When Southerners objected, Douglas proposed the division of the Nebraska Territory into two prospective states, Kansas and Nebraska. The Missouri Compromise of 1820 had banned slavery from territories and states formed from the Louisiana Purchase north of the southern boundary of Missouri. In order to make it possible for its inhabitants to choose to make Kansas a slave state if they wanted to, the Missouri Compromise was re-pealed.

In the territory itself the result was a small-scale civil war as Northerners and Southerners rushed to Kansas and struggled for control, fighting and sometimes killing one another. In the nation as a whole, the result was con-fusion and conflict as well. Suddenly the future not only of the newly ac-quired Mexican Cession but also of the older Louisiana Purchase territory was unclear. Yet another shock came in 1857, when in *Dred Scott*, a case about the rights of a runaway slave in the free state of Ohio, Chief Justice Roger Taney, a conservative Southern slave owner, and a majority of the Supreme Court ruled that Congress lacked the power to ban slavery from any territory. The constitutionality of the Northwest Ordinance, which was a congressional statute, was now unclear. It was also unclear whether states, in their own constitutions, could ban slavery, or whether the protection of property rights by the federal Constitution permitted slave owners to take their slave "property" anywhere in the country. The Dred Scott decision raised the possibility that every state in the Union might become a slave state. Northerners debated whether they were required to assist Southern slave owners to retrieve runaway slaves under a fugitive slave law passed as part of the Compromise of 1850 that was harsher than its predecessors.

Both Free-Soilers and abolitionists in the North began to organize against what they called the "slave power." Of the two groups, the Free-Soilers were far more numerous and politically important. White abolitionists who argued for the abolition of slavery in the South, and, in some but not all cases, equal rights for free black Americans, were a small if idealistic minority. Most white Americans in the North were hostile to the idea of social equality among whites and blacks, and many members of the white working class in the North feared they would have to compete with blacks for jobs in the North if Southern slaves were emancipated. Racist working-class mobs in the North often attacked abolitionist leaders and institutions as well as free blacks.

The Free-Soil movement reflected the interests and values of the racist white majority in the Midwest and Northeast. Most Free-Soilers, while they sought to prevent the extension of slavery, did not want to abolish it in the South. The policy of nonextension served the economic interests of both Northern white farmers and the urban white working class in the North. Small farmers would not have to compete with rich slave owners for desirable farms and ranches in the Western territories. Many working-class Americans in the cities of the East, who had no intention of moving West, believed that the westward migration of some of their fellow workers would create a tighter labor market in the East and raise their own wages. For this reason the early American labor movement supported Western homestead legislation.

The Free-Soil movement tended to be antiblack as well as antislavery. The majority of Free-Soilers wanted to prevent free blacks as well as black slaves from emigrating to the West, which was to be a white-only society from which Indians had been removed (and into which Asian immigration would later be banned). The goal of a white West was served by the maintenance of slavery in the South, where the majority of the black population could be indefinitely confined. The peaceful emancipation of slaves in the South itself appeared to be a distant prospect. In the unlikely event that such emancipation did occur, most Northern states already had laws to keep out black immigrants from the South, and it was reasonable to expect that Western territories, on becoming states, would enact similar laws against free black migration. Whether slave or free, the South, walled in all along its northern border by laws against both free black migration and slavery, would function in the role assigned to it by the white racist majority in the North: a racial ghetto stretching from Virginia to Texas, where most of the black population of the United States, if it did not emigrate, indefinitely would be confined, protecting the wages and the "racial purity" of Northern whites. The economic logic of the Free-Soil movement was explained by W. E. B. DuBois in *Black Reconstruction in America* (1935): "The attitude of the West toward Negroes, therefore, became sterner than that of the East. Here was the possibility of direct competition with slaves, and the absorption of Western land into the slave system. This must be resisted at all costs, but beyond this, even free Negroes must be discouraged. On this the Southern poor white immigrants insisted."[7] The abolitionists opposed slavery in the West because they were against slavery anywhere. The Free-Soilers opposed both slavery and free black migration to the West, and were willing to tolerate slavery in the South because they wanted a white West.

The campaign against slavery extension was the first of two nineteenth-century political movements to create a white-only West. The second was the Oriental exclusion movement of the 1880s. Both the Free-Soil movement and the movement to restrict Asian immigration arose to protect white workers and farmers in the American West from economic competition with nonwhite labor and the alleged threats of racial equality and racial amalgamation. Most of the same arguments made by those who opposed enslaved black labor in the West in the mid-nineteenth century were also made by those who opposed the introduction of Chinese contract or "coolie" labor a generation later. The migrants (blacks or Asians) were said to be intellectually inferior by nature and unassimilable with America's white majority; they worked for lower wages and would take jobs away from native and immigrant whites. The immigration restrictionists added an argument about the superiority of "free labor" to slave labor, in the case of black slaves; and to contract labor, in the case of "coolies" from China and other Asian countries. However, race was more important than condition; most Free-Soilers wanted to keep free blacks as well as enslaved blacks out of the West, and the Oriental exclusion movement sought to ban all Asian immigrants, not just contract laborers.

All of this explains why, in response to the confusion about the future status of the Western territories in the 1850s, the dominant issue was the geographic extension of slavery rather than its abolition in the South, a reform favored by only a tiny minority of white and black abolitionists in the North. And it explains the meteoric rise of Lincoln in national politics, not as a pro-black abolitionist, but as a leader of the Free-Soil movement whose goal was a white West.

"I WAS LOSING interest in politics when the repeal of the Missouri compromise aroused me again," Lincoln wrote in the autobiographical sketch he prepared for the 1860 presidential campaign.[8]

Lincoln was quick to see an opportunity for himself when an "anti-Nebraska" movement arose in national politics. In addition to dividing the Democratic Party along pro- and anti-Nebraska lines, the repeal of the Missouri Compromise catalyzed the formation of the Republican Party in 1854 from a coalition of anti-Nebraska Democrats, former Whigs, Free-Soilers, and abolitionists. The Dred Scott decision of 1857, which held that attempts to restrict slavery anywhere in the United States were unconstitutional, further enraged Northern opinion. Identified with Southern slave owners and their Northern allies, the Democratic Party suffered serious losses. Between 1852 and 1856, 70 percent of Northern Democrats in the House lost their seats, and the number of Northern Democrats plummeted from 91 to 25.[9]

Lincoln stayed aloof from the new Republican Party for a while. When it became clear that the Whig Party had collapsed over the slavery issue, he joined it and quickly became one of its leaders in Illinois. In 1856 Lincoln, who was already prominent enough to receive 110 votes for the party's vice presidential nomination at the convention, supported the Republican Party's first presidential candidate, the Mexican War hero John C. Fremont, and worked to persuade former Whigs to abandon the rival American Party for the Republican Party. Running for the United States Senate as a Republican, Lincoln was passed over twice by the Illinois legislature, which chose the state's U.S. senators at the time. In 1855, when it became clear that he would not be chosen by the Illinois legislature, Lincoln threw his support to Lyman Trumbull, an anti-Nebraska Democrat who later became a Republican. In 1858 Lincoln lost the race for the other Illinois Senate seat to the Democrat Stephen A. Douglas, the author of the hated Kansas-Nebraska Act. Lincoln's debates with Douglas, reprinted in newspapers across the country, made him a national celebrity, a status confirmed when he gave a stirring and closely reasoned critique of the South's campaign to extend slavery in an address at Cooper Union in New York on February 27, 1860. The repeal of the Kansas-Nebraska Act and the issue of slavery extension had transformed Abraham Lincoln from an obscure Whig disciple of Henry Clay into a potential presidential candidate.

For Lincoln, as for most white Free-Soilers, the purpose of preventing the extension of slavery to the territories was to keep the West white. Banning slavery from the territories and the new free states to be formed from them was an auxiliary precaution against black migration, supplementing the state laws against free black migration that had existed for years or decades. As long as slavery was confined to the South, most blacks would remain confined to the South as well, because most black Americans were slaves.

During the campaign that turned him from a little-known former Whig congressman into President of the United States, Lincoln explained the system in great detail. Preventing the extension of slavery until blacks could be colonized abroad, he explained, was the best way to prevent economic competition between Northern whites and blacks: "Is it not rather our duty to make labor more respectable by preventing all black competition, especially in the territories?"[10] Lincoln emphasized that he and other Republicans sought to protect whites in the North and West from competing with blacks: "Negro equality will be abundant, as every White laborer will have occasion to regret when he is elbowed from his plow or his anvil by slave niggers."[11] Lincoln explained: "The whole nation is interested that the best use shall be made of these territories. We want them for the homes of free white people. This they cannot be, to any considerable extent, if slavery shall be planted within them." Why did Lincoln, a master of language, say "free white people" instead of "free people"? He was opposed to the presence of free blacks as well as enslaved blacks in the territories that were to become new states. Perhaps thinking of his own family, he declared: "Slave States are places for poor white people to remove from; not to remove to. New free states are the places for poor people to go to and better their condition."[12] Lincoln, like many of his neighbors and constituents in Illinois, was an immigrant from the South who had flourished in two states, Indiana and Illinois, where laws against both slavery and the migration of free blacks protected whites like him against nonwhite competition. In Peoria, Illinois, in 1854, Lincoln predicted that the territories were to be "The happy home of teeming millions of free, white, prosperous people, and no slave among them"—and no free black either, by implication.[13]

Lincoln insisted on the link between the wages of white workers in the East and the outlet provided for "our surplus population" in the West in a campaign speech for Fremont in Kalamazoo, Michigan, on August 27, 1856:

"As our Northern States are growing more and more in wealth and population, we are continually in want of an outlet, through which it may pass out to enrich our country." Lincoln elaborated: "I think we have some interest [in the territories]. I think that as white men we have. Do we not wish for an outlet for our surplus population, if I may so express myself?"[14] To prevent wages in the East from falling as a result of overcrowding, the territories "should be kept open for the homes of free white people." White immigrants provided the major economic competition to white workers in the East, but Lincoln, who welcomed European immigration, never acknowledged this inconvenient fact.

For Lincoln, as for most Free-Soilers, the movement against the extension of slavery was half of a program to create a white West, the other half of which consisted of state laws designed to keep free blacks out of Northern and Western states. For example, the Indiana territorial legislature outlawed black court testimony in cases involving whites (1803), black membership in the militia (1807), and black voting (1810). In 1815 an annual tax was imposed on all adult black and mulatto men. The nearby Illinois territorial legislature in 1813, one historian observes, "passed a bill requiring justices of the peace to order every incoming free Negro or mulatto to leave the territory. Failure to comply with the order subjected the offender to a whipping of 39 lashes, repeated every fifteen days until he left."[15] Lincoln was well aware of such Black Laws. He had voted for them in Illinois and repeatedly told voters that they were necessary to prevent the evils of racial integration and racial intermarriage. For rhetorical purposes he seldom mentioned the Black Laws. He portrayed the development of antislavery legislation in the Old Northwest and the states formed from it solely as the result of an idealistic commitment to the principles of 1776. In reality it was simply half of a two-pronged effort by white Midwesterners who were determined not to permit the immigration of any blacks, including free blacks, to protect whites in the region not only from economic competition with blacks but from the alleged danger of racial amalgamation. "What I would most desire would be the separation of the white and black races," Lincoln said in Springfield on July 17, 1858.[16]

Lincoln, who made the issue his own only after passage of the Kansas-Nebraska Act, was a relative latecomer to the Free-Soil controversy. For the most part he repeated the arguments made by other Free-Soilers in the decade following the war with Mexico and the annexation of vast northern Mexican territories. David Wilmot, the Pennsylvania Democrat in the House whose Wilmot Proviso would have banned black emigration to the Western territories won from Mexico, explained: "I plead the cause and the rights of white freemen [and] I would preserve to free white labor a fair country, a rich inheritance, where the sons of toil, of my own race and own color, can live without the disgrace which negro slavery brings upon free labor."[17] Lincoln's fellow Illinois Republican, Lyman Trumbull, who shared Lincoln's support for colonizing blacks abroad, declared in 1859: "We, the Republican Party, are the white man's party. We are for the free white man, and for making white labor acceptable and honorable, which it can never be when negro slave labor is brought into competition with it."[18] The Republican editor Horace Greeley declared that if the Republicans won, then "all the unoccupied territory . . . shall be reserved for the benefit of the white Caucasian race—a thing which cannot be except by the exclusion of slavery."[19] Republican proponents of colonization, such as the brothers Francis and Montgomery Blair, played up their plans to allay the fears of white voters, particularly those in the border states, that the gradual end of slavery might produce a migration of free blacks out of the South to other parts of the country. The goal of denying the West to all blacks, free as well as slave, was made clear by some Republicans, such as Iowa senator James Harlan in a Senate speech entitled "Shall the Territories Be Africanized?"[20]

In the 1850s Lincoln was thought of as a moderate Republican compared to New York governor William H. Seward, who became Lincoln's Secretary of State. Seward had acquired a reputation as an antislavery radical when he spoke of an "irrepressible conflict" between free society and slave society. And yet Seward no more supported racial equality in the

United States than did Lincoln. In 1860 Seward described black Americans as a "foreign and feeble element, like the Indian, incapable of assimilation [and] unwisely and unnecessarily transplanted to our fields."[21] According to Seward, "the motive of those who protested against the extension of slavery" had "always really been concern for the welfare of the white man" rather than an "unnatural sympathy for the negro."[22] Seward, in 1856, to an audience made up largely of European immigrants in Oswego, New York, made a speech entitled "Immigrant White Free Labor or Imported Black African Slave Labor?": "Only grant now that this great end of the slaveholders can be attained, and you will need no argument to prove that African slaves will be found in the ports, not merely of New York, New Orleans, and Philadelphia, and in the fields of Kansas and Nebraska, but even in the ports of Oswego, Rochester, and Buffalo, and in the fields of Western New York, forcing the free white labor, equally of native Americans, and of Englishmen, Irishmen, and Germans, no matter whether they be Protestants or Roman Catholics, into Canada, Russian America [Alaska], Australia, and wherever else throughout the whole earth, free white industry can find refuge."[23] After the Civil War, Seward, then Secretary of State in the Grant administration, dismissed the plight of former slaves: "The North has nothing to do with the Negroes. I have no more concern for them than I have for the Hottentots. . . . They are not of our race."[24]

The examples of Lincoln and Seward, along with many other leading opponents of the extension of slavery, demonstrate that Alexis de Tocqueville was correct when he observed: "In the United States people abolish slavery for the sake not of the Negroes but of the white men."[25]

ALTHOUGH LINCOLN LOST the campaign for the office of U.S. Senator from Illinois to Stephen A. Douglas in 1858, the Lincoln–Douglas debates made Lincoln a star of the new Republican Party and helped him obtain the Republican nomination for president in 1860. Generations of Americans have been taught to treat the Lincoln–Douglas debates as a struggle between an antiracist abolitionist, Lincoln, and a proslavery theorist, Douglas. Few Americans know that proslavery Southern Democrats were so hostile to Douglas that they abandoned the Democratic Party when he was nominated for the presidency in 1860, or that Douglas was a fervent Unionist who supported the Lincoln administration in the Civil War until his death in 1861.

Both Lincoln and Douglas were Unionists who wanted a white-only West. They disagreed about how best to achieve this common goal. Lincoln wanted the federal government, with the Northwest Ordinance as its model, to outlaw slavery in all territories and the new states to be formed from them. Douglas wanted the settlers in each new state to decide. Douglas assumed that most if not all of the new states, as a result of the exercise of "popular sovereignty," would be free states, or rather white states from which both slaves and free blacks would be kept out. By promoting popular sovereignty he hoped to appease the powerful slave owners in the Democratic Party while thwarting their desire for the extension of slavery. The Southern slave owners were not fooled by the ruse of popular sovereignty, and they turned against Douglas in 1860 on the assumption that a President Douglas would be almost as resistant to their demands as a President Lincoln was certain to be.

While they shared the same goal of a white West, Douglas and Lincoln disagreed profoundly on the philosophical question of human rights. Both Lincoln and Douglas supported racial segregation for free blacks in Illinois and elsewhere. But Lincoln affirmed the natural equality of all races in theory while Douglas denied it. Lincoln ridiculed "popular sovereignty" as the doctrine that "if one man chooses to enslave another, no third man has a right to object."[26]

During his debates with Lincoln, Douglas sought to emphasize the practical issues on which they agreed, such as the system of racial segregation in Illinois. On October 16, 1854, Lincoln declared, "In the course of his reply, Senator Douglas remarked, in substance, that he had always considered this government was made for the white people and not for the Negroes. Why, in point of mere fact, I think so too."[27] Challenged by Douglas on the question of granting free blacks citizenship, Lincoln replied: "I tell him very frankly that I am not in favor of Negro citizenship. . . . Now, my opinion is that the different States have the power to make a Negro a citizen under the Constitution of the United States, if they choose. The Dred Scott decision decides that they have not that power. If the State of Illinois had that power, I should be opposed to the exercise of it."[28] On September 18, 1858, Lincoln said: "I will say then that I am not, nor ever have been in favor of bringing about in any way the social and political equality of the white and black races, [applause]—that I am not nor ever have been in favor of making voters or jurors of Negroes, nor of qualifying them to hold office, nor to intermarry with white people; and I will say in addition to this that I believe that there is a physical difference between the white and black races which I believe will for ever forbid the two races living together on terms of social and political equality. And inasmuch as they cannot so live, while they do remain together there must be the position of superior and inferior, and I as much as any other man am in favor of having the superior position assigned to the white race."[29] And on August 21, 1858, Lincoln insisted: "I, as well as Judge Douglas, am in favor of the race to which I belong having the superior position. I have never said anything to the contrary."[30] The other senator from Illinois, Lyman Trumbull, an ally of Lincoln, also dismissed the charge of Democrats like Douglas that Republican support for the principle of equality meant racial integration in the United States: "When we say that all men are created equal, we do not mean that every man in organized society has the same rights. We don't tolerate that in Illinois."[31]

It was in Lincoln's interest to change the subject from the nearly nonexistent rights of free blacks in the state of Illinois to the abstract rights of humanity for two reasons. First, both the racist Free-Soilers and the antiracist abolitionists in the Republican Party agreed on the universality of the principles of the Declaration of Independence, even if they disagreed about their application to black Americans. Even more important, Douglas insisted that human rights did not exist; there were only the rights of Europeans and their descendants. In the debate of October 15, 1858, Douglas argued that the signers of the Declaration of Independence "did not mean negro, nor the savage Indians, nor the Feejee Islanders, nor any other barbarous race . . . They alluded to men of European birth and European descent—to white men, and to none others, when they declared that doctrine." According to Douglas, arguing that the principle of equality applied to white men alone did not require whites to enslave blacks or "other dependent races." However, nonwhites had no rights, merely "privileges" granted to them by benevolent whites: "Humanity requires that we should give them all these privileges; Christianity commands that we should extend those privileges to them." Those privileges, however, were to be determined by the white majority in each state of the Union, "consistently with the safety of society."[32]

The idea that racial "science" had discredited the universalist ideals of the Founding Fathers was often endorsed in the 1850s. Of the Declaration of Independence's claim that all men were created equal, Senator John Pettit of Indiana declared: "I hold it to be a self-evident lie. . . . You talk of carrying to all the races of the world your institutions, your religion, your arts and your sciences. You can no more do it than you can give to all the races your color, form, and development."[33] In the Dred Scott case, Chief Justice Roger B. Taney had declared that blacks, slave or free, "had no rights which the white man was bound to respect." After quoting the Declaration of Independence—"We hold these truths to be self-evident: that all men are created equal; that they are endowed by their Creator with certain inalienable rights; that among them is life, liberty, and pursuit of happiness; that to secure these rights, governments are instituted, deriving their just powers from the consent of the governed"—Taney wrote: "The general words quoted above would seem to embrace the whole human family, and if they were used in a similar instrument at this day, would be so understood. But it is too clear for dispute, that the enslaved African race were not intended to be included, and formed no part of the people who framed and adopted this Declaration . . ."[34] As early as 1832 Thomas Dew was replacing the traditional Southern description of slavery as an evil that could not immediately be abolished with the claim that "slavery was the necessary result of the laws of mind and matter, that it marked some benevolent design, and was intended by our Creator for some useful purpose."[35]

In his Lyceum address of 1838 Lincoln had called for making the Enlightenment ideals of the American Revolution a "political religion." The Lincoln-Douglas debates as well as other speeches and debates provided Lincoln with an opportunity to defend the American Creed against the political heresy that the rights named in the Declaration of Independence belonged to Caucasians alone. Lincoln, following Henry Clay and Thomas Jefferson, argued that all human beings had abstract natural rights, even if in the United States most civil rights were and should be limited to whites only. "Negroes have natural rights, however, as other men have, although they cannot enjoy them here, and even Taney once said that 'the Declaration of Independence was broad enough for all men.' But though it does not declare that all men are equal in their attainments or social position, yet no sane man will attempt to deny that the African *upon his own soil* has all the natural rights that instrument vouchsafes to all mankind."[36] Using one of his favorite phrases from Clay, Lincoln accused Douglas and others who denied human equality of "blowing out the moral lights around us, when he contends that whoever wants slaves has a right to hold them; that he is penetrating, so far as lies in his power, the human soul, and eradicating the light of reason and the love of liberty . . ."[37]

Seeking to win votes from white populist Democrats who revered Jefferson, Lincoln defended the idealism of the author of the Declaration of Independence. "I should like to know if, taking this old declaration of independence, which declares that all men are created equal upon principle, and making exceptions to it where will it stop. If one man says it does not mean a negro, why may not another say it does not mean some other man? If that declaration is not the truth let us get the statute book in which we find it and tear it out!"[38] Speaking of Jefferson's disapproval of slavery, Lincoln recalled "the strong language" that Jefferson used in saying that "he trembled for his country when he remembered that God was just . . ."[39] Lincoln told Illinois voters: "In those days, our Declaration of Independence was held sacred by all, and thought to include all; but now, to aid in making the bondage of the negro universal and eternal, it is assailed, and sneered at, and construed, and hawked at, and torn, till, if its framers could rise from their graves, they could not at all recognize it."[40]

Lincoln quoted Jefferson selectively to serve his own purposes. Lincoln was correct to claim that Jefferson believed that all human beings, not whites alone, had innate rights and that slavery was an evil. And Jefferson had devised the program of graduated emancipation followed by colonization that Clay and Lincoln later adopted as their own. But Jefferson had favored the extension of slavery throughout the territories as a way of "diffusing" the black population. Jefferson had denounced the Compromise of 1820 as "treason against the hopes of the world" because it banned slavery from the area north of 36 degrees, 30 minutes in the Louisiana Purchase. He called the compromise "a firebell in the night" which he considered "the death knell of the Union." Raging against those who sought to confine slavery to the South, Jefferson wrote: "A geographical line, coinciding with a marked principle, moral and political, once conceived and held up to the angry passions of men, will never be obliterated; and every new irritation will mark it deeper." Jefferson argued that every state had an "exclusive right" to regulate "the different descriptions of men composing a state . . . Could Congress, for example, say that the nonfreemen of Connecticut shall be freemen, or that they shall not emigrate into any other state?" Jefferson hoped that the diffusion of slaves throughout the Union "would make them individually happier, and proportionally facilitate the accomplishment of their emancipation [and colonization], by dividing the burden on a greater number of coadjutors."[41] Jefferson thus had taken a position on the question of slavery extension that was the opposite of the policy that Lincoln and other Free-Soilers advocated, and identical to the popular sovereignty position defended by Steven A. Douglas.

Lincoln's passionate defense of the ideas of 1776 was sincere. At the same time, it served a political purpose. By defining the issue as the principles of the Declaration of Independence, Lincoln minimized the need to talk about issues that divided Free-Soilers and abolitionists—such as civil rights for free blacks, which abolitionists favored and most Free-Soilers opposed, and the enforcement of the fugitive slave laws and the protection of slavery in the South, which Free-Soilers, afraid of being overwhelmed by black immigrants from the South, tended to support, and which abolitionists opposed. With the aid of this rhetorical strategy, Lincoln not only helped form a new alliance in American politics, but quickly became one of its national leaders.

NORTHERN POLITICIANS LIKE Douglas made a strategic mistake when they jettisoned the idealism of the American Revolution in order to argue that only Anglo-Americans or Caucasians in general had any rights, even in theory. Some Southern proslavery thinkers made an even more disastrous political error when they rejected the idea of human rights altogether and declared that slavery was good for whites as well as blacks.

This was the thesis of George Fitzhugh, a maverick Virginia planter who had a talent for the shocking paradox. In two books, *Sociology for the South, or the Failure of Free Society* (1854) and *Cannibals All!* (1857), as well as in editorials for the *Richmond Enquirer,* the *Richmond Examiner,* and *DeBow's Review,* Fitzhugh rejected modern liberalism as the source of all evil. Influenced by Counter-Enlightenment thinkers in contemporary Britain and Europe, such as Thomas Carlyle, Fitzhugh opposed an idealized feudal order, in which benevolent masters looked after serfs and slaves, to a ruthless industrial capitalist society whose "wage slaves" were tossed aside by the rich and powerful when they were ill or old. Not only abolitionism but the other "isms" of Yankee moral reformers, such as temperance, women's suffrage, and socialism, were to be rejected along with the Lockean idealism of the American Founders. Taking his counterrevolution to its logical conclusion, Fitzhugh rejected John Locke for his seventeenth-century rival, Sir

Robert Filmer, who traced the descent of social authority not from an original social contract but from the partriarchal authority of Adam.

As several historians have pointed out, Filmer was part of the aristocracy of Kent in England whose offshoots included many of the great families of the South, including the Washingtons, Jeffersons, Randolphs, and Byrds. In defending the patriarchal, slave-based social order of the Southern ruling class, Fitzhugh abandoned the eighteenth-century idealism they had adopted in favor of the patriarchal theory of authority of the earliest Virginia planters, who had sided with the royalists against the republicans in the English Civil War.[42] The existence of a conscious "Kentish" tradition of illiberal, Anglophile conservatism in the South is demonstrated by a newspaper account of the remarks made by Virginia senator John Randolph of Roanoke (as he styled himself), a descendant of one of the founders of Jamestown, John Rolfe, and the Indian "princess" Pocahontas, during a filibuster in the U.S. Senate on May 2, 1826: "Then he spoke of his land at Roanoke, saying he had it by a royal grant. He then spoke of a song about the men of Kent, saying Kent had never been conquered by William the Norman. He was about to sing it when the editor Niles left."[43]

"I had a Southern work called Sociology by Fitzhugh, I think," Lincoln's law partner William Herndon recalled. "It defended slavery in every way. This aroused the ire of Lincoln more than most pro-slavery books."[44] In a speech at Bloomington, Illinois, on May 29, 1856, a newspaper quoted Lincoln as saying: "The sentiment in favor of white slavery now prevailed in all the slave state papers, except those of Kentucky, Tennessee and Missouri and Maryland. Such was the progress of the National Democracy."[45] Lincoln also referred to editorials, which he may not have known were written by Fitzhugh, in "the Richmond Enquirer, an avowed advocate of slavery, regardless of color."[46]

To clarify its position, the *Richmond Enquirer* published editorials renouncing any desire for white slavery, including this one in May 1856: "We do not hope, nor wish, to see slavery like ours introduced at the North. There is no room for black slaves, and we never wish to see white men made slaves."[47] But the damage had been done. Republicans treated Fitzhugh's eccentric and inflammatory statements—"The principle of Slavery is in itself right, and does not depend on differences of complexion"—as though they were typical of Southern elite thought. Fitzhugh's importance was magnified by foreign journalists as well. After touring the United States and Canada in 1857–58, the British journalist Charles Mackay published *Life and Liberty in America* (London, 1859). In a chapter entitled "Pro-Slavery Philosophy," Mackay observed: "Within the last two or three years a change has come over the philosophy and the tactics of the slaveholders. . . . In one sentence they allege Slavery to be the normal and only proper condition of society. . . . [Mr. Fitzhugh] would not only enslave the negroes, but the poor Irish and German immigrants, as fast as they arrive in New York, and either send them off to till the ground in the cotton and sugar regions, or sell them at Charleston, or New Orleans, by public auction, to the highest bidder."[48]

If the South's repudiation of the ideals of 1776 did not convert Northern whites to the Republican Party, perhaps the claim that Southern slave owners wanted to enslave them would. During the presidential campaign of the first Republican candidate, John C. Fremont, in 1856, the Republican Party circulated a broadside entitled "White Slavery: The New 'Democratic Doctrine,' " which declared: "The South now maintains that *Slavery is Right, natural and necessary, and does not depend upon COMPLEXION.* The laws of the Slave States *justify* the HOLDING OF WHITE MEN IN BONDAGE." The pamphlet quoted from a proslavery theorist in South Carolina: "Slavery is the natural and normal condition of the *Laboring Man,* whether WHITE or black. . . . Master and slave is a relation in society as necessary as that of parent and child; and the Northern States will yet have to introduce it. Their theory of Free Government is a delusion." The anonymous authors also quoted a Democratic paper from Muscogee, Alabama: "Free society! We sicken of the name. What is it but a conglomoration [*sic*] of GREASY MECHANICS, FILTHY OPERATIVES, SMALL FISTED FARMERS, and moon-struck THEORISTS? All the Northern and especially the New

England States are devoid of society fitted for well bred gentlemen. The pre-vailing class one meets with, is that of mechanics struggling to be genteel, and small farmers who do their own drudgery; and yet who are hardly fit for associating with a Southern gentleman's body-servant." Another Repub-lican publication declared: "The New York Day Book, one of the two pa-pers in New York City that support James Buchanan, proposes to enslave Poor *AMERICANS, GERMANS, and Irish,* who may fall into poverty, and be unable to support their families. . . ."[49]

In addition to fueling fear of the enslavement of working-class whites, speculations by a few radical Southern proslavery theorists such as Fitzhugh permitted Lincoln and other Northern Republicans to defend the dignity of white labor against the slurs of Southern aristocrats. "I have noticed in Southern newspapers, particularly the Richmond Enquirer, the Southern view of the Free States," Lincoln told an audience at Kalamazoo, Michigan, on August 27, 1856. Lincoln went on: "[The Southerners] insist that their slaves are better off than Northern freemen. What a mistaken view do these men have of Northern laborers! They think that men are always to remain laborers here—but there is no such class. The man who labored for another last year, this year labors for himself, and next year he will hire others to la-bor for him. These men don't understand when they think in this manner of Northern free labor."[50] At a speech given on March 6, 1860, at New Haven, Connecticut, Lincoln said: "I am glad to see that a system of labor prevails in New England under which laborers can strike when they want to [Cheers], where they are not obliged to work under all circumstances, and are not tied down and obliged to labor whether you pay them or not! [Cheers.] I like the system which lets a man quit when he wants to, and wish it might prevail everywhere. [Tremendous applause.] One of the reasons why I am opposed to Slavery is just here. . . . I want every man to have the chance—and I believe a black man is entitled to it—in which he can better his condition—when he may look forward and hope to be a hired laborer this year and the next, work for himself afterward, and finally to hire men to work for him! That is the true system. Up here in New England, you have a soil that scarcely sprouts black-eyed beans, and yet where will you find wealthy men so wealthy, and poverty so rarely in extremity? There is not another such place on earth! [Cheers.] I desire that if you get too thick here, and find it hard to better your condition on this soil, you may have a chance to strike and go somewhere else, where you may not be degraded, nor have your family corrupted by forced rivalry with negro slaves. I want you to have a clean bed, and no snakes in it. [Cheers.] Then you can better your condition, and so it may go on and on in one ceaseless round so long as man exists on the face of the earth! [Prolonged applause.]"[51]

The labor theory of value, familiar to Lincoln from the American school economists Wayland and Carey, found a new use in polemics against aristocratic slave owners. In Lincoln's Annual Message to Congress of December 1861, he asserted: "Labor is prior to, and independent of, capital. Capital is only the fruit of labor, and could never have existed if labor had not first existed. Labor is the superior of capital, and deserves much the higher consideration." In later generations, supporters of organized labor would often quote these lines out of context. What Lincoln actually said was that in the United States in 1861, a majority of Americans were neither capitalists nor laborers: "A large majority belong to neither class—neither work for others, nor have others working for them. . . . Men with their families—wives, sons, and daughters—work for themselves, on their farms, in their houses, and in their shops, taking the whole product to themselves, and asking no favors of capital on the one hand, nor of hired laborers on the other." What is more, according to Lincoln, "there is not, of necessity, any such thing as the free hired laborer being fixed to that condition for life. . . . The prudent, penniless beginner in the world, labors for wages awhile, saves a surplus with which to buy tools or land for himself; then labors on his own account another while, and at length hires another new beginner to help him. This is the just, and generous, and prosperous system, which opens the way to all— gives hope to all, and consequent energy, and progress, and improvement of condition to all." Lincoln ended this disquisition with a paean to upward mobility: "No men living are more worthy to be trusted than those who toil up from poverty—none less inclined to take, or touch, aught which they have not honestly earned."[52]

Lincoln, the former Whig, enhanced his personal appeal to Jacksonian populists in the Democratic Party tradition by emphasizing his frontier background. In May 1860 the Republican state convention in Decatur, Illinois, resolved that Lincoln should be the Republican Party's candidate for president. Lincoln arranged to have his speech interrupted by the entry of his cousin John Hanks, identified as an "Old-time Democrat of Macon County," who ceremoniously carried two aged fence rails supporting a banner that read: "ABRAHAM LINCOLN FOR PRESIDENT / The Rail Candidate for President in 1860 / Two rails from a Lot of 3,000 Made in 1830 by Thos. Hanks [sic—John Hanks] and Abe Lincoln—Whose Father was the First Pioneer of Macon County."[53]

In its report of a speech by Lincoln at Belleville, Illinois, on October 18, 1856, the *Belleville Weekly Advocate* emphasized Lincoln's credentials as a Southerner as well as a laborer: "A Kentuckian, as he is, familiar with Slavery and its evils, he vindicated the cause of free labor. . . . He showed the tendency and aim of the Sham Democracy to degrade labor to subvert the true ends of Government and build up Aristocracy, Despotism and Slavery. . . . The Kentuckian, LINCOLN, defended the Declaration of American Independence against the attacks of the degenerate Vermonter, DOUGLAS, and against BRECKENRIDGE and the whole ruling class of the South. Here was a Southerner, with eloquence that would bear a comparison with HENRY CLAY's, defending Liberty and the North against the leaders of the Border Ruffians and Doughfaces of Illinois."[54]

FOLLOWING THE PASSAGE of the Kansas–Nebraska Act in 1854, Lincoln and like-minded politicians saw an opportunity to create a realignment in American politics that would end the hegemony of the Southern-dominated Democratic Party in the federal government. The debate over the extension of slavery could be used to detach populist

Democrats in the Midwest and upper South from the slaveholders of the Deep South and bring them into an alliance with former Whigs and abolitionists in the Republican Party. In seeking to win over populist Democrats to their new party, Lincoln and other Republicans appealed both to their racism—their desire to keep blacks, slave or free, out of the West—and to their idealism—their patriotic attachment to the principles of 1776, best expressed by Thomas Jefferson, the author of the Declaration of Independence and a hero to Democratic farmers and workers.

Other former Whigs sought to achieve a similar coalition of onetime Whigs and former Democrats by raising the issue of European immigration rather than the issue of the migration of black slaves to the West. Making immigration restriction and changes in naturalization laws its rallying cry, the American Party did well in congressional elections in 1854 and 1855. As its presidential candidate in 1856, the American Party nominated former president Millard Fillmore.

Fillmore was typical of American Party nativists. A New York Whig and Zachary Taylor's vice president, he became president in 1850 when Taylor died in office. Fillmore had been elected to the U.S. Congress from western New York as an anti-Mason before becoming a Whig. His causes were those of Clay and Lincoln, such as the protective tariff and internal improvements. In the 1840s the Whig Party in New York was divided between those like William Seward, who wanted to woo Irish and German immigrants, and an anti-immigrant faction led by Fillmore; both factions were anti-Southern and antislavery. When Fillmore ran for governor of New York as a Whig, he was defeated by Catholics and radical abolitionists. Succeeding Taylor, who had been an opponent of the compromise proposals of 1850, Fillmore played a key role in the passage of the compromise, supporting Clay, Webster, and other Whigs. His support for the enforcement of the Fugitive Slave Act of 1850, which Lincoln also supported, endeared him to Southern Whigs while alienating abolitionists. He was the first president to approve federal aid for building railroads, a policy Lincoln would promote later as the first Republican president.

The Whig Party, like its predecessor the Federalist Party and its successors in the 1850s, the American and Republican parties, had been predominantly a party of Northern Anglo-American Protestants whose ancestors had brought their dislike of Irish Catholics with them from the British Isles. Their opposition to Irish immigration was based both on their dread of Catholicism, which they considered incompatible with an enlightened republic, and their resentment of the fact that Irish-Americans in the Northern cities tended to ally themselves in national politics with Southern slave owners like Jefferson and Jackson against the Northern elite. The Federalists, alarmed by the appeal of the French Revolution to many Irish-Americans, enacted the Alien and Sedition Acts. In the 1830s and 1840s the massive wave of Irish and German immigration, most of which went to Northern cities, rekindled Northern Protestant nativism. Fearing Catholic and foreign conspiracies, American nativists who joined fraternal organizations like the Order of United Americans adopted a code of secrecy. If asked about the order, they were supposed to say: "I know nothing"—thus their nickname, the Know-Nothings. In contemporary American public discourse, the term "Know-Nothing" is used indiscriminately for populists, whatever their views on immigration; the implication is that they are ignoramuses. In fact, the original Know-Nothings tended to belong to the professional and business elite in the North, with which Whigs like Lincoln identified. They were far more educated and prosperous than the largely Catholic working-class immigrants whom they feared. Henry Clay's loss of New York to Polk in the presidential election of 1844 was blamed by many Whigs on the immigrant vote.

Except on the question of European immigration, the views of Americans in the North and the Republicans tended to be identical: opposition to the territorial extension of slavery, and support for the Hamilton-Clay program of internal improvements, national banking, and protective tariffs. Indeed, Northern nativists could argue with some plausibility that since most Irish Catholic immigrants in the North were allied with Southern conservatives in the Democratic Party, the best way to check the

Slave Power was to reduce the numbers of its ally, the Immigrant Power. Both the Americans and the Republicans claimed to be protecting liberal democracy and the ideals of 1776 from threats: the foreign threat of illiberal Catholicism and the internal threat of the Southern oligarchy that sought to jettison American ideals in order to defend slavery.

Lincoln rejected anti-European nativism in a letter of August 24, 1855, to his former partner Joshua F. Speed: "I am not a Know-Nothing. That is certain. How could I be? How can any one who abhors the oppression of negroes, be in favor of degrading classes of white people? Our progress in degeneracy appears to me to be pretty rapid. As a nation, we begin by declaring that 'all men are created equal.' We now practically read it 'all men are created equal, except negroes.' When the Know-Nothings get control, it will read 'all men are created equal, except negroes, and foreigners, and catholics.' "[55] In a debate with Douglas on October 15, 1858, Lincoln called for the territories to be "an outlet for free white people everywhere the world over—in which Hans and Baptiste and Patrick, and all other [white] men from all the [white] world, may find new homes and better their conditions in life."[56] Earlier, in 1844, Lincoln had sought to refute the Whig Party's nativist reputation, which had led the Democrats to label them "Native Whigs." According to a Democrat who reported one of Lincoln's speeches at the time, "Mr. Lincoln also alleged that the Whigs were as much the friends of foreigners as democrats; but he failed to substantiate it in a manner satisfactory to the foreigners who heard him."[57]

But Lincoln's friendliness to European immigrants was less a function of idealism than of a white-racial nationalism that was more inclusive than that of many of his fellow Whigs. Lincoln did not hold a nativist past against his allies and appointees. Among former American Party supporters who rose to high positions in the Republican Party during and after the Lincoln years were Simon Cameron, Lincoln's Secretary of War, and General Ulysses S. Grant. Lincoln's appointed director of the U.S. Mint at Philadelphia, James Pollock, had been elected governor of Pennsylvania on the American Party ticket; his Protestant fervor, in addition to making him an anti-Catholic nativist, inspired him to persuade Congress to add "In God We Trust" to American currency.[58]

There was no theoretical disagreement about natural equality between Free-Soilers like Lincoln and nativists like Fillmore. Lincoln argued that while blacks had the same natural rights as everyone else, they should not have more than minimal civil rights while residing in the United States before colonization abroad. Again and again, Lincoln quoted Clay's distinction between abstract and actual rights. The American Party made the same distinction. The natural rights of the Irish and Germans did not include the right to relocate from their native countries to New York or Philadelphia. The right of immigration was a civil privilege, bestowed or withdrawn, with various conditions, by a nation-state in its own interest. With this Lincoln evidently agreed. While Lincoln opposed restrictions on European immigration and signed legislation promoting it during the Civil War, he never questioned the U.S. immigration law which, throughout his lifetime, limited immigrants to "free white persons." Lincoln would hardly have devoted so much effort to promoting the colonization of blacks abroad if he had not assumed that white-only immigration and naturalization laws would be a permanent feature of American policy, forever keeping black and other nonwhite immigrants out.

The nativists were as eager to protect the ideals of the Declaration of Independence from the Vatican as the Free-Soilers were to protect those ideals from the Southern slaveocracy. Most Free-Soilers, like Lincoln, believed that a racially homogeneous population was necessary as the basis for a republican polity. Most nativists agreed; but they argued that religious homogeneity was an additional requirement. The most extreme nativists would have extended the naturalization period in the United States and denied more political offices to the foreign-born (the Constitution is a "nativist" document in requiring that the president be a U.S. citizen by birth). Compare these proposals to the much harsher Black Laws supported by Lincoln and most Free-Soilers, which provided that blacks could not vote, could not serve on juries, could not serve in militias, and in some cases had to post bond or be sponsored by a white in order to stay in a state overnight.

Despite these parallels, generations of American historians have judged Fillmore and the American Party by a stricter standard than they have applied to Lincoln and the Republican Party. Historians routinely refer to the American Party by the derogatory nickname, the Know-Nothings. The equivalent would be to write about Lincoln's party in standard histories as "the Black Republicans." Fillmore is condemned for believing that religious homogeneity was a precondition of republican government, while Lincoln is excused for believing the same about racial homogeneity. Lincoln is forgiven for wanting to keep blacks out of the West, prevent them from marrying whites, and ship them out of the country, but Fillmore is condemned for wanting to keep Catholics out of the United States and prevent those here from holding a small number of high political offices.

What explains the double standard according to which American historians have routinely treated the anti-European bias of the American Party as far more despicable than the antiblack bias of most Republicans? Most American historians are white, and since the early twentieth century many have been descendants of non-English European immigrants. They have been much more hostile to nineteenth-century Anglo-American Protestants who wanted to keep their ancestors out of the East than to similar nineteenth-century Anglo-American Protestants who wanted to keep blacks out of the West. If most American historians were black, it is doubtful that they would condemn the anti-Irish sentiments of Millard Fillmore far more severely than the antiblack sentiments of Abraham Lincoln, William Seward, Lyman Trumbull, David Wilmot, and other racist Free-Soilers.

The historical record is further distorted by the common practice of treating Lincoln's crusade against slavery extension as a precursor to the pro-black reforms of the abolitionists, some Radical Republicans, and the civil rights movement of the twentieth century. But this puts Lincoln in the wrong political family tree. For all of his sincere theoretical belief in human equality, he does not belong in the civil rights family tree that includes

William Lloyd Garrison, Wendell Philips, Charles Sumner, Thaddeus Stevens, Frederick Douglass, and Martin Luther King, Jr. Instead, Lincoln belongs in the immigration restriction family tree—on a branch not too far from the one on which his fellow former Whig, Millard Fillmore, sits. Opposition to a group of migrants—foreign Catholics or black Americans, enslaved or free—was the issue that defined each of the two parties that vied in the 1850s to be the successor of the mostly Northern Hamiltonian party that would replace the Whigs, oppose the Democrats, and promote the American System of internal improvements, protective tariffs, and national banking. The political posterity of both Lincoln and Fillmore includes the politicians—most of them Northern Republicans in the Lincoln tradition— who enacted Asian immigration restriction laws in the 1880s and European immigration laws in the 1920s.

The American Party did not give way to the Republican Party in the mid-1850s because the Free-Soil movement's goal of a white West and Lincoln's vision of a white-only United States from which all blacks, slave and free, had been deported was morally superior to the nativist vision of an Anglo-Saxon Protestant America with fewer Catholic immigrants. The American Party collapsed in 1856 because it split between its Northern and Southern wings over the issue of slavery extension, as the Whigs had done earlier, and as the Democrats would do in 1860.

The Republicans proved to be more competitive in the North than the American Party for several reasons. To begin with, the threat that the Southern elite, by spreading slavery, would further increase its power in Washington was plausible. As a correspondent wrote to the economist Henry C. Carey, who like Lincoln was a Whig who joined the Republicans in the mid-1850s, "neither the Pope nor the foreigners ever can govern the country or endanger its liberties, but the slavebreeders and slavetraders do govern it, and threaten to put an end to all government but theirs. Here is . . . an issue" that could succeed.[59]

Another comparative advantage of the Republican Party was the fact that it could appeal to immigrant voters, as Republican opponents of nativism such as Lincoln and Seward realized. It was difficult for the ex-Whigs to have a chance at becoming a majority party in the North without winning over most of the German-American vote concentrated in the Midwest. German Protestants as well as German Catholics were offended by Anglo-American nativism and the allied temperance movement. When members of the American Party denounced Catholicism, they offended German Catholics as well as Irish Catholics, and if they took potshots at the serving of wine in an Irish-American Catholic mass, the bullet might richochet and strike a German-American beer garden. Prohibition, a perennial cause of Northern Protestants, passed (like those other longtime Yankee causes, the abolition of slavery and restrictions on European immigration), as a war measure; during World War I, German-American brewers were portrayed as fifth columnists for the Kaiser, sapping the health and morals of Americans.

The Republican Party could win over populist Democrats who did not see Irish and other European immigrants as a threat but loathed the idea of allowing the black population of the South, whether slave or free, to migrate to the West, and perhaps to the North as well. On the Pacific Coast the movement to protect white labor from nonwhite competition produced support for banning Chinese immigration as well as black migration to the West. During the constitutional convention that produced the first Oregon state government in 1857, the antislavery activist George Williams spoke of his wish to "consecrate Oregon to the use of the white man, and exclude the negro, Chinaman, and every race of that character."[60] On November 9, 1857, the voters of Oregon overwhelmingly voted both to ban slavery and forbid the immigration of free blacks to the state. In 1858 Walt Whitman, who made his living as a Democratic journalist in New York City, praised the way that the new Oregon state constitution banned blacks from living in the state: "We shouldn't wonder if this sort of total prohibition of colored persons became quite a common thing in new Western, Northwestern, and even Southwestern States. . . . [There] will be a conflict between the totality of White Labor, on the one side, and on the other, the interference and competition of black labor, or of bringing in colored persons on *any* terms. Who believes that Whites and Blacks can ever amalgamate in America? . . . Besides, is not America for the Whites? And is it not better so?"[61] On another occasion Whitman wrote: "Nature has set an impassable seal upon it. No race can ever remain slaves if they have it in them to become free. Why do the slave ships go to Africa only?"[62] Whitman, a Jacksonian Democrat who came to admire Lincoln, had been an admirer of the South Carolina senator John C. Calhoun, the South's leading proslavery, states' rights theorist.[63] In short, Whitman was exactly the sort of racist Democrat whom Free-Soil Republicans like Lincoln were hoping to lure into the Republican Party with the slavery extension issue.

In 1856 Fillmore received the presidential nomination both of the American Party and the Southern remnant of the Whig Party, but at the convention the American Party split over the slavery extension issue. In the fall election, won by the Democrat James Buchanan, Fillmore came in third with 21 percent of the vote behind the first Republican presidential candidate, John C. Fremont, who got 33 percent of the vote. Most Northern American Party members voted for Fremont in 1856. Fillmore carried only Maryland in the election while winning more than 40 percent of the vote in ten other states in the South. The collapse of the American Party swelled the ranks of the Republicans. In 1860 former nativists helped Lincoln win five hundred thousand more votes than Fremont won in 1856.

After the campaign of 1856, in a letter to her half sister Emilie Todd Helme in Kentucky, Mary Todd Lincoln expressed her preference for Fillmore over Fremont, the Republican presidential candidate for whom her husband was campaigning. "My weak woman's heart was too Southern in feeling to sympathize with any but Fillmore. I have always been a great admirer of his, he made so good a President & is so just a man & feels the *necessity* of keeping foreigners within bounds."[64] Thinking, no doubt, of her own experience with a succession of Irish-American maids in Springfield—one of whom said of Mrs. Lincoln: "I was never so unhappy in my life as while living with her"—Mary told Emilie: "If some of you Kentuckians had to deal with 'the wild Irish,' as we householders are sometimes called to do, the South would certainly elect Mr. Fillmore next time."[65] In 1856 Mary would have been astonished to be told that the president elected in 1860 would not be Mr. Fillmore, but her husband.

AFTER LINCOLN LOST the race for U.S. senator from Illinois to Douglas in 1858, some of his friends blamed the bold speech he gave at the Republican State Convention in Springfield on June 16, 1858, in which he declared, "A house divided against itself cannot stand. I believe this government cannot endure, permanently half slave and half free."[66] Although Lincoln was defeated by Douglas, his debates with the Illinois Democrat had made him a national figure. And by campaigning for other Republican candidates in other states, he gained allies who were useful when he made his own bid for the presidency.

Douglas, for his part, had suffered even though he retained his position as United States senator from Illinois. While the Lincoln-Douglas debates had helped Lincoln's standing in the Republican Party, they had made Douglas a controversial figure in the Democratic Party. Proslavery Southern Democrats knew that popular sovereignty, the alternative that Douglas offered to Lincoln's policy of the nonextension of slavery, was likely to accomplish the same result—the exclusion of slavery from most or all of the states formed from Western territories in the future. Convening in Charleston, South Carolina, on April 23, 1860, the Democratic convention broke down in squabbles over slavery and the territories. Fifty Southern Democrats stormed out of the convention. After fifty-seven ballots failed to give either Douglas or anyone else the presidential nomination, the convention adjourned. Following the breakdown of the Democratic convention, on May 9 a group of politicians—many of them Southern Whigs who dreaded Southern secession but thought that the Republican Party was too extreme—met in Baltimore and organized the Constitutional Union Party, nominating Tennessee senator John Bell for president and former

Massachusetts senator and former Harvard University president Edward Everett.

The splintering of the Democratic Party during the presidential campaign of 1860 was preceded by a split among Democrats in Congress. In Congress the Democratic delegation was divided between a majority of proslavery Democrats and a minority of Northern Free-Soil or "anti-Lecompton" Democrats, who opposed to the admission of Kansas as a slave state under its "Lecompton" constitution. Like the Democrats, the old Whig coalition had split into two parties, the antislavery Republicans and the nativist Americans. Congress by 1859 therefore had a de facto four-party system in which the swing votes were provided by the anti-Lecompton Democrats and the American Party.[67]

On May 15, 1860, Republican delegates gathered in the cavernous "Wigwam" in Chicago. They knew that if the Democratic vote was split between a Northern and a Southern candidate, and if Bell and Everett did not drain away many voters, the Republican Party, after losing when it ran its first candidate, Fremont, for president in 1856, had a good chance of winning the presidency this time.

The front-runner for the presidential nomination in 1860 was the former governor of New York, William Seward. Although Seward was a former Whig like Lincoln, he had won a reputation for radicalism on the slavery question by saying in 1850 that "there is a higher law than the Constitution" and using the phrase "irrepressible conflict" to describe the rivalry of the North and South in 1857. In addition, Seward's friendliness to Irish Catholic immigrants in New York alienated many Protestant Republicans of the kind who had been drawn to the nativist American Party. These nativists were particularly strong in Pennsylvania, one of the key states that the Republicans needed in 1860. Finally, many Midwesterners viewed New York with suspicion and dislike.

Lincoln's support of high protective tariffs, popular in Pennsylvania, helped him win the nomination. Morton McMichael, an ally of Carey and a Republican delegate at the Chicago convention, told the readers of his pro-tariff newspaper, the *North American*: "Mr. Lincoln was, throughout, well known for his firm and unwavering fidelity to Henry Clay, and the great policy of protection to American industry."[68] In 1859 the Republican editor Horace Greeley told a friend: "Now about the Presidency: I want to succeed this time, yet I *know* the country is not Anti-Slavery. It will only swallow a little Anti-Slavery in a great deal of sweetening. An Anti-Slavery man *per se* cannot be elected; but a Tariff, River and Harbor, Pacific Railroad, Free Homestead man *may* succeed *although* he is Anti-Slavery."[69] The historic Abraham Lincoln was not just "Anti-Slavery"; he was "a Tariff, River and Harbor, Pacific Railroad, Free Homestead man."

According to Joshua Giddings, the Republican congressman whom Lincoln appointed as consul general to Canada, the fact that Lincoln's opposition to slavery had been more measured than Seward's worked in his favor: "Indeed, Lincoln was selected . . . because he was supposed to be able to carry [Illinois] and Indiana and [was] acceptable to Pennsylvania and his antislavery sentiment had been less prominent" than the antislavery views expressed by Seward and Salmon P. Chase.[70] Fearing that Seward would alienate too many voters, many Republican delegates rallied behind Lincoln, who won 102 votes to Seward's 173½ on the first ballot. By the third ballot, after Lincoln's representatives had made various deals—the War Department for Pennsylvania's Simon Cameron, the Department of the Interior for Indiana's Caleb Smith—Lincoln became the second Republican presidential nominee.

Following the Republican convention, the Democratic Party convened again in June in Baltimore. When Douglas and his vice presidential candidate, former Georgia governor Herschel V. Johnson, won the nomination, a number of Southern Democrats met across town in Maryland Institute Hall. They nominated John C. Breckinridge, the vice president of the incumbent Buchanan administration, and Oregon senator Joseph Lane. The new Southern Democratic Party supported slavery in the territories and the American seizure of Cuba, a potential new slave state.

The Republican Party platform in 1860 appealed to former Democrats in two ways: It promised Jeffersonian farmers Western homesteads protected from black labor competition, and it promised no new restrictions on immigration in the hope of winning over immigrant Democrats whom the American Party had alienated. Lincoln knew that he would win in the electoral college if his ticket carried all the states carried by Fremont in 1856, plus Illinois, Indiana, and Pennsylvania. Even though Lincoln was not on the ballot in any Southern state, he received 39.8 percent of the popular vote and 180 electoral votes. Douglas won only in Missouri. Bell carried the moderate border states of Kentucky and Tennessee as well as Virginia. Breckinridge won in eleven of the fifteen slave states. The second-place winner of the popular vote was Douglas, with 29.5 percent—but because his vote was spread thinly, he came in last in the electoral college with only 12 electoral votes. In the electoral college Breckinridge came in second with 72 votes, even though he came in third in the popular vote (18.1 percent) And Bell came in last in the popular vote (12.6 percent) but third in the electoral vote (39 percent). If the Democratic Party had not split and if the votes of Douglas and Bell had been combined, the result would have been a popular vote exceeding Lincoln's by more than 100,000. But Lincoln still would have won in the electoral college.

On December 20, 1860, South Carolina's state convention announced that the state had seceded from the Union. In January Florida, Mississippi, Alabama, Georgia, and Louisiana followed. In February 1861 their representatives gathered at Montgomery, Alabama, to adopt a constitution for what they called "the Confederate States of America." As Texas and other Southern states moved toward secession, the Southern states that had already seceded went on to seize federal forts and military arsenals in their territory. By January only Fort Pickens at Pensacola, Florida, remained, along with a federal garrison in Charleston Harbor, which had been besieged by Southern troops. Its name was Fort Sumter.

THE COMPLICATED POLITICAL realignment of the 1850s resulted in the secession of the South. During the 1850s the Whig Party disintegrated as a result of the controversy over the extension of slavery out-side of the South, and many white, populist Jeffersonians in the Midwest left the Democrats and joined with former Whigs, nativists, and abolitionists to create the new Republican Party. And the breakup of the Democratic Party into Northern and Southern factions that backed different presidential can-didates in the election of 1860 permitted Abraham Lincoln to become pres-ident with less than 40 percent of the popular vote.

The Republican Party, like its rival American Party, was dominated by former Whigs. The Republican Party succeeded, where the American Party failed, for two reasons. First, the Republicans managed to win the votes of former white Jeffersonian Democrats who in the Midwest and elsewhere worried more about competing with black farm labor in the West than about competing with Catholic immigrant labor in the East. The Pope and the Jesuits were far away while the Southern plantation owners and millions of Southern blacks were near. Second, the Republican Party was immune from an internal North-South split. The Whig, American, and Democratic parties all split along sectional lines. The only reason the Republican Party did not split along sectional lines was that it was already a purely sectional party of the North. Its nature as the only party without a disruptive, proslavery Southern wing permitted it to avoid extinction in the Darwinian political environment of the 1850s. Having broken up three national parties in a single decade with their demand to extend slavery, Southern extremists had no one to blame but themselves when the party that won the presidency in 1860 was a sectional Northern party which, because of its very lack of a Southern wing, was im-mune to extortion by the South.

The leaders of the South committed moral suicide by rejecting the lib-eral universalist ideals of the American Revolution. Then they committed political suicide by disrupting the three national parties that had substantial Southern wings. And finally they committed military suicide by leading the South to attempt to secede from the United States.

FIVE

LINCOLN AND
THE UNION

DURING THE PRESIDENTIAL campaign of 1856, when John C. Fremont ran as the first presidential candidate of the new Republican Party, many radical "fire-eaters" in the South threatened that their region would secede from the United States if a Republican were elected president. Following Lincoln's election in November 1860, one Southern state after another carried out that threat.

As Southern officials seized federal forts and arsenals in the South, President James Buchanan, a Democrat from Pennsylvania with Southern sympathies, in his final message to Congress anticipated one of Lincoln's arguments against the breakup of the Union: "By such a dread catastrophe the hopes of the friends of freedom throughout the world would be destroyed, and a long night of leaden despotism would enshroud the nations. Our example for more than eighty years would not only be lost, but it would be quoted as conclusive proof that man is unfit for self-government." Nevertheless, Buchanan explained to Congress that, although secession was illegal, his constitutional powers as president were not sufficient for him to prevent it.[1] Throughout the crisis in the winter of 1860–61, Northern opinion was divided. Some argued that the United States was better off without the Southern states. Before the Civil War, the Northern abolitionists Wendell Phillips and William Lloyd Garrison called upon the North to separate from the slave South. Still others speculated that the United States would disintegrate into smaller confederacies—perhaps a New England federation or a Pacific union. Clement L. Vallandigham, a Democratic representative from Ohio whom the Lincoln administration later deported to the South during the Civil War because he criticized its policies, proposed on February 20, 1861, that the United States be reorganized as a confederation with four sections: North, West, Pacific, and South.[2] One New York congressman proposed that Manhattan become an independent city-state, like contemporary Hamburg or Bremen.[3] While the *New York Times* argued that the federal Constitution prohibited secession, the *New York Tribune* declared: "Whenever a considerable portion of our Union shall deliberately resolve to go out, we shall resist all coercive measures designed to keep it in. We hope never to live in a republic whereof one section is pinned to the residue by bayonets."[4]

For his part, Lincoln never doubted that the federal government had the right as well as the strength to prevent unilateral secession. Campaigning for Fremont in 1856, in response to the threat that the South would secede if Fremont won the presidency, Lincoln told an audience: "The Union, in any event, won't be dissolved. We don't want to dissolve it, and if you attempt it, we won't let you. With the purse and sword, the army and navy and treasury in our hands and at our command, you couldn't do it. . . . We do not want to dissolve the Union; you shall not."[5]

In his ardent Unionism no less than in his adoption of the Hamiltonian nationalist view of the U.S. Constitution, Lincoln emulated his "beau ideal of a statesman," Henry Clay. Accused of being a traitor to the South, Clay replied on February 13, 1850: "I know no South, no North, no East, no West, to which I owe allegiance. . . . My allegiance is to this Union and to my own State; but if gentlemen suppose they can exact from me an acknowledgment of allegiance to any ideal or future contemplated confederacy of the South, I here declare that I owe no allegiance to it; nor will I, for one, come under any such allegiance if I can avoid it."[6] In his last great oration in the Senate during the debates on the Compromise of 1850, on July 22, 1850, Clay vowed to support the federal government if it needed to put down Southern secession: "If Kentucky to-morrow unfurls the banner of resistance unjustly, I never will fight under that banner. I owe a permanent allegiance to the whole Union—a subordinate one to my own State. When my State is right—when it has a cause for resistance, when tyranny, and wrong, and oppression insufferable arise—I will then share her fortune, but if she summons me to the battle-field or to support her in any cause which is unjust against the Union, never, never will I engage her in such a cause." If any other Southern state tried to secede, Clay warned: "Thousands, tens of thousands, of Kentuckians would flock to the standard of their country to dissipate and repress their rebellion. These are my sentiments. Make the most of them."[7] When civil war did come, Clay's adopted state of Kentucky remained in the Union, and the president who restored the Union was not only a disciple of Henry Clay but also, by birth, a Kentuckian.

THE REPUBLICAN PRESIDENTIAL platform of 1860 had called for a guarantee against federal interference with slavery in states in which it existed. However, when a constitutional amendment containing that guarantee came before Congress, a majority of Republican senators and representatives voted against it.[8] While continuing to declare his commitment to leaving slavery untouched in the states where it already existed, as president-elect, Lincoln rejected other proposals intended to conciliate the South.

A month before Lincoln's inauguration, the Washington Peace Conference began on February 4, 1861. The Southern states that had seceded refused to send delegates, but all of the other states except Arkansas, California, Michigan, Oregon, and Wisconsin sent representatives. Most of the attention focused on a scheme devised by Kentucky senator John Crittenden. The Crittenden Plan, consisting of six proposed constitutional amendments, would have affirmed the protections afforded to slavery and restored the Missouri Compromise line of 36 degrees, 30 minutes N. However, opponents of slavery extension feared that this would inspire the South to agitate for the conquest and annexation of parts of Mexico, Cuba, and Central America as slave states. A majority of Republican members of Congress voted against Crittenden's compromise. President-elect Lincoln used his influence behind the scenes to encourage this result, telling one ally that "no concession by the free States short of a surrender of every thing worth preserving, and contending for would satisfy the South, and that Crittenden's proposed amendment to the Constitution in the form proposed ought not to be made."[9]

On January 11, 1861, president-elect Lincoln wrote a letter to James T. Hale, a Republican member of Congress from Pennsylvania who had suggested a similar measure. Lincoln rejected the proposed compromise, arguing that it would only encourage the South to make new demands on the rest of the country: "A year will not pass, till we shall have to take Cuba as a condition upon which they will stay in the Union. They now have the Constitution, under which we have lived over seventy years, and acts of Congress of their own framing, with no prospect of their being changed; and they can never have a more shallow pretext for breaking up the government, or extorting a compromise, than now."[10] In the same letter Lincoln justified a refusal to be blackmailed by the threat of secession in the same terms in which, later, he would justify action to repress secession: "We have just carried an election on principles fairly stated to the people. Now we are told in advance, the government shall be broken up, unless we surrender to those we have beaten, before we take the offices. In this they are either attempting to play upon us, or they are in dead earnest. Either way, if we surrender, it is the end of us, and of the government."

During the tense period between his election and the outbreak of the war, as one Southern state after another seceded, Lincoln rejected compromise measures that many others, including other Republicans, were discussing. "Stand firm," he declared on December 10, 1860. "The tug has to come, and better now, than any time hereafter."[11] On another occasion he said: "I will suffer death before I will consent or will advise my friend to consent to any concession or compromise which looks like buying the privilege to take possession of this government to which we have a constitutional right."[12] Lincoln told an acquaintance "that he would rather be hung by the neck till he was dead on the steps of the Capitol, before he would buy or beg a peaceful inauguration."[13]

DIFFERING VIEWS ABOUT the constitutionality of unilateral secession by states have always reflected disagreements about the nature of the United States itself. Between the Founding and the Civil War, three major theories of the federal union were expounded: the nationalist theory; the unilateral compact theory; and the multilateral compact theory. The nationalist interpretation holds that there is a single sovereign American "people," while the two variants of the compact theory hold that, for purposes of constitutional law, there are as many sovereign "peoples" as there are American states.

Joseph Story, appointed to the Supreme Court by Madison in 1811, wrote the definitive account of the nationalist theory in his *Commentaries on the Constitution of the United States* (1833). According to Story, "In our republican form of government, the absolute sovereignty of the nation is in the people of the nation." The Continental Congress, formed by delegates from what were then British colonies, "exercised de facto and de jure sovereign authority, not as the delegated agents of the governments de facto of the colonies, but in virtue of original powers derived from the people." The Declaration of Independence was "implicitly the act of the whole people of the united colonies," not of separate states that individually seceded from the

British Empire.[14] Story's version of the nationalist theory of popular sovereignty holds that the United States was always a nation-state, never an alliance of sovereign states. Even under the Articles of Confederation, which gave the central government almost no powers, the Union was a decentralized nation-state rather than a confederation or league of independent polities. In favor of this theory is the United States Code. The first section, entitled "The Organic Laws of the United States of America," contains four documents: the Declaration of Independence (1776), the Articles of Confederation (1777), the Ordinance of 1787: The Northwest Territorial Government, and the Constitution of the United States of America (1787). Story and other nationalists argued that this sequence reflected the gradual "perfecting" of a Union that was created by the Declaration. The significance of the Northwest Ordinance was its exclusion of slavery from that territory, in keeping with the principles of 1776.

The most important rival to the nationalist theory has been the compact theory, which holds that the American Union is a compact or treaty among the states. The most familiar version of the compact theory, held by Thomas Jefferson, John C. Calhoun, and the Confederate secessionists, can be described as the unilateral compact theory. In this interpretation, the people of each state are to be the judges of whether the constitutional compact among the states has been violated by other states or the federal government. A state has the unilateral right to secede from the Union, as the Confederate states sought to do. Many advocates of the compact theory also claimed that in addition to possessing a right of unilateral secession, individual states have the right to "nullify" laws they consider to have violated the federal Constitution. This argument was made by the legislatures of Virginia and Kentucky in 1798 when they passed the Virginia and Kentucky Resolutions drafted by Thomas Jefferson, and repeated by the government of South Carolina during the Nullification Crisis of 1830 to 1832. In his posthumously published *A Discourse on the Constitution and Government of the United States* (1851), Calhoun argued that both the right of states unilaterally to veto or nullify federal laws and the right of unilateral secession were necessary inferences from the nature of the Union as a treaty among sovereign states.[15]

A different version of the compact theory might be called the multilateral compact theory. Its best-known advocate was James Madison, known as the Father of the Constitution for his role at the constitutional convention of 1787 and his coauthorship, with Alexander Hamilton and John Jay, of *The Federalist Papers.* Madison's version of the compact theory was significantly different from that of his philosophical adversary in his old age, John C. Calhoun.

On March 15, 1833, the retired president wrote a letter to Massachusetts senator Daniel Webster, who in February, following the Nullification Crisis of 1832, had delivered a rebuttal to Senator John C. Calhoun's argument that each individual state possessed the power to reject or "nullify" a federal law of which it disapproved. "I return my thanks for the copy of your late very powerful speech in the Senate of the United States," Madison wrote Webster. "It crushes 'nullification' and must hasten the abandonment of 'secession.' " Having agreed with Webster's conclusions, Madison dissented from the logic of the nationalist theory that Webster shared with Story and Lincoln. "It is fortunate when disputed theories can be decided by undisputed facts. And here the undisputed fact is that the Constitution was made by the people, but as embodied into the several states, who were parties to it and therefore made by the States in their highest authoritative capacity. They might, by the same authority and by the same process have converted the Confederacy [the United States under the Articles of Confederation] into a mere league or treaty; or continued it with enlarged or abridged powers; or have embodied the people of their respective states into one people, nation or sovereignty; or as they did by a mixed form make them one people, nation, or sovereignty, for certain purposes, and not so for others." In Madison's view, the present Union was created by the ratification of the federal Constitution by the states in 1787–88.

After restating the conventional theory of the Constitution as a compact among the people of each state, Madison went on to argue that "whilst the

Constitution, therefore, is admitted to be in force, its operation in every respect must be precisely the same," whether the Constitution is thought to
have been authorized by one national people or by the separate states.[16] In
other words, according to Madison acceptance of the compact theory does
not require acceptance of the idea that states are free at their own initiative
to nullify federal laws or secede from the Union at will. The compact can
be revised or dissolved—but only with the agreement of all of the parties,
not just of one or a few.

It is impossible to know how Madison, who died in 1836, would have
responded to the secession crisis and the Civil War. Although he probably
would have opposed secession, this Virginian, like many former Southern
Unionists, might have sided with his native state once the war began. What
is important is the fact that the multilateral compact theory of Madison, no
less than the nationalist theory shared by Story and Webster, held that unilateral secession by a state was unconstitutional.

IN 1859 LINCOLN joked: "The position taken by the advocates of
State Sovereignty always reminds me of the fellow who contended that the
proper place for the big kettle was inside of the little one."[17] Lincoln's own
theory of the Union was the one he had learned from nationalist scholars
and statesmen in the Federalist and Whig parties, such as Story and Webster
as well as the New York jurist Joseph Kent, whose *Commentaries on American
Law* (1826–30) he cited on more than one occasion. To help him clarify his
ideas while composing his inaugural address in a room across the street from
the Illinois Statehouse in Springfield, he studied the U.S. Constitution,
Henry Clay's 1850 speech, Andrew Jackson's proclamation against nullification, and Webster's Reply to Hayne, which, according to his law partner
William Herndon, "he always regarded as the grandest specimen of
American oratory."[18]

Before turning to Lincoln's restatement of the nationalist theory of the
U.S. Constitution, it is worth briefly examining two minor, subsidiary ar-

guments he made for the territorial integrity of the United States. One was an argument from geography: "That portion of the earth's surface which is owned and inhabited by the people of the United States, is well adapted to be the home of one national family; and it is not well adapted for two, or more. . . ."[19] The weakness of this line of argument is evident from the fact that the United States and Canada, two federal states created in the aftermath of the sundering of Britain's North American empire, form two "national families" that exist side by side on the same landmass.

As unconvincing as his argument from geography was Lincoln's claim that the Confederates rejected majority rule in favor of minority rule. In his inaugural address, Lincoln argued: "If a minority . . . will secede rather than acquiesce, they make a precedent which, in turn, will divide and ruin them; for a minority of their own will secede from them, whenever a majority refuses to be controlled by such minority. . . . Plainly, the central idea of secession, is the essence of anarchy."[20] But the Confederate theory of state sovereignty did not justify the secession, from the states themselves, of counties, cities, neighborhoods, or individuals. From a Confederate perspective, neither the secession of 1776 nor that of 1860–61 necessarily justified secession by entities smaller than colonies or states. One could, without contradiction, support both the right of South Carolina to secede from the Union and the right of South Carolina to repress the attempted secession of one of its counties or cities. By the same logic, nationalists like Lincoln were perfectly consistent when they, locating sovereignty in the nation rather than in the individual state, assumed that the American people as a whole possessed both the right to secede from the British Empire and the right to defeat the attempt of the Southern states to secede from the United States. It was precisely the constitutional question of *which* majority possessed the authority to authorize the secession of individual states—a majority in each state or a national majority?—that divided the Confederates from the Unionists.

Lincoln devoted much of his First Inaugural Address to restating the nationalist theory of the U.S. Constitution that he had inherited from Story and others. "[We] find the proposition that, in legal contemplation, the

Union is perpetual, confirmed by the history of the Union itself. The Union is much older than the Constitution. It was formed, in fact, by the Articles of Association in 1774. It was matured and continued by the Declaration of Independence in 1776. It was further matured and the faith of all the then thirteen states expressly plighted and engaged that it should be perpetual, by the Articles of Confederation of 1778. And finally, in 1787, one of the declared objects for ordaining and establishing the Constitution was 'to form a more perfect union.' "[21]

It was not necessary, however, to adopt the nationalist theory of the Constitution in order to agree with Lincoln that unilateral secession was unconstitutional. Lincoln himself acknowledged this in his First Inaugural, when he argued that secession was unlawful not only according to the nationalist theory but also according to the compact theory. Using the same logic that Madison had employed in his letter to Webster, Lincoln argued: "Again, if the United States be not a government proper, but an association of States in the nature of contract merely, can it, as a contract, be peaceably unmade, by less than all the parties who made it? One party to a contract may violate it—break it, so to speak; but does it not require all to lawfully rescind it?"[22]

Lincoln's predecessor as president, James Buchanan, a Democrat of the states' rights school, had agreed that secession was unconstitutional. In his annual message to Congress of December 1860, delivered as the crisis deepened, Buchanan pointed out that during the debates in the individual states over the ratification of the federal Constitution in 1787–88 "it never occurred to any individual, either among its proponents or advocates, to assert or even to intimate that their efforts were all in vain labor, because the moment that any State felt herself aggrieved she might secede from the Union. What a crushing argument would this have proved against those who dreaded that the rights of States would be endangered by the Constitution! The truth is that it was not until many years after the origin of the Federal Government that such a proposition was first advanced."[23]

While denying that individual states possessed a right of unilateral secession, Lincoln acknowledged that the national majority had the authority to "dismember" the Union by either constitutional or revolutionary methods: "This country, with its institutions, belongs to the people who inhabit it. Whenever they shall grow weary of the existing government, they can exercise their constitutional right of amending it, or their revolutionary right to dismember or overthrow it."[24] By referring to "their constitutional right of amending it," Lincoln seemed to suggest that the Constitution could be amended in order to permit states to leave either by the ordinary process of constitutional amendment by a majority of the states or by the never-used alternative, a constitutional convention.[25] The fact that the federal Constitution, by containing procedures for amendment, provides not only for its own alteration or replacement but also, at least in theory, for the peaceful division of the United States into two or more countries is difficult to reconcile with Lincoln's statement, elsewhere in the First Inaugural, that "no government proper, ever had a provision in its own organic law for its own termination."[26]

In addition to the option of secession by means of constitutional amendment, there remained the possibility of extraconstitutional revolution, which proponents of both the nationalist and compact theories of the American Union acknowledged as legitimate in some circumstances. In his letter to Webster, Madison warned against confusing "the claim to secede at will, with the right of seceding from intolerable oppression. The former answers itself, being a violation, without cause, of a faith solemnly pledged. The latter is another name only for revolution, about which there is no theoretic controversy"—by which he meant that no Americans of any school doubted the existence of a right of revolution by an oppressed people.[27] In a speech on the Mexican War, Lincoln, then a Whig member of Congress, observed on January 12, 1848: "Any people, anywhere, being inclined and having the power, have the right to rise up and shake off the existing government, and form a new one that suits them better. This is a most valuable, a most sacred right, a right which we hope and believe is to liberate the world. Nor is this right confined to cases in which the whole people of an existing government may choose to exercise it. Any portion of such people, that can, may revolutionize, and make their own of so much of the territory as they inhabit. More than this, a majority of any portion of such people may revolutionize, putting down a minority, intermingled with, or near about them, who may oppose their movements."[28] However, Lincoln stressed that such a revolution had to be "exercised for a morally justifiable cause" if it were not to be "simply a wicked exercise of physical power."[29] Without referring again to the alleged right of a "portion of such people" to revolutionize a government, Lincoln in his First Inaugural acknowledged the American people's "revolutionary right to dismember, or overthrow" their government. For their part, many Confederates, while claiming that unilateral secession was legal under the federal Constitution, hedged their bets by invoking extra-constitutional, revolutionary legitimacy for their actions. Southern state legislatures passed secession laws, which were then ratified by state conventions that purported to represent the citizens of the state in a revolutionary mode.

Whether a revolution is justified or not is an ethical and political question, not an issue of constitutional law. In both 1776 and 1860, majorities of the citizens (if not of the inhabitants) of South Carolina supported a revolution. But the goal in 1776 was to preserve and increase republican government in North America, whereas the goal in 1861, according to most of the Confederate leaders themselves, was to preserve if not extend the zone of chattel slavery in North America. The United States in 1776 had been a slave society as well, but the perpetuation of slavery was not the cause of the secession of the American colonies, as it was the fundamental cause of the secession of the Southern states. Lincoln had no doubt that the secession of the Confederate states was not "for a morally justifiable cause."

Echoing Story, Lincoln, and others in the nationalist tradition of constitutional interpretation, the Supreme Court formally rejected the constitutionality of secession in 1869 in *Texas v. White,* writing that the Union "began among the Colonies . . . It was confirmed and strengthened by the necessities of war, and received definite form, and character, and sanction from the Articles of Confederation."[30] The military defeat of the Southern minority's unconstitutional attempt at unilateral secession in 1865 did not mean that the constitutional method of secession was no longer available. At any time since 1865, Southerners—or Americans in any other region or individual state—could have introduced a constitutional amendment to permit secession or could have worked for a constitutional convention with the goal of producing the same result. Since 1865 hundreds of constitutional amendments have been proposed and fifteen have been adopted, beginning with the Reconstruction Amendments (the Thirteenth, Fourteenth, and Fifteenth). The absence of proposals for the division of the United States into two or more countries by constitutional amendment suggests that the outcome of the Civil War discredited the very idea of secession by any method, including the constitutional and peaceful methods acknowledged as legitimate by Lincoln. Furthermore, the complete absence of proposals for secession by American political leaders since slavery was abolished by the Thirteenth Amendment tends to discredit the argument that the protection of slavery was not the ultimate cause of the South's attempted secession from the United States.

WHEN LINCOLN RESUPPLIED the besieged federal garrison at Fort Sumter, the new Confederate regime of South Carolina began to bombard it on April 12, 1861. Thirty-six hours later the garrison surrendered. The Civil War had begun.

Lincoln's call for seventy-five thousand volunteers to support the Union backfired, by provoking the secessions of Virginia, North Carolina, Arkansas, and Tennessee in April and May. The first major military setback for the Union came on July 16. Union forces dispatched to capture Richmond, Virginia, which had replaced Montgomery, Alabama, as the capital of the Confederate States of America, were routed at Bull Run Creek near Richmond. Demoralized federal troops retreated to Washington, D.C. Lincoln responded to the humiliation of Bull Run by putting General George B. McClellan in charge of the Army of the Potomac.

McClellan had won fame when, as commander of the Ohio militia, he had invaded West Virginia and detached it from the Confederacy (in 1863, West Virginia became a state, boosting the votes of the Republican Party in the U.S. Senate and the presidential electoral college).

By the beginning of 1862, the U.S. Army had swelled to six hundred thousand troops. The Confederacy had only a quarter of a million soldiers. The war lasted longer and cost more than either side expected. But from the beginning, the champions of the Union had reason to expect success. In 1860 the free states, with 19 million inhabitants, outnumbered the slave states, whose population of 12 million included 4 million slaves. The North, with five times as much industrial production as the South and three times as much wealth, accounted for 100 percent of America's rolled iron, which was needed for railroad tracks, as well as most of its production of ships (98 percent), firearms (97 percent), and locomotives (96 percent).[31] As long as the majority in the North opposed disunion, material factors ensured that the attempt of the South to secede was almost certain to fail.

LINCOLN DERIVED A distinctive theory of the nature of the Civil War from the nationalist theory of the federal Union. In Lincoln's view the Civil War, or rather "the rebellion," was not a "war between the states" much less a war between two countries, the United States of America and the Confederate States of America. The federal government was seeking to suppress an uprising in its jurisdiction. Neither federal authority nor the proper constitutional authority of the state governments had ever ceased to exist. Parts of the country had merely been taken over by the "so-called" Confederate state and federal governments, which were nothing more than criminal conspiracies. In effect the Civil War was a colossal riot, and the goal of federal forces was to restore law and order.

One of the clearest expositions of Lincoln's theory of the "rebellion," which may have been written at his direction by his aide John Hay, appeared in the *Illinois Daily State Journal* on January 22, 1861. The anonymous writer denounced outgoing president James Buchanan and his attorney general Jeremiah S. Black for alleging that the federal government lacked the power to go to war to coerce a state. After quoting Article 6, Section 2 of the federal Constitution, providing that the "Constitution, and the laws of the United States which shall be made in pursuance thereof . . . shall be the supreme law of the land . . . anything in the Constitution or laws of any State to the contrary notwithstanding," the author continues: "There being no power then in the Legislature of South Carolina to secede from the Union—no power to nullify the laws of the United States—no power to absolve their citizens from their allegiance or their fealty to the laws—it remains only for the execution of the laws to go right on. If resisted, the resistance must be overcome. If the civil arm cannot do it, the military must aid. If organized insurrection follows, it is the duty of the President to 'see that the laws be faithfully executed.' And if ten thousand armed men are necessary to execute the laws of Congress within a State, it does not follow that a single law of that State need be disturbed in its operation, or a single State right infringed. These things involved legal 'coercion,' not of the *State,* but of the offender who resists. . . . A State has no more right to oppose its legislation to an act of Congress than a county or city has to oppose *its* resolves or ordinances to the law of a State. . . ."[32]

While the Lincoln administration defined the Civil War as an attempt to repress a rebellion, it was forced to make concessions to the rival view of the conflict as a struggle between two countries. Under a strict interpretation of the rebellion theory, Lincoln should have ordered the closure of Southern ports rather than a blockade of the South. As Thaddeus Stevens, a leading Republican member of Congress, pointed out, the latter policy meant that "we were blockading ourselves."[33] Lincoln, however, believed that a blockade was less likely to cause conflict with European naval powers than an order closing the ports.[34] The Lincoln administration also deviated from a consistent application of the rebellion theory when it treated captured Confederate soldiers as prisoners of war rather than as common criminals. Lincoln further undermined the rebellion theory of the war by engineering the secession of West Virginia from the rest of Virginia over the objection of Attorney General Edward Bates that this was unconstitutional.[35]

The Lincoln administration resolved some of these dilemmas by adopting, from international law, the concept of an organized "belligerent," an entity that was less than a sovereign state but more than a collection of individual lawbreakers. The Supreme Court agreed with this interpretation, ruling that as of July 13, 1861, when Congress passed a Non-Intercourse Act with the areas in rebellion, the South had assumed the character of a belligerent. This created a situation in which the federal government, in addition to attempting to enforce federal law by conventional means, could employ tactics and strategies traditionally used in international conflicts as well as in civil wars in other countries.

To His Nationalist theory of the Constitution and his definition of the war as a rebellion rather than a conflict between countries, Lincoln added an expansive view of his war powers as president. He claimed that between sessions of Congress, the president was entitled to exercise all of the war powers of Congress. After Congress convened at his request for a special session on July 4, 1861, he explained: "It is believed that nothing has been done beyond the constitutional competency of Congress." According to Lincoln, "It was with the deepest regret that the Executive found the duty of employing the war-power, in defence of the government, forced upon him." Lincoln explained that his actions "whether strictly legal or not, were ventured upon, under what appeared to be a popular demand, and a public necessity; trusting then, as now, that Congress would readily ratify them."[36]

Lincoln's conception of the powers assigned specifically to the president by the Constitution was just as expansive. Lincoln told Carl Schurz: "Looked at from a constitutional standpoint, the executive could do many things by virtue of the war power which Congress could not do in the way of ordinary legislation."[37] Lincoln told his aide John Nicolay, "The very existence of a general and national government implies the legal power, right, and duty of maintaining its own integrity."[38] Lincoln claimed that "as Commander in Chief of the Army and Navy, in time of war, I suppose I have a right to take any measure which may best subdue the enemy."[39]

When a former Massachusetts Whig, William Whiting, published a defense of practically illimitable presidential wartime authority, *The War Powers of the President,* in 1862, Lincoln was so pleased that he appointed Whiting solicitor general of the War Department. Of the war powers of the president Whiting wrote: "They are principally contained in the Constitution, Art. II, Sect. 1, Cl. 1 and 7; Sect. 2, Cl. 1; Sect. 3, Cl. 1; and in Sect. 1, Cl. 1, and by necessary implication in Art. I, Sect. 9, Cl. 2. By Art. II, Sect. 2, The President is made commander-in-chief of the army and navy of the United States, and of the militia of the several states when called into the service of the United States."[40] In defending an elastic interpretation of these constitutional grants of authority, Whiting belonged in the Hamiltonian tradition of the Federalist, Whig, and Republican parties. In favor of what he calls "liberal construction," Whiting cited Hamilton in *Federalist* 23: "It must be admitted as a necessary consequence, that there can be no limitation of that authority, which is to provide for the defence and protection of the community in any matter essential to its efficacy,—that is, in any matter essential to the formation, direction, or support of the national forces."[41] Further indicating his Hamiltonian intellectual lineage, Whiting alluded to the nationalist constitutional theories expounded by "Chief Justice Marshall, and approved by Daniel Webster, Chancellor Kent, and Judge Story . . ."[42] In Whiting's view, during wartime ordinary constitutional provisions are set aside, and the entire country, not merely areas of combat, may legitimately be subject to martial-law rule, which is regulated by the international laws of war rather than by the domestic Constitution or statutes. "Necessity arbitrates the rights and the methods of war. Whatever hostile military act is essential to public safety in civil war is lawful."[43]

LINCOLN'S MOST CONTROVERSIAL exercise of war power was his suspension of the writ of habeas corpus, the right of a court to insist that a citizen who has been arrested either be charged with a crime or released. The suspension of habeas corpus permits the military to detain individuals indefinitely in areas where martial law has been imposed. The Constitution assigns Congress the power to suspend habeas corpus, but Lincoln claimed that the president has the authority to provide for its suspension in an emergency while Congress is not in session.

The reason for Lincoln's initial suspension of habeas corpus during the early months of the war was uncertainty about the loyalty of officials in the state of Maryland. A state more Southern than Northern, Maryland was home to many Southern sympathizers. If Maryland seceded, then Washington, D.C., would be cut off and might have to be abandoned by the federal government. Following attacks on federal troops who were passing through Baltimore, city officials burned key bridges there on the night of April 19, 1861, arguing that by preventing federal troops from crossing the city they were preventing a second riot. Viewing this as a pro-Confederate plot, Lincoln and others worried that the Maryland legislature, scheduled to convene on April 26, would pass a secession ordinance. Even though the Maryland legislature refused to consider a secession ordinance, Lincoln ordered the arrest and preventive detention of a number of Maryland state legislators and other officials early in the summer of 1861. Lincoln authorized General Scott to suspend habeas corpus first in Maryland, Delaware, Pennsylvania, and the District of Columbia, and then in the entire East Coast.

Neither the administration nor the military informed federal courts that habeas corpus had been suspended. On May 25 a citizen of Maryland named John Merryman was arrested on a charge of conspiring with others to join the Confederate Army. Roger B. Taney, the Chief Justice of the Supreme Court and author of the controversial Dred Scott decision that had overturned the Missouri Compromise, issued a writ of habeas corpus. After the military refused to obey Taney's writ, the Chief Justice issued an opinion that Lincoln's action was unconstitutional because only Congress could suspend habeas corpus. Taney's opinion was hailed and reprinted by Democratic critics of Lincoln in the North and used by Confederate leaders as evidence of federal tyranny. In his July 4 address to Congress, which he convened in special session, Lincoln seemed to concede that his action might have been illegal, when he pleaded necessity—"To state the question more directly, are all the laws, but one, to go unexecuted, and the government itself go to pieces, lest that one be violated?"—and insisted: "It was not believed that any law had been violated."[44]

Throughout the Civil War Lincoln expressed hostility toward federal judges who questioned his power to suspend habeas corpus. Reportedly he talked of arresting Chief Justice Taney. In a Cabinet meeting on September 14, 1863, Lincoln threatened to exile judges who used writs of habeas corpus to free conscripts from the draft, the way he had exiled Vallandigham, and the next day he read the Cabinet a proposed order that would have authorized the military to resist police carrying out court orders to produce a person under a writ of habeas corpus. Several members of his Cabinet, however, persuaded Lincoln to soften the language of what became the proclamation of September 15, 1863, which suspended habeas corpus throughout the United States for the duration of the war.[45] Lincoln's contempt for federal judges like Chief Justice Taney, who questioned presidential decisions in wartime, was shared by William Whiting in *The War Powers of the President*: "Are the black gown and wig to be the protection of traitors?"[46]

Congress ratified Lincoln's nationwide suspension of habeas corpus when it passed the Habeas Corpus Act on the same day in March 1863 that it passed the Enrollment Act, a national conscription act to replace the previous militia draft, which limited a soldier's service to nine months. The passage of martial-law and draft legislation on the same day was not a coincidence. The adoption of the first national draft provoked upheavals throughout the North, including the Draft Riots in New York City, the bloodiest riots in U.S. history. The Lincoln administration was so concerned about New York State, which had 20 percent of the population of the North, that in order to enforce the draft it stationed more troops in New York than the draft obtained in the summer of 1863.[47] The draft law was profoundly unfair because it permitted wealthy young men to buy their way out of military service by paying for substitutes. Lincoln, while sending the sons of other men to their deaths, ensured that his own adult son Robert would avoid combat, first as a student at Harvard College and then as a member of the staff of General Ulysses S. Grant.

The argument that the federal government was tyrannical because it temporarily suspended the right of habeas corpus and enacted a draft law cannot be made by defenders of the Confederate government, which undertook identical actions. Unlike Lincoln, Jefferson Davis suspended the writ only after receiving authority from the Confederate Congress, which passed four acts authorizing suspension between February 27, 1862, and February 15, 1864.[48] As with Lincoln, Davis began by suspending the writ in the area of his government's capital, when the Richmond area was threatened by an invasion of federal forces. Nor can the federal draft be interpreted as evidence of tyranny unless a similar charge is leveled at the Confederacy, whose first conscription act, enacted on April 14, 1862, created a draft for all able-bodied white males between eighteen and thirty-five.[49] The Confederate law, preceding the Union conscription act by a more than a year, created the first draft in American history. As the war went on, the Confederate government became stricter in enforcing its draft.

SECRETARY OF STATE William Seward, who presided for a time over internal security, told the British ambassador: "I can touch a bell on my right hand and order the imprisonment of a citizen of New York; and no power on earth except the President can release them."[50] Between 10,000 and 15,000 people were detained. Most were arrested in or around the front lines, on suspicion of smuggling or of being Confederate soldiers.[51] The overwhelming majority were held briefly and then released. But a number were tried by military commissions rather than civilian courts, convicted, and sentenced to imprisonment, hard labor, or death.

Because the power to suspend the writ of habeas corpus was delegated to officers in the field, it was sometimes abused by soldiers, who arrested politicians or shut down newspapers for criticizing the president or questioning the war. When this happened, the Lincoln administration sometimes backed the overzealous officer in order to save face. This is what happened when General Ambrose Burnside arrested the Ohio Democrat Clement Laird Vallandigham after he gave a speech criticizing the Lincoln administration. Burnside had Vallandigham arrested, tried by a military commission, and summarily sentenced to imprisonment for the duration of the war. Lincoln commuted the sentence to banishment to the Confederacy.

Following the arrest of Vallandigham, Lincoln provided his major defense of his administration's policy of military arrests in a public letter of June 12, 1863, to Erastus Corning, an Ohio Democrat. Without citing any constitutional provisions, laws, or judicial precedents other than the Constitution's provision for the suspension of habeas corpus, Lincoln claimed that "arrests by process of courts, and arrests in cases of rebellion, do not proceed altogether upon the same basis. . . . In the latter case, arrests are made, not so much for what has been done, as for what probably would be done." Lincoln cited the examples of Confederate generals, including Robert E. Lee, who "were all within the power of the government since [sic] the rebellion began, and were nearly as well known to be traitors then as now. Unquestionably if we had seized and held them, the insurgent cause would be much weaker. But no one of them had then committed any crime defined in the law." The idea that citizens should be subject to arrest, not only for treasonable deeds but also for treasonable sentiments, is as profoundly illiberal as the notion that citizens can be arrested for crimes that they have not committed but might commit in the future. Equally disturbing is Lincoln's argument that behavior that could justify preventive arrest in wartime includes both silence and ambiguous speech: "The man who stands by and says nothing, when the peril of his government is discussed, can not be misunderstood. If not hindered, he is sure to help the enemy. Much more, if he talks ambiguously—talks for his country with 'buts' and 'ifs' and 'ands.' "

According to Lincoln, the suspension of habeas corpus allowed the military to arrest any U.S. citizen, and imprison him indefinitely without recourse to the courts, for no reason other than that the president or military officers consider that citizen's public expressions of patriotism too qualified or insufficiently enthusiastic. Lincoln seemed to equate all criticism of his administration with incitement to desertion by soldiers: "Must I shoot a simple-minded soldier boy who deserts, while I must not touch a hair of a wiley agitator who induces him to desert? This is none the less injurious when effected by getting a father, a brother, or friend, into a public meeting, and there working upon his feelings, till he is persuaded to write the soldier boy, that he is fighting in a bad cause, for a wicked administration of a contemptible government, too weak to arrest and punish him if he shall desert." By Lincoln's logic, any politician or citizen who opposes a war or criticizes its conduct, once it has begun, is even worse than a soldier who deserts his post. Under this theory, Lincoln, who as a young member of Congress accused President James K. Polk during the Mexican War of provoking the conflict and lying about its origins, could have been imprisoned by the military at the command of President Polk.

Lincoln further justified his administration's policy of military arrests by observing that during the War of 1812, General Andrew Jackson, the military commander of New Orleans, had arrested not only a writer who criticized him in a newspaper but the writer's lawyer and the judge who issued a writ of habeas corpus. After hostilities ended, Jackson released the prisoners and paid the thousand-dollar fine imposed upon him by the judge. In the 1840s Congress reimbursed Jackson for the fine. After describing the incident, Lincoln wrote that "the permanent right of the people to public discussion, the liberty of speech and the press, the trial by jury, the law of evidence, and the Habeas Corpus, suffered no detriment whatever by that conduct of Gen. Jackson, or its subsequent approval by the American Congress." The fact that constitutional government survived Jackson's actions, however, hardly justifies them. On the contrary, by reimbursing Jackson for the fine, Congress acknowledged its lack of constitutional power to reverse the judge's holding by means of ex post facto legislation. Lincoln did not even bother to suggest that Jackson's arrest of his critic, the lawyer, and the judge had been necessary to help the United States win the War of 1812.

At one point in his open letter to Corning, the president lied to the American public: "The military arrests and detentions, which have been made, including those of Mr. V. which are not different in principle from the others, have been for prevention, and not for punishment—as injunctions to stay injury, as proceedings to keep the peace—and hence, like proceedings in such cases, and for like reasons, they have not been accompanied with indictments, or trials by juries, nor, in a single case by any punishment whatever, beyond what is purely incidental to the prevention." This was untrue. Many of those arrested by the military had been tried by military tribunals and sentenced to imprisonment, hard labor, or, in a few cases, execution, as Lincoln knew because he had reviewed many of the punishments. Indeed, following his assassination, the accused coconspirators of John Wilkes Booth were tried by a military commission on the grounds that they had assassinated the commander in chief of the armed forces in wartime, even though the war was over and civilian courts were functioning. Four of Booth's associates were hanged, including Mary Surratt, on July 7, 1865; three others were given life sentences. Lincoln's assertion that military arrests were solely "for prevention, and not for punishment . . ." was therefore an outright lie.

In his letter to Corning, Lincoln conceded: "If Mr. Vallandigham was not damaging the military power of the country, then his arrest was made on mistake of fact, which I would be glad to correct, on reasonably satisfactory evidence."[52] It was clear even then, as a matter of fact, that Vallandigham could have denounced Lincoln until the end of the war without significantly affecting the outcome. Unfortunately, instead of overruling General Burnside's arrest of Vallandigham, Lincoln not only endorsed it but compounded the harm done to constitutional government by his public defense of preventive detentions on mere suspicion and his equation of wartime dissent with treason and desertion.

Replying on June 23, Corning observed that Lincoln, instead of arguing that military necessity overrode the Constitution, invoked the Constitution's habeas corpus clause: "You claim to have found not outside, but within the Constitution, a principle or germ of arbitrary power, which in time of war expands at once into an absolute sovereignty, wielded by one man; so that liberty perishes, or is dependent on his will, his discretion or his caprice. This extraordinary doctrine, you claim to derive wholly from that clause of the Constitution, which, in case of invasion or rebellion, permits habeas corpus to be suspended. . . . You must permit us, to say to you with all due respect, but with the earnestness demanded by the occasion, that the American people will never acquiesce in this doctrine."[53]

In his earlier letter to Corning, Lincoln declared: "I think the time not unlikely to come when I shall be blamed for having made too few arrests rather than too many."[54] Few historians would agree that Lincoln and the U.S. military should have arrested more Americans than they did, including more opposition politicians and more newspaper editors critical of the Lincoln administration. Even some of Lincoln's closest friends and advisers were disturbed by the administration's military arrests. Lincoln's longtime Illinois supporter and presidential campaign manager David Davis recalled later: "Mr. Lincoln was advised, and I also so advised him, that the various military trials in the Northern and Border States, where the courts were free and untrammeled, were unconstitutional and wrong; that they would not and ought not to be sustained by the Supreme Court; that such proceedings were dangerous to liberty. He said that he was opposed to hanging; that he did not like to kill his fellow-man; that if the world had no butchers but himself it would go bloodless."[55] By asserting his own benevolence in reviewing the death sentences assigned by military tribunals, Lincoln evaded the issue his old friend had raised.

Appointed to the Supreme Court by Lincoln, Davis wrote the opinion in *Ex parte Milligan* (1866), in which the Court repudiated Lincoln's expansive interpretation of presidential war power in the course of overturning the death sentence of Lambdin P. Milligan, a Democratic politician from Ohio found guilty of disloyalty by a military commission in 1864 and sentenced to hang. On behalf of the majority of the Supreme Court, five of whose members had been appointed by Lincoln, Davis wrote: "No graver question was ever considered by this court, nor one which more nearly concerns the rights of the whole people; for it is the birthright of every American citizen when charged with crime, to be tried and punished according to law." Davis summarized the Lincoln administration's theory as the claim that "when war exists, foreign or domestic, and the country is subdivided into military departments for mere convenience, the commander of one of them can, if he chooses, within his limits, on the plea of necessity, with the approval of the Executive, substitute military force for and to the exclusion of the laws, and punish all persons, as he thinks right and proper, without fixed or certain rules." According to Davis, "Martial law, established on such a basis, destroys every guarantee of the Constitution. . . . Civil liberty and this kind of martial law cannot endure together; the antagonism is irreconcilable; and, in the conflict, one or the other must perish." The majority held that the Constitution's suspension of habeas corpus limits the government to temporary preventive detention: "It does not say after a writ of habeas corpus is denied a citizen, that he shall be tried otherwise than by the course of the common law. . . ." This implied that most if not all of the military trials of civilians during the Civil War, and the penalties that resulted, including in some cases execution, were unconstitutional.

The Court sought to restrict not only the scope but the geographic application of the martial-law authority of the federal government: "Martial law cannot arise from a threatened invasion. The necessity must be actual and present; the invasion real, such as effectually closes the courts and deposes the civil administration. . . . Martial rule can never exist where courts are open" but is "confined to the locality of actual war." Davis and his fellow justices believed that Lincoln's extension of martial law throughout the North had not been justified: "It is difficult to see how the safety of the country required martial law in Indiana. If any of her citizens were plotting treason, the power of arrest could secure them, until the government was prepared for their trial, when the courts were open and ready to try them. It was as easy to protect witnesses before a civil as a military tribunal; and as there could be no wish to convict, except on sufficient legal evidence, surely an ordained and established court was better able to judge of this than a military tribunal composed of gentlemen not trained to the profession of law."

On the question of civil liberties in wartime, the eloquent opinion of Justice Davis in *Ex parte Milligan* is more persuasive than the sophistical reasoning and deliberate lies contained in President Lincoln's letter to Erastus Corning: "The Constitution of the United States is a law for rulers and people, equally in war and in peace, and covers with the shield of its protection all classes of men, at all times, and under all circumstances. No doctrine involving more pernicious consequences, was ever invented by the wit of man, than that any of its provisions can be suspended during any of the great exigencies of government. . . . [T]he government, within the Constitution, has all the powers granted to it, which are necessary to preserve its existence; as has been happily proved by the result of the great effort to throw off its just authority."[56]

IN THE AREA of habeas corpus law, Lincoln's theory and practice provided a bad example that subsequent presidents could invoke to excuse unjustified abuses of the civil liberties of Americans and foreigners. In another area of military law, however, the Lincoln administration helped to raise standards in the world as well as in the United States.

In the midst of the Civil War, President Lincoln asked Francis Lieber, the great German-American scholar and friend of Alexis de Tocqueville, to codify the laws of war for the U.S. Army. In 1863 Lieber published *Instructions of the Government of Armies of the United States in the Field*, known as General Order No. 100 or "the Lieber Code." Lieber knew that he had to balance the practical needs of armies with the principles of morality if his code was to be taken seriously in the United States and elsewhere. Even so, the Lieber Code was remarkable for its humanity. According to Article 56: "A prisoner of war is subject to no punishment for being a public enemy, nor is any revenge wreaked upon him by the intentional infliction of any suffering, disgrace, by cruel imprisonment, want of food, by mutilation, death, or any other barbarity." Article 75: "Prisoners of war are subject to confinement or imprisonment such as may be deemed necessary on account of safety, but they are to be subjected to no other intentional suffering or indignity." Article 76: "Prisoners of war shall be fed upon plain and wholesome food, whenever practicable, and treated with humanity."[57]

The document, commissioned by President Lincoln, became the basis not only of U.S. military law but also of all subsequent international treaties regarding the treatment of prisoners of war and civilians in occupied countries. The Lieber Code inspired the Hague Conventions of 1899 and 1907, which in turn were modified by the Geneva Conventions of 1929 and 1949. The world owes the ongoing attempt to regulate warfare in the interests of justice and decency in part to the administration of Abraham Lincoln.

DENOUNCED AS A tyrant by critics, Lincoln did not think of himself as a dictator. Notwithstanding his broad view of his war powers, Lincoln demonstrated his respect for property rights and constitutional government when he overruled General John C. Fremont's proclamation of August 30, 1861, emancipating slaves in Missouri. In addition to considering Fremont's action a usurpation of presidential authority, Lincoln believed that it was inconsistent with the Confiscation Act recently passed by Congress. Writing to a friend, Lincoln asked, "Can it be pretended that it is any longer the government of the U.S.—any government of Constitution and laws wherein a General, or a President, may make permanent rules of property by proclamation?"[58] Such a policy, Lincoln argued, would be "simply 'dictatorship.' " After he issued the Emancipation Proclamation in 1863, he lobbied for the passage of the Thirteenth Amendment to the Constitution to permanently ban slavery, because in his own view the proclamation was a temporary war measure that did not necessarily have permanent legal force.

Lincoln mocked the idea of an American dictator in a letter he sent on January 26, 1863, to Major General Joseph Hooker. Hooker, appointed to command the Army of the Potomac, had allegedly complained that to win the war the government needed a dictator. Lincoln wrote: "I have heard, in such a way as to believe it, of your recently saying that both the Army and the Government needed a Dictator. Of course it was not for this, but in spite of it, that I have given you the command. Only those generals who gain successes, can set up dictators. What I now ask of you is military success, and I will risk the dictatorship."[59]

Even though he was convinced for a time that he would lose his bid for reelection in 1864, Lincoln dismissed the idea of suspending elections until the Union was restored. "We cannot have free governments without elections, and if the rebellion could force us to forego, or postpone a national election, it might fairly claim to have already conquered and ruined us."[60] Lincoln declared after the election that it had "demonstrated that a people's government can sustain a national election, in the midst of a great civil war. Until now it has not been known to the world that this was a possibility."[61]

This achievement, however, was tainted by the Lincoln administration's corruption of the electoral process. The Republican Party in its guise as the Union party compelled federal officeholders to make financial contributions to and in some cases work for Lincoln's reelection campaign.[62] Afraid of offending the commander in chief, most officers declared they would not support General George McClellan, the former commander of the Army of the Potomac who won the Democratic presidential nomination.[63] Corruption was widespread. For example, pro-Lincoln members of the 60th Massachusetts Infantry were permitted to vote in Indiana's election. "It is estimated that the Sixtieth Massachusetts Regiment cast about 6,000 votes for Governor Morton last Tuesday," a correspondent wrote in an Indianapolis newspaper. "And I know that some of the boys of Company I voted ten and twelve times each one."[64] Although only 53 percent of the civilian population voted for Lincoln, 78 percent of voters in uniform supported him.[65]

In addition to treating the military and the federal government as an extension of the Republican/Union Party, Lincoln's allies calumniated the

Democratic Party. On September 3, 1864, in a speech entitled "The Allies of Treason," Secretary of State William Seward made the false accusation that documents published in the *London Times* proved that the nomination of McClellan as the Democratic presidential candidate was the result of a "treaty formally contracted between the democratic traitors at Richmond, and the democratic opposition at Chicago, signed, sealed, attested, and delivered."[66]

Almost all of the alleged "Copperhead" conspiracies were as imaginary as the one to which Seward referred. Most Northern Democrats were War Democrats who opposed the abolition of slavery but favored restoration of the Union by force, even if they criticized the Lincoln administration's strategy and tactics.[67] And most of the Peace Democrats who wanted to negotiate with the South sought a negotiated reunion, not Southern independence.

Nor was there any basis to the charge, made by Lincoln's partisans in 1864 and repeated by many uncritical historians since, that if the much-maligned General George McClellan had won the presidency in 1864, the Union cause would have been lost. In accepting the Democratic nomination for president in 1864, McClellan insisted that the restoration of the Union was his goal: "I could not look in the face of my gallant comrades, who have survived so many bloody battles, and tell them that their labors and the sacrifice of many of our slain and wounded brethren had been in vain, that we had abandoned the Union for which we have so often periled our lives."[68] He distanced himself from the Democratic Party platform, which contemporary Republicans and many later historians misrepresented as one calling for peace at the price of union; in fact it merely suggested an armistice.

The truth is that Lincoln's determination to preserve the Union was shared by a majority of Northern Democrats. Patriotic Democrats were often vilified by the Republicans, but without their assistance the Republican Party alone might not have been able to create a solid consensus in the North for anything less than the unconditional surrender of the South.

During the Civil War Lincoln's longtime rival Stephen A. Douglas, in his capacity as an Illinois senator, led the War Democrats in support of the Union cause until his death in 1861. After the firing on Fort Sumter, Douglas told a friend: "I've known Mr. Lincoln a longer time than you have, or than the country has. He'll come out right, and we will all stand by him."[69]

In addition to claims that Northern Democrats, including even General McClellan, were pro-Confederate traitors and members of "Copperhead" plots to sabotage the war and dismember the Union, assertions flourished in the Republican Party and the Republican press that Jewish financiers and their allies on Wall Street and in the City of London were seeking to profit from the war and the destruction of the United States. A Jewish citizen of Baltimore asked sarcastically whether the war was "inaugurated or fostered by Jews exclusively? Is the late democratic party composed entirely of Israelites?"[70] The depth of wartime anti-Semitism in the North can be judged from General Ulysses S. Grant's notorious General Orders Number 11, which banned "Jews" from Tennessee; Grant identified all peddlers, who annoyed him, with Jews (Lincoln quickly ordered Grant to rescind the order).

Demagogy and corruption, to be sure, were not monopolies of the Republican Party. Throughout the war, Democratic politicians and journalists vilified Lincoln as a tyrant and—what was just as bad in the eyes of their constituents—a promoter of racial equality. In the mid-nineteenth century, before the adoption of civil service reforms and the professionalization of the military, most officeholders and many military officers were political patronage employees who seldom distinguished between their official and their partisan duties. All parties manipulated elections when they could. For example, fearing that soldiers would vote disproportionately for Lincoln, the Democrats who controlled New Jersey, Indiana, and Lincoln's home state of Illinois refused to enact absentee ballot legislation.[71] The level of political honesty in the South can be inferred from the fact that, in 1860, Lincoln's name was not even on the ballot in most Southern states.

Lincoln's allies engaged in massive electoral cheating in the 1864 election, but there is no evidence that in the absence of their activities Lincoln would not have defeated McClellan and won a second term as President of the United States.

IN HIS SECOND inaugural address on March 4, 1865, Lincoln said: "With malice toward none, with charity for all, with firmness in the right as God gives us to see the right, let us strive to finish the work we are, to bind up the nation's wounds, to care for him who shall have borne the battle and for his widow and his orphan, to do all which may achieve and cherish a just and lasting peace among ourselves and with all nations."[72]

At a time when many Northerners were insisting on mass executions of Confederate leaders, Lincoln rejected the idea. According to Lincoln's bodyguard Ward Hill Lamon, an intervention by General John A. J. Creswell on behalf of a Confederate friend soon after the South's surrender inspired this response: "Creswell," said Mr. Lincoln, "you make me think of a lot of young folks who once started out Maying. To reach their destination, they had to cross a shallow stream, and did so by means of an old flatboat. When the time came to return, they found to their dismay that the old scow had disappeared. They were in sore trouble, and thought over all manner of devices for getting over the water, but without avail. After a time, one of the boys proposed that each fellow should pick up the girl he liked best and wade over with her. The masterly proposition was carried out, until all that were left upon the island was a little short chap and a great, long, gothic-built, elderly lady. Now, Creswell, you are trying to leave me in the same predicament. You fellows are all getting your own friends out of this scrape; and you will succeed in carrying off one after another, until nobody but Jeff Davis and myself will be left on the island, and then I won't know what to do. How should I feel? How should I look, hugging him over? I guess the way to avoid such an embarrassing situation is to let them all out at once."[73]

———

" M U S T   A   G O V E R N M E N T , of necessity, be too strong for the liberties of its own people, or too weak to maintain its own existence?"[74] This was the rhetorical question President Lincoln asked Congress, which he had called into special session to address the crisis of the Civil War on July 4, 1861, the eighty-fifth anniversary of the American Declaration of Independence. Could a liberal democracy defend itself against insurrection without losing its liberal and democratic character?

Lincoln had no doubt about the answer. He believed that the U.S. Constitution not only permitted but required him to suppress the illegal attempted secession of the Southern states. Lincoln was a politician, not a theorist, and he frequently sacrificed principle to pragmatism. Even so, he and his administration waged the war for reunion on the basis of a relatively coherent constitutional theory that answered two questions: Was the unilateral secession of individual states from the United States legal, under the federal Constitution? And: What powers to defeat an illegal attempt at secession did the president possess? Lincoln found the answers to these questions in the writings of statesmen and jurists in the Hamiltonian tradition, which influenced both the Whig Party, in which he spent most of his political career, and the Republican Party, which he led as president.

Lincoln's theory of the Union was that of Hamiltonian nationalists who believed not only that the federal Constitution outlawed unilateral secession by states, but also that the Union itself predated both the present federal Constitution and the states themselves. The Whig Party had been organized by members of Congress like Henry Clay and Daniel Webster to oppose a powerful president, Andrew Jackson, and opposition to the aggrandizement of the executive in domestic policy had become part of Whig ideology. At the same time, former Whigs like Lincoln showed their Hamiltonian heritage in arguing that the war powers of the president were extensive. Except in the case of congressional powers he exercised in the early months of the war, Lincoln never argued that necessity made extraconstitutional presidential action possible. Instead, he and members of his administration always sought to ground the administration's actions in specific grants of constitutional authority. However, the Lincoln administration's interpretation of presidential power was so broad that in practice it acknowledged few constitutional constraints on the president's authority in wartime.

Lincoln's view of the U.S. Constitution shaped his policy toward two subjects that consumed much of his time and attention during the war: the restoration of the Southern states to the Union and the future of slavery in the United States. How both his views and his policies with respect to these challenges changed in the course of the Civil War is the subject of the next chapter.

S I X

———❧———

RACE AND
RESTORATION

ON APRIL 12, 1861, learning that the Confederates had begun the bombardment of Fort Sumter, Senator Charles Sumner of Massachusetts, one of the leading abolitionists in the Republican Party, hurried to the White House. In his discussion with the president, he recalled later, "I . . . told [Lincoln] that under the war power the right had come to him to emancipate the slaves."[1]

Sumner was referring to a theory popularized a few decades earlier by former president John Quincy Adams, who after his retirement served in Congress and became a bitter critic of slavery and the Southern elite. In congressional debates in the 1830s and 1840s, Adams had argued that in the event of civil or foreign war, "not only the President of the United States but the commander of the army has the power to order the universal emancipation of the slaves."[2] According to Adams, the wartime emancipation power would exist not only during a civil war, but also during a "servile war," or slave rebellion, that the federal government sought to put down and a foreign invasion of the United States. "From the instant that your slave-holding States become the theatre of a war, civil, servile, or foreign war, from that instant the war powers of Congress extend to interference with the institution of slavery, in every way by which it can be interfered with, from a claim of indemnity for slaves taken or destroyed, to the cession of States burdened with slavery to a foreign power."[3]

In addition to Sumner, a number of Republicans including Horace Greeley, the ex-Whig who edited the *New York Tribune,* publicized Adams's argument for using presidential war powers to abolish slavery. Lincoln, how-ever, did not intend to use the war power to free slaves in the South, if he could avoid it. "In his conduct of the war he acted upon the theory that but one thing was necessary, and that was a united North," Lincoln's old friend Leonard Swett observed.[4] Lincoln had to hold together a coalition of radi-cal, moderate, and conservative Republicans and nationalist War Democrats in which abolitionists were a minority.

In addition, strategy required him to be sensitive to the slave states that had not defected to the Confederacy. In the early years of the war, Lincoln's hopes for preventing further disintegration rested on keeping the border states of Missouri, Kentucky, Maryland, and Delaware in the Union. By May 1861 Federal forces had ensured the safety of Washington, D.C., by se-curing Maryland and Delaware. Before being killed at the battle of Wilson's Creek, General Nathaniel Lyon secured Missouri for the Union by dis-banding the secessionist state militia and gaining control of the local railroad system. When Kentucky's pro-Southern governor declared the state's neu-trality, Lincoln adopted a passive policy that was justified when, in the sum-mer, Kentucky sided with the Union. "I hope to have God on my side, but I must have Kentucky," the Kentucky-born president declared.[5]

THE DISAGREEMENT BETWEEN Sumner and Lincoln at the beginning of the Civil War marked the beginning of a clash of visions about the restoration of the Union that would outlive Lincoln himself. While the details changed, the basic outlines of Lincoln's conservative plan for reconstruction emerged early in the war. Following his death, his successor President Andrew Johnson continued his approach.

Lincoln argued that the Southern states had never left the Union, but had been taken over by a conspiracy of criminal insurrectionists. This theory gave the president, empowered by the Constitution to enforce federal law, the chief responsibility for putting down the insurrection and restoring constitutional government in the South. Initially Lincoln sought to restore self-government within the Union to the Southern states without any changes. By 1863 he had decided that slavery had to be abolished by the states themselves. Later, he favored abolition by means of a constitutional amendment, which became the Thirteenth Amendment. By the time of his death, loyalty to the U.S. federal government and the ratification of the Thirteenth Amendment were the only requirements he wanted to impose for the rehabilitation of the South. Lincoln did not make full equality in civil and political rights for blacks a precondition of Southern "restoration," but viewed these as matters that the federal Constitution left to the authority of individual states.

Although the Radical Republicans were a varied group, most agreed on a theory of the war and a corollary theory of reconstruction that were different from Lincoln's. The radical theory of the war held that the states had actually left the Union. In doing so they had committed "state suicide" and reduced themselves to the status of territories. The model for the readmission of the seceded states was the admission of territories applying for statehood. This theory permitted Congress to impose any conditions it liked on the would-be states.

The differences between the radicals and moderates and conservatives like Lincoln were not limited to constitutional theory. Lincoln sometimes spoke as though slavery was the only issue dividing the South from the North. For example, on October 16, 1854, in a speech at Peoria, Illinois, he said: "I have no prejudice against the Southern people. They are just what we would be in their situation. If slavery did not now exist among them, they would not introduce it. If it did now exist among us, we would not instantly give it up."[6] In contrast, the Radicals had what might be called a "sociological" theory of the Southern problem—the South was an aristocratic, agrarian region in a middle-class, industrial nation-state. The problem was not just formal slavery, but the entire Southern caste and class system, which degraded poor whites as well as blacks. The mere abolition of slavery was not enough; the quasi-feudal social structure of the South needed to be revolutionized, if necessary with the help of Yankee colonists who would bring middle-class virtues into a postwar South.

Lincoln, a Hamiltonian in the Whig tradition, interpreted the federal Constitution loosely when it came to federal and presidential powers. But even he did not believe that the federal government had the constitutional authority to undertake the remaking of Southern society that some of the radicals envisioned. Lincoln and his young aides John Nicolay and John Hay were in the habit of referring to the radicals as "Jacobins," after the bloodthirsty, doctrinaire extremists of the French Revolution. The struggle between these two visions of the restoration of the Union survived Lincoln's assassination in 1865 and shaped the period of Reconstruction that followed the Civil War. In January 1865 Lincoln complained that the radical Massachusetts senator Charles Sumner hoped "to change this Government from its original form and make it a strong centralized power."[7] Instead of using the war as an occasion to reshape the United States as it should be, Lincoln intended to restore it as closely as possible to the condition in which it had been. Lincoln emphasized his conservative approach to reunion in his address to Congress on December 3, 1861, stressing that "in considering the policy to be adopted for suppressing the insurrection, I have been anxious and careful that the inevitable conflict for this purpose shall not degenerate into a violent and remorseless revolutionary struggle."[8]

BEFORE THE OUTBREAK of war, Lincoln had insisted upon his support for a constitutional amendment to guarantee federal noninterference with slavery in the South. In his First Inaugural Address of March 4, 1861, he declared: "I understand a proposed amendment to the Constitution . . . has passed Congress, to the effect that the federal government, shall never interfere with the domestic institutions of the States, including that of persons held to service. To avoid misconstruction of what I have said, I depart from my purpose not to speak of particular amendments, so far as to say that, holding such a provision to now be implied constitutional law, I have no objection to its being made express, and irrevocable."[9] Congress passed what would have been the Thirteenth Amendment and sent it to the states for ratification. Ohio and Maryland ratified it, but then the beginning of the Civil War rendered it irrelevant.

Congress, not President Lincoln, led the way to the abolition of slavery in the United States. On August 6, 1861, Congress passed the first Confiscation Act, which authorized federal authorities to seize rebel property and emancipate slaves. This inspired General John C. Fremont, the Republican candidate for the presidency in 1856, to issue a proclamation emancipating all slaves in Missouri on August 30, 1861. Arguing that this was an order that only the president could give, Lincoln overruled Fremont's emancipation declaration.

Lincoln persisted in promoting versions of the solution to the problem of slavery proposed by Henry Clay and other colonizationists: gradual, compensated emancipation of slaves accompanied by the emigration both of former slaves and free blacks from the United States. On assuming the presidency, Lincoln appointed James Mitchell, his ally in the colonization campaign in Illinois state politics in the 1850s, to an informal post as director of black colonization in the Department of the Interior. As early as the spring of 1861, Lincoln approved of private efforts to obtain coal-rich land in Chiriqui, Colombia (now part of Panama), as a colony for emancipated slaves and free blacks from the United States.

In his first annual message to Congress in December 1861, Lincoln proposed that slaves freed by a program of compensated emancipation be colonized "at some place, or places, in a climate congenial to them. It might be well to consider, too, whether the free colored people already in the United States could not, so far as individuals may desire, be included in such colonization."[10] With their use as possible destinations for black emigrants in mind, Lincoln called for the recognition of Haiti and Liberia, which previously had been denied diplomatic recognition because of the influence of Southern slave owners on the federal government.

On April 10, 1862, Congress passed a resolution endorsed by Lincoln that proposed providing "pecuniary aid" to "any state which may adopt gradual abolition of slavery . . ."[11] The resolution, which did not have the force of law, was opposed by members of Congress from the slaveholding border states. A few days later, on April 16, Lincoln signed into law a bill that provided for the compensated emancipation of slaves in the District of Columbia and also appropriated money for their emigration "to the Republic of Haiti or Liberia, or such other country beyond the limits of the United States as the President may determine." Lincoln declared that he was "gratified that the two principles of compensation, and colonization, are both recognized, and practically applied in the act."[12]

ON MAY 18, 1862, the U.S. Government Printing Office published a report by Lincoln's colonization adviser, James Mitchell: *Letter on the Relation of the White and African Races of the United States, Showing the Necessity of the Colonization of the Latter: Addressed to the President of the U.S.* Mitchell began by asserting: "The rebellion that is now shaking the foundation of the nation, is the struggle of *Imperialism* to establish itself in a republican land." Mitchell defined imperialism, which he identified with aristocratic Britain and the Southern slave-owner elite, as "the government of the many by the few, the dominion of unchecked, despotic will. . . . *Republicanism*, on the other hand, is a deliverance from this curse of despotic rule—a condition in which all men are equal before the law—and the law is supreme—meting out equal protection and equal justice."

That successful republics required a "homogeneous" population was a truism of traditional republican political theory, which held that political parties were illegitimate "factions" that sacrificed the public interest. Republicans feared that, in a country with two or more racial or religious groups in its population, the political competition among the groups might lead to civil war or tyranny. Using the same reasoning that led Protestant nativists to oppose Catholic immigration to largely Protestant America, Mitchell made the criterion of republican homogeneity, rather than allegations of black inferiority, the basis for his public argument for an all-white America: "Our institutions require a homogeneous population to rest on as a basis; without this basis, the continuance of republicanism, for any great length of time, is impossible." Mitchell discussed the racial problem in the republican language of factional "interest": "Our danger in the future arises from the fact that we have 4,500,000 persons, who, whilst among us, cannot be of us—persons of a different race, forming necessarily a distinct interest . . ."

Lincoln's colonization expert considered the possibility of granting equal rights to black Americans and allowing intermarriage to blend them and whites into a "homogeneous" population: "We are free to admit that such a system of assimilation or amalgamation is necessary, *provided you wish to retain those people here,* under the jurisdiction of our *republican form of government;* nay, we maintain, that our fundamental laws require equal rights to all our citizens." But white Americans, especially those in the South and Midwestern border states, would reject this alternative, Mitchell argued. Lincoln's fellow Midwesterner observed that "the fear of having African blood engrafted on the future population of the great [Mississippi] valley" was what "has nerved the arms of thousands in this conflict; it has said to the slave despots, '*you shall not Africanize this land,*' the heritage of our children." Whatever "that small class of northern theorists who defend amalgamation" might believe, Southern and Western whites would "erect legal protections against this possible admixture of blood . . ." But laws against interracial marriage would not prevent extra-legal amalgamation, which according to Mitchell "is giving to this continent a nation of bastards." Ostracized by white society, the mixed-race Americans might unite with black Americans in an antiwhite race war: "[T]he period will come when this mixed population will assume the offensive, and possibly the next great civil war will be the conflict of this race for dominion and existence."

Mitchell then considered the option of "a restrictive franchise for the freed men of the country . . . they will make you a valuable peasantry, say our English friends of the court end of London." But those who propose replacing black slavery with black serfdom "forget, or affect to forget, that slaves and peasants deprived of the right of citizenship, and suffering social degradation, are incompatible with the genius of our republicanism." To create a laboring class without civil and political rights would be "the overthrow of republicanism and the establishment of imperialism."

Thus a heterogeneous, biracial society was incompatible with republicanism for practical reasons, because politics would degenerate into race war, and the existence of different categories of citizens with different rights could not be reconciled with republican ideals. The alternative that Lincoln and Mitchell endorsed, colonization, would preserve the racial homogeneity of the American republic while permitting expatriated blacks to be full citizens of one or more nonwhite countries in which they would find new homes. Mitchell proposed that "the tropical lands of our own hemisphere should be devoted to their use, and that all available means should be seized to pour a flood of Anglo-African colonization on the tropical lands of the old hemisphere most accessible to us (Western Africa)." In addition, the United States and Mexico should agree "to divide this continent between the Anglo-American and mixed races . . ." The United States should not add any more territory "on the south, unless that territory is uninhabited; for every square mile added which is encumbered with a mixed race of local and fixed habits (unused to migration like the Mexican and Central American Indian, and Negro races), adds danger, trouble, and sure decay to republicanism." Mitchell concluded: "In doing this we take from imperialism its temptation to tamper with our republicanism."

The ideology of republicanism has sometimes encouraged paranoia; if the homogeneous people are divided among themselves, surely some hidden, outside force is to blame. Mitchell devoted much of his "Letter" to the paranoid claim that British imperialists were responsible for the criticism of the colonization policy by New England abolitionists and proslavery Southerners alike. "We were thus divided, while the people of England were a unit . . .'Emancipation on the soil' was their watch cry, and the creation of a colored peasantry out of the freed men. To enforce this plan upon us two agencies were used, the Puritan and the Cavalier; the first addressed himself to the North, the last to the South." At one point in this government document Mitchell actually wrote: "Thus the plot thickened . . ." Mitchell told Lincoln and the public: "Well do the nobility of England know that the negro race constitute the vulnerable point in our republicanism . . ." The abolitionists who opposed colonization formed a fifth column for Britain's aristocratic imperialists: "These English agencies found a ready people amongst the polished thinkers, the benevolent and philosophic minds of cold and calm New England . . . Here an English party and an English interest formed a lodgment." At the same time, the "old tory party" of the South were also pawns of Britain, advocating "a colored peasantry under bonds of perpetual servitude." Now that New England and the South were unwitting pawns in Britain's scheme to destroy American republicanism by creating a biracial society or a black peasantry in the United States, the true American republican tradition "found its most able advocates in the Middle States and the Mississippi Valley. Amongst the chief advocates of this policy, stood that true representative of American statesmen, Henry Clay . . ." The Midwestern Anglophobe took a final shot at Britain in his conclusion: "Will not the men of England enable us to respect, if not love, the land which has given us our language, most of our institutions, and national life [that is Britain], by permitting us to mature plans and opinions . . . undisturbed by the doctrines of imperial society and life?" Mitchell's Anglophobic conspiracy theory, in which both New England abolitionists and Southern Confederates were promoting the British goal of destroying republican society in the United States, resembled later anti-

Semitic conspiracy theories which claimed that both capitalism and communism, although apparently opposed, were mutually reinforcing elements
of a single plan devised by hidden but all-powerful Jews.

Mitchell's *Letter* contains much that is idiosyncratic. Nevertheless,
Mitchell's argument echoes a number of themes found in Lincoln's own
speeches and writings: the opposition to black-white intermarriage; the goal
of an all-white West which is not "Africanized" by free blacks or black
slaves; the identification of Southern slavery with British monarchy, aristocracy and imperialism; the argument that the first principles of republicanism
are at stake in the struggle over slavery and secession; and, not least, the veneration of that leading colonizationist and "true representative of American
statesmen, Henry Clay." Lincoln's approval of Mitchell's essay can be inferred from the fact that he asked Mitchell to arrange a meeting between
him and black representatives in an attempt to win the support of free blacks
in the North for colonization.[13]

IN THE SAME month, May 1862, Lincoln annulled General David
Hunter's proclamation emancipating slaves in South Carolina, Georgia, and
Florida, as he had countermanded General Fremont's similar order almost a
year before. In response, on July 17, 1862, the House and Senate passed the
Second Confiscation Act, which would have freed the slaves of all rebels.
Although the bill provided half a million dollars for the resettlement of for-
mer slaves outside of the country, Lincoln threatened to veto it because it
permanently deprived slave owners of their property without compensation.
Congress passed a joint resolution to address Lincoln's objections, but many
Republicans were furious at Lincoln's conservative policy.

Under pressure from Congress, Lincoln met with his Cabinet on July
21 and 22 to discuss the administration's policy toward slavery. After Seward
and Blair argued against it, Lincoln decided to postpone issuing a presidential emancipation proclamation. At this point Lincoln's only plan remained
the plan for compensated emancipation, which the border states had already

rejected. Lincoln may have been persuaded by Seward's argument that unless it followed a Union victory, an emancipation proclamation would appear to the world to be "the last measure of an exhausted government, a cry for help; the government stretching forth its hands to Ethiopia, instead of Ethiopia stretching forth her hands to the government."[14]

ON AUGUST 14, 1862, James Mitchell, whom Lincoln had put in charge of colonization, escorted five black leaders into the White House. This was not only the first time a president had met with black leaders in an official capacity in the White House, it was also Lincoln's first meeting with black leaders. During the campaign of 1860, Lincoln had angrily written to a correspondent that he did "not hold the black man to the equal of the white, unqualifiedly as Mr. S. states it . . . I was never in a meeting of Negroes in my life. . . ."[15]

To the black leaders Mitchell had assembled, Lincoln launched immediately into the reasons he supported colonization: "You and we are different races. We have between us a broader difference than exists between almost any other two races. Whether it is right or wrong I need not discuss, but this physical difference is a great disadvantage to us both, as I think your race suffer very greatly, many of them by living among us, while ours suffers from your presence. In a word we suffer on each side. If this is admitted, it affords a reason at least why we should be separated."

Lincoln told the black representatives: "Your race are suffering, in my judgment, the greatest wrong inflicted on any people." But he blamed the Civil War on the presence of blacks: "But for your race among us there could not be war, although many men engaged on either side do not care for you one way or the other." Lincoln proceeded to attempt to pressure the black delegates into endorsing colonization in condescending language: "You may believe you can live in Washington or elsewhere in the United States the remainder of your life, perhaps more so than you can in any foreign country, and hence you may come to the conclusion that you have nothing to do with the idea of going to a foreign country. This is (I speak in no un-kind sense) an extremely selfish view of the matter. . . . It is exceedingly im-portant that we have men at the beginning capable of thinking like white men, and not those who have been systematically oppressed. . . . For the sake of your race you should sacrifice something of your present comfort for the purpose of being as grand in that respect as the white people. . . ." In arguing that black Americans should depart for Central America, Lincoln alluded to "the similarity of climate with your native land [Africa]—thus being suited to your physical condition."[16] The belief that blacks could flourish only in tropical climates was part of nineteenth-century white racist ideology.

The August 15 *New York Tribune* carried the headline: THE COLONIZA-TION OF PEOPLE OF AFRICAN DESCENT / Interview with President Lincoln / SPEECH OF THE PRESIDENT / He Holds that the White and Black Races Cannot Dwell Together / He Urges Intelligent Colored Men to Exert Themselves for Colonization / He Suggests Central America as the Colony.[17] The next day the same newspaper editorialized, "with all defer-ence to the President, we suggest that before our country begins the ardu-ous, expensive task of exporting to some foreign shore Four Million of her loyal people, she should finish up the little job she has at hand by [expatria-tion] of some thousands of her leading traitors. . . ."[18] William Lloyd Garrison remarked, "President Lincoln may colonize himself if he choose, but it is an impertinent act, on his part, to propose the getting rid of those who are as good as himself."[19]

A minority of black Americans had long supported colonization. In 1852, in *The Condition, Elevation, Emigration, and Destiny of the Colored People of the United States,* Martin Delany had argued that black Americans could find freedom only in a country in which they were the majority. Delany helped organize an emigrationist convention in Cleveland in 1854, and in his utopian novel *Blake; or the Huts of America* (1859–62), he imagined the establishment of a black republic in Cuba.[20] But the overwhelming majority of free blacks in the North were quick to denounce Lincoln's colonization scheme in mass meetings, and Frederick Douglass asserted that it showed "his contempt for Negroes."[21] The prospect of exchanging slavery in the cotton South for drudgery in the coal mines of Central America failed to inspire most black Americans, who, unlike Lincoln, Mitchell, Clay, Jefferson, and other white colonizationists, thought of the United States, not Africa, as their "native land."

ON SEPTEMBER 22, 1862, the battle of Antietam was only a partial success because Lee's army escaped from the forces of George McClellan, commander of the Union army. But Antietam was enough of a victory that Lincoln could issue the preliminary Emancipation Proclamation without his action appearing to be evidence of Northern weakness.

On that day Lincoln issued the Preliminary Proclamation. To pressure the Southern rebels into laying down their arms, Lincoln threatened that as of January 1, 1863, slaves in states or areas still in rebellion would be declared free. At the same time, in an attempt to cement the slaveholding border states to the Union, Lincoln recommended to Congress that it compensate slave states not in rebellion to induce them to emancipate their slaves. If the Confederate rebels ended the insurrection within one hundred days, the Southern states would be readmitted to the Union without interference with the institution of slavery.

In the Preliminary Proclamation, Lincoln promised "that the effort to colonize persons of African descent, with their consent, upon this continent, or elsewhere, with the previously obtained consent of the Governments existing there, will be continued."[22] The Emancipation Proclamation is usually treated in isolation from Lincoln's plans for shipping both freeborn blacks and freed slaves out of the United States. However, emancipation and colonization were inextricably linked in his mind.[23] "Following the preliminary proclamation, and as a part of the plan, was the question of deporting and colonizing the colored race," Secretary of the Navy Gideon Welles recalled in 1872. "This was a part of the President's scheme, and had occupied his mind some time before the project for emancipation was adopted, although the historians, biographers, and commentators have made slight, if any, allusion to it. The president, however, and a portion of his Cabinet considered them inseparable, and that deportation should accompany and be a part of the emancipation movement."[24] The Cabinet meeting of September 22, 1862, at which Lincoln read the Preliminary Emancipation Proclamation, which was published the next day, was followed two days later, on September 24, by another Cabinet meeting convened to discuss the removal of blacks from the country. Welles, who was present at the meeting, recorded Lincoln as saying that he "thought it essential to provide an asylum for a race which we had emancipated, but which could never be recognized or admitted to be our equals."[25] Welles supported colonization as did all of the Cabinet except for Secretary of the Treasury Salmon P. Chase, who was closest to the abolitionists in his views, and Secretary of State William Seward. Seward believed that blacks were inferior to whites, but he objected to colonization because of "the self evident principle that all *natives* of a country have an *equal* right to its soil."[26]

On September 26, Lincoln convened the Cabinet again to hear Attorney General Edward Bates read a paper on the subject. According to Welles, "Mr. Bates was for compulsory deportation," but, "The President objected unequivocally to compulsion. Their emigration must be voluntary and without expense to themselves."[27] According to Welles: "Opposed to the whole system of enslavement, but believing the Africans were mentally an inferior race, [Lincoln] believed that any attempt to make them and the whites one people would tend to the degradation of the whites without materially elevating the blacks, but that separation would promote the happiness of each." Lincoln believed that emancipation and colonization were "to be parts of one system, and that must be carried forward together."[28] For his part, Welles shared Lincoln's doubts about black competence: "Until I can be satisfied that they are capable of enjoying and maintaining civil rights, I shall be opposed to their having and exercising in this country the privileges of freemen."[29]

The South did not take up Lincoln's offer to lay down arms in return for the preservation of slavery. Karl Marx observed in November 1862: "Of

Lincoln's emancipation, one still sees no effect up to the present, save that from fear of a Negro inundation the Northwest has voted Democratic."[30]

LINCOLN OFFERED THE South yet another bargain in his annual message to Congress of December 1, 1862. His plan for what he called "gradual emancipation and deportation" required three amendments to the Constitution. The thirteenth would have required the states to abolish slavery by January 1, 1900; the fourteenth would have required the federal government to pay compensation to the owners of the minority of slaves who had already been set free "by the chances of war"; and the fifteenth would have authorized Congress to "appropriate money, and otherwise provide, for colonizing free colored persons, with their own consent, at any place or places without the United States." The vast majority of the "free colored persons" initially colonized abroad would have been the free blacks of the North, not the slaves of the South, whose emancipation could be delayed until the beginning of the twentieth century. In other words, Lincoln's scheme was designed to remove free blacks from the North while confining enslaved blacks to the South until they could be deported as well.

Trying to allay the fear of black competition by Northern white workers, Lincoln argued that freed blacks would not move north in great numbers: "Their old masters will give them wages at least until new laborers can be procured; and the freed men, in turn, will gladly give their labor for the wages, till new homes can be found for them, in congenial climes, with people of their own blood and race. This proposition can be trusted on the mutual interests involved. And, in any event, cannot the north decide for itself, whether to receive them?"[31]

"And, in any event, cannot the north decide for itself, whether to receive them?" Lincoln is pointing out that if freed blacks in the South attempted to move north, the Northern states had the power to keep them out by means of Black Laws, such as those of Illinois, which imposed cruel penalties on free blacks found inside their borders.

In all of the volumes of commentary on Lincoln, this sentence has never been emphasized. And yet it is a key to Lincoln's thought about race and slavery. In chapter 3 it was pointed out that the nonextension of slavery and the enactment of Black Laws deterring immigration by free blacks to the Northern and Western states were two complementary halves of a single system to confine as many blacks as possible, slave and free, to the South. In Lincoln's plan for compensated emancipation and colonization, at least as of 1862, the South was to be a holding pen in which former slaves, in a state of quasi-serfdom as "apprentices" or wage laborers working on the same plantations, would be held until they could be "deported" to a foreign country. Needless to say, Lincoln's system would collapse if ex-slaves had the right to move anywhere in the United States to obtain jobs and homes. Ever logical, Lincoln has anticipated that possibility and devised the solution: The ex-slaves would be fenced into the South by state laws in the North that ban black immigration. Lincoln's reminder to the Northern states that they could outlaw immigration by free blacks was consistent with the Free-Soil ideology that he shared with most of his fellow Republicans. With the exception of the abolitionist minority in the party, most Republicans thought that the purpose of their movement was not simply to keep slavery confined to the South; it was to keep most blacks, slave or free, confined to the South. And even if Lincoln's panacea of colonization failed, state black laws in the North and West would make it possible for free blacks to be ghettoized in the South indefinitely, reducing the possibility of economic competition and racial intermarriage among whites and blacks in the rest of the country.

"And, in any event, cannot the north decide for itself, whether to receive them?" Here is a summary of the Black Laws of Indiana, which ensured that the state in which Lincoln spent much of his childhood would not "receive" large numbers of free blacks: "1. Negroes and mulattoes not allowed to come into the State. 2. All contracts with such negroes and mulattoes declared to be void. 3. Any person encouraging them to come, or giving them employment, to be fined from $10 to $500. 4. Negroes and mulattoes not to be allowed to vote. 5. No negro, or mulatto having even one-eighth part of negro blood, shall marry a white person; and punishes a violation of the law with from one to ten year's imprisonment, and fine of from $1,000 to $5,000. 6. Any person counseling or assisting such marriage shall be fined from $100 to $1,000, and the marriage to be void. 7. Negroes and mulattoes are not allowed to testify against white persons, or send their children to the free schools with white children, or hold any office."[32]

The antiblack laws of Illinois that Lincoln supported, like those of Indiana, were successful in deterring large numbers of free blacks from seeking to live there. At the beginning of the Civil War, blacks, totaling 7,628, made up less than one-half of 1 percent of the Illinois population.[33] The Black Laws continued to be enforced during the Civil War. Former slaves, or "contrabands," began to migrate to Illinois, some of them to a federal camp established for them. In order to deter further black migration, city officials in Carthage, Illinois, convicted six blacks of violating the state Black Laws and sold them into slavery to the highest bidders. This had the desired effect of discouraging flight by freed slaves to Lincoln's state.[34] Lincoln had both voted for these laws and expressed approval of them—for example, in Charleston, Illinois, on September 18, 1858. "Now, my opinion is that the different States have the power to make a Negro a citizen under the Constitution of the United States, if they choose. The Dred Scott decision decides that they have not that power. If the State of Illinois had that power, I should be opposed to the exercise of it."[35]

"And, in any event, cannot the north decide for itself, whether to receive them?" This sentence in the annual message of 1862 is ignored by those who quote the grand rhetoric of Lincoln's conclusion: "Fellow-citizens, we cannot escape history. . . . In giving freedom to the slave, we assure freedom to the free—honorable alike in what we give, and what we preserve. We shall nobly save, or meanly lose, the last best hope of earth." Read carefully: The "freedom" to be given to the slave was not to include the freedom to move from Mississippi or Alabama to Detroit, Michigan, or Chicago, Illinois. According to Lincoln, the "freed men" could be prevented by state Black Laws from living in most of the United States—but they would be perfectly free to leave the country.

"And, in any event, cannot the north decide for itself, whether to receive them?" This sentence marks the moral low point of Lincoln's career.

LINCOLN'S OPPOSITION TO racial integration did not matter to the many blacks and Northern abolitionists who responded with jubilation to his issuance of the final Emancipation Proclamation on January 1, 1863. The proclamation designated the areas in rebellion and ordered the U.S. military to recognize freedom of all slaves within them, and would take freed slaves as soldiers in the U.S. Army. Slavery remained intact in Maryland, Delaware, Kentucky, West Virginia, Missouri, and in one Confederate state, Tennessee. In a letter of January 8, 1863, Lincoln explained that the South had refused to accept the bargain he had offered—reunion in return for no interference with slavery—and the proposed offer had expired: "After the commencement of hostilities I struggled nearly a year and a half to get along without touching the 'institution'; and when finally I conditionally determined to touch it, I gave a hundred days fair notice of my purpose, to all the States and people, within which time they could have turned it wholly aside, by simply again becoming good citizens of the United States. They chose to disregard it, and I made the peremptory proclamation on what appeared to me to be military necessity."[36]

The limited nature of the proclamation as a war measure incapable of effecting the abolition of slavery, which only the states or a federal constitutional amendment could do, was stressed by Lincoln in a letter to Salmon P. Chase, one of the most radical members of his Cabinet. The "original proclamation has no constitutional or legal justification, except as a war measure." If he sought to abolish slavery by presidential power, "must I not do so, without the argument of military necessity, and so, without any argument, except the one that I think the measure politically expedient, or morally right? Would I not thus give up all footing upon constitution or law? Would I not thus be in the boundless field of absolutism? . . . Could it fail to be perceived that without any further stretch, I might . . . change any law in any state?"[37]

At this stage Lincoln proposed that the ex-slaves, instead of being granted full civil rights and political equality, would exist in a legal and constitutional limbo of "apprenticeship." A few days after issuing the Emancipation Proclamation, on January 8, 1863, Lincoln told General John A. McClernand that the Southern states would be free to adopt "systems of apprenticeship for the colored people, conforming substantially to the most approved plans of gradual emancipation."[38]

On July 11, 1863, on the first day that draftees in New York City were called up, the New York Draft Riots began. They escalated into the bloodiest urban riots in American history. Mobs of working-class whites, many of them Irish immigrants, massacred blacks. Mitchell reported that when, on August 18, seven months after the Emancipation Proclamation was signed, he asked Lincoln whether "colonization was still the policy of the Administration," Lincoln replied, "I have never thought so much on any subject and arrived at a conclusion so definite as I have in this case, and in after years found myself wrong." According to Mitchell, Lincoln mused that "it would have been much better to separate the races than to have such scenes as those in New York the other day, where Negroes were hanged to lamp posts."[39]

While Lincoln wanted to enlist black troops, he worried about spontaneous slave insurrections in the South. On November 24, 1863, John Hay recorded in his diary a conversation with the president: "He thinks that the enormous influx of slave population into the Gulf states does not strengthen slavery in them. He says, 'It creates in those states a vast preponderance of the population of a servile and oppressed class. It fearfully imperils the lives and safety of the ruling class. Now, the slaves are quiet, choosing to wait for the deliverance they hope from us, rather than endanger their lives by a frantic struggle for freedom. . . . But if they [white Southerners] should succeed in secession the Gulf states would be more endangered than ever. The slaves, despairing of liberty through us would take the matter into their own hands, and no longer opposed by the government of the United States they would succeed.' "[40]

THE NEXT IN a series of Lincoln's plans for reconstruction, which continued to change under the pressure of events, was found in his Proclamation of Amnesty and Reconstruction of December 8, 1863. Lincoln promised to grant a full pardon to everyone who had "directly or by implication, participated in the existing rebellion," with the exception of Confederate political and military officers, and promised "restoration of all rights of property, except as to slaves." Those applying for a pardon would have to take an oath to "faithfully support, protect, and defend the Constitution of the United States and the Union of the States thereunder" and to "abide by and faithfully support all acts of congress passed during the existing rebellion with reference to slaves, so long and so far as not repealed, modified, or held void by congress" as well as "all proclamations of the President made during the existing rebellion having reference to slaves, so long and so far as not modified or declared void by decision of the supreme court."

Under Lincoln's plan, he would grant recognition to a state as soon as a group of citizens equal in number to 10 percent of those who took part in the presidential election of 1860 took the oath and established a state government that abolished slavery. (The so-called Restored Government of Virginia had already been recognized by Lincoln and Congress.) A commitment to abolish slavery was introduced stealthily into the 10 percent plan, because everyone taking the loyalty oath was obliged to abide by all presidential and congressional measures affecting slavery undertaken to date. However, Lincoln softened the blow by proposing "apprenticeship" as an alternative to full black equality. He said that he would not object "to any provision which may be adopted by such State government in relation to the freed people of such State, which shall recognize and declare their permanent freedom, provide for their education, and which may yet be consistent, as a temporary arrangement, with their present condition as a laboring, landless, and homeless class." Lincoln almost certainly had separate-but-equal systems of segregated public education in mind along with compulsory labor contracts for the ex-slaves, modeled possibly on those that General Nathaniel Banks imposed on former slaves in Louisiana requiring them to remain on plantations and continue to work in their former tasks.[41] The Radical Republicans in Congress opposed Lincoln's plan.

On December 8, 1863, the same day that he issued his Proclamation of Amnesty and Reconstruction, Lincoln delivered his annual message to Congress. In it he justified the Emancipation Proclamation and the subsequent enlistment of black soldiers as well as his Proclamation of Amnesty and Reconstruction. "Thus we have the new reckoning," Lincoln told Congress, signaling the shift from reunion with slavery intact to reunion without slavery. At first Lincoln hoped that the states would abolish slavery individually, perhaps with federal compensation and colonization of the freed blacks abroad. Now, as a condition of readmission to the Union, the states would have to treat Lincoln's Emancipation Proclamation and other wartime orders in connection with slavery as permanent law. "I may add at this point, that while I remain in my present position I shall not attempt to retract or modify the emancipation proclamation; nor shall I return to slavery any person who is free by the terms of that proclamation, or by any of the acts of Congress."[42]

For a time Lincoln feared that he would not be reelected, and a group of Radical Republicans dissatisfied with his leadership engaged in an abortive attempt to nominate John C. Fremont for president. However, military successes by Union forces in Virginia and Georgia helped Lincoln win. Bolstered by his reelection, Lincoln, in his annual message to Congress on December 6, 1864, called on both houses to pass the Thirteenth Amendment so the states could ratify it. The Thirteenth Amendment would ensure that all prior actions by Lincoln and Congress to undermine slavery were legal and could never be overturned by the Supreme Court. Section 1 read: "Neither slavery nor involuntary servitude, except as a punishment of crime whereof the party shall have been duly convicted, shall exist within the United States, or any place subject to their jurisdiction." While Lincoln used his political skills to ensure that Congress enacted the Thirteenth Amendment, he did not live to see it ratified.

The evolution of Lincoln's approach to restoring the Union is illustrated by the three possible Thirteenth Amendments that Lincoln endorsed or proposed between 1861 and 1865. On March 4, 1861, he endorsed a proposed amendment to prevent the federal government from interfering with slavery where it existed; on December 1, 1862, he proposed that the federal government fund the abolition of slavery by the states; and in January 1865 he endorsed the abolition of slavery by an amendment to the federal Constitution, signed by him on February 1, 1865, which became the actual Thirteenth Amendment when it was ratified after his death.

Initially Lincoln prosecuted the Civil War with a single goal in mind: the restoration of the Union as it had been before the war, with antebellum institutions including slavery intact. If Confederate resistance had crumbled and the war had been brief, as Lincoln hoped, this would have been the result. In the course of what became a prolonged and ever more devastating conflict, he changed his mind and added a second goal that many abolitionists and others had urged on him from the beginning—the abolition of slavery by the states themselves with federal compensation, or by the option he finally favored, the Thirteenth Amendment to the U.S. Constitution. To the two political goals of reunion and emancipation, many Radical Republicans added a third: the achievement of full political and social equality for black Americans. Lincoln never viewed this as one of his wartime goals. For him it was sufficient that the Union was restored and that slavery was abolished.

Lincoln's last offer to the rebel South was made to the Confederate commissioners, including Confederate vice president Alexander Stephens, with whom he met at Hampton Roads, Virginia, on February 3, 1865. Lincoln refused to abandon his demand for the unconditional surrender of the South. However, he promised to use his presidential power to grant pardons generously, and he proposed that the Southern states ratify the Thirteenth

Amendment in return for federal compensation to slave owners. When Lincoln returned to Washington and proposed that the government pay $400 million to Southern slave owners in return for the abolition of slavery, his entire Cabinet opposed the idea and he dropped it. The war continued.

Ironically, emancipation as a war measure was adopted by the South out of desperation in the final days of the Civil War. On March 13, 1865, Jefferson Davis signed a bill passed by the Confederate Congress that permitted the enlistment of black soldiers. The presidential directive implementing the law, General Order No. 14, commanded: "No slave will be accepted as a recruit unless with his own consent and with the approbation of his master by a written instrument conferring, as far as he may, the rights of a freedman."[43] The measure came too late and was never implemented.

By the time the war ended, Lincoln's plans for colonization had collapsed. The project of resettling blacks in Central America came to an end after the governments of Honduras, Nicaragua, and Costa Rica protested against the scheme in the summer and fall of 1862. Having abandoned the idea of a Central American colony, Lincoln, in December 1862, contracted with a businessman to settle five thousand blacks on Ile a Vache, an island off the coast of Haiti, at government expense. That same month, in his annual message to Congress, Lincoln explained that "several of the Spanish American republics have protested against the sending of such colonies to their respective territories. . . . Liberia and Haiti are, as yet, the only countries to which colonists of African descent from here, could go with certainty of being received and adopted as citizens; and I regret to say such persons, contemplating colonization, do not seem so willing to migrate to those countries, as to some others, nor so willing as I think their interest demands."[44]

Early in 1863 Lincoln reportedly spoke of a plan "to remove the whole colored race of the slave states into Texas." Evidently, Lincoln also considered Florida as a reservation for blacks.[45] In the spring of 1864, after many of the black colonists on Ile a Vache died of disease and starvation, the survivors were brought back to the United States and Congress canceled the money it had appropriated for colonization.

THE CIVIL WAR formally ended on April 9, 1865, when Lee surrendered to Grant at Appomattox. The controversy over Reconstruction remained. In July 1864 critics of Lincoln's policy in Congress had passed the Wade-Davis Bill. Under this plan, before a state could be restored, 50 percent of its male voters would have to take an "ironclad" oath that they had never voluntarily supported the confederacy. Lincoln used a "pocket veto" to prevent the Wade-Davis Bill from becoming law. Ignoring it, he proceeded on the basis of his own plan. By the time the war ended, under his scheme new governments had been organized in Louisiana, Arkansas, Tennessee, and Virginia. Congress refused to seat the representatives and senators from these states.

The debate over reconstruction was the subject of Lincoln's last public address, an impromptu speech he gave to a jubilant crowd that gathered on the White House lawn on April 11, two days after the surrender of Lee to Grant. He dismissed arguments about whether the states had reverted to territorial status or not: "Finding themselves safely at home, it would be utterly immaterial whether they had ever been abroad." Lincoln concluded with the mysterious promise that he was preparing "to make some new announcement to the people of the South . . . I am considering, and shall not fail to act, when satisfied that action will be proper."[46] Lincoln's plan, if any, remained a mystery, because a few days later, on April 14, he was murdered at Ford's Theater by one of the spectators who had listened to him on the White House lawn the night of the eleventh: John Wilkes Booth.

Following Lincoln's assassination, Vice President Andrew Johnson succeeded to the presidency. He issued an amnesty proclamation of his own on May 29, 1865. It was harsher than Lincoln's had been. Johnson, a War Democrat who had briefly been the Unionist governor of Tennessee, was a populist who despised the rich slave-owning oligarchy almost as much as he detested blacks. His plan to put yeoman farmers and white artisans in charge in the South included a provision to disenfranchise all Southerners who had estates worth twenty thousand dollars or more. Initially the radicals were pleased that Johnson, unlike Lincoln, vehemently denounced the rebels and shared their goal of a social revolution in the South.

Under Johnson's plan the Southern states were swiftly reorganized during the period in which Congress was adjourned between April and December 1865. Provisional governors appointed by Johnson supervised state conventions that repealed secession ordinances and abolished slavery.

The ratification of the Thirteenth Amendment by the states posed a political challenge. Three-fourths of the states must ratify an amendment to the U.S. Constitution. When the Civil War began there were 34 states, Kansas having been admitted on January 29, 1861. The three-fourths rule meant that 26 states were needed to ratify an amendment. But there were 15 slave states and only 19 free states—a number that grew to 20 when Maryland abolished slavery in 1864. During the war two more free states—Nevada and West Virginia—were added by Congress, which also abolished slavery in the nine territories that were to become states in the future. However, increasing the number of states also increased the number required to ratify a constitutional amendment by the three-fourths amendment rule. Having been approved by Congress in January 1865, the Thirteenth Amendment was finally ratified after the war at gunpoint on December 6, 1865, by all Confederate states except Florida, Mississippi, and Texas.

When state legislative elections were held, many of the winners were former Confederate officers who had been disenfranchised. Instead of ordering new elections, Johnson began issuing numerous pardons. The new legislatures of every state except Mississippi ratified the Thirteenth Amendment. At the same time, however, many of the new state legislatures, beginning with Mississippi in 1865, enacted "black codes" that reduced the freedmen to a status of quasi-slavery. The newly created Ku Klux Klan began to terrorize freedmen as well as Southern white Unionists and Union soldiers, white and black.

Perceiving an attempt to restore slavery in a disguised form, Congress passed the Civil Rights Act of 1865. Johnson vetoed it, but Congress overrode his veto and passed it in 1866. Northern opinion turned against Johnson's lenient policy, and Congress refused to seat Southern senators and representatives when it convened in December 1865. Over Johnson's veto, Congress passed reconstruction laws such as the Civil Rights Act and the Freedmen's Bureau Bill. The new president, a former Southern Democrat, denounced radical members of Congress and alienated moderate Republicans. Opposition to Johnson in Congress coalesced around the members of the Joint Committee on Reconstruction. On April 28, 1866, the committee declared that the elections in the South were invalid because the region had been in a state of civil disorder.

While most congressional Republicans agreed on the importance of enacting a Fourteenth Amendment that would outlaw the black codes and similar attempts by Southern states to re-create the substance of slavery without the name, the radicals and the moderates disagreed about the method. Radicals like Wendell Phillips and Thaddeus Stevens wanted to amend the Constitution to prevent discrimination on the basis of race by federal, state, or local governments. Stevens introduced a resolution to this effect on December 5, 1865: "All national and State laws shall be equally applicable to every citizen, and no discrimination shall be made on account of race and color."[47] But earlier, in a fight against a nondiscrimination provision in the Civil Rights Act of 1866, the moderate John Bingham of Ohio had pointed out that most Northern as well as Southern states discriminated against blacks in their constitutions and their laws: "By the constitution of my own State neither the right of the elective franchise nor the franchise of office can be conferred upon any citizen of the United States save upon a white citizen of the United States. What do you propose to do by this bill? You propose to make it a misdemeanor, punishable upon conviction by fine and imprisonment in the penitentiary, for the Governor of Ohio to obey the requirements of the constitution of the State. . . ."[48] Bingham offered an alternate, weaker amendment that would protect the "privileges and immunities" of everyone in every state. What did "privileges and immunities" mean? From the legislative history it is clear that Bingham and other members of Congress intended to guarantee black citizens minimal property and procedural rights without guaranteeing them the political right of suffrage or the right to hold office or striking down "separate but equal" treatment in education and public accommodations. A good statement of the rights that moderate Republicans like Bingham sought to protect were those enumerated in the Civil Rights Act of 1866: the "right to make and enforce contracts, to sue, be parties, and give evidence, to inherit, purchase, lease, sell, hold, and convey real and personal property, and to full and equal benefit of all laws and proceedings for the security of person and property, and shall be subject to like punishment, pains and penalties, and to none other, any law, statute, ordinance, regulation, or custom to the contrary notwithstanding."[49]

The Fourteenth Amendment was intended therefore to provide blacks with minimal legal and property rights while leaving suffrage and jury service to the discretion of the states. The Fourteenth Amendment's only penalty for not granting black suffrage was diminishing the state's representation in Congress. Even while the Radical Republicans, motivated in part by a desire to forestall the return of white conservative Democrats to Washington, promoted black suffrage in the South, Northern states were hastily disenfranchising blacks. Between 1865 and 1868 Wisconsin, Connecticut, Minnesota, Nebraska, New Jersey, Ohio, Pennsylvania, and Michigan enacted legislation against black voting.[50]

In 1863 the *New York Times,* expressing the opinion of most Northern whites, derided the abolitionist Wendell Phillips for his suggestion that the Constitution be made color-blind: "He would not content himself with compelling every State to make an end of Slavery forthwith, but would also force them to clear their statute books of every distinction between the black man and the white. If Maine law doesn't allow black men upon juries, the Federal arm must force it; if Massachusetts law don't [*sic*] allow them to muster indiscriminately into the militia, the Federal arm must force it. So, too, must the Federal arm force New-York to abolish all of her property limitations upon the elective franchise possessed by black men; Ohio to strike down every bar against the election of black men to any and all offices; Illinois to abrogate her statutes against black immigration into her borders; . . . Maryland to expunge every law forbidding amalgamation by marriage; and Georgia, and Mississippi, and Alabama, and Louisiana to remit the entire civil control to the black majority now within their limits."[51] Thanks to the deeply rooted racial prejudices of the majority of white Northern Republicans, slavery was replaced by segregation rather than by a color-blind political and social order in many Northern states as well as in the South.

In 1866 Congress approved the Fourteenth Amendment. Except for Tennessee, every Southern state refused to ratify it. Antiblack pogroms followed in Memphis on May 1 and in New Orleans on July 30, 1866. The Northern congressional elections of 1866 strengthened the radicals, who benefited from Northern fears that ex-Confederates would regain power in the South and in the national government. In 1867 the First, Second, and Third Reconstruction Acts passed over Johnson's veto. The First Reconstruction Act, which went into effect on March 2, 1867, abolished the reconstructed governments of the Southern states and returned the South to federal military rule. With the exception of Tennessee, rewarded for its ratification of the Fourteenth Amendment, the South was divided into five military districts.

The radicals claimed that Congress rather than the presidency had the right to control military reconstruction. To reduce the power of the president over the military, Congress passed the Tenure of Office Act, which held that the president needed the consent of the Senate for the removal as well as the appointment of certain federal officials. In practice this created an alliance against the president between Radical Republicans in Congress and their allies in the executive branch. When Johnson insisted on firing Edwin M. Stanton, the radical Secretary of War, without congressional approval, the House impeached him in February 1868. By one vote the Senate failed to convict and remove Johnson in May. But Johnson had been isolated and defeated. A fourth and final reconstruction act was enacted by Congress over his opposition in 1868. Also in 1868 the Fourteenth Amendment was finally ratified with the help of the reconstruction regimes in the South. The Fifteenth Amendment, ratified in 1870, guaranteed the right to vote to all male citizens regardless of color or previous condition of servitude.

In 1868 Ulysses S. Grant, allied with the Radical Republicans in Congress, was elected president. Most of the Southern states had been readmitted by 1870 under the rules of the radical Congress, after they ratified the Fourteenth Amendment (and also the Fifteenth Amendment, in the case of the last states to be reconstructed). However, the Ku Klux Klan and other groups continued to wage a guerrilla war against federal troops as well as blacks and white Republicans. In 1871 Congress passed the Act to Enforce the Fourteenth Amendment (Ku Klux Klan Act). But the Northern public was growing weary of the cost of Reconstruction, and white Southerners had coalesced as a bloc to support the national Democratic Party against the hated Republicans.

On March 1, 1875, Congress passed a civil rights act giving blacks the right to equal treatment in transportation and public places. The Supreme Court later held that it was unconstitutional. But the tide was turning. A small number of black representatives were elected to the House and Senate, and a mixed-race politician, P. B. S. Pinchback, briefly served as acting governor of Louisiana in the winter of 1872–73. But in 1876 Wade Hampton, a former Confederate leader, was sworn in as governor of South Carolina while the U.S. Senate voted not to seat Pinchback as senator from Louisiana.

During the 1876 presidential election, each of the three Southern states that still had Republican "carpetbagger" governments—Florida, South Carolina, and Louisiana—sent in two sets of returns from rival forces. A rigged electoral commission with eight Republicans and seven Democrats gave the presidency to the Republican Rutherford B. Hayes instead of the Democrat Samuel J. Tilden. In return, the Republicans agreed to end Reconstruction and all federal troops were withdrawn from the South.

The result of the Compromise of 1877 was what Southern conservatives called the "redemption" of the South. In state after state, ex-Confederates rose to power. Reconstruction-era constitutions were scrapped. Violence and intimidation were used to prevent blacks and white dissidents from voting or running for office. In the early 1900s the Southern elite in a number of states—alarmed by the challenge to its authority of Southern Populism, which followed the Reconstruction challenge—enacted measures such as literacy tests and poll taxes to strip the right to vote from all blacks and as much as half of the white population. A harsh regime of racial apartheid was formalized, and poor whites as well as blacks found themselves reduced to peonage as sharecroppers. The Southern oligarchy had lost its battle for independence, but by 1900 it had won the war to restore its domination of regional society. Its supremacy was not challenged significantly again until the civil rights revolution that followed World War II.

During and after the civil rights revolution, Reconstruction was viewed as a precedent by many civil rights activists. While many Radical Republicans sincerely believed in racial integration in the 1860s and 1870s, they were a minority in their own party. Reconstruction was motivated more by the desire of Republican politicians to maintain control of the federal government than by any interest in the welfare of black Southerners. Lincoln's party was a sectional party in danger of losing its majority status in the federal government. After the war began, seventeen of the nineteen states in the North had Republican governors. And as a result of the withdrawal of most Southern Democrats from Congress, only 50 out of 181 members of the House were Democrats, and only 14 out of 66 senators when Congress convened in special session at Lincoln's request on July 4, 1861.[52] The 1862 midterm congressional elections, which gave the Democrats a few more seats in the House, did not endanger Republican control of that body, and the Republicans picked up five seats in the Senate.

But the end of the Civil War threatened Republicans with the prospect that with the help of votes from the restored Southern states, the Democratic Party would recapture not only the House and the Senate but also the presidency. Between 1876 and 1892 the Republican presidential candidate lost the popular vote to the Democratic candidate in four out of five elections, never getting more than 48.25 percent of the popular vote.[53]

Radical Reconstruction, for any purpose, was doomed to fail because of the lack of adequate federal force. As a result of postwar demobilization, the U.S. military shrank from more than 1 million on May 1, 1865, to fewer than 200,000 by November 12, 1865. The number of troops assigned to occupy the South, never more than 10,000, declined to a mere 3,000 by the time of the 1876 election, which led to the end of Reconstruction.[54] The outcome of both the Civil War and Reconstruction resulted from the consensus in the white North. Northerners were willing to fight and expend vast sums to prevent the South from leaving the Union. But they were not willing to pay a high price to eliminate white supremacy and one-party Democratic monopoly in the South. And so the elite of the South lost the battle for independence but won the war for regional autonomy within the Union.

WHAT IF LINCOLN had not been murdered by John Wilkes Booth? If Lincoln had completed his second term, what form would Reconstruction have taken? Unfortunately, Lincoln left no hints about his plans for Reconstruction. Nevertheless, on the basis of his policies and his philosophy, informed speculation is possible.

It seems likely that Lincoln, like Johnson, would have been opposed by Radical Republicans in Congress for being too lenient toward the defeated South. However, it seems equally likely that relations between Congress and the White House would not have degenerated into political warfare, as they did under Johnson, for several reasons. To begin with, Lincoln, unlike Johnson, would have been the popular president, elected twice, who had led the Union to victory in the war. His prestige would have deterred all but the fiercest critics in Congress. And while Johnson was a Democrat, Lincoln was the leader of the Republican Party.

In addition, Lincoln, unlike Johnson, was a master politician. He would have done anything necessary to prevent being isolated by a coalition of political enemies. He might have sided with moderates in Congress to isolate the radicals. Or—if Northern anger at the unrepentant attitude of white Southerners had led to calls for harsh punishment—he might have placated the Radical Republicans by adopting a stricter policy, moderating it in his characteristically cautious way.

While it is easy to imagine Lincoln adopting a harsher attitude toward the South in response to postwar Southern provocations, it is difficult to believe that he would have repudiated the theory under which he had waged the war. Against the radicals who claimed that the Southern states had left the Union and become mere territories, Lincoln had consistently maintained that the states remained intact and should be readmitted with a minimum of political upheaval. This approach committed Lincoln to a minimal reconstruction plan—the abolition of slavery by state ratification of the Thirteenth Amendment, and the swift restoration of functioning governments and Southern representatives in the House of Representatives and the U.S. Senate. If Lincoln had lived it is almost certain that there would have been nothing like Radical Reconstruction.

What is more, if Lincoln had lived it is unlikely that he would have supported anything like the Fourteenth and Fifteenth Amendments. On August 28, 1860, the *New York Times* described Lincoln's views: "He declares his opposition to negro suffrage, and to everything looking towards placing negroes upon a footing of political and social equality with the whites;—but he asserts for them a perfect equality of civil and personal rights under the Constitution."[55] There is no evidence that he ever changed his mind about black social and political equality. Lincoln envisioned something like the black codes in the form of "apprenticeship," which his own Secretary of the Treasury denounced, in a private letter to Henry Ward Beecher, as "qualified involuntary servitude."[56] Most blacks in the United States would exist in a condition above slavery but below full citizenship, with property rights and basic civil rights but not the right to vote.

He seems to have gone to his grave without imagining any amendments to the Constitution beyond the abolition of slavery. The Fourteenth

Amendment eradicated Black Laws by preventing the restriction of black migration by individual states. However, Lincoln apparently did not envision a constitutional amendment like the Fourteenth that would create national citizenship. Lincoln seems to have assumed that in the future, as in the past, states would be able to ban blacks from entering and taking up residence, as Illinois and many antebellum free states had done. Freedom for ex-slaves, it seems, would not necessarily mean freedom to move out of the South and live and work wherever black Americans chose. If Lincoln had lived, the Thirteenth Amendment might well have been the only constitutional amendment to emerge from the Civil War and Reconstruction. Slavery would have been abolished in every state, but the states would have retained their discretion to deny citizenship to blacks. Lincoln was willing to let the states deny the suffrage to black citizens; at most, he would "suggest" that black citizens be subject to literacy tests and property qualifications. Rejecting his advice, the reconstructed Unionist governments of which he approved denied black suffrage altogether.

In the aftermath of the civil rights revolution, some American historians argued that Lincoln experienced a late-life conversion to the ideal of a color-blind America, a conversion that had gone unnoticed not only by his contemporaries but also by American historians before the late twentieth century.[57] The evidence for this is slight, consisting chiefly of Lincoln's discussion four days before his death of the new constitution for the state of Louisiana: "It is . . . unsatisfactory to some that the elective franchise is not given to the colored man. I would myself prefer that it were now conferred on the very intelligent, and on those who serve our cause as soldiers."[58] Far from signaling Lincoln's conversion to a color-blind vision of society, this statement shows that he remained a segregationist to the very end of his life. Black and white abolitionists—the group Lincoln referred to as "some"—were demanding suffrage for all black men. Lincoln, however, was willing to exclude all black men from voting rights except for "the very intelligent, and . . . those who serve our cause as soldiers." How were the "very intelligent" to be distinguished from the rest of the adult black male population? Presumably by means of something like the "literacy tests" used in the segregated South to deny voting rights to most blacks for generations. Far from embracing the ideal of racial equality, Lincoln assumed that only some black men were "intelligent" enough to be entrusted with a right given to all white men, no matter how unintelligent.

While it is unlikely that Lincoln would have expended much if any political capital on behalf of black voting rights, one of the people who knew him best speculated that Lincoln, if he had lived, would have approved of the late-nineteenth-century movement to give women the vote. As a candidate for the legislature from New Salem in 1836, Lincoln wrote that he favored "admitting all whites to the right of suffrage who pay taxes or bear arms (by no means excluding females)." Of this his later law partner William Herndon wrote, "His broad plan for universal [sic] suffrage certainly commends itself to the ladies, and we need no further evidence to satisfy our minds of his position on the subject of 'Woman's Rights,' had he lived." Lincoln said that "the great questions of moral and social reforms, under which he classed universal suffrage, temperance, and slavery," according to Herndon, "must first find lodgment with the most enlightened souls who stamp them with their approval. In God's own time they will be organized into law and thus woven into the fabric of our institutions."[59]

I T   I s   N o t clear that by his death Lincoln had abandoned his belief in colonization. "I am happy that the President has sloughed off that idea of colonization," Lincoln's secretary John Hay wrote in his diary on July 1, 1864.[60] As late as November 30, 1864, Attorney General Edward Bates gave an affirmative answer to Lincoln's question of whether Mitchell could continue as "your assistant or aid [sic] in the matter of executing the several acts of Congress relating to the emigration or colonizing of the freed Blacks," even though Congress had embargoed funds for further experiments with colonization.[61] General Benjamin F. Butler claimed that shortly before his death, Lincoln had told him in a meeting in the White House: "I wish you would carefully examine the question and give me your views upon it and go into the figures, and you did before in some degree, so as to show whether the Negroes can be exported. . . ." According to Butler, he told Lincoln two days later: "Mr. President, I have gone very carefully over my calculations as to the power of the country to export the Negroes of the South, and I assure you that, using all your naval vessels and all the merchant marine fit to cross the seas with safety, it will be impossible for you to transport to the nearest place for them . . . half as fast as Negro children will be born here."[62] Although some historians have questioned Butler's veracity, there is no reason to doubt his account in light of Lincoln's obsession with the colonization scheme.

"Lincoln was a colonizationist, as Jefferson, Madison and Henry Clay were," his old Illinois acquaintance Henry Clay Whitney recalled in 1892. Whitney speculated that Lincoln "would have made still more heroic efforts, looking to that end, had he completed his second term; and his policy of emancipation was adopted, against both his judgment, desire and conscience . . ."[63]

As president, Ulysses Grant revived the colonization scheme, promoting the annexation of the Dominican Republic as a new home for "the entire colored population of the United States, should it choose to emigrate."[64] In 1898 Samuel Gompers, the president of the American Federation of Labor, proposed protecting white labor by expatriating blacks to Liberia or Cuba.[65] In the twentieth century the idea of colonization was kept alive by black nationalists and white supremacists such as the members of the Ku Klux Klan.

In June 1938 Theodore Bilbo, United States senator from Mississippi, proposed an amendment to a New Deal unemployment relief bill. His plan was to have the U.S. government "voluntarily" ship 12 million blacks to a "Greater Liberia" created by forcing Britain and France, in payment of their debts to the United States from World War I, to turn over four hundred thousand square miles of their African territories. As evidence that many blacks would voluntarily leave, he submitted a petition with signatures from forty-five states gathered by a black woman from Chicago, Mrs. Mattie Lena Gordon, the leader of a black nationalist group called the Peace Movement of Ethiopia. Bilbo, one of the most vicious racists in American politics at the time, cited Jefferson and Lincoln as his inspirations, and claimed correctly that his proposal was "the solution to the race problem which they advocated . . . When this task has been accomplished, what a great problem we will have solved for ourselves and our posterity."[66] Bilbo sought to avert what Jefferson, Madison, Clay, and Lincoln had sought to avert as well—the possibility of racial amalgamation. In his debate with Stephen A. Douglas on June 26, 1857, Lincoln had insisted, "I have said that the separation of the races is the only perfect preventive of amalgamation." Following World War II, Senator Bilbo published a book entitled *Separation or Mongrelization: Take Your Choice.*[67]

The history of Liberia provides a sad footnote to the colonization policy of Jefferson, Clay, Lincoln, and the rest. Only a small number of black Americans migrated to the country founded to provide a home for former slaves from the United States. In Liberia the former Americans and their descendants formed an oligarchy that exploited the native Africans. Until Liberia in the late twentieth century disintegrated completely amid scenes of horrifying carnage, it was ruled from the capital, Monrovia, named after the colonizationist and U.S. president James Monroe, by a party that took its name from the party of Henry Clay and the young Abraham Lincoln: the True Whig Party.

FOLLOWING RECONSTRUCTION, THE North abandoned the majority of black Americans to their fate as landless farmworkers or sharecroppers in the South, emancipated from slavery but stripped of rights. The plan of some Radical Republicans to break up Southern plantations and give former slaves "forty acres and a mule" probably would not have succeeded. Most freedmen, like many white farmers, might have lost their land during the depressions of the late nineteenth century and found themselves reduced to the status of tenant farmers. An alternative that was considered by Lincoln but never carried out was the federally sponsored industrialization of the South.

Henry Carey, the leading economist of the Republican Party, dreamed of promoting an industrial revolution in the South that would shatter the power of the plantation oligarchy in national politics. Already before the Civil War, German immigrants had operated the foundries at Selma, Alabama.[68] In the 1850s Carey's writings had inspired the Massachusetts Republican Eli Thayer and John C. Underwood, a New Yorker who had moved to Virginia, to found the North American Emigrant Aid and Homestead Company. In 1857 the company created a colony in West Virginia, intending to create the kind of diversified economy of farms and factories that Carey advocated. The enterprise failed, but not before it had excited Northern financiers, businessmen, and journalists as a model for Southern modernization.[69] Simon Cameron, a leading Republican, declared in 1858: "These poor white men of the South, who are our brothers, and our natural allies, must be taught . . . that we are battling for their rights. They will learn in time, that by acting with us, they will cease to be the 'mudsills of society.' "[70] In 1868 Horace Greeley suggested making the South safe for the Republican Party by sending Northern colonists to Florida (3,000), Arkansas, Alabama, Louisiana, and Mississippi (5,000 each), and Virginia, North Carolina, and Texas (1,000 each).[71]

In 1861 Carey lobbied Lincoln to encourage construction of a North-South railroad in order to promote the industrialization of the highland South, including Lincoln's native Kentucky: "How much more firm and stable might the antebellum union have been, had there developed then a policy which would have filled the hill country of the South with free white men engaged in mining coal and ore, making iron and cloth, and building school houses and churches, and establishing little libraries. . . ." Carey told his fellow disciple of Clay in the White House: "If Henry Clay's tariff views would have been carried out sooner there would have been no secession because the southern mineral region would long since have obtained control of the planting area. Some means must be found to enable these people of the hill country to profit of our present tariff. . . ."[72]

Lincoln, himself the child of "these people of the hill country" in the

South, acted on Carey's proposal. In a section of his December 3, 1861, address to Congress is buried the Carey-Lincoln plan for creating a social revolution in the Appalachians and Ozarks by means of government-catalyzed industrialization: "I deem it of importance that the loyal regions of East Tennessee and North Carolina should be connected with Kentucky, and other faithful parts of the Union, by railroad. I therefore recommend, as a military measure, that Congress provide for the construction of such road, as speedily as possible. Kentucky, no doubt, will co-operate, and, through her legislature, make the most judicious selection of a line."[73]

The immigration of skilled labor, merchants, and professionals—not only to a booming, almost all-white industrial Kentucky, Tennessee, and West Virginia but also to the plantation regions—was also part of their vision for the modernization of the South. In his next message to Congress on December 1, 1862, Lincoln argued that even if the emancipation of the slaves was not followed by their immediate colonization, jobs for white immigrant laborers would open up because the freedmen as wage laborers would choose to do less work: "If they stay in their old places, they jostle on white laborers; if they leave their old places, they leave them open to white laborers. . . . Thus, the customary amount of labor would still have to be performed; the freed people would surely not do more than their old proportion of it, and very probably, for a time, would do less, leaving an increased part to white laborers, bringing their labor into greater demand, and, consequently, enhancing the wages of it."[74] E. Pershine Smith, a Northern politician, wrote to Henry Carey in 1859: "Abolish slavery in Virginia tomorrow, and the exodus from New England would be tremendous."[75]

Carey and Lincoln wanted to do no less than "Midwesternize" the highland South—to create a society like that of the Northern states in the poor Southern mountain region. Whites from the East would move not only to the West but to the South in search of opportunity, and be joined by streams of European immigrants, like the Irish and Germans who had poured into Illinois and other Midwestern states before the war. The collaboration of Carey and Lincoln in furtherance of this vision gives the lie to historians who claim that Lincoln hoped to base the postwar Republican Party in the South on conservative business elites, many of them former Whigs. The logic of Carey's plan for Southern modernization suggested a postwar Republican Party based on an alliance between newly industrialized highland Southern factory owners and their workers, and white workers and farmers in the coastal South allied against the plantation oligarchs.

Something like the Carey-Lincoln plan for federal encouragement of industrialization of the poor, mostly white highland South was carried out generations later, in the 1930s and 1940s, as part of Franklin Roosevelt's New Deal. The prototype of the Tennessee Valley Authority (TVA) and the Lower Colorado River Authority (LCRA)—infrastructure projects intended to serve as the nucleus of the modernization of the poorest parts of the upland South and the Texas hill country—was the North–South railroad envisioned by Henry Carey and proposed to Congress by Abraham Lincoln. The prototype for this, in turn, was New York governor DeWitt Clinton's Erie Canal, which had catalyzed much of the industrialization of the Northeast. With good reason had the young Lincoln once said that he wanted to be "the DeWitt Clinton of Illinois."[76] Far from being trivial, this was a very honorable ambition indeed.

If Lincoln had lived and promoted the industrialization of the highland South, American economic and political history might have been quite different. The poor mining areas of the Appalachians and Ozarks might have become the sites of industrial cities like Pittsburgh, Detroit, and Chicago, providing employment for Southern blacks as well as poor Southern whites and white immigrants from Europe and other parts of the United States. In national politics the industrialized highland South might have been detached from the solid South (which would have been much smaller and weaker) and attached to the Midwest and Northeast.

The result would not have been a color-blind society. As it was, until the civil rights revolution, the white working class in the industrial North used both politics and violence to limit black competition. And when low-wage Southern states created a textile industry in the early twentieth century, the good jobs went to white workers, not to blacks. But even the partial industrialization and urbanization of the South in the late nineteenth century would have weakened the Southern racial system as well as the Southern class system. That kind of erosion of Southern hierarchy occurred when the South was finally and belatedly urbanized and industrialized beginning with the New Deal in the middle of the twentieth century.

It was not to be. Most poor, white highland Southerners deserted the Republican Party during Reconstruction, leaving in the South an almost exclusively black party that was soon marginalized.[77] The failure of the nineteenth-century federal government to promote the industrialization of the South before the New Deal in the 1930s created social disasters from which the United States still suffered in the twenty-first century, ranging from the continuing political power of the Southern oligarchy, which had captured the Republican Party by 2000, to the diaspora of poor black and white Southerners in ghettoes and trailer parks throughout the nation. In 1862, when he had encouraged blacks to emigrate and work in Central America, Lincoln had said: "As to the coal mines, I think I see the means available for your self-reliance."[78] Lincoln had the wrong coal mines in mind. The coal mines that counted, for poor black and white Southerners alike, were those in Appalachia. And generations of Southern black workers no less than Southern white workers paid the price for the failure of the plan of Henry Carey to make those mines the nuclei of manufacturing towns.

THE GREAT EMANCIPATOR was a title that Lincoln welcomed. Discussing the Emancipation Proclamation with his friend Joshua Speed, Lincoln "alluded to an incident in his life, long passed, when he was so much depressed that he almost contemplated suicide. At the time of his deep depression he said to me that he had 'done nothing to make any human being remember that he had lived,' and that to connect his name with the events transpiring in his day and generation, and so impress himself upon them as to link his name with something that would redound to the interest of his fellow man, was what he desired to live for. He reminded me of that conversation, and said with earnest emphasis, 'I believe that in this measure [meaning his proclamation] my fondest hope will be realized.' "[79]

But the credit for emancipation arguably goes to the Confederate generals and politicians. If they had been less skillful, and if the white Southern majority had been less determined to win independence from the United States, the Civil War might have ended quickly, with slavery not only intact but protected from federal interference by the first of several proposed Thirteenth Amendments that Lincoln supported.

The Great Emancipator was not the Great Integrationist. Most Americans today, like black Americans and a small number of Radical Republicans in Lincoln's own time, view the full social and political equality of Americans of all races as the logical sequel to the abolition of slavery. But Lincoln, like most of his white contemporaries, as well as most white Americans in the century that followed, did not share their view. Lincoln's opposition to slavery was sincere. As he declared on October 7, 1858, in Galesburg, Illinois, "Now, I confess myself as belonging to that class in the country who contemplate slavery as a moral, social and political evil . . . [and] desire a policy that looks to the prevention of it as a wrong, and looks hopefully to the time when as a wrong it may come to an end."[80] Lincoln denounced efforts to "dehumanize the negro—to take away from him the right of ever striving to be a man . . ."[81]

At the same time Lincoln believed that, if the voluntary deportation of all blacks to another country could not be arranged, the United States should be a separate-but-equal society, not a racially integrated society. It is inaccurate to call the civil rights revolution the long-delayed fulfillment of the "promise" of the Civil War and Reconstruction, because neither Lincoln nor the majority of white Northerners ever made any such promise to black Americans and other nonwhite Americans. Like many successful revolutions, the civil rights revolution was disguised as a restoration. But in reality it was part of a global process of overturning white supremacy and white colonialism that occurred simultaneously throughout the world in the decades following World War II. The other English-speaking democracies—Britain, Canada, Australia, and New Zealand—all abolished their white-supremacist civil rights laws and white-only immigration policies at the same time that the United States did, and they did so for reasons that had nothing to do with the American Civil War.

Discussing Lincoln's attitude toward black Americans, Lincoln's friend and law partner William Herndon observed that "Mr. Lincoln was a cold man. . . . The African was enslaved and deprived of this right; a principle was violated in doing so. . . . When he freed the slaves there was no heart in the act."[82] The great black abolitionist Frederick Douglass, who met several times with Lincoln in the White House, agreed. Douglass provided his most considered assessment of Lincoln in a speech he delivered at the unveiling of a monument to Lincoln at Lincoln Park in Washington, D.C., on April 14, 1876. While he praised Lincoln's sincere opposition to slavery, and celebrated his role in its destruction, Douglass noted that "the Union was more to him than our freedom or our future. . . ." According to Douglass, "President Lincoln was a white man, and shared the prejudices common to his countrymen towards the colored race." Douglass observed: "He was preeminently the white man's President, entirely devoted to the welfare of white men. He was ready and willing at any time during the first years of his administration to deny, postpone, and sacrifice the rights of humanity in the colored people to promote the welfare of the white people of this country. . . . The race to which we belong were not the special objects of his consideration. . . . Knowing this, I concede to you, my white fellow-citizens, a pre-eminence in this worship at once full and supreme. First, midst, and last, you and yours were the objects of his deepest affection and his most earnest solicitude. You are the children of Abraham Lincoln. We are at best only his step-children. . . ."[83]

—∞∞∞—

SEVEN

LINCOLN'S AMERICA:
THE RISE AND FALL OF THE
SECOND REPUBLIC

THE VICTORY OF the Union in the Civil War ensured that the United States as a whole would continue to exist under the Constitution of 1787. The federal Constitution was modified by the Reconstruction Amendments—the Thirteenth, Fourteenth, and Fifteenth—that abolished slavery, established national citizenship, and, in theory, established universal male adult suffrage without regard for race. Apart from these amendments, the formal structure of the United States following the Civil War was the same as it had been before the conflict. This would have pleased Lincoln, whose approach to constitutional change had always been cautious and conservative.

Nevertheless, American government and society changed dramatically and permanently during and after the Civil War. Although still small by later standards, the federal government in the second half of the nineteenth century was much larger and more powerful than it had been before. And industrial capitalism, encouraged by the policies of Lincoln and his Republican successors, transformed American society. These changes were the result not of constitutional alteration, but of legislation and executive and judicial policy. Notwithstanding the continuity in the realm of the formal Constitution, these transformations added up to what has been called a second American revolution—a second founding of the United States.[1] Lincoln and his fellow Republicans constructed the Second Republic of the United States, which collapsed between the Great Depression and the civil rights revolution, to be succeeded by the Third Republic established by Franklin D. Roosevelt and his successors between the 1930s and the 1960s.

The fact that the Civil War and Reconstruction permitted Lincoln and the Republicans to reshape the United States does not mean—as some critics of Lincoln have charged—that Lincoln and his party deliberately provoked the Civil War to provide themselves with an excuse to carry out their Hamiltonian domestic policy program of high tariffs, national banking, and railroad subsidies. Had the Southern states not seceded, sacrificing their seats in Congress, Southern representatives and senators could have blocked or diluted much of the legislation that the Republican Party enacted in their absence in the 1860s and early 1870s, just as previous generations of Southerners had blocked the earlier programs for national industrial capitalist development of Alexander Hamilton and Henry Clay. If the South had not seceded, or if the Southern states had accepted the mild terms for reunion that Lincoln offered at the beginning of the Civil War, the window of opportunity for the Republicans to enact their Hamiltonian agenda would have been brief. If the Jeffersonians of the South disliked the second American republic that Lincoln and his party constructed during the voluntary absence of their representatives from Washington, D.C., they had no one to blame but themselves.

THE FIRST REPUBLIC of the United States was dominated by Southern politicians, who controlled the presidency, Congress, and the Supreme Court for most of the period between 1789 and 1861. The Second Republic was dominated by the North. Between 1860 and 1932 Republican presidents held the White House for all but sixteen years: Ulysses S. Grant, Rutherford B. Hayes, James A. Garfield, Chester A. Arthur, Benjamin Harrison, William McKinley, Theodore Roosevelt, William Howard Taft, Warren G. Harding, Calvin Coolidge, and Herbert Hoover. (Andrew Johnson, Lincoln's second vice president and successor, had been a Unionist Democrat.) Between 1868 and 1950, in all of the presidential elections except one, at least one of the two presidential candidates of the two national parties came from one of five states: Ohio, New York, Illinois, Indiana, and New Jersey.[2]

From the 1860s until the 1880s the Republicans failed to consolidate their majority status in the country. The Republicans originated as a minority party that succeeded in the Darwinian competition of the 1850s only because the rival successor to the Whig Party, the American Party, split over the issue of slavery extension in 1856, while the Democrats split over the same issue in 1860. They controlled the government from 1860 to 1865 only because of the secession of the mostly Democratic South. From 1868 until 1896 they never won more than a minority of the popular vote in presidential elections. Republicans became a genuine majority party only in 1896, in an economic recession in which the party attracted voters who favored the agrarian populism of William Jennings Bryan.

The Republicans artificially boosted their power in the federal government by rapidly admitting first West Virginia and then Western states, with small populations chiefly of New Englanders and Midwesterners of Yankee Protestant ancestry and, in some places, culturally similar Germans and Scandinavians—Nebraska (1867), Colorado (1876), North Dakota (1889), South Dakota (1889), Montana (1889), Washington (1889), Idaho (1890), Wyoming (1890), Utah (1896), Oklahoma (1907), New Mexico (1912), and Arizona (1912). The overrepresentation of these thinly populated Western states exaggerated Northern Republican power in the Senate and in the electoral college.

DESPITE THEIR PRECARIOUS status as a minority party that controlled Congress only because of the absence of Southern representatives during the Civil War and Reconstruction, the Republicans between 1861 and 1877 used legislation to push through a Hamiltonian revolution. The Hamiltonian nationalist agenda had been blocked for half a century by Southern members of Congress and their Northern allies, or, on the rare occasions when Hamiltonian legislation passed, by the veto of a president who was Southern or had a Southern constituency. In 1841, when the first of two Whig presidents, William Henry Harrison, was inaugurated, it looked as though the Federalist-Whig program of national modernization might pass, at least in part. But Harrison died later that year, and John Tyler, the vice president who succeeded him, revealed his true colors as a Southern champion of states' rights once he was in the White House. Only after the Southern states seceded were Northern Hamiltonians, no longer blocked by Southern obstructionism, able to realize the triad of internal improvements, national banking, and protective tariffs to foster American manufacturing industries that made up the American System of Henry Clay and his disciple Lincoln.

From the earliest years of the Washington administration, when Treasury Secretary Hamilton sparred with Secretary of State Jefferson over the constitutionality of the First Bank of the United States, to the 1830s, when Clay led the unsuccessful fight to prevent Andrew Jackson from destroying the Second Bank of the United States, a centralized banking authority and rational currency laws had been goals of the modernizing Hamiltonians in their successive incarnations as Federalists, National Republicans, Whigs, and Lincoln Republicans.

The Republican Party was divided in its attitudes toward banking. Former Whigs like Lincoln supported a national banking system. But many Western Republican farmers who had earlier been Jacksonian Democrats had a populist suspicion of Northeastern financiers and British finance. Their suspicions seemed to be confirmed when New York bankers refused to extend loans to the U.S. government during the early part of the Civil War when asked to do so by Secretary of the Treasury Salmon P. Chase.

When the Civil War began, currency consisted exclusively of notes issued by banks chartered by the states and redeemable in gold or silver. As president, Lincoln signed a series of banking reforms. The Legal Tender Act of 1862 allowed the Secretary of the Treasury to issue paper money based on federal government debt in the form of "greenbacks." The National Currency Acts of 1863 and 1864 created a new federal banking system. Under its provision, state bank notes were eliminated by a 10 percent tax on them, and a system of nationally chartered banks authorized to issue bank notes supplied by the Treasury was created. The *New York Times* wrote on March 9, 1863, "The legal tender act and the national currency bill crystallized . . . a centralization of power, such as Hamilton might have eulogized as magnificent."[3] But the Republicans did not create a Third Bank of the United States. That came later. In response to the financial panic of 1907, the Federal Reserve system—in effect the Third Bank of the United States—was created by the Glass-Owen Act in 1913, realizing the hopes of Hamilton and his successors, including Clay and Lincoln.

During the Civil War the federal budget increased from $63 million in 1860 to $1.2 billion in 1865. After Lincoln's death, Mary Lincoln told Herndon that her husband had planned to take the family to Europe following his retirement from the presidency: "After his return from Europe, he intended to cross the Rocky Mountains and go to California, where the soldiers were to be digging out gold to pay the national debt."[4]

To pay for the war, the federal government instituted income, inheritance, and excise taxes, and ran up a deficit of $2.5 billion. To cope with this, the Lincoln administration and its congressional allies created the Internal Revenue Service within the Treasury Department as part of legislation that Lincoln signed on July 1, 1862. The law created the first U.S. income tax, with rates of 3 to 5 percent. After the federal income tax was abolished in 1872, a new income tax was enacted by Congress in 1894 but then ruled unconstitutional by the Supreme Court in 1895. In 1913 the Sixteenth Amendment, permitting federal taxation of incomes, was adopted.

Internal improvements, another part of Clay's Hamiltonian American System, were also established on a grand scale under Lincoln and his successors. Before 1860 no bill providing federal aid for the construction of a rail-road from the East to the Pacific had ever passed in Congress.[5] In 1862 Congress appropriated millions for a Pacific rail line to be built and operated by two companies, the Union Pacific and Central Pacific. Corrupt practices on the part of company officials, including allies of Lincoln, produced the Credit Mobilier scandal during the Grant administration and contributed to the bankruptcy of the Union Pacific and Central Pacific prior to the completion of the line in May 1869.[6] Notwithstanding such corruption, between 1860 and 1870 the U.S. railroad system grew from 29,000 miles to 49,000 miles.[7] The United States had the greatest proportion of railroad mileage to inhabitants in the world by 1868.[8]

The centerpiece of Henry Clay's plan for the industrialization of the United States had been a high protective tariff (Hamilton by contrast had preferred government subsidies, or "bounties," for infant industries). Clay's political disciple Abraham Lincoln had always supported protective tariffs, first as a Whig and then as a Republican. But while seeking the Republican nomination for the presidency, Lincoln kept quiet, afraid of offending former Jacksonian Democrats in the Western farming regions who had been attracted to the new party because of its opposition to slavery extension but supported low tariffs and free trade. In October 1859 he wrote to a correspondent in Pennsylvania that "it is my opinion that, just now, the revival of that question, will not advance the cause itself, or the man who revives it."[9] But he discreetly reminded Pennsylvania protectionists that he was on their side, a factor that helped win him the nomination. The tariff was the subject of the twelfth plank of the Republican Party platform of 1860, which promised "such an adjustment of imports as to encourage the development of the industrial interests of this country."[10] In 1860, after he had been nominated as the Republican presidential candidate, Lincoln took part in a political rally in Springfield. In the parade, the local woolen mill was represented, in the words of one historian, by "an immense wagon containing a power loom driven by a steam engine. Several yards of jean cloth, from which a garment was fashioned for Lincoln, were publicly made. The wagon bore the significant motto 'Protection to Home Industry.' "[11] The electoral votes of Pennsylvania and New Jersey were crucial in helping Lincoln and the Republicans win the White House in 1860. "Protection made Mr. Lincoln president," the economist Henry C. Carey asserted.[12]

Following his election and before his inauguration, Lincoln assured an audience in Pittsburgh on February 15, 1861, that the pro-tariff plank on the subject in the Republican platform would be "a general law to the incoming Administration."[13] In May 1860, before the election, the House had passed the Morrill Tariff, which was passed by the Senate between Lincoln's election and his inauguration. This began a period, lasting until World War II, in which the United States had the most protected home market in the world. Between 1867 and 1914 the U.S. tariff on dutiable imports hovered between 40 and 50 percent.[14]

William McKinley, who published a book on the tariff, succeeded Justin Morrill as the leading spokesman for protectionism in the Republican Party and gave his name to the 1890 McKinley Tariff. His vice president and successor, Theodore Roosevelt, wrote in 1895: "Thank God I am not a freetrader. In this country pernicious indulgence in the doctrine of free trade seems inevitably to produce fatty degeneration of the moral fibre."[15]

Corporate capitalism assumed its present form only during the era of the Second Republic of the United States. Modern corporations are based on the principle of limited liability, which means that shareholders are not responsible for the debts of a corporation. Without that protection, most private investment in large-scale enterprises would be too risky. Limited liability made possible enormous private corporations capable of funding research and development, mass production, and mass marketing.

Before the widespread enactment of limited liability laws, companies often had to be granted charters for particular purposes by state legislatures in the same way that corporations in colonial America and monarchical Europe had required royal charters. This system was often abused and created resentment and suspicion. Only in the second half of the nineteenth century did limited liability become routine in Britain, the United States, and other leading countries. Even in the 1860s, most U.S. manufacturing was undertaken by unincorporated companies that were not protected by limited liability laws.[16]

The explosive growth of American industrial capitalism began in the North during the Civil War. Between 1862 and 1864 alone, Philadelphia built an additional 180 factories.[17] In 1860 Britain had 19.9 percent of world manufacturing output compared to only 7.2 percent for the United States and 4.9 percent for Germany. In 1900 the United States had 23.6 percent, Britain had fallen to the second position at 18.5 percent, and Germany with 13.2 percent was catching up rapidly.[18] By 1913 the United States surpassed Britain as the most industrialized country in the world. In per capita terms the United States had a 10 percent advantage over Britain, and by 1932 its lead in industrialization per capita had risen to 50 percent.[19] In 1850 the United States had only one-quarter of the industrial capability of Britain, then the richest society on earth. Half a century later, thanks to the triumph of a version of Henry Clay's American System under Lincoln and his successors, the United States, with more than 1.6 times the industrial power of Britain, had become the wealthiest country in the world.[20]

The wealth was not evenly shared among the regions of the United States. The South had been ruined by the Civil War. Two hundred fifty thousand Confederates died of wounds from battle or disease. If the Union forces had suffered proportional losses, instead of losing 360,000 men, they would have lost more than a million. The equivalent to the South's losses by the United States in World War II, in which the nation lost more than 300,000, would have been more than 6 million.[21] In addition to conquest and occupation, Southerners experienced losses on a scale suffered by European nations in the world wars of the twentieth century. The abolition of slavery erased $2 billion of capital. Two-thirds of Southern wealth vanished. Between 1860 and 1870 the South's share of U.S. wealth shrank from 30 percent to 12 percent.[22] By 1880 the gap in per capita wealth between the North and South was comparable to that between Germany and Russia.[23]

Lincoln, like Clay, Carey, and other protectionists of the American School, had claimed that all regions and industries benefited from high tariffs. In reality the benefits of the tariff were shared by capitalists and industrial workers in the North while the costs fell on farmers, who were concentrated in the South and West. In addition to subsidizing Northern industry by paying higher prices for manufactured goods as a result of tariffs, Southerners were taxed to subsidize government pensions for Civil War veterans and their widows, a form of welfare that helped to keep the agrarian West in the Republican coalition despite the attempts of agrarian populists such as William Jennings Bryan to unite the farmers of the South and West against the industrial Northeast. The Southern oligarchy, having survived the Civil War and Reconstruction and gone into business with Northeastern investors, was insulated by its wealth. Poor black and white Southerners suffered the most from the conversion of the conquered South into an unfairly taxed resource colony of the booming industrial Northeast under the Republicans who succeeded Lincoln in the White House. Hamilton's proposal to promote American infant industries by means of government subsidies, rather than high tariffs, might have inspired a more equitable policy.

THE ECONOMY OF the Second Republic of the United States was based on what might be called a system of "dual protection." While American industry was protected against foreign competition by tariffs, white American workers were protected against nonwhite competition by racial segregation and immigration restriction.

The 1790 immigration law that limited naturalization to free white persons was amended by the 1870 Naturalization Act, which limited U.S. citizenship to "white persons and persons of African descent" in order to acknowledge the grant of citizenship to former slaves by the Fourteenth Amendment. Between 1851 and 1900 more than 16.7 million immigrants came to the United States, most of them European immigrants who could become naturalized citizens under America's white-supremacist immigration regime. Ellis Island, opening in 1892, processed 12 million immigrants from Europe over thirty years. Of the 76 million Americans in 1900, 34.2 percent were born abroad or had a foreign-born parent.[24] Most of them went to the Northern states.

The California Gold Rush, beginning in 1849, stimulated the migration of Chinese workers to California. The reaction of white Californians (most of them recent immigrants from other parts of the United States and Europe) was swift. In 1854 Chinese immigrants were prohibited from testifying against whites in California courts. Other anti-Chinese measures included the Foreign Miner's Tax of 1853 and the Immigrant Tax of 1855. The segregation of the Chinese on the West Coast was similar to the segregation regime in Illinois, Indiana, and other states that had Black Laws. Chinese immigrants were forbidden to testify in court, to own property, to vote, and to marry non-Chinese.

In 1855 Hinton Helper, a white Southern populist critic of slavery who opposed black migration to the West, had argued that Asian migration to the West ought to be banned as well: "I should not wonder at all, if the copper of the Pacific yet becomes so great a subject of discord and discussion as the ebony of the Atlantic."[25] The parallel between the "yellow slavery" of coolie labor and black slavery as threats to the white worker and farmer in the American West was drawn in an 1880 song, "The Chinamen Must Go": Praising "These men who struck for homesteads less / Than thirty years ago," the song warned that "Asia poured her heathen hosts / In floods upon our shore, / And filled the land with slaves, and still / Is sending us some more."[26]

In 1877 Denis Kearney, an Irish-American, organized the Workingman's Party with the slogan, "The Chinese must go!" His campaign inspired anti-Chinese pogroms. The Chinese Exclusion Act passed by Congress in 1882 restricted Chinese immigration. The Immigration Act of the same year imposed a tax on each immigrant. In 1885 the Alien Contract Labor Law prevented employers from bringing in immigrants under labor contracts, with the exception of domestic servants and some skilled workers. Then in 1907 the "Gentleman's Agreement" with Japan effectively banned Japanese immigration except to Hawaii, then a territory. In 1917 another immigration law specifically prohibited all immigration from Asia, except for Japan and the Philippines. In the case of *United States v. Bhaghat Singh,* the Supreme Court ruled that immigrants from India could not become U.S. citizens.[27]

Meanwhile, the California constitution of 1879 declared: "The presence of foreigners ineligible to become citizens of the United States is dangerous to the well-being of the State." In 1913 California enacted the Alien Land Law, which prevented "aliens ineligible for citizenship" (all Asians, since they could not be naturalized under the 1870 act) from owning property in the state. Other states imitated California. In 1942 the California State Federation of Labor declared: "[T]he true credit for the agitation against Oriental Immigration should go where it belongs—to the pioneers of the trade union movement in San Francisco, Denis Kearney, Frank Rooney, John O. Walsh, John I. Nolan, and many others of that day who in and out of season preached the gospel of exclusion of Orientals."[28] Many Latin American republics followed the U.S. example and passed laws banning black and Asian immigration.[29]

In the nineteenth century, Irish-American and German-American voters had used their political influence to block attempts by Anglo-American nativists to limit their numbers. However, they had no objection to the restriction of Asian immigration. And in the 1920s, threatened by competition from Southern and Eastern European immigrants, many German- and Irish-Americans allied themselves with Anglo-Americans to restrict European immigration using a system that magnified German- and Irish-American shares of the immigration quota at the expense of other ethnic groups. The Johnson-Reed Act discriminated in favor of German and Irish immigrants by limiting annual immigration from Europe to 2 percent of each nationality defined by the U.S. Census in 1890, before the wave of Southern and Eastern European immigration had begun. In 1952 the McCarran-Walter

Immigration Act, passed by Congress over the veto of President Truman, reinvigorated the national origins system by limiting annual immigration to one-sixth of 1 percent of the population of the continental United States in 1920 (immigrants born in the Western Hemisphere were exempted from numerical limits).

While many manufacturers, interested in cheap labor, were opposed to immigration restriction, union leaders generally supported the policy. Between the Civil War and World War I, American labor leaders viewed the restriction on European immigration, along with the abolition of slavery, the outlawing of Asian contract (coolie) labor, and bans on prison labor and child labor and female labor, as mutually reinforcing policies that would raise American wages by reducing the supply of labor relative to the demand. Theodore Roosevelt praised the protection of "the free [white] working-man" in the United States by convict labor laws and Asian immigration restriction, as well as the conversion of black slaves into wage laborers.[30]

The kind of white-labor populism identified with Lincoln and the Free-Soil wing of the Republican Party in the 1850s found a champion around the turn of the century in Samuel Gompers, president of the American Federation of Labor (AFL). Like Lincoln and most of his fellow Whigs, who feared in the 1840s and 1850s that U.S. territorial expansion would bring large nonwhite populations into the country, Gompers opposed American imperialism. In a speech entitled "Imperialism: Its Dangers and Wrongs," on October 18, 1898, Gompers warned: "If the Philippines are annexed what is to prevent the Chinese, the Negritos and the Malays coming to our country?" Gompers asserted: "This massive entry of labor is intended to loosen the labor market. In other words, to organize unemployment and permit the bosses to more easily resist the demands of the working class." In 1911 Gompers wrote in the *American Federationist*, "The lines have been drawn by America's workingmen against the indiscriminate admission of aliens to this country. It is simply a case of the self-preservation of the American working class." Like Denis Kearney, Samuel Gompers was an immigrant from the British Isles, and, like Kearney, he wanted to protect white Americans from nonwhite competition. In 1905 Gompers declared that "the Caucasians are not going to let their standard of living be destroyed by Negroes, Chinamen, Japs, or any others." Gompers also proposed protecting white labor by colonizing native-born black Americans in Liberia or Cuba.[31]

By the 1920s the Euro-American majority in the Northern states was made up predominantly of Anglo-Americans and "old immigrants," German- and Irish-Americans. While they were protected from competition by Asian and European immigrants, black competition was still possible. Lincoln had failed to eliminate that possibility by colonizing blacks outside of the United States. But the other part of the black exclusion policy succeeded—most blacks were kept out of the North and West. The Fourteenth Amendment and a series of court cases gutted state Black Laws, of the kind which Lincoln hinted might keep blacks walled into the South. Black citizens had the legal right to move and work anywhere in the United States. In practice, however, blacks were deterred from moving to the North and West because of informal white discrimination by employers, unions, officials, and landlords. When blacks did move North to work for Northern employers, white working-class gangs often attacked them in pogroms that are described somewhat misleadingly as "race riots." In August 1908, in Lincoln's adopted town of Springfield, Illinois, six died and sixty were wounded before the Illinois National Guard put an end to a race riot in which whites, determined to lynch a black man accused of assaulting a white woman, went on a rampage, yelling, "Lincoln freed you, we'll show you where you belong." The incident inspired a number of black and white reformers to found the National Association for the Advancement of Colored People (NAACP).

If the North, minus the South, is thought of as having formed a country-within-a-country between the Civil War and the 1930s, then the Second Republic of the United States was a close approximation of the all-white, industrializing America planned by Clay, Lincoln, and their allies, and blacks in Mississippi, from the perspective of most Northern whites, might as well have been in Liberia, Haiti, or Nicaragua. By 1900 a *New York Times* editorial could explain that white Northerners no longer objected to the denial of voting rights to blacks in the South: "The necessity of it under the supreme law of self-preservation is candidly recognized."[32]

ELSEWHERE IN THE world, the American School of economic nationalism proved to be far more influential than the British School of free trade and laissez-faire economics in the nineteenth and early twentieth centuries. The German-American writer Friedrich List published the theoretical treatise of the school that became best known outside of the United States, *The National System of Political Economy,* in 1841.[33] In the words of one scholar, "This work is the great classic of modern economic nationalism, as Smith's *Wealth of Nations* is of liberalism."[34] List, who died by his own hand in 1848, did not live to see his economic dreams for Germany realized by Bismarck's Imperial Germany, which followed a policy of economic nationalism modeled on that of the United States. List wanted a democratic as well as an industrial Germany and would have disapproved of Bismarck's authoritarian Reich—and approved of the contemporary Federal Republic of Germany.[35]

List was the transitional figure between the American School of "national economy" or economic nationalism in the first half of the nineteenth century and the German Historical School of economics in the second half of the century. Theorists of the German Historical School developed a nuanced, historical approach to economics as an alternative to the abstract, pseudoscientific approach of British classical economists such as Smith and Ricardo. From Germany the theory and program of economic nationalism was disseminated to Japan. During a visit to Germany in the 1870s, Okubo Toshimichi, one of the leaders of the Meiji restoration, became acquainted with the Hamilton-Clay-List-Lincoln tradition. Returning to Japan, Okubo founded the Ministry of Home Affairs *(Naimusho)* to promote Japanese industry, and in 1874 he issued an equivalent of Hamilton's Report on Manufactures in the form of his influential Proposal for Industrial

Promotion *(Shokusan Kogyo ni kansuru Kengisho),* which called for the government to "induce and monitor the weak entrepreneurs to produce industries."[36]

The adoption of a high protective tariff by Germany in July 1879 inaugurated a global trend toward protectionism. Between 1870 and 1890 many
Latin American countries, whose industrialization had been retarded by the
"free trade" mandated by unequal treaties with the British Empire, adopted
protectionist tariffs to encourage the development of their own manufacturing sectors.[37] In the words of a leading economic historian, "It is no exag-
geration to claim that, with the exception of Britain, the developed world
was an ocean of protectionism. It was an ocean that did not recede until after World War II."[38] Clay, Carey, List, Lincoln, and other politicians and
publicists of the American School and the German Historical School had argued that the worldwide adoption of economic nationalism would bring
British global economic and military supremacy to an end. They proved to
be right. Britain's policy of unilateral free trade had been adopted between
the 1840s and the 1860s in the hopes of encouraging other countries to specialize in agriculture and mining and to buy their manufactured goods from
Britain. Instead, manufacturers in America, Germany, and other protectionist countries, with exclusive access to their own domestic markets, took advantage of Britain's free trade policies to add the British consumer markets
to their own. By the early twentieth century, then, the United States,
Germany, and Japan had successfully used economic nationalism to catch up
with Britain and, in the case of the first two nations, surpass it.

By 1900, however, American manufactured goods were pouring into
markets in Europe and around the world. In 1870, 60.2 percent of
American exports had been accounted for by cotton; by 1900 cotton accounted for only 17.7 percent while manufactured goods had risen to 35.4
percent.[39]

Supporters of "imperial preference" such as Joseph Chamberlain argued
that the only way that the British Empire could compete with giant states
like the United States, Germany, and Russia in the twentieth century was to

abandon free trade and to consolidate the smaller markets of Britain and its dominions into a single imperial common market with a common external tariff. However, Britain persisted in the free trade policy it had adopted in the 1840s, when it dominated the world's manufacturing. Meanwhile, the economic primacy of the British Empire was subverted by the influence of Lincoln's Second Republic of the United States on the "white dominions" of Canada, Australia, and New Zealand.

In 1876 the British government—concerned that the U.S. government, having subdued the South, might turn its ambitions northward—created a more consolidated federal system in Canada with the British North America Act. In an 1878 speech to the Canadian Parliament arguing for industrial protection, John A. Macdonald, the first prime minister of Canada, echoed the themes of Clay, Carey, List, Lincoln, and other members of the school of "national economy," to the extent of regarding British industry as the adversary: "I say then that, if our manufacturers had a reasonable protection, if they had a hold upon our four millions of people in the same way as the manufacturers in the United States, then there would be a basis whereby they might be enabled to go in by degrees and develop their resources like those of the United States, who, as I have pointed out, can compete with and undersell England in every part of the world."[40] Macdonald's "national policy" was the Canadian version of Clay's American System. Between 1879, when high tariffs went into effect, and 1913, the per capita level of manufacturing in Canda, which had been only 40 to 45 percent of that of the already industrialized nations, rose to 82 to 87 percent.[41] Another element inspired by the Clay-Lincoln American System was construction of the transcontinental Canada-Pacific railroad, which brought settlers from eastern Canada, Britain, Europe, and even the United States to homesteads on the Canadian prairie created by the Dominion Land Act of 1872, the Canadian equivalent of the U.S. Homestead Act.

Like the United States, Canada encouraged immigration from the British Isles and Europe and sought to ban nonwhite immigration. In 1882, the year that the United States passed its Chinese Exclusion Act, Macdonald

argued that Canada should emulate its southern neighbor because Asian immigrants "would not and could not be expected to assimilate with our
Aryan population."[42] In 1885 Canada passed the Chinese Immigrant Act,
which required any Chinese immigrant to pay the federal government a
"head tax" of five hundred dollars per person. This discouraged Chinese
workers from bringing their families to Canada. Between 1923 and 1947
immigration from China was halted altogether. Canadian immigration officials also discouraged black Americans from moving to Canada.

Another British dominion, Australia, also emulated Lincoln's Second
Republic of the United States. Like the United States and Canada, Australia
became more centralized while remaining, unlike Britain, a federal state.
Alfred Deakin, leader of the Protectionist Party in Australia, played the role
of Abraham Lincoln in the United States and John A. Macdonald in Canada.
Deakin was converted to the doctrine of economic nationalism by David
Syme, a media magnate and tireless promoter of industrialization who was
the Australian equivalent of Henry Carey or Friedrich List. As the second
prime minister of Australia, from 1903 to 1904, and again from 1905 to
1908, Deakin emulated the United States and Canada in overseeing enactment of a high-tariff industrial policy and a "White Australia" immigration
policy. The Australian colony of Victoria, which contained about half the
population of Australia by 1900, had enacted a tariff to promote industry in
1867.[43] Australia's version of the system of dual protection for domestic industry and white labor endured until the second half of the twentieth century and was known as the Deakinite Settlement.

New Zealand, which had maintained a relatively low tariff for the purpose of revenue, adopted a tariff policy designed to promote its manufacturing in 1888.[44] Both New Zealand and Australia were far more radical than
the United States in their egalitarian policies, with centralized government
wage arbitration and expensive welfare state programs. New Zealand in the
1900s inspired American progressives with its egalitarianism. As this suggests, influence within the English-speaking world was not entirely one-
way. Political reformers in the United States campaigned for the "Australian

ballot" (secret voting, to replace the public polling that then existed) and the New Zealand system of workmen's compensation (itself inspired by legislation in Bismarck's newly united Germany).

In the United States and the white dominions, the expropriation of the natives—Indians in the United States and Canada, aborigines in Australia, Maori in New Zealand—was the precondition for the settlement of interior lands by white homesteaders and the development of regional agricultural and mining economies linked by railroads to new national manufacturing centers that sprang up as a result of protective tariffs. In all of these countries, governments experimented with different policies toward the natives, ranging from assimilation to giving them semisovereign status on reservations, usually with unhappy results made worse by the racist attitudes of the majority white populations. In all of these English-speaking settler states in this period, liberal parties supported by agrarian interests espoused free trade and promoted trade liberalization on the rare occasions when they were in power. In the United States the Democratic Party, still dominated by the Southern agrarian elite, reduced U.S. industrial protection with the Underwood Tariff of 1913. Woodrow Wilson, the Southern-born head of the Southern-dominated Democrats, made international free trade one of his Fourteen Points. In Canada the Liberal Party favored freer trade, as did liberal parties in Australia and New Zealand. In the first half of the twentieth century, however, political coalitions of manufacturers and white industrial workers, like the coalition which came to power in the United States with Abraham Lincoln, dominated the British white dominions.

The costs of protection for manufacturers and high wages for their workers fell on farmers in these countries. Agrarian discontent sometimes flared into political rebellion of the kind that produced the Populist movement in the American South and West in the late nineteenth century. In the 1930s agrarian Western Australia threatened to secede, but was mollified by a program of federal revenue-sharing.

Ironically, although they remained within the British Empire, Canada, Australia, and New Zealand modeled their nation-building efforts—

centralized federations, industrial tariffs, white-only immigration policies, railroad development, and homestead policies on land expropriated from the natives—on Henry Clay's American System, in the form in which it was finally adopted by Lincoln and his successors. These developments vindicated the observation of Karl Marx in a letter written to Friedrich Engels on March 6, 1862, in which he accurately predicted that the end of Britain's global market hegemony "is further hastened by the protectionist policy of the United States, which now, if only to revenge themselves on John Bull, will assuredly not give it up soon. Moreover, John Bull discovers to his horror that his principal colonies in North America and Australia become protectionist in precisely the same measure as John Bull becomes a free trader."[45]

THE SECOND REPUBLIC of the United States founded by Lincoln and his allies during the Civil War and Reconstruction reached its maturity in the 1920s. Under the leadership of presidents Warren G. Harding and Calvin Coolidge and of Northern and Midwestern Republicans in Congress, the United States was more or less the country that Henry Clay and Abraham Lincoln had envisioned: a nation-state with the world's leading industrial economy, a protected home market, an overwhelming white majority whose status was secured by white-only immigration laws and formal and informal segregation of the relatively small number of nonwhites, and a Whiggish preference for "dollar diplomacy" instead of the foreign military intervention favored by the Southern-born president Woodrow Wilson during the World War I era.

Between the Great Depression and the end of the civil rights revolution in the 1960s, the America of Lincoln crumbled and was replaced by the America of Franklin D. Roosevelt. The New Deal and its aftershocks, up to Lyndon Johnson's Great Society, and the civil rights revolution were part of a Third American Revolution that transformed the United States as much as the Civil War and Reconstruction had done. In many ways the Third

Republic of the United States was based on the repudiation of the ideas and policies of the Second.

The Great Depression devastated Lincoln's party. In 1932 Hoover won less than 40 percent of the vote and only six states. After the 1932 elections the Republicans were outnumbered 313 to 117 in the House and 60 to 35 in the Senate (Farmer–Labor politicians collaborated with the Democrats). After the 1936 elections the ratio dropped to 435 to 89 in the House and 96 to 16 in the Senate.

While Lincoln's Second Republic had been dominated by the North and Midwest, the national politics of the Third Republic was dominated by the South and the "sun belt" that included southern California and Florida. The Democrats who swept the Republican Party from power in the 1930s were a coalition of Southerners, urban Catholic workers, and progressive Yankees and German-Americans, in which Southerners, both conservative and populist, were dominant. With the exceptions of Franklin Roosevelt, the Hudson River squire, and the Irish-American John F. Kennedy, every Democratic president between 1932 and 2000 was a Southerner: Truman (from the southern part of Missouri), Johnson, Carter, Clinton. Congress was dominated by Southerners in the New Deal era, many of them reactionary segregationists. To maintain a conservative, one-party Democratic "solid South," the Southern oligarchy used methods ranging from terrorism to literacy tests, poll taxes, and grandfather clauses to prevent not only blacks but also poor whites from voting.

Until the middle of the twentieth century the racial views of most white Americans and the presidents they elected changed little from Lincoln's time. White supremacist attitudes were shared by progressives and liberals with conservatives. Of blacks, Theodore Roosevelt wrote to his friend Owen Wister: "I entirely agree with you that as a race and in the mass they are altogether inferior to whites."[46] Woodrow Wilson, the first Southern-born president since before the Civil War, resegregated Washington, D.C., and, joining the British, rejected a proposal by the Japanese government at the Versailles Conference in 1919 that the League of Nations outlaw racial discrimination worldwide. As vice president, Calvin Coolidge declared: "America should be kept American. . . . Biological laws show that Nordics deteriorate when mixed with other races."[47] Although his wife Eleanor campaigned for black civil rights, Franklin Roosevelt refused to confront the Southern segregationist wing of the Democratic Party and shared the genteel racism of his class. During World War II Roosevelt interned Japanese-Americans and Japanese nationals while leaving German-Americans alone. In 1925 Roosevelt had written in an editorial: "In this question, then, of Japanese exclusion from the United States, it is necessary only to advance the true reason—the undesirability of mixing the blood of the two peoples." According to Roosevelt, "Californians have properly objected on the sound basic ground that Japanese immigrants are not capable of assimilation into the American population . . . Anyone who has traveled in the Far East knows that the mingling of Asiatic blood with European or American blood produces, in nine cases out of ten, the most unfortunate results." Roosevelt asserted that the Japanese "would feel the same repugnance and objection to having thousands of Americans settle in Japan and intermarry with the Japanese as I would feel in having large numbers of Japanese come over and intermarry with the American population."[48] Roosevelt's successor Harry S Truman integrated the armed forces and promoted civil rights legislation, triggering the defection of many Southern Democrats. But in 1911 the young Truman had written: "I am strongly of the opinion that negroes ought to be in Africa, yellow men in Asia, and white men in Europe and America."[49]

The discrediting of racism by Hitler's genocidal policies and the need for the United States to appeal to postcolonial nations in Africa and Asia and Latin America in its Cold War with the Soviet Union provided additional incentives for the American political elite to overcome its prejudices and dismantle racial segregation in the North as well as in the South. The federal judiciary led the way in *Smith v. Allwright* (1944), which held that the Fourteenth Amendment forbade discrimination in primaries, a ruling expanded on in subsequent voting rights cases.[50] The Civil Rights Act of 1957 was followed by the Voting Rights Act of 1965, strengthened in 1970, which empowered the Justice Department to oversee voting. A century after its ratification, the Fifteenth Amendment was finally enforced: "The right of citizens of the United States to vote shall not be denied or abridged by the United States or by any state on account of race, color, or previous condition of servitude." Along with segregation, racially biased immigration laws were abolished between the 1940s and the 1970s. The Chinese Exclusion Act was repealed in 1943, and bans on the acquisition of U.S. citizenship by Asians were abolished. In 1965 the Immigration and Nationality Act abolished the national origins system of the 1920s. The new emphasis on family reunification soon benefited chiefly Latin American and Asian immigrants.

By the late 1960s the White America policies of Jefferson, Clay, and Lincoln, and their successors had been dismantled. The similar White Canada, White Australia, and White New Zealand policies were dismantled around the same time.

T H E   E N D   O F segregation, paradoxically, produced a renaissance of Southern cultural and political conservatism. The rise of the Republican Party in the late twentieth century masked an underlying continuity in national politics, insofar as most of the conservative Republican leaders were from the South and many were former Democrats. By the beginning of the twenty-first century the core territory of the Republican Party consisted of the states of the former Confederacy. Dominated by conservative whites in the Deep South, the Republicans now stood for states' rights and Christian fundamentalism. Republican presidential candidates felt compelled to endorse, or avoid criticizing, official displays of the Confederate flag by Southern state governments. The party of Abraham Lincoln had become the party of Jefferson Davis.

Meanwhile, old-fashioned Lincoln-to-Hoover Republicans from Maine to the Midwest to the Pacific Northwest converted in great numbers to the

Democratic Party, which they found more appealing than a Republican Party taken over by former Dixiecrats. Regional realignment produced particularly striking results in Wisconsin, where the Republican Party of Lincoln was first formed in the town of Ripon in 1854 in response to the Kansas-Nebraska Act. In 1902 Wisconsin had two Republican U.S. senators, and its House delegation included ten Republicans and only one Democrat. In 1998 both of Wisconsin's senators were Democrats while Democratic representatives outnumbered Republicans five to four.[51]

The reversal of foreign policy positions by the Democratic and Republican parties between the 1950s and the 1980s is easily explained by the transformation of their regional bases. When Greater New England was the regional base for the Republican Party, it was the more isolationist and antimilitary of the two parties; by the 1980s Greater New England had become the new homeland of the national Democratic Party, whose positions on presidential power, defense spending, and military intervention accordingly resembled those of Taft rather than those of Truman. The internationalism of many Democrats between the presidencies of Woodrow Wilson and Lyndon Johnson reflected the influence of Southerners who, when they switched to the Republican Party, brought their internationalist, free trade, promilitary attitudes with them.

THE SYSTEM OF dual protection of industry and labor that had been the basis of Lincoln's Second Republic was eliminated by new generations of American leaders between the 1920s and the 1970s. The Southern conservatives who wielded disproportionate power in the federal government between the 1930s and the early twenty-first century, first as Democrats and then as Republicans, inherited the Jeffersonian preference for the free market economics of Adam Smith over the economic nationalism of the Carey-List American School. Following World War II, the influence of Southerners like Secretary of State Cordell Hull, a former Tennessee senator with the Southern exporter's devotion to free trade, explains in part why the United States—the most protectionist country in the world under the leadership of Northern Republicans from manufacturing states—adopted the global abolition of tariffs as a policy goal. Even in the late twentieth century, the South and West remained heavily dependent on export-oriented agriculture and mining rather than manufacturing. While using their political predominance to subsidize commodity exporting enterprises, Southern and Western members of Congress between World War II and the early 2000s were indifferent to the deindustrialization of the old manufacturing belt in the Midwest and Northeast.

However, the shift away from protection toward trade liberalization by the United States following World War II cannot be explained entirely in terms of the preferences of the dominant Southern elite. Franklin D. Roosevelt, concerned to eliminate competition over colonies and resources as a source of great-power war, wanted to construct a rule-based global economy as an alternative to imperial spheres of influence. In addition, the initial goal of import-substitution tariff protection in the United States— allowing America's "infant industries" to catch up with those of Britian— had been achieved by the early 1900s. The supporters of infant-industry protection, including Hamilton, Carey, List, and other leading thinkers of the American School of economic nationalism, sometimes argued that protectionism was a temporary measure to help establish new industries. As the strength of American manufacturing rendered the infant-industry argument for protection irrelevant, protectionists began emphasizing the defense of high wages for American labor. For example, in 1892 William McKinley emphasized the protection from low-wage foreign competition that the tariff provided to American labor: "Open competition between high-paid American labor and poorly paid European labor will either drive out of existence American industry or lower American wages, either of which is unwise."[52]

The economic depression of the 1890s convinced many American business leaders and policymakers that the economy was suffering from industrial overproduction. Indiana senator Albert J. Beveridge declared in 1897:

"American factories are making more than the American people can use; American soil is producing more than they can consume. Fate has written our policy for us; the trade of the world must and shall be ours."[53] Secretary of State James Blaine explicitly attributed the new problem of overproduction to the success of the Clay-Lincoln system: "Under the beneficent policy of protection we have developed a volume of manufactures which, in many departments overruns the demands of the home market." He called for "expansion of trade with countries where we can find profitable exchanges," and then emphasized his rejection of colonialism: "We are not seeking annexation of territory."[54] Following this logic, Republican presidents such as Theodore Roosevelt began to favor moderate trade liberalization in the first decades of the twentieth century.

Following World War II, both parties favored the establishment of global trade liberalization. In 1945 the United States accounted for roughly half of all global industrial production. Like Britain, with its near monopoly of industry a century earlier, the United States did not need to protect its industries and sought to gain access to foreign markets. The United States prevailed in making the reduction of tariffs—first by means of successive GATT negotiations, and then through the mechanism of the WTO—central to global economic negotiations. Labor as well as capital in the United States benefited from the monopoly profits that U.S. industry reaped in Europe, Asia, and elsewhere for a generation after the Second World War. By the 1970s, however, European and Japanese industry had recovered to become competitive with U.S. industry. As a consequence, the free trade consensus in the United States began to fray in the 1970s and 1980s.

Despite official rhetoric about free trade and globalization, throughout the second half of the twentieth century Hamiltonian economic nationalism flourished in the United States. While the U.S.-led effort to reduce tariffs around the world had almost eliminated the tariff as a tool in American industrial policy, the United States retained other instruments of national economic statecraft. Hamilton himself had preferred "bounties," or government subsidies, to favored industries. The federal government showered money on the computer, aerospace, and medical industries in which the United States led the world. And the U.S. military, acting as a venture capitalist, created a computer network linking universities with defense research contracts called DARPANET, which came to be known as the Internet and formed the global communications infrastructure—an example of Hamiltonian "internal improvements" on a planetary rather than a merely national scale. After 1945 Uncle Sam may have quoted Adam Smith, but he acted like Alexander Hamilton.

THE FREE LABOR morality of Lincoln and his fellow Whigs and Republicans, with its exaltation of the self-reliant producer, was a casualty of the success of the industrial capitalism that they promoted. The evolution of large-scale industry made impossible the kind of society of small producers that Clay and Lincoln and their contemporaries had hoped to reconcile with machine technology. Although Lincoln favored industrial modernization, he lived before the era of giant corporations and vast industrial proletariats. Without conscious hypocrisy, in defending the dignity of labor against proslavery theorists Lincoln could claim that the North was a model for a future America in which most people, even if they worked as laborers for a short time when young, would be self-employed entrepreneurs, professionals, artisans, or farmers. By 1900 this vision was anachronistic. It was possible for a blacksmith's apprentice to work for a few years in order to save money to start his own smithy. It was absurd to suggest that a steelworker need work in a factory or forge only until he could save enough money to buy his own personal steel mill.

In *Life on the Circuit with Lincoln* (1892), Henry Clay Whitney was nostalgic for the era when his old acquaintance Abraham Lincoln could discuss property without "strike" and "lockout" being brought to mind.[55] As industrialization created growing inequality and class conflict in the United States, both conservative and progressive Republicans claimed Lincoln. The conservatives continued to recite the rhetoric of Lincoln about the self-made man, true to the letter, while progressives claimed to be true to the spirit of Lincoln by promoting schemes of workplace regulation, social insurance, or reforms that favored organized labor. In his lifetime, Lincoln never had to confront the conflict between the equality of opportunity he favored and the industrial capitalism he promoted. But the issue moved to the center of American political life in the late nineteenth and early twentieth centuries, and in doing so it split the Republican Party into conservatives and progressives.

Theodore Roosevelt tried to enlist Lincoln for the progressive cause. In his "New Nationalism" speech at the dedication of the John Brown cemetery in Osawatomie, Kansas, Roosevelt interpreted the Civil War in terms of a connection between a strong national government and individual upward mobility: "The National Government belongs to the whole American people, and where the whole American people are interested, that interest can be guarded effectively only by the National Government." The United States "means nothing unless it means the triumph of a real democracy, the triumph of popular government, and, in the long run, of an economic system under which each man shall be guaranteed the opportunity to show the best that there is in him." In his speech, Roosevelt quoted Lincoln's statement that "Labor is prior to, and independent of, capital" and observed, "If that remark was original with me, I should be even more strongly denounced as a Communist agitator than I shall be anyhow. It is Lincoln's. I am only quoting it."[56] Conservative Republicans, of course, could respond by quoting Lincoln as well.

The conservatives, such as William Howard Taft, claimed that they were following Lincoln in revering the rights of property and defending economic individualism. The progressives, such as Theodore Roosevelt, claimed that they were following Lincoln in defending social equality and the rights of workers. Both Republican progressives and Republican conservatives claimed to be the heirs of Lincoln. And both were.

LINCOLN'S ALTERNATIVE TO a welfare state and minimum wage laws had been homestead legislation. The American West was supposed to act as a "safety valve" for the white working class. In settling the West, workers-turned-farmers would not only improve their own living standards, but they would indirectly help raise wages in the areas they left behind, where labor markets would grow tighter. As Lincoln had explained: "I am in favor of cutting up the wild lands into parcels, so that every poor man may have a home."[57]

The policy was a failure from the beginning. To this day a number of American families can trace modest amounts of wealth back to homestead grants. But only a small percentage of the population ever settled in the Western interior—and many of those lost their homes when they were bankrupted by depressions, including the Great Depression. What is more, the experiment in Western settlement became an agricultural and ecological disaster, turning Lincoln's dream of the American West into a nightmare during the "dust bowl" era of the 1920s and 1930s. The Great Plains never recovered. By the beginning of the twenty-first century, the area between the Rocky Mountains and the Mississippi River contained only 12 percent of the U.S. population. Vast stretches of the plains were losing population, and parts qualified for the definition of "frontier." Some suggested making the interior a "buffalo commons" or giving the land back to the Indians. The campaign for a white-only West before the Civil War looked, in retrospect, like a mistake because it turned out that almost nobody wanted to live in the former Western territories.[58]

The great white migration to the prairies and plains for which Lincoln had hoped never took place; but the great black migration out of the South that Lincoln dreaded did occur. Ironically, it resulted from something of which he would have approved—the industrialization of Southern agriculture. The Southern plantation system, which had survived both the Civil War and Reconstruction, was finally destroyed by the mechanical cotton picker. The percentage of Southern cotton that was harvested mechanically rose from 6 percent in 1949 to 78 percent in 1964 to 100 percent in 1972.[59] Rural blacks were being pushed from the land, at the same time that the restriction of European immigration in the North in the 1920s was opening up jobs for black workers in manufacturing cities.

In 1900 more than 90 percent of black Americans still lived in the South.[60] Between 1940 and 1970 more than 5 million black Americans moved out of the South in search of work in one of the greatest internal migrations in American history. By the 1970s more than half of black Americans had become urban Northerners, many of them marooned in impoverished inner cities.

Millions of poor rural white Southerners left the South as well.[61] The migration of more than 2 million Appalachian whites to the Northern industrial cities between 1940 and 1970 created a white underclass similar to the inner-city underclass of black Southern migrants. "The City's toughest integration problem has nothing to do with Negroes," Albert Votaw wrote in *Harper's* in 1958 in an article entitled "Hillbillies Invade Chicago." "It involves a small army of . . . migrants from the South—who are usually poor, proud, primitive and fast with a knife. . . . [Their] sex habits . . . are clearly at variance with urban legal requirements . . . On the job they are said to lack ambition. . . ."[62] In 1951 natives of Detroit answered a polling question about "undesirable people" who were "not good to have in the city." Thirteen percent named "Negroes"; 21 percent named "poor Southern whites, hillbillies."[63]

The rhetoric of the Free-Soil movement about protecting the white workingman was revived as the black migration accelerated. In 1917 a union-led demonstration in East St. Louis against black immigration from the South produced rioting that left thirty-nine blacks dead. Labor leader Samuel Gompers denounced local employers who had "lur[ed] colored men into that city to supplant white labor." The link between black immigrants from the South and immigrants from abroad as threats to the white working class was clear in the mind of Representative Robert Bacon, a Republican from Long Island. Bacon introduced a statement from thirty-four academics calling for restriction on immigration from nations "in which the population is not predominantly of the white race" into the *Congressional Record*. In 1931 he cosponsored the Davis-Bacon Act, which favors unions in federal construction projects. The purpose of the act, and not merely its effect, was to protect Northern white labor from being in economic competition with Southern black labor. AFL president William Green testified in favor of Davis-Bacon: "Colored labor is being brought in to demoralize wages." John Cochran (D-Missouri) agreed: "I have received numerous complaints in recent months about southern contractors employing low-paid colored mechanics getting work and bringing in employees from the south."[64] Southern employers had replaced Southern slave owners, and the blacks they brought in were poorly paid workers rather than unpaid slaves, but the fears of Northern white workers and their political champions were the same as those of their predecessors in the 1850s. Indeed, the Great Migration of the black poor from the South to the North and West was exactly what Lincoln's twin policies of nonextension of slavery and black colonization had been designed to prevent.

LINCOLN'S AMERICA TOOK shape between 1860 and 1877, and was replaced by a different America between 1932 and 1965. The result of the Civil War—contrary to the wishes of a tiny minority of abolitionists—was not a color-blind society, but a segregated society with a racist immigration policy. Antiracist abolitionists like Frederick Douglass and Wendell Phillips were defeated by Lincoln and like-minded moderate and conservative Republicans, who represented popular and elite sentiment. Lincoln's America was realized by the 1920s—an isolationist, high-tariff, segregated society with a white-only immigration policy. The United States of Harding, Coolidge, and Hoover was more or less what the Republican Party of Lincoln's day had wanted the United States to be. The same forces that produced White America also worked to produce White Australia and White Canada, each with a more centralized government that promoted local industrialization by means of American-style internal improvements and protective tariffs.

The Third Republic of the United States, in the mature form it assumed between the 1960s and the end of the twentieth century, was the opposite in many ways of the Second Republic. The North dominated the Second

Republic, the South and the Sun Belt the Third. Midwestern states like Illinois, Indiana, and Ohio provided most of the presidents in the Second Republic; Southern and Western states like Texas, California, Georgia, and Arkansas sent their citizens to the White House in the Third Republic. In the Second Republic, agrarian interests were sacrificed to those of manufacturing; in the Third, agribusiness in the South and West had more clout in Washington than the declining manufacturing industries of the "rust belt." The Second Republic combined segregation with a European-only immigration policy; the Third Republic combined racial preferences for nonwhites with immigration chiefly from Latin America and Asia. The Second Republic was a great power with a limited foreign policy, reflecting the suspicion of militarism of Greater New England elites; the Third Republic was a global superpower whose frequent recourse to war was caused to some degree by the militaristic culture of Southern and Western elites.

Not least among the differences between Lincoln's America and its successors was the geography of race. The Third Republic witnessed the diffusion of the black population from the South throughout the United States. And one of the places where Southern blacks congregated, a major center of black American culture, was Chicago, Illinois.

In the presidential race of 2000, the only candidate who espoused the policies of Lincoln-McKinley Republicans—a high tariff instead of high income and payroll taxes, high wages instead of welfare payments, and immigration restriction—was Patrick J. Buchanan. Like Pauline Hanson, the old-fashioned populist who defended the abandoned Deakinite Settlement in Australia, Buchanan was considered anachronistic by members of the political mainstream. In the twenty-first-century public mind, America's civil rights tradition was identified with the antiracist ideology of the abolitionists, and its economic tradition was identified with the free trade dogma long associated with export-oriented Southern agrarians and the nineteenth-century British empire. The system of "dual protectionism" on which the Second Republic of the United States had rested between Lincoln and

Hoover, combining industrial protection with the protection of white labor from nonwhite competition, was all but forgotten.

What remains of Lincoln's legacy? The debate between proponents of laissez-faire and economic nationalism continues in the United States and other industrial capitalist societies. However, the infant-industry protectionist measures supported by Lincoln succeeded long ago and therefore lost their relevance in the United States, if not necessarily in other countries at earlier stages of industrial development. Lincoln's racial policies, intended to produce a homogeneous, all-white America, seem repugnant in a postracist United States where not only racial integration but also racial intermarriage increase with each generation.

But while Lincoln's policies are obsolete, his principles remain relevant. Lincoln the protectionist and white supremacist is a figure of the past. But Lincoln the champion of liberal democracy continues to inspire people throughout the world. To use the phrase uttered by his Secretary of War Edwin Stanton at Lincoln's deathbed, Lincoln the Great Democrat "belongs to the ages."

─◆◆◆─

EIGHT

THE GREAT DEMOCRAT:
ABRAHAM LINCOLN AND THE
MEANING OF THE CIVIL WAR

THE PRESIDENT DECIDED to use his Second Inaugural Address to explain his view of the meaning of the Civil War. Great numbers of soldiers had died, much of the country had been laid waste, and more suffering was to come. What political goals could possibly justify the continuation of this carnage? The president would make the purpose of the war clear.

The president was Jefferson Davis, and the occasion was his second inauguration as President of the Confederate States of America at a ceremony in Richmond, Virginia, the second capital of the Confederacy (the first had been Montgomery, Alabama). Davis noted that the date, February 22, 1862, was the birthday of George Washington, "the man most identified with the establishment of American independence," and told the crowd that "under the favor of Divine Providence, we hope to perpetuate the principles of our revolutionary fathers."

If any of his listeners expected Davis to identify "the principles of our revolutionary fathers" as liberty or democracy or equality, they must have been surprised by his definition of the cause for which the Confederacy fought: "When a long course of class legislation, directed not to the general welfare, but to the aggrandizement of the Northern section of the Union, culminated in a warfare on the domestic institutions of the Southern States—when the dogmas of a sectional party, substituted for the provisions of the constitutional compact, threatened to destroy the sovereign rights of the States, six of those States, withdrawing from the Union, confederated together to exercise the right and perform the duty of instituting a Government which would better secure the liberties for the preservation of which the Union was established."

What "liberties" were threatened by the majority in the North who were opposed to the South's secession—a majority that included most Northern Democrats, as well as members of the young Republican Party? Elsewhere in his Second Inaugural, Davis denounced the violation of Southern rights and property by invading Federal armies. But he did not directly answer the question of what Southern rights had been threatened by the mere election of Abraham Lincoln, a threat so powerful that secession was the only alternative. Before the South seceded, had Republicans and Northern Democrats threatened to interfere with Southern elections? To end freedom of speech? To abolish trial by jury? Of course not. The only liberty of Southerners that the new Northern majority had threatened was the liberty of Southern slave owners to create slave plantations in Western states. It was the Northern consensus against the extension of slavery to which Davis referred obliquely, when he said that Southerners "believed that to remain longer in the Union would subject them to a continuance of a disparaging discrimination, submission to which would be inconsistent with their welfare, and intolerable to a proud people."

The new Confederacy, however, stood for more than its own selfish interests, according to Davis. It was also "full of promise for mankind." What exactly was "the promise for mankind" embodied in the Confederacy? The "promise," Davis's listeners soon learned, was the purely economic benefit to the world economy of Southern commodity exports and the Southern market for foreign manufactured goods: "Yet the interest involved is not wholly our own. The world at large is concerned in opening our markets to its commerce. When the independence of the Confederate States is recognized by the nations of the earth, and we are free to follow our interests and inclinations by cultivating foreign trade, the Southern States will offer to manufacturing nations the most favorable markets which ever invited their commerce. Cotton, sugar, rice, tobacco, provisions, timber and naval stores will furnish attractive exchanges." Humanity had an interest in the triumph of the Confederacy for another reason. The confederated Southern States would be a force in the world for peace, not because of their ideals, but because of their agricultural interests: "By the character of their productions, they are too deeply interested in foreign commerce wantonly to disturb it."

Davis had almost finished his Second Inaugural—and what had he said? He had said that the possibility that a Northern majority in the federal government would prevent the minority of Southerners who owned slaves from creating slave-worked farms and ranches in the West justified the destruction of the United States. And he had said that this would promote international peace, because the Confederacy, as an agrarian supplier of "cotton, sugar, rice, tobacco, provisions, timber and naval stores," would have an economic interest in trade with, and a disinclination to war upon, the industrial countries such as Britain, France, and perhaps the remnant of the United States that would supply most of its manufactured goods.

So far Davis, in justifying the Confederate War of Independence, had carefully avoided mentioning any ideals identified with the American War of Independence. Now, however, as he neared the end of his speech, he finally referred to the principles of the Patriots of 1776: "Fellow-citizens, after the struggle of ages had consecrated the right of the Englishman to constitutional representative government, our colonial ancestors were forced to vindicate that birthright by an appeal to arms."[1] To this, three decades of proslavery thought in the South had reduced the Enlightenment ideals of the American Founders: not universal human rights, not the principles of liberty and equality, but only the "birthright" of "the Englishman." The source of the rights of "the Englishman," in the British Isles and in North America, was "the struggle of ages," not philosophy. What the Founders and most Americans had mistaken for universal rights, in principle if not in practice, were merely the ancient tribal customs of the English tribe—irrelevant to the Scots, Welsh, and Irish to say nothing of Africans and African-Americans.

Davis offered a similar interpretation of the Declaration of Independence in the speech he gave when he resigned as U.S. Senator from Mississippi on January 21, 1861. The state of Mississippi "has heard proclaimed the theory that all men are created free and equal, and this made the basis of an attack upon her social institutions; and the sacred Declaration of Independence has been invoked to maintain the position of the equality of the races." According to Davis, however, "That Declaration of Independence is to be construed by the circumstances and purposes for which it was made." Davis construed the phrase "men" in the assertion "that men were created equal" to mean "the men of the political community." The "great principles" of the Declaration "have no reference to the slave."[2] On the contrary, Thomas Jefferson, the man for whom Davis was named, wrote in a passage of the Declaration of Independence that was deleted by the Continental Congress: "He has waged cruel war against human nature itself, violating its most sacred rights of life and liberty in the persons of a distant people who never offended him, captivating and carrying them into slavery in another hemisphere, or to incur miserable death in their transportation thither. . . . Determined to keep open a market where men should be bought and sold, he has prostituted his negative for suppressing every legislative attempt to prohibit or to restrain this execrable commerce."[3]

The rejection of the universalist idealism of the American Revolution by Davis remained implicit in his reference to the time-honored rights of Englishmen rather than the abstract rights of humankind. A little less than a year earlier, the Vice President of the Confederacy, Alexander Stephens, had made explicit what Davis only hinted at when he gave what became known as the Cornerstone Speech in Savannah, Georgia, on March 21, 1861. The Founding Fathers such as Jefferson, Stephens admitted, had believed that slavery was a moral wrong: "The prevailing ideas entertained by him and most of the leading statesmen at the time of the formation of the old constitution, were that the enslavement of the African was in violation of the laws of nature; that it was wrong in principle, socially, morally, and politically. It was an evil they knew not well how to deal with, but the general opinion of the men of that day was that, somehow or other in the order of Providence, the institution would be evanescent and pass away. This idea, though not incorporated in the constitution, was the prevailing idea at that time."

Stephens, in this remarkable passage, conceded that the opponents of slavery in the North were correct about the belief of the Founding generation that slavery was immoral and their hope that the institution would ultimately be abolished. So much the worse for the Founders, said Stephens: "Those ideas, however, were fundamentally wrong. They rested upon the assumption of the equality of the races. This was an error. . . . Our new government is founded upon exactly the opposite idea; its foundations are laid, its cornerstone rests upon the great truth, that the Negro is not equal to the white man; that slavery—subordination to the superior race—is his natural and normal condition. [Applause.] This, our new government, is the first, in the history of the world, based upon this great physical, philosophical, and moral truth. This truth has been slow in the process of its development, like all other truths in the various departments of science."

The Founders could be forgiven for believing in human equality. They did not know any better. But now that racial "science" has discredited the notion, said Stephens, anyone who shares the ideals of Thomas Jefferson, George Washington, Benjamin Franklin, Alexander Hamilton, and Tom Paine is literally insane: "One of the most striking characteristics of insanity, in many instances, is forming correct conclusions from fancied or erroneous premises; so with the anti-slavery fanatics; their conclusions are right if their premises were. They assume that the negro is equal, and hence conclude that he is entitled to equal privileges and rights with the white man. If their premises were correct, their conclusions would be logical and just—but their premise being wrong, their whole argument fails."

The ideals of the American Revolution, then, were nothing but errors based on bad biology, according to the Vice President of the Confederacy. The Confederate States of America is superior to the United States of America because the Confederacy is based on a "physical" or scientific truth—blacks are subhuman and therefore legitimately enslaved and bought and sold and used like draft animals: "[The Negro] by nature, or by the curse against Canaan, is fitted for that condition which he occupies in our system. . . . The substratum of our society is made of the material fitted by nature for it, and by experience we know that it is best, not only for the superior, but for the inferior race, that it should be so. . . ." Eventually, Stephens argued, the rest of the civilized (that is, white) world will acknowledge the scientific status of racial inequality. "Thousands of people who begin to understand these truths are not yet completely out of the shell; they do not see them in their length and breadth. We hear much of the civilization and christianization of the barbarous tribes of Africa. . . ."[4]

Indeed, "the civilization and christianization of the barbarous tribes of Africa" had been one of the avowed goals of the abolition of slavery and colonization of freed slaves in Africa, according to Henry Clay. In his address to the Colonization Society of Kentucky on December 17, 1829, Clay had held out the democratization and Christianization of Africa as two of the reasons to emancipate American slaves: "And may we not indulge the hope, that in a period of time, not surpassing in duration, that of our own Colonial and National existence, we shall behold a confederation of Republican States on the western shores of Africa, like our own, with their Congress and annual Legislatures thundering forth in behalf of the rights of man, and making tyrants tremble on their thrones?" Clay also looked forward to the role of Christian former slaves in Africa working as "missionaries, of the descendants of Africa itself, with the same interests, sympathies and constitutions of the natives, to communicate the benefits of our religion and of the arts."[5]

Stephens dismissed such visions: "We hear much of the civilization and christianization of the barbarous tribes of Africa. In my judgment, those ends will never be attained, but by first teaching them the lesson taught to Adam, that 'in the sweat of his brow he should eat his bread,' [applause] and teaching them to work, and feed, and clothe themselves."[6] Stephens implied that all blacks in Africa, too, should be enslaved by whites for their own good.

The remarks of Jefferson Davis and Alexander Stephens, despite their different emphases, present a consistent vision of the ideals of the Confederate States of America. The Confederacy rejects the belief of the American Founders in human equality. Liberty was merely the tribal birthright of people of English descent (Davis) or the white race (Stephens was somewhat more generous—he would include all Caucasions).

In the 1850s, before they led the attempt at secession and purged the U.S. Constitution of liberal elements in order to create the Confederate Constitution, Jefferson Davis and other proslavery Southerners tried to purge anything suggestive of liberty and equality from the iconography of the American government as well as from its structure and philosophy. As Secretary of War under Franklin Pierce between 1853 and 1857, Jefferson Davis was responsible for supervising the enlargement and rebuilding of the United States Capitol. When the sculptor Hiram Powers, commissioned to design a statue to adorn the peak of the new Capitol dome, modeled America as a goddess trampling manacles and holding aloft a liberty cap, the design was rejected in favor of a statue to which Secretary of War Davis gave the title *Armed Liberty*. This goddess is an icon of militarism, wearing a helmet with eagle feathers and resting her hands on a sword and a shield. The future Confederate president had ordered the removal of a liberty cap from an early version of this statue. Powers complained, "I regard 'America' rather the apostle of Liberty and self government—than the armed champion. Our business is to persuade and lead mankind, not to coerce them."[7]

When the statue was finally installed atop the dome during the Civil War in 1863, a writer for *New York Times* complained that Jefferson Davis, "worshipping slavery," had replaced the liberty cap with "the barbarous device" of the military helmet.[8]

When the artist Thomas Crawford planned to include a pileus—the "liberty cap" of the freed slave that was an ancient Roman symbol of liberty—in a cornice design depicting Justice and Liberty, he received a tart message from his immediate supervisor: "Mr. Davis says that he does not like the cap of Liberty introduced into the composition. That American Liberty is original & not the liberty of the freed slave—that the cap so universally adopted & especially in France during its spasmodic struggles for freedom is desired [derived?] from the Roman custom of liberating slaves thence called freedmen & allowed to wear this cap." Under pressure from Davis, the artist replaced "Liberty" with "History," symbolizing the transition in Southern thought from timeless universal rights to Anglo-American history as the basis for the freedom of white Americans—and white Americans only.[9]

THE PRESIDENT AND Vice President of the Confederate States of America, while they differed in details, shared a common theory of the meaning of the Civil War. The President of the United States had a quite different conception.

"This is essentially a People's contest," Lincoln insisted in his statement to Congress of July 4, 1861. "On the side of the Union, it is a struggle for maintaining in the world, that form, and substance of government, whose leading object is, to elevate the condition of men—to lift artificial weights from all shoulders—to clear the paths of laudable pursuit for all—to afford all, an unfettered start, and fair chance, in the race of life."[10] The Union was willing to accept the costs of prosecuting the war not only to maintain the practical benefits of the integrity of the United States, but also in order to vindicate democracy as a form of government capable of crushing insurrection.

Capable of crushing insurrection? Most contemporary Americans, asked the meaning of the Civil War, would refer to the abolition of slavery or the promotion of the idea of equality—not the capacity of democratic governments to muster enough force and resolve to smash rebellions. And yet this was Lincoln's view of the meaning of the struggle, repeated many times.

"Our popular government has often been called an experiment," Lincoln told Congress on July 4, 1861, after he had convened it in special session. "Two points in it, our people have already established—the successful establishing, and the successful administering of it. One still remains—its successful maintenance against a formidable internal attempt to overthrow it. It is now for them to demonstrate to the world, that those who can fairly carry an election, can also suppress a rebellion—that ballots are the rightful, and peaceful, successors of bullets; and that when ballots have fairly, and constitutionally, decided, there can be no successful appeal, back to bullets; that there can be no successful appeal, except to ballots themselves, at succeeding elections. Such will be a great lesson of peace; teaching men that whatever they cannot take by an election, neither can they take it by a war. . . ."[11]

In his diary, Lincoln's private secretary John Hay recorded Lincoln's statement that the "central idea" of the Civil War was to prove that democracies can defend themselves against insurrection: "We must settle this question right now, whether in a free government the minority have the right to break up the government whenever they choose. If we fail it will go far to prove the incapacity of the people to govern themselves."[12]

The Gettysburg Address, delivered by Lincoln on November 19, 1863, was his classic formulation of this theme. The American nation—by which Lincoln means the American nation-state—was "conceived in Liberty and dedicated to the proposition that all men are created equal." The United States was undergoing "a great civil war, testing whether this nation, or any nation so conceived and so dedicated, can long endure." If the United States disintegrated because the losers in an election resorted to arms, people everywhere might conclude that democratic government is inherently unstable and cannot "long endure." Not only elsewhere in the world but also in North America, most people might conclude that only authoritarian governments were capable of providing law and order and stability. Democracy, which Lincoln famously defined as "government of the people, by the people, for the people" would "perish from the earth" because it would be considered an impractical way of organizing a large-scale, modern society. [13]

Lincoln, then, believed that democracy, as a form of government, would be discredited worldwide if the United States proved incapable of suppressing the Southern insurrection. In his view, the test of American democracy—and, by implication, of democracy in general—had begun months before the South fired the first shot at Fort Sumter.

During the tense period between his election and the outbreak of the war, Lincoln rejected compromise measures on the grounds that they would reward extortion. The challenge to American democracy, with all its implications for the future of democracy in the world, did not begin with the secession of the Southern states; it began with the mere threat that the South would use violence to achieve goals that it had failed to achieve by peaceful political action. For the bullet to trump the ballot, it was not necessary that the bullet be used. The successful threat of the bullet's use by the losers of an election to intimidate the winners into making concessions would cripple democracy in the United States and tend to discredit it in the eyes of the world.

The centrality of free and democratic elections in Lincoln's explanation of the global significance of the American Civil War refutes those who, at the time and in later eras, sought to draw parallels between the secession of the thirteen colonies from the British Empire in 1776 and the secession of the Southern states from the United States in 1860–61. The British Empire was not democratic as a whole. The colonies were partly democratic; and interference with colonial legislatures by British authorities convinced a majority of Americans that even this partial democracy was in danger of being replaced by direct, autocratic imperial rule. Even then, however, secession was the last resort of the American patriots. In the mid-1770s American leaders proposed several ways to democratize the British Empire in order to avert a rupture with the colonies. The colonies could send representatives to the London Parliament, as Scotland and Ireland did. Alternately, each colonial legislature could be elevated to equality with the London Parliament; or the colonies could send representatives to an American federal parliament, which would be responsible for domestic legislation, while the imperial government retained responsibility for imperial defense and trade. Had London not dismissed these proposals for giving the American colonies the equivalent of the dominion status granted in the nineteenth century to Canada, Australia, and New Zealand, the American War of Independence might have been avoided. Part or all of the North American population might have seceded in later generations for one or another reason, to be sure. But like the South in 1860–61, Americans in a hypothetical democratic British Empire would have been hard pressed to justify a violent rebellion in 1776 against a government in which they were free to try to redress their grievances by democratic and constitutional methods. The point was made by Edward Everett in his oration at Gettysburg, which preceded Lincoln's more famous speech: "What would have been thought by an impartial posterity of the American rebellion against George III., if the colonists had at all times been more than equally represented in parliament, and James Otis, and Patrick Henry, and Washington, and Franklin, and the Adamses, and Hancock, and Jefferson, and men of their stamp, had for two generations enjoyed the confidence of the sovereign and administered the government of the empire?"[14]

THE VICTORY OF the federal government in the Civil War, then, was necessary, according to Lincoln, to demonstrate that democracy—a rare and novel kind of government in the mid-nineteenth century—was not inherently unworkable and doomed to produce anarchy or despotism, as many contemporary European political theorists and most Western political philosophers had maintained.

In saying that the vindication of democracy gave the Civil War its universal significance, Lincoln did not ignore the issue of slavery. By the time he gave the Gettysburg Address, he had issued the Emancipation Proclamation and endorsed a constitutional amendment abolishing slavery in every state. But early in the war, Lincoln had made it clear that the abolition of slavery was a goal subordinate to preservation of the Union. He wrote to the newspaper editor Horace Greeley on August 22, 1862, "My paramount object in this struggle is to save the Union, and is not either to save or destroy slavery."[15] The abolition of slavery, in addition to eliminating a contradiction between America's principles and America's practice, would make the United States more attractive as a model of democracy for foreigners. But the immediate threat to democracy in the United States was not slavery; it was unlawful rebellion against democratic government. This rebellion was started by slave owners, but insurrections or coups d'etat by other groups, with different purposes, would have threatened democracy in the United States—and by implication, in the world—in the same way. When Lincoln said that the "great civil war" is a test of whether a democratic government "can long endure," he was not referring to the evil of slavery, but rather to the evil of armed insurrection against a democratic government. His lifelong disgust with slavery notwithstanding, Lincoln's horror of anarchy and veneration of law and order led him to support constitutional provisions that supported slavery, until the Constitution could be mended. And his law-and-order attitude inspired him to applaud the execution in 1859 of the antislavery terrorist John Brown. Under different circumstances, President Lincoln can easily be imagined sending federal troops to occupy New England, if New England abolitionists of the "disunionist" school had gained power and attempted to take their states out of the Union in protest against the Constitution's protections of slavery.

Lincoln was criticized by abolitionists for whom the emancipation of the slaves was as important, or more important, than the preservation of the Union. But if the United States was the world's model democracy, Lincoln's ordering of priorities made sense. An American democracy stained by slavery was an imperfect inspiration to democrats around the world, but it was still an example of a functioning modern republic on a large scale. But an American democracy that fell to pieces after the losers in an election took up arms would dishearten democrats everywhere, while reinforcing the belief of monarchists, aristocrats, and authoritarian militarists that democracy was destined to result in chaos followed by autocracy.

In the Gettysburg Address, Lincoln distinguished between the campaign to eliminate slavery in the United States and the campaign to vindicate the authority of the democratic federal government. The abolition of slavery was a local matter—"that this nation, under God, shall have a new birth of freedom"—while the preservation of democracy in the United States had global significance. When referring obliquely to slavery, Lincoln used the term "this nation," whereas in referring to democracy, he repeatedly made it clear that he was also referring to potential democratic states elsewhere: "this nation, or any nation so conceived and so dedicated . . ." American democracy would emerge from the contest morally improved by the abolition of slavery. But that reform would be the result of a campaign that was of global significance because it proved to the world that democrats can defeat rebellions and enforce their democratically made laws and constitutions.

Lincoln's subtle and often overlooked distinction in the Gettysburg Address between the local significance of the campaign against slavery and the global significance of the campaign to vindicate democratic government was justified. The British Empire had emancipated its black slaves in the 1830s, and the British fleet had largely succeeded in suppressing the African slave trade. Outside of parts of Africa and the Middle East, chattel slavery survived only in the United States, Brazil, and Cuba. The abolition of chattel slavery might have had global significance if it had been conceived of as the first step toward racial equality. In the United States, however, only the black minority and a few white radicals thought in these terms. Lincoln, like most white Americans, saw no contradiction between the abolition of slavery and subsequent racial segregation or separation by means of the colonization of blacks abroad.

Lincoln believed that by fighting for the Union, black Americans could promote both the local cause of emancipation and the globally significant struggle to vindicate American democracy. He made this clear in a public letter to James C. Conkling on August 26, 1863, that foreshadows the Gettysburg Address. Most of the letter was a defense of Lincoln's refusal to negotiate with the Confederates before the rebel army was defeated and a defense of the enlistment of black soldiers. Lincoln concluded by saying "The signs look better" and mentioned the recent victories "at Antietam, Murfreesboro, Gettysburg, and on many fields of lesser note." Four sentences after his passing mention of Gettysburg, Lincoln declared that when victory comes, "It will then have been proved that, among free men, there can be no successful appeal from the ballot to the bullet; and that they who take such appeal are sure to lose their case, and pay the cost. And then, there will be some black men who can remember that, with silent tongue, and clenched teeth, and steady eye, and well-poised bayonet, they have helped mankind on to this great consummation; while, I fear, there will be some white ones, unable to forget that, with malignant heart, and deceitful speech, they have strove [sic] to hinder it."[16]

Like many famous Lincoln passages, this excerpt is widely known and generally misunderstood. Lincoln was not saying that black soldiers are noble only because they have taken part in a war against slavery; he is saying that they are noble because they have taken part in a war to defend democratic government against criminal insurrection. Both white and black Union soldiers were fighting to prove to the rest of the world that a democratic government could be powerful enough to crush treason. The black Union troops "with silent tongue, and clenched teeth, and steady eye, and well-poised bayonet" were fighting to prove "that, among free men, there can be no successful appeal from the ballot to the bullet; and that they who take such appeal are sure to lose their case and pay the cost." The Civil War was about law and order in the service of democracy.

Some readers may be inclined to believe that Lincoln referred obliquely to the end of slavery in the same letter in expressing his hope that peace "will come soon, and come to stay, and come so as to be worth the keeping in all future time." But in the context of the need to vindicate "the ballot" against "the bullet" it is more likely that Lincoln meant, by a peace that "comes so as to be worth the keeping in all future time," a peace in which the democratically elected and constitutional government of the United States had vindicated its legal authority without giving in to extortion by insurrectionists.

LINCOLN'S UNDERSTANDING OF the significance of the Civil War as a test of the effectiveness of democratic government was far from original. The idea of the United States as a model democracy, with a moral obligation to demonstrate that democratic republicanism is practical as a form of government, dates back to the Founding. On the eve of his retirement as commander in chief of the Continental Army on June 8, 1783, George Washington wrote to the state governors: "It is yet to be decided whether the Revolution must ultimately be considered as a blessing or a curse: a blessing or a curse, not to the present age alone, for with our fate will the destiny of unborn Millions be involved."[17] In the first essay in the *Federalist,* Alexander Hamilton wrote: "It has been frequently remarked that it seems to have been reserved to the people of this country, by their conduct and example, to decide the important question, whether societies of men are really capable or not, of establishing good government from reflection and choice, or whether they are forever destined to depend, for their political constitutions, on accident and force. If there be any truth in the remark, the crisis, at which we are arrived, may with propriety be regarded as the era in which that decision is to be made, and a wrong election of the part we shall act, may, in this view, deserve to be considered as the general misfortune of mankind."[18] In *The Columbian Orator,* which neighbors recalled as one of his textbooks, the youthful Lincoln might have read an "Extract from an Oration Delivered at Boston, July 4, 1794, in Commemoration of American Independence": "Americans! . . . You have a government deservedly celebrated as 'giving the sanctions of law to the precepts of reason;' presenting, instead of the rank luxuriance of natural licentiousness, the corrected sweets of civil liberty. . . . We indulge the sanguine hope, that her equal laws and virtuous conduct will hereafter afford examples of imitation to all surrounding nations."[19] In his farewell address, Andrew Jackson told the American people: "Providence . . . has chosen you as the guardians of freedom, to preserve it for the benefit of the human race."[20] John C. Calhoun, as a young nationalist, declared: "[W]e are charged by Providence, not only with the happiness of this great people, but . . . with that of the human race. We have a government of a new order . . . founded on the rights of man . . . If it shall succeed . . . it will be the commencement of a new era in human affairs."[21]

The phrase "the American experiment" does not refer to a utopian attempt in social engineering, like "the Soviet experiment." Rather, in its original usage it means the "trial" or "test" of American institutions to determine whether they are capable of enduring in time while providing all of the genuine goods, and few or none of the evils, provided by nondemocratic forms of government such as monarchy, aristocracy, and dictatorship. These other forms of government, however odious they might be, at least could provide some basic goods, like public order and military defense—the Founders, and subsequent American thinkers and statesmen such as Lincoln, conceded that. This is why, in the eighteenth and nineteenth centuries, instead of rejecting the state, as anarchists did, America's liberal democrats were concerned to prove to skeptics that a democratic state could do what traditional states do, as well or even better. Many Americans claimed that the War of 1812 proved that a republic could hold its own against an empire, and that the Mexican War demonstrated that a republic could defeat a dictatorship modeled on those of the Old World (the Mexican dictator Santa Anna styled himself "the Napoleon of the West"). Nondemocratic states survived by now and then crushing insurrections and rebellions against their authority. The Civil War was yet another "experiment," or test, to determine whether a democratic republic could succeed in that traditional exercise of state power as well.

In the Gettysburg Address and his other statements about the meaning of the Civil War, Lincoln distilled the perceptions of many ordinary American citizens. Robert T. McMahan, a private in the 2nd Ohio Cavalry, wrote in his diary on September 13, 1863, of "the great principles of liberty and self-government at stake, for should we fail, the onward march of Liberty in the Old World will be retarded at least a century, and Monarchs, Kings and Aristocrats will be more powerful against their subjects than ever."[22] Lincoln would have been pleased to learn of the views of Peter Welsh, an Irish-American immigrant who fought in the Irish Brigade of the 28th Massachusetts, in 1863: "This is my country as much as the man who was born on the soil. . . . This is the first test of a modern free government in the act of sustaining itself against internal enemys [*sic*] . . . if it fail, all tyrants will succeed [and] the old cry will be sent forth from the aristocrats of europe that such is the common lot of all republics. . . ."[23]

"I THINK YOU should admit that we already have an important principle to rally and unite the people, in the fact that constitutional government is at stake. This is a fundamental idea," Lincoln told religious leaders in Chicago on September 13, 1862.[24] For Lincoln, democracy itself as a form of government was on trial in the U.S. Civil War. But what precisely was Lincoln's conception of democracy?

Lincoln was a politician, not a political theorist. In his statements Lincoln assumed an identity between democratic government, liberal government, and constitutional government. He never discussed, and may never have reflected on, hard cases that appeal to political theorists: illiberal democracies, liberal autocracies, and constitutional regimes that are neither liberal nor democratic.

Lincoln was a democrat because he was a liberal. He valued democracy and equality because they protect and promote liberal individualism. Like most of the Founders, Lincoln was not a civic republican, for whom the exercise of civic duty is the highest good. Nor was he a radical egalitarian. He made it clear that he was in favor of equality of opportunity, not equality of result, and he thought of equality of opportunity chiefly in terms of economic self-betterment. As he told an audience in New Haven, Connecticut, on March 6, 1860, "What is the true condition of the laborer? I take it that it is best for all to leave each man free to acquire property as fast as he can. Some will get wealthy. I don't believe in a law to prevent a man from getting rich; it would do more harm than good. So while we do not propose any war upon capital, we do wish to allow the humblest man an equal chance to get rich with everybody else. [Applause.] When one starts poor, as most do in the race of life, free society is such that he knows he can better his condition; he knows that there is no fixed condition of labor, for his whole life."[25] In a speech to German immigrants in Cleveland, Ohio, on February 12, 1861, Lincoln observed that "working men are the basis of all governments" because "there are more of them than of any other class." He continued, "I hold the value of life is to improve one's condition. Whatever is calculated to advance the condition of the honest, struggling laboring man, so far as my judgment will enable me to judge of a correct thing, I am for that thing."[26] On February 22, 1861, Lincoln defined democracy as the form of government "which gave promise that in due time the weights should be lifted from the shoulders of all men, and that all should have an equal chance."[27] By definition, monarchies and aristocracies assigned places in the socioeconomic scale on the basis of heredity rather than individual effort. A democratic society was the only one in which the normal type would be Henry Clay's "self-made man," the ideal for Lincoln and like-minded Americans. A view of democracy that treats it not as an end in itself, but as the political precondition for efforts by individuals to improve their economic status, may not appeal to adherents of other schools of democratic thought. But this is what Lincoln believed.[28]

Many British and continental European thinkers along with some Americans argued that liberal governments need not be democratic, in the sense of abolishing monarchical or aristocratic institutions or providing for universal manhood or adult suffrage. Daniel Webster in 1824 seems to have classed the United States and Britain together as constitutional or "regulated" liberal governments, even if Britain was not democratic: "There are, happily, enough of regulated governments in the world, and those among the most distinguished, *to operate as constant examples,* and to keep alive an unceasing panting in the bosoms of men for the enjoyment of similar free institutions" (emphasis added).[29]

Lincoln, by contrast, always spoke as though monarchical and aristocratic regimes were inherently illiberal. He denounced both monarchy and slavery as deviations from the democratic republican ideal in a campaign speech for the first Republican presidential candidate, John C. Fremont, at Kalamazoo, Michigan, on August 27, 1856: "We find a people on the North-east, who have a different government from ours, being ruled by a Queen. Turning to the South, we see a people who, while they boast of being free, keep their fellow beings in bondage. Compare our Free States with either, shall we say here that we have no interest in keeping the principle [of equality] alive?"[30]

Lincoln also criticized the idea that partial democratic participation in an aristocratic and royalist regime was sufficient to qualify such a polity as a free society. In his Annual Message to Congress of 1861, Lincoln argued that "the insurrection is largely, if not exclusively, a war upon the first principle of popular government—the rights of the people. Conclusive evidence of this is found in the most grave and maturely considered documents, as well as in the general tone of the insurgents." By "the most grave and maturely considered documents" he seems to be referring to the polemics by George Fitzhugh and others arguing that slavery or serfdom is the natural condition of most human beings of all races. "In those documents we find the abridgement of the existing right of suffrage and the denial to the people of all right to participate in the selection of public officers, except the legislative boldly advocated, with labored arguments to prove that large control of the people in government, is the source of all political evil. Monarchy itself is sometimes hinted at as a possible refuge from the power of the people."[31] Note that Lincoln conceded that some antiliberal thinkers admitted the right of "the people" to participate in selecting "legislative" officers while rejecting the democratic election of executive officials—that is, the king and his ministers. From Lincoln's point of view, parliamentary monarchy was merely another version of monarchy, notwithstanding the election of some legislators, and the claim of a hereditary monarch to rule people who had not elected him was no more legitimate than the claim of a slave owner to rule a slave. In his last debate with Stephen A. Douglas at Alton, Illinois, on October 15, 1858, Lincoln equated monarchy with slavery: "It is the eternal struggle between these two principles—right and wrong—throughout the world. They are the two principles that have stood face to face from the beginning of time; and will ever continue to struggle. The one is the common right of humanity and the other the divine right of kings. . . . No matter in what shape it comes, whether from the mouth of a king who seeks to bestride the people of his own nation and live by the fruit of their labor, or from one race of men as an apology for enslaving another race, it is the same tyrannical principle."[32] Lincoln associated monarchy with militarism and the economic exploitation of the majority. "Kings had always been involving and impoverishing their people in wars, pretending generally, if not always, that the good of the people was the object," Lincoln wrote to his friend and law partner William Herndon on February 15, 1848, in a letter justifying his opposition as a member of Congress to President James K. Polk's policy in the Mexican War. "This, our [Constitutional] Convention understood to be the most oppressive of all Kingly oppressions; and they naturally resolved to frame the Constitution that no one man should have the power of bringing this oppression upon us."[33]

The evidence indicates that Lincoln viewed constitutional monarchy not as an equally legitimate form of liberal society, but as a variant of autocracy. The record of many parliamentary monarchies in the twentieth century may be thought to have refuted his view. But inasmuch as most of these, like Britain, have become democratic republics in all but name, with ceremonial monarchs and largely vestigial aristocracies, perhaps Lincoln was right after all.

———

IN 1920 H.L. Mencken raised a question that has occurred to many readers of the Gettysburg Address: In what way would the success of the Southern states in seceding have caused democracy to "perish from the earth"? "The doctrine is simply this: that the Union soldiers who died at Gettysburg sacrificed their lives to the cause of self-determination—that government of the people, by the people, for the people, should not perish from the earth. It is difficult to imagine anything more untrue. The Union soldiers in the battle actually fought against self-determination; it was the Confederates who fought for the right of their people to govern themselves."[34]

Was Lincoln wrong to believe that the disintegration of the United States would discredit democracy as a form of government? Neither Lincoln nor other Unionists expected that the Confederacy, if it won its freedom, would adopt a monarchical or aristocratic constitution, much less that royal rule and titles of nobility would return to a rump U.S. shorn of the Southern states. Many Unionists feared, rather, that the secession of the South would be followed by a series of civil wars and wars among the successor states to the United States. The argument that successful secession would have produced two functioning democracies instead of one—the USA and the CSA—ignores the likelihood of further disintegration. Texas might have seceded from the Confederacy, and California from the United States. Different former American states and regions might have gone to war over contested borders. Seeking foreign military aid, they might have turned to rival European great powers—the South to Britain, the North to Russia or France or Prussia/Germany. From the seventeenth to the nineteenth century, British-settled North America had been an arena for struggles among Britain and France, and France took advantage of the distraction of the United States by the Civil War to invade Mexico. John Quincy Adams wrote in 1796: "There is no one article of my political creed more clearly demonstrated to my mind than this, that we shall proceed with giant strides to honor and consideration, and national greatness, if the union is preserved; but that if it is once broken, we shall soon divide into a parcel of petty tribes at perpetual war with one another, swayed by rival European powers, whose policy will agree perfectly in the system of keeping us at variance with one another."[35] During the Civil War the fear that the successful secession of the Confederacy, instead of producing two enduring countries in place of one ephemeral union, would result in a cycle of further secessions, civil wars, coups d'etat, and dictatorships, was widely discussed, and not only by politicians and intellectuals. Samuel Evans, a blacksmith fighting for the Union in the 7th Ohio Regiment, wrote to his father on September 13, 1863: "Admit the right of the seceding states to break up the Union at pleasure . . . and how long will it be before the new confederacies created by the first disruption shall be resolved into still smaller fragments and the continent become a vast theater of civil war, military license, anarchy, and despotism? Better settle it at whatever cost and settle it forever."[36]

Although he seems to have believed that secession was constitutional, in 1798 Thomas Jefferson had rejected an argument for secession by Southerners upset at New England's temporary predominance in the federal government on the grounds that it might lead to endless political disintegration: "If on a temporary superiority of the one party, the other is to resort to a scission of the Union, no federal government can ever exist. If we rid ourselves of the present rule of Massachusetts and Connecticut, we break the Union, will the evil stop there? Suppose the New England states alone cut off, will our nature be changed? . . . Immediately, we shall see a Pennsylvania and a Virginia party arise in the residuary confederacy, and the public mind will be distracted with the same party spirit. . . . If we reduce our Union to Virginia and North Carolina, immediately the conflict will be established between the representatives of these two States, and they will end by breaking into their simple units."[37]

Latin America provided an example to be avoided. Like Anglophone North Americans, most Latin Americans shared a common language, culture, traditions, and religion. But attempts to unite the former colonies of

Spain had failed, and independence had been followed by endless civil wars and secessions, such as the secession of the Central American states and Yucatán and Texas from Mexico (Yucatán was reconquered, and Texas annexed to the United States, but Honduras, Guatemala, Nicaragua, El Salvador, and Costa Rica remained independent). While most of the Latin American states were republics in form, in practice they were usually military or civilian dictatorships; and there were repeated attempts to restore monarchy in Mexico, culminating in the support of many Mexicans for the French-installed Emperor Maximilian.

Latin America was not the only example of a cultural community divided among warring states that illustrated the dangers of division to American Unionists. In the 1860s Germany and Italy, nations divided for centuries among weak and often mutually hostile governments, provided American Unionists with a similar negative example. In his address at Gettysburg, Edward Everett drew the parallel with both countries: "In Germany, the wars of the Reformation and of Charles V, in the sixteenth century, the Thirty Years' war in the seventeenth century, the Seven Years' war in the eighteenth century, not to speak of other less celebrated contests, entailed upon that country all the miseries of internecine strife for more than three centuries. . . . In Italy, on the breaking up of the Roman Empire, society might be said to be resolved into its original elements—into hostile atoms, whose only movement was of mutual repulsion." Everett, after warning of the dangers of geopolitical disintegration in North America, went on to claim that the major historical trend of the mid-nineteenth century was the unification of divided nations like Germany and Italy: "There is no country in the world in which the sentiment of national brotherhood is stronger [than in Germany]. . . . [N]ow Tuscan and Lombard, Sardinian and Neapolitan, as if to shame the degenerate sons of America, are joining in one cry for a united Italy."[38] As a result of the Franco-Prussian War in 1870, both Germany (outside of the Habsburg domains) and Italy would be united.

Everett's assumption that the national unification of Germany and Italy was part of the same progressive trend as the preservation of the American

Union was widely shared. Many Americans celebrated what they saw as the creation of a United States of Germany and a United States of Italy. Even though the new German and Italian unions were monarchies rather than republics, they were viewed initially as enlightened federal governments similar to the United States. The hostility of Bismarck to the Catholic Church and the defeat of the Vatican by the new Italian monarchy of Victor Emmanuel further endeared the new nation-states to many Protestant and secular Americans.

The belief in a spiritual affinity between the American Civil War and the wars of Italian unification seems odd today. But it was held by none other than Julia Ward Howe, author of "The Battle Hymn of the Republic," who, to the same tune, was inspired to write a "Hymn for the Celebration of Italian Unity":

> *Let them sound a victor strophe from the mountains to the sea!*
> *Sweep away the old defences! Let the tide of life run free*
> *As the thought of God commissioned, that outleaps captivity.*
> *Let Italy be one!*
> CHORUS: *Glory, hallelujah!*
>
> *Sound the trumpet of resurrection! let the noble dead arise!*
> *Let the hour long wept and wished for make God present to their eyes!*
> *Let one joy illume the heavens and the earthly paradise,*
> *Since Italy is one!*[39]

Before the Civil War William Ware, an American visitor to Italy, had observed that the short-lived Roman Republic of Giuseppe Mazzini could have survived only in the context of a united federal Italy with a strong national government. Referring to the rivalries of the petty Italian states, he wrote: "They are all of them what our South Carolina is, alone fortunately, in its character—all for self—ready to throw the world into universal confusion and war, rather than not be able to have her own way—like a petted baby. A few Carolinas would reduce our country to the miserable condition of the Italian republics. The want of a spirit of union and amity has destroyed them."[40]

The argument that the disintegration of the American republic would discredit democracy in Europe, Asia, and elsewhere, then, did not assume that monarchy or aristocracy would be reintroduced into the two or more successor states of the American Union. The prestige of democratic republicanism would be damaged severely, even if the petty and weak states that emerged from the disintegration of the United States were republics in form. The lesson for the rest of the world would not be lost: republicanism was less suited than monarchy or dictatorship as a form of government for a modern nation-state.

The atrocities committed by authoritarian and totalitarian nationalist movements in the twentieth century have persuaded many that "democracy" and "nationalism" are somehow opposed. In the nineteenth century, however, many liberals supported nationalism as an alternative both to despotic empires and to small-scale princedoms and oligarchic republics dominated by hereditary aristocracies. Liberal nationalism was espoused by some of the greatest liberal philosophers, including J. S. Mill and Giuseppe Mazzini and Friedrich List, who envisioned a world of liberal democratic nation-states in place of a world of dynastic empires.

The most influential American proponent of the theory that modern democracy should take the form of the liberal nation-state was Francis Lieber, the political scientist and jurist who advised the Lincoln administration. Lieber summed up his ideas about democracy, liberalism, nationalism, and the replacement of a world of empires by a world of nation-states in a single cumbersome sentence in "Nationalism: A Fragment of Political Science" (1868): "The National Polity is the normal type of Modern Government; Civil Liberty resting on Institutional Self-Government is the highest political calling of the period; Absolutism, whether Monarchical or Democratic, intelligent or brilliant or coarse, its pervading danger; and increasing International Neighborliness with growing Agreement of National

Forms and Concepts, its fairest Gauge of the Spreading Progress of our Kind." Elaborating, Lieber explained that forms of government other than the nation-state were anachronistic: "The universal monarchy . . . ; a single leading nation; confederacies of petty sovereigns; a civilization confined to one spot or portion of globe—all these are obsolete ideas, wholly insufficient for the demands of advanced civilization, and attempts at their renewal have led and must lead to ruinous results, the end of all anachronisms recklessly pursued." Most other Lincoln Republicans would have agreed with Lieber that "the three main characteristics of the political development which mark the modern epoch are: The national polity; The general endeavor to define more clearly, and to extend more widely, human rights and civil liberty (not unconnected as this movement is with the pervading critical spirit of the age, and the wedlock of Knowledge and Labor which marks the nineteenth century); And the decree which has gone forth that many leading nations shall flourish at one and the same time, plainly distinguished from one another; yet striving together, with one public opinion, under the protection of one law of nations, and in the bonds of one common moving civilization."[41]

The assumption that liberalism, democracy, and nationalism were allied against illiberalism, autocracy, and empire explains the expressions of support by Americans for the Greek revolt against the Ottoman Empire, for the wars of independence from the Spanish Empire waged by the Latin American republics, and for the nationalist revolutions that swept Europe in 1848. Daniel Webster, like Clay one of Lincoln's Whig heroes, offered moral support to the Greek war of independence from the Ottoman Empire, declaring in 1824: "The civilized world has done with 'the enormous faith, of many made for one' [the phrase is from the eighteenth-century English poet Alexander Pope's "Essay on Man"]. Society asserts its own rights, and alleges them to be original, sacred and unalienable. It is not satisfied with having kind masters; it demands a participation in its own government; and in states much advanced in civilization, it urges this demand with a constancy and an energy that cannot well nor long be resisted."[42] Lacking the power to influence the world beyond the Western Hemisphere, President James Monroe and his successors announced the Monroe Doctrine, which declared that the United States would oppose the incorporation of independent countries in the Americas into European empires, without threatening existing British, Spanish, and French imperial domains in the Americas.

Lincoln's first public statement in support of self-determination by foreign nationalities came on September 6, 1849, when he took part in a committee of leading citizens in Springfield that drafted "Resolutions of Sympathy with the Cause of Hungarian Freedom," which were published in the *Illinois Journal* on September 7. Then on January 8, 1852, Lincoln spoke to a meeting of Illinois Whigs seeking to formulate resolutions in response to the American tour of the exiled Hungarian leader Louis Kossuth. Lincoln "spoke in favor of sympathy but non-intervention." A committee drew up resolutions, which Lincoln reported on January 9; they were published and sent to Kossuth and each member of the U.S. Congress from Illinois. The resolutions demonstrate that Lincoln and his fellow citizens of Springfield hoped that the revolutions of 1848 would lead to the end of multinational empires and the emergence of a world of democratic nation-states. They denounced tsarist Russia for invading Hungary, affirming that "it is the right of any people, sufficiently numerous for national independence, to throw off, to revolutionize, their existing form of government, and to establish such other in its stead as they may choose." They resolved further that "it is the duty of our government neither to foment, nor assist, such revolutions in other governments" except in cases such as that of "the late interference of Russia in the Hungarian struggle." They resolved that, while supporting the battle for Hungarian independence, "we should not fail to pour out the tribute of our praise and approbation to the patriotic efforts of the Irish, the Germans and the French, who have unsuccessfully fought to establish in their several governments the supremacy of the people." And they concluded by denouncing Britain for supporting the multinational monarchies of continental Europe: "[T]here is nothing in the past history of the British government, or in its present expressed policy, to encourage the belief that she will aid, in any manner, in the delivery of continental Europe from the yoke of despotism; and that her treatment of Ireland, of O'Brien, Mitchell, and other worthy patriots, forces the conclusion that she will join her efforts to the despots of Europe in suppressing every effort of the people to establish free governments, based upon the principles of true religious and civil liberty.[43]" Lincoln's references to the significance of the American Civil War for the fate of democracy in Europe and the world must be understood in the context of his support for the unsuccessful liberal nationalist revolutions in Europe in 1848.

IN THE SECOND half of the twentieth century, many liberal and democratic thinkers sought to sever democracy from nationalism. Some invoked the Gettysburg Address as evidence that American patriotism is a matter of pure idealism and has nothing to do with a particular historic American national community.

This is a misreading of Lincoln's thought. Lincoln was not only a nationalist but also a white-racial nationalist who thought that the American national community should be limited to Anglo-Americans and European immigrants. Black Americans, no matter how much they shared the culture of white Americans, could never participate in the white American national community nor, by implication, could nonwhite immigrants, whose exclusion by white-only naturalization laws Lincoln never questioned. Lincoln favored the immigration only of white Europeans: "Inasmuch as our country is extensive and new, and the countries of Europe are densely populated, if there are any abroad who desire to make this the land of their adoption, it is not in my heart to throw aught in their way, to prevent them from coming to the United States."[44] In Lincoln's mind, the white American nation was dedicated to the Enlightenment ideals of liberty, equality, and democracy. But those ideals alone did not define the American people, and could not. Indeed, there would have been no point in Lincoln's calling on the American people to dedicate themselves to democratic ideals, if the American people were already defined by those ideals rather than by nonpolitical criteria of nationality, criteria which, in Lincoln's view, included race.

Lincoln's conception of American patriotism as a compound of particularistic nationalism and universalist idealism is evident in speeches he gave on his journey to be inaugurated in Washington, D.C., in 1861. To the New Jersey Senate on February 21, preceding his inauguration as president, Lincoln described the American Revolution as having two objects—one local and national, one global. Discussing his childhood reading "of the battlefields and struggles for the liberties of the country," Lincoln said: "I recollect thinking then, boy even though I was, that there must have been something more than common that those men struggled for." That "something" was "even more than National Independence" and "held out a great promise to all the people of the world to all time to come . . ."[45] In a speech in Independence Hall, Philadelphia, a few days later on February 22, 1861, Lincoln returned to this theme: "I have often inquired of myself, what great principle it was that kept this Confederacy so long together. It was not the mere matter of the separation of the colonies from the mother land; but something in that Declaration giving liberty, not alone to the people of this country, but hope to the world for all future time. It was that which gave promise that in due time the weights should be lifted from the shoulders of all men, and that all should have an equal chance."[46] Lincoln was not disparaging "national independence" and "the separation of the colonies from the mother land." He was saying that in addition to those legitimate goals, of interest to Americans alone, the American Revolution stood for principles valid everywhere.

On different occasions, for different purposes, Lincoln emphasized particular national sentiment, which was limited by its nature to the American national community, and universal ideals, which other nations could and should share. In the Gettysburg Address, rallying Northerners to continued struggle, he appealed to America's universalist political ideals. In his first inaugural, however, when he was trying to conciliate white Southerners, he emphasized the shared sentiments of Anglo-Americans in North and South whose ancestors had fought together against the British and other enemies. Adapting a concluding paragraph suggested by William H. Seward, Lincoln wrote: "Though passion may have strained, it must not break our bonds of affection. The mystic chords of memory, stretching from every battle-field, and patriot grave, to every living heart and hearthstone, all over this broad land, will yet swell the chorus of the Union, when again touched, as surely they will be, by the better angels of our nature."[47] This appeal to the communal sentiment of the nation was just as legitimate as appeals to the ideals of the Declaration of Independence. In Lincoln's mind, sentimental nationalism and democratic idealism were complementary, not exclusive.

When Lincoln applauded struggles for national independence abroad, it never occurred to him to argue, as later antinationalist proponents of democracy would argue, that there was something sinister or illiberal about celebrating the nonpolitical traditions that distinguish nations from others. Lincoln hoped that eventually democratic republicanism would be adopted by all of the nations of the earth. But Lincoln neither expected nor wanted nations to disappear. On the contrary, like most of his American contemporaries, he thought that democracy required the conversion of a small number of multinational empires into a great number of nation-states defined by language, culture, and ethnicity, like an independent Ireland and an independent Hungary.

Today racial homogeneity of the kind favored by Lincoln and most white Americans before the mid-twentieth century has been discredited as a basis for national identity. However, most nation-states in the world, including multiracial countries like the United States, cohere on the basis of a common language and common majority customs. And even in countries with high levels of immigration like the United States, the majority of citizens inherit their citizenship from their parents rather than acquire it by choice. Academic philosophers may defend the idea of citizenship as a matter of choice rather than descent and argue that a common political philosophy is sufficient to provide a sense of community among groups who share nothing else in common. But the idea of postnational democracy, like the idea of world federalism, is alien to the political philosophy of Abraham Lincoln.

I T   W O U L D   B E   inaccurate, to portray Lincoln as a provincial American idealist who naïvely expected that the entire world could adopt American liberal and democratic institutions overnight. Utopian hopes for the rapid and painless spread of liberal and democratic institutions were more characteristic of twentieth- and twenty-first-century Americans than of their eighteenth- and nineteenth-century predecessors. Earlier generations of American statesmen and thinkers, including Lincoln, distinguished between ideal human rights and actual civil rights. They also recognized that republican government might not succeed in all societies.

Lincoln rejected arguments that only Caucasians, or Anglo-Saxons, had human rights. However, like most eighteenth- and nineteenth-century liberals, Lincoln distinguished between innate human rights, which to use the language of the Declaration of Independence were "unalienable," and civil and political rights, which could be bestowed by the government on some groups and withheld from others. Slavery was incompatible with liberalism, but in his mind the denial of political and social equality to black Americans was not.

A typical statement of Lincoln's distinction between ideal and practical rights is this one: "I have all the while maintained, that in so far as it should be insisted that there was an equality between the white and black races that should produce a perfect social and political equality, it was an impossibility. . . . [A]nd with it I have said, that in their right to 'life, liberty and the pursuit of happiness,' as proclaimed in that old Declaration, the inferior races are our equals."[48] Speaking of the Declaration, Lincoln said: "I think the authors of that notable instrument intended to include all men, but they did not mean to declare men equal in all respects. . . . They meant simply to declare the right so that the enforcement of it might follow as fast as circumstances should permit." Lincoln continued: "They meant to set up a standard maxim for free society which should be familiar to all: constantly looked to, constantly labored for, and even though never perfectly attained, constantly approximated and thereby constantly spreading and deepening its influence and augmenting the happiness and value of life to all people, of all colors, everywhere."[49]

As authority for his argument that the ideal of equality required neither immediate emancipation of the slaves nor social and civil equality for free blacks, Lincoln in his October 15, 1858, debate with Douglas quoted Henry Clay on the meaning of the phrase "all men are created equal" in the Declaration of Independence. According to Clay: "Now, as an abstract principle, there is no doubt of the truth of that declaration; and it is desirable in the original construction of society, and in organized societies, to keep it in view as a great fundamental principle. But, then, I apprehend that in no society that ever did exist, or ever shall be formed, was or can the equality asserted among the members of the human race be practically enforced and carried out." As examples of people whose abstract human rights did not translate into actual civil rights and voting rights, Clay cited "women, minors, insane, culprits, transient sojourners, that will always probably remain subject to the government of another portion of the community."[50] In this category Clay and Lincoln included free blacks living in the United States. But as colonizationists they held out the possibility that blacks could have complete political and legal equality in an all-black or majority-nonwhite nation other than the United States.

Just as it was a commonplace in Lincoln's America that abstract human equality could not, and need not, be translated into full civic and social equality for all groups, so it was widely assumed that some societies, because of their racial composition, religious traditions, or other factors, might fail to achieve successful republican government. In a letter to John Adams on September 4, 1823, referring to struggles in Europe and Latin America, Jefferson predicted that in the long run "all will attain representative government, more or less perfect." In some cases, however, Jefferson thought that this would take the form of constitutional monarchy rather than dem-

ocratic republicanism: "[Representative government] is now well understood to be a necessary check on kings, whom they will probably think it
necessary to chain and tame, than to exterminate. To attain all this however
rivers of blood must yet flow, and years of desolation pass over."[51] As president, Jefferson carried on a friendly correspondence with Tsar Alexander,
whom he regarded as an enlightened autocrat capable of gradually preparing the Russian people for representative government in future generations.[52]

Henry Clay also combined a passionate belief in democracy as an ideal
with an acknowledgment that the ideal could not immediately be realized in
some societies. Clay denied the equation of Protestant and republican society: "There is nothing in the Catholic religion unfavourable to freedom. All
religions, united with government, are more or less inimical to liberty. All,
separated from government, are compatible with liberty. . . ."[53] But he conceded that as a result of their political traditions, some nations might be un-
prepared for immediate success with republican, constitutional government.
Following the abdication of King Louis Philippe of France in the spring of
1848, Clay wrote to a correspondent: "Poor France. I fear she is destined to
undergo another bloody Revolution. It is preposterous to suppose her capable of establishing and maintaining a Republic."[54] In 1852 Clay told the
exiled Hungarian leader Louis Kossuth that the failure of republican government in France "teaches us to despair of any present success for liberal institutions in Europe. Far better is it for ourselves, for Hungary, and for the
cause of liberty, that, adhering to our wise, pacific system, and avoiding the
distant wars of Europe, we should keep our lamp burning brightly on this
western shore as a light to all nations, than to hazard its utter extinction amid
the ruins of fallen or falling republics in Europe."[55]

Many liberals in the nineteenth and early twentieth centuries who
made the distinction between abstract and realizable rights defended
European imperialism by arguing that it was a school for eventual self-
government on the part of nonwhite nations after a period of benevolent
white rule. Similar arguments were made to justify U.S. rule in the

Philippines between the Spanish-American War and World War II. Despite his support for white supremacy in the United States, Lincoln was a consistent opponent of white supremacy in the world. As president he gave diplomatic recognition to Haiti after decades in which the influence of Southern slaveholders had prevented acknowledging the existence of a black republic and also recognized Liberia. And as president he provided moral support to the Mexican republican leader Benito Juárez, an Indian, in his struggle against the forces of the French-installed Habsburg monarch Maximilian. In the Mexican city named for Juárez, both an Avenida Lincoln and a statue of Lincoln can be found.

Unlike the French Jacobins, who claimed they had a moral duty to revolutionize other countries, most American republicans rejected the idea that the United States had a duty to take part in democratic revolutions abroad or to impose democracy on other societies by force. In his speech on Discoveries and Inventions on February 11, 1859, Lincoln mocked "Young America," the symbol of Manifest Destiny, and suggested that talk about spreading democracy on the part of American expansionists was a disguise for other motives: "He is a great friend of humanity; and his desire for land is not selfish, but merely an impulse to extend the area of freedom. He is very anxious to fight for the liberation of enslaved nations and colonies, provided, always, they *have* land, and have *not* any liking for his interference. As to those who have no land, and would be glad of help from any quarter, he considers *they* can afford to wait a few hundred years longer" (emphasis in original).[56] Lincoln "did not believe in enlarging our field, but in keeping our present possession, making it a garden, improving the morals and education of the people."[57] Others could and should adopt their versions of the American model because of America's example, not America's arms.

As an exemplary republic, the United States belonged to a small category of states that included the Most Serene Republic of San Marino, a city-state in Italy that traced its republican heritage to the Middle Ages and offered asylum to Garibaldi after the collapse of the short-lived Roman republic in 1849. After the citizens of San Marino made Lincoln an honorary citizen, he wrote: "Although your dominion is small, nevertheless your state is one of the most honored throughout history." In the government palace of San Marino is a bust of Lincoln.

BY DEFEATING "THE Rebellion," Lincoln and his allies believed that they had proved that modern, national republics were as capable as monarchies and dictatorships of defending themselves against internal insurrections. Lincoln, like most Americans of his era, hoped that the United States would inspire nations around the world to break free from multinational empires, create nation-states, replace royal with republican governments, and abolish aristocracy, as the United States had done.

Was the American example critical to the development of democracy in the world? Skeptics might answer in the negative. Democracy might be inevitable, either because of an innate, irrepressible human desire for democratic government, or because democracy is the by-product of industrial and social modernization.

The fact that democracies have been rare in history suggests the absence of a universal human demand for democratic government. Is democracy, however, inevitable in modern conditions? In industrial societies, in which the majority of people are literate and urban, concessions to populism have been more common than in preindustrial agricultural societies. But modern populism has often taken the form of mobilization of the masses by fascist and communist dictatorships and by other kinds of authoritarian regimes. Some kind of populism may be inevitable in modern conditions; multiparty liberal democracy is not.

Another possibility is that France or Britain might have inspired modern democracy in the absence of the example of the United States. Of the two republican traditions that originated in the eighteenth century, the tradition of the French Revolution inspired far more democrats in Europe and throughout the world than the tradition of the American Revolution, before the world wars of the twentieth century.

The American and French Revolutions turned out quite differently. But republicans in the United States and France, despite significant differences, shared a common political language. The American Founders and those who admired them, like Lincoln, spoke of the American "experiment" in the same way that a French journalist in 1794 wrote: "The French Revolution might be described as the first experiment performed on the grand scale on a whole nation." In the nineteenth century Lincoln argued that the American republic was the hope of humanity, while the French historian Michelet argued that France, a nation "that has best merged its own interest and destiny with those of humanity," had a duty as "the moral ideal of the world" and a "universal fatherland" to "help every nation born to liberty."[58] In 1917 Henri Barbusse wrote: "Some assure that in order to walk to one's death and sacrifice one's life, it is necessary to be stimulated by a narrow patriotism or inebriated by hatred for a given race. No, it is rather the lofty promise of final progress which leads the true men to give their blood. We, who fought as Frenchmen, and above all as men, can say proudly that we are living proof of this."[59]

American republicanism had its greatest international impact through its influence on France itself, during the early, liberal phase of the French Revolution. The French philosopher Condorcet wrote in 1786: "It is not enough that the rights of man be written in the books of philosophers and inscribed in the hearts of virtuous men; the weak and ignorant must be able to read them in the example of a great nation. America has given us this example."[60] In *Ruins of Empires* by the French philosopher Constantine Volney, which Lincoln read as a young man, is a footnote which states that "the science of the rights of man is a new science: it was invented yesterday by the Americans, to-day the French are perfecting it, but there yet remains a great deal to be done. . . ."[61]

Because France was the leading continental power in Europe, which was the dominant region of the world until the mid-twentieth century, the French republican example had far more global influence than the model of the American republic. Modern political movements—liberalism, conservatism, socialism—defined themselves largely by their attitude toward the French Revolution. The very terms "left" and "right" derive from seating arrangements in the French National Assembly. The idea of universal human rights was familiar to most people in the world from the French Declaration of the Rights of Man and the Citizen, not from the U.S. Declaration of Independence or Bill of Rights. Liberal, democratic, and nationalist reformers and revolutionaries in Europe and the world identified with one or another faction in the French Revolution, such as Jacobins or Girondists. Nobody outside of the United States modeled themselves on Jeffersonians or Hamiltonians. The French revolutionary leaders—Robespierre, Danton, Marat, Lafayette, Napoleon—were world famous. Outside of the United States, hardly anyone could name any American Founders, except for Washington, about whom little was known. When liberal and leftist revolutionaries in Europe took to the streets in 1830 and 1848, they often saw themselves as the heirs of one or another strain within the French Revolution. None of them, not even moderate, bourgeois liberal republicans, waved copies of the U.S. Constitution or the *Federalist Papers.* Lincoln and other Americans might have identified the cause of humanity with the cause of the United States, but for most liberals and democrats around the world, France was the "universal nation." For example, the Russian radical Bakunin wrote in 1867: "Only in those rare moments when a nation really represents the general interest, the right and freedom of all mankind, can a citizen who calls himself a revolutionary be a patriot too. . . . The French patriots of 1793 struggled, fought and triumphed in the name of the freedom of the world; for the future fate of all mankind was identical with the cause of revolutionary France. . . ."[62]

Throughout the nineteenth and early twentieth centuries, however, movements inspired by the republican tradition of France were failures. European republicans were defeated by monarchists during the Napoleonic Wars and again during the revolutions of 1848. Monarchical and aristocratic elites feared republican subversives, but before World War I, dynasties and empires were firmly in control of most of Europe and the world.

An alternative to French and American republicanism was provided by the British model of parliamentary monarchy. In the late eighteenth century, British elites were shocked first by the loss of their American colonies to republican rebels, and then by the destruction of the monarchy and aristocracy in France by other republicans. The conservative British establishment rejected both republicanism and the Lockean theory of the sovereignty of the people in favor of the theory of "chartered liberties" promulgated by Edmund Burke. There was no such thing as "liberty" in the abstract, only particular "chartered" liberties or privileges in particular countries. These privileges were not the birthright of all human beings. Instead, they were bestowed upon particular populations by benevolent monarchical regimes. Monarchs and aristocrats did not owe their legitimacy to the people and were not acting as their agents. The divine right theory of politics having lost favor, British conservatives and their foreign admirers tended to substitute "History" for the "Nature" of the French and American liberal republicans. Progress was gradual and evolutionary, not revolutionary, said the Burkean Right. Even in the United States, liberty was not the result of the American Revolution; it was based on an inheritance of centuries of British precedents going back to the Magna Carta in the thirteenth century and the Glorious Revolution of 1689. Different nations and ethnic groups—whether for reasons of "race" or culture—were at different levels of development, and the amount of liberty and democracy they could be entrusted with by a benevolent elite therefore varied. Guided by this approach, the British upper class managed to co-opt and dilute popular pressure for democracy in Britain itself. In 1865 most of the Cabinet posts in Britain were filled by members of leading aristocratic families, while half of the House of Commons belonged to or was connected by marriage to peers or barons.[63]

Having rejected popular sovereignty and universal human rights as the basis for government, the British conservatives and the foreign thinkers they influenced detached liberalism from both democracy and nationalism. A liberal society, they argued, did not require universal-suffrage democracy.

Constitutionalism and chartered liberties might be safer in a system in which the authority of a democratic branch of the legislature was balanced by the participation of a hereditary monarch and hereditary aristocrats in government (this was the classical theory of the "mixed constitution" that the American republicans and the more radical French republicans had rejected in the eighteenth century). And the rejection of popular sovereignty led logically to the rejection of national self-determination in favor of multinational systems like the British Empire, in which particular nations and ethnic groups were granted political privileges depending on their level of "development." The corollary, in international relations, to the British theory of limited, chartered democracy was the British theory of limited, chartered sovereignty. Call it the British Creed.

In Britain, public opinion about the Civil War was divided. Radicals and many liberals identified with the Union cause. On January 19, 1863, Lincoln wrote a letter of thanks to a committee of industrial workers in Manchester, England, who had expressed their hope for a Union victory. Praising the idealism they showed by putting their principles above their economic interest in a resumption of the cotton trade with the Southern states, Lincoln observed: "It has been often and studiously represented that the attempt to overthrow this government, which was built on the foundation of human rights, and to substitute for it one which should rest exclusively on the basis of human slavery, was likely to obtain the favor of Europe."[64]

Most conservatives and many conservative liberals in Britain hoped for the victory of the aristocratic South over the middle-class North. Thackeray preferred Southern aristocrats to the "Dutch traders of New York and the money-getting Roundheads of Pennsylvania and New England." The *Times* of London wrote that "excepting a few gentlemen of republican tendencies, we all expect, we nearly all wish, success to the Confederate cause."[65] Following the war, Lord Acton, a British liberal thinker who opposed nationalism, explained to Robert E. Lee in a letter: "The institutions of your Republic have not exercised on the old world the salutary and liberating influence which ought to have belonged to them, by reason of those defects and abuses of principle which the Confederate Constitution was expressly and wisely calculated to remedy. . . . Therefore I deemed that you were fighting the battles of our liberty, our progress, and our civilization; and I mourn for the stake which was lost at Richmond more deeply than I rejoice over that which was saved at Waterloo."[66]

It Was Semidemocratic parliamentary monarchy of the British kind, not democratic republicanism of the French or American kind, that became the dominant form of representative government for most of the new countries created between the American Civil War and World War I. Lincoln and like-minded Americans hoped for the spread of republican government and national self-determination. Their hopes were disappointed. Germany and Italy were consolidated from above by militaristic, bureaucratic monarchies, and their societies were based on gradations of aristocratic rank instead of on civic equality. Monarchs in Germany and Russia, trying to co-opt middle classes and working classes, cautiously liberalized their societies. But they made it clear that power flowed from the top downward. The emperor "gave" the people a constitution, the people did not impose one upon him.

The apparent exception to the rule, France, confirms it. In 1870, as a result of the defeat of France in the Franco-Prussian War, the dictator Louis Napoleon fell from power. On September 4, 1870, Victor Hugo, having returned to France from exile following the abdication of Louis Napoleon, addressed a gargantuan crowd in Paris, exhorting his fellow citizens to defend Paris from the Prussian army in the name of republican idealism. According to the American ambassador, Elias Washburne: "Seeing our flag, he called attention to it, and said, 'That banner of stars speaks to-day to Paris and France, proclaiming miracles of power which are easy to a great people, contending for a great principle, the liberty of every race and the fraternity of all.' "[67]

However, many of the politicians who created the Third Republic were conservatives who hoped to pave the way to a monarchical restoration. Because of the rivalry of conflicting dynastic claimants, the royal restoration never came, but the Third Republic was animated by a traditionalist outlook similar to that of the parliamentary monarchies of Europe. The conservative French elites who competed with the British to build colonial empires in Africa and Asia and the Middle East were not bothered by the incompatibility of this project with the French revolutionary idea of a world of republican nation-states.

The story was equally disappointing where national self-determination was concerned. Italy was united and freed from French and Habsburg control, but Ireland and India did not gain their independence from the British Empire, nor was Poland freed from Russian, German, and Austrian rule. Beginning with Greece, the new countries created by Britain and the other European great powers out of the former Balkan empire of the Ottomans, such as Bulgaria, Serbia, and Romania, were saddled with kings and aristocrats of their own. Meanwhile, between the Civil War and 1914, Africa and much of Asia were carved up by Britain and other European imperial powers. The amount of the earth's territory controlled by Western empires expanded from 35 percent in 1800 to 67 percent in 1878 and then to 85 percent in 1914.[68] Following World War I, the British and French empires divided the former Ottoman Empire's lands in the Middle East among themselves.

In 1900 there were forty-eight more or less independent states in the world. Only eight of these countries—whose inhabitants made up only 10 to 12 percent of humanity—could be described as democracies. And among the great powers in 1900, only two—the United States and France—were republics.[69] Most human beings in the world outside of the Americas were ruled by a handful of European empires—and with the exception of France, the major imperial powers were ruled by kings and aristocrats. Most of the European monarchies had adopted constitutions of some kind and established legislatures in which commoners could serve in the lower houses. But hereditary nobles or royal appointees dominated the upper houses in Britain, Germany, the Habsburg Empire, and the Russian Empire. The dominant social class in Europe remained the landed, titled nobility, whose members not only tended to monopolize the military, politics, and higher positions in the bureaucracy, but also controlled most wealth.

There is one major exception to the generalization that Lincoln's words and actions had little direct effect on the development of democracy before 1945. The founder of the Chinese republic, Sun Yat-sen, was taught the Gettysburg Address as a student in Honolulu, Hawaii. The "three people's principles" he promulgated as a political creed for China were government "of the people *[Min you],* by the people *[Min chih],* and for the people *[Min hsiang].*"[70] The connection between Lincoln and the first Chinese republic does not end there. John Hay, who in his twenties had been one of Lincoln's closest aides, while serving as Secretary of State under McKinley and Theodore Roosevelt formulated the U.S. policy of opposition to European imperial control over China—the "Open Door" Doctrine, an Asian corollary to the anti-imperial Monroe Doctrine in Latin America. While the United States, like the other great powers, intervened in Chinese affairs, American determination that China, like Latin America, should not be absorbed into the European imperial system, like India and Africa, helped make a Chinese nation-state possible, just as Lincoln's example influenced the adoption of republicanism as its new form of government.

In the world as a whole, however, the British Creed of an aristocratic, imperial world order and chartered liberties prevailed over the French and American dream of a world of sovereign nation-states and universal human rights. Around the world the principles with which Lincoln identified the Union cause diminished in influence following the Union victory—while the principles of leading Confederates, like the doctrine of nonwhite racial inferiority and a rejection of Enlightenment beliefs in human rights and self-determination, were shared by a majority of the statesmen in London, Paris, Berlin, Vienna, and Moscow. The Confederates lost their war of independence. But in the world beyond the United States, the philosophical allies and well-wishers of the Confederates won in the war of ideas.

During World War I Woodrow Wilson's enthusiasm for national self-determination and democracy, shared by many liberals and democrats in Britain and continental Europe, held out the prospect of a postimperial world order. But following the war the United States withdrew from European affairs, and Britain and France carved up the former Ottoman Empire in the Middle East, where they created new monarchies instead of republics. It was not until 1945 that the United States was in a position to reshape global order in light of American republican values. President Franklin Delano Roosevelt himself was a sincere anti-imperialist who believed that the British and French had shamelessly exploited the peoples they had conquered. Although the British and French fought to preserve portions of their overseas empires, by the 1960s the hostility of both the United States and the Soviet Union had brought about the decolonization of Africa, Asia, and the Middle East. The conservative British Creed of limited democracy provided as a gift to subjects by monarchs, and of limited national self-government within vast imperial structures provided as a gift to "natives" by white-skinned colonial rulers, was soon forgotten, even in postimperial Britain itself. Human rights and national self-determination became the basis of the United Nations system devised and promoted by Roosevelt and his successors.

Abraham Lincoln's hope that the democratization of the world would result from the American example, then, was realized in the middle of the twentieth century in a way he could not have expected. The principles of the post-1945 world order enshrined in the U.N. Charter, the U.N. organization, and the Universal Declaration of Human Rights are those of the eighteenth-century American and French tradition of liberal republicanism. These principles were adopted worldwide, in theory if not always in practice, following World War II, not because of America's example, as Lincoln had hoped, but because of America's primacy. The chief credit for this goes to Franklin Delano Roosevelt and his allies among America's liberal internationalists, a group that included anti-imperial Republicans in the Lincoln tradition such as Wendell Willkie.

But Lincoln deserves credit as well. By identifying the cause of the

Union with the universalist liberal republicanism of his idol Henry Clay and the Founders, Lincoln may have given that philosophical tradition a new lease on life, initially in the United States and then, after 1945, in the world.

IN LINCOLN'S LIFETIME there was a danger that most Americans, not merely Confederate apologists for slavery, would reject the universalist, eighteenth-century rationale for democracy and human rights in favor of the more recent understanding of both democracy and liberty as products of historical evolution relevant only to the Anglo-Saxon or Germanic nations or "races." In 1847, at the age of eighty-seven, Albert Gallatin, the Swiss-American émigré who had been Jefferson's Secretary of the Treasury, penned a polemic entitled "Peace with Mexico," in which he accused the American racial theorists of the 1840s of betraying the democratic idealism of the Founding generation to which he belonged. He scoffed at claims of Anglo-Saxon superiority, pointing out that China and India had achieved high civilizations when the Anglo-Saxons had been barbarians. According to Gallatin, the "allegations of superiority of race and destiny neither require nor deserve any answer; they are but pretences under which to disguise ambition, cupidity, or silly vanity." The superiority of the American people, Gallatin wrote, in words which Lincoln may have read, was to be found in American institutions, not an American "race": "Your mission is to improve the state of the world, to be the 'model republic,' to show that men are capable of governing themselves, and that this simple and natural form of government is that also which confers most happiness on all, is productive of the greatest development of the intellectual faculties, above all, that which is attended with the highest standard of private and political virtue and morality."[71]

But Gallatin's old-fashioned Enlightenment optimism was being eclipsed in the United States as well as in Britain and Europe by pessimistic theories of racial determinism. Some versions of the Anglo-Saxon theory of democracy held that other races not only were incapable of liberal democracy, but would suffer from it. In 1845 a representative from Ohio, Alexander Duncan, claimed that there was "something in our laws and institutions peculiarly adapted to our Anglo-Saxon-American race, under which they will thrive and prosper, but under which all others wilt and die."[72] James Russell Lowell, in a speech at Harvard in July 1865, declared that the Union victory in the Civil War signaled the advent of "a new imperial race."[73] In an 1885 essay in *Harper's* entitled "Manifest Destiny," John Fiske justified the expansion of American territory and power in terms of Social Darwinism—the influential if scientifically illiterate attempt to describe world history in terms of racial competition. In Fiske's essay, American expansionism degenerated into American exterminism—other races would actually become extinct, allowing the Anglo-Saxons to repopulate the world from the British islands and North America: "The work which the English race began when it colonized North America is destined to go on until every land on the earth's surface that is not already the seat of an old civilization shall become English in its language, in its political habits and traditions, and to a predominant extent in the blood of its people. The day is at hand when four fifths of the human race will trace its pedigree to English forefathers, as four fifths of the white people in the United States trace their pedigree today."[74] The racism of Fiske is hardly distinguishable from the genocidal racism of Hitler a few generations later.

The appeal of this kind of imperial racism to all white Americans, and not merely Southern slave owners, made all the more important the distinction that Lincoln, following Clay and Jefferson, maintained between "unalienable" universal human rights and civil rights, their moderate racist views notwithstanding. Like Clay, the champion of self-determination and republicanism in Latin America and Africa, Lincoln and those of his contemporaries influenced by the eighteenth-century universalist tradition could envision something like the post-1945 world order, a world composed mostly of sovereign nation-states with nonwhite populations, at least some of which, in favorable conditions, could be liberal democracies. The nineteenth-century historicists, whose influence was growing in the United

States, Britain, and Europe, could not envision such a world. The more racist among them considered the idea of an African or Asian republic comical. Other historicists, who emphasized culture more than biological race, conceded that the Indians and Africans and Asians might be prepared for self-government—but only in the remote future.

It is not difficult to imagine scenarios in which Confederate-style racism and historicism replaced the old-fashioned eighteenth-century Enlightenment idealism that Lincoln defended as the basis of the public philosophy of the United States. Suppose, for example, that the Civil War had been averted by a compromise that permitted the addition of new slave states. If such a compromise had averted Southern secession, the slave South, its political power in Washington augmented by new slave states, might have dominated the federal government in the second half of the nineteenth century as it had done in the first half. Whether formal slavery remained would have been irrelevant. The character of the United States would have been radically different. Almost certainly Southerners would have used their control of Washington, D.C., to conquer islands in the Caribbean and Pacific and parts or all of countries in Latin America either as states or territories. On October 29, 1860, the *Vicksburg Weekly* predicted that "the overthrow of the Union would not only perpetuate slavery where it now exists and establish it more firmly, but would necessarily lead to its widespread extension. The Southern States once constituted as an independent republic, the acquisition of Mexico, Central America, Cuba, Santo Domingo, and other West India Islands would follow as a direct and necessary result . . ."[75] If the North had appeased the South, the price paid to keep the South in the Union might have been the annexation of some of these areas. The United States might have had an overseas empire far larger than its tiny post-1898 empire, one comparable to those of Britain and other maritime colonial powers. Unlike Britain and Germany, which did not have universal suffrage until the twentieth century, the United States would have retained universal suffrage for white men. But the "typical American" of 1900, in the eyes of the world, might have been the aristocratic Southern colonel ruling this or that tropical protectorate rather than the Pittsburgh industrialist or the Wall Street financier.

The Southern elite of an Imperial America might have championed global free trade in order to sell the products of their American and colonial plantations. But it would not have used its influence in the twentieth century to champion a world order based on national self-determination and democracy. A Southern-dominated Imperial America would have been committed to global white supremacy and racial imperialism as the organizing principles of world politics, even if it had rejected radical and genocidal variants of racial imperialism such as German National Socialism. Liberal democratic nationalism as an ideology might have had no great-power sponsors at all. The battle of ideas in the twentieth century may have been between racial imperialism, in its American, British, and other versions, and one or another form of socialism. Both the imperial racists and the socialists might have agreed that liberal republicanism, with its ideals of human rights and national self-determination, was a discredited eighteenth-century ideology of no relevance in the contemporary world. The ideas of Jefferson and Lincoln and Paine and Lafayette, of the American Declaration of Independence and the French Declaration of the Rights of Man and the Citizen, would have been displaced by notions of race and hierarchy and the heroic ethic found in the writings of philosophers like Carlyle and Gobineau and in the practice of politicians like Disraeli and Bismarck and their equivalents in the American South. George Fitzhugh, the Confederate proslavery apologist, might have been better known in the United States and the world than Emerson or Thoreau.

The result might have been similar, even if the North had defeated Southern secessionists and forgone territorial imperialism, under the leadership of Unionist Democrats, Whigs, or conservative Republicans who deemphasized or rejected the universalist idealism of the Founders. If Stephen A. Douglas had been elected president in 1860, one or more Southern states might have seceded, fearing that Douglas's popular-sovereignty formula would result in the effective exclusion of slavery from the territories, and might even encourage the abolition of slavery in Southern states by the sovereign people of each state. In such circumstances it is quite likely that Douglas, an ardent Unionist, would have rallied most Northern Democrats to team up with the Republican Party in order to defeat secession. Unlike Lincoln, however, Douglas agreed with the Confederates that the Declaration of Independence was merely a white man's charter of customary English liberties. If the Union had defeated the South under the leadership of President Stephen A. Douglas, generations of Americans might have been taught that the colonists rebelled in 1776 solely to preserve their particular historic privileges as English subjects, and that the Civil War was a contest between Unionist advocates of popular sovereignty and Southern secessionists. Later generations might have agreed with many Northern Democrats and Confederates that the Lincoln Republicans had been fanatics seduced by discredited and utopian eighteenth-century ideas about human equality.

A similar outcome might have occurred had William H. Seward rather than Lincoln, as the Republican nominee, won the presidency in 1860 and presided over the defeat of an attempt at Southern secession. Like Lincoln, Seward denounced aristocracy in the name of democracy and free labor. In his speech entitled "The Irrepressible Conflict," delivered on October 25, 1858, in New York, Seward similarly claimed that what was occurring was "a dynastical struggle of two antagonistical systems, the labor of slaves and the labor of freemen, for mastery in the Federal Union. One of these systems partakes of an aristocratic character; the other is purely democratic."[76] Unlike Lincoln, however, Seward was an imperialist who predicted that one day the United States would encompass all of North America and have its capital in Mexico City (Alaska, purchased by Secretary of State Seward from Russia in 1867, became known as Seward's Folly.) The most important thing at stake in the Civil War, Seward believed, was not America's principles but America's future glory as a military and diplomatic superpower. In an address to Congress on January 12, 1861, Seward, then a senator from New York, described how impressed Europeans had been at an American man-of-war in the Mediterranean: "I imagine the same noble vessel again entering the same haven. The flag of thirty-three stars and thirteen stripes has been hauled down, and in its place a signal is run up, which flaunts the device of a lone star or a palmetto tree. Men ask, 'Who is the stranger that thus steals into our waters?' The answer contemptuously given is, 'she comes from one of the obscure republics of North America. Let her pass on.' "[77]

If Seward instead of Lincoln had been the Republican nominee in 1860 and the president who steered the Union to victory in the Civil War, generations of Americans and others might have studied Seward's explanation of what was at stake in the struggle: "The population of the United States consists of native Caucasian origin, and Exotics [immigrants] of the same derivation. The Native mass rapidly assimilates to itself and absorbs the Exotic, and these therefore constitute one homogenous people. The African race, bond and free, and the Aborigines, savage and civilized, being incapable of such assimilation and absorption, remain distinct, and owing to their peculiar condition remain inferior masses, and may be regarded as accidental, if not disturbing political forces. The ruling Homogenous family was planted at first on the Atlantic shore, and following an obvious law is seen continually and rapidly spreading itself westward year by year, subduing the Wilderness and the Prairie, and thus extending this great political community, which as fast as it advances, breaks into distinct States for municipal purposes only, while the whole constitutes one entire contiguous and compact nation. . . . The question now arises, Shall this one great People, having a common origin, a common language, a common religion, common sentiments, interests, sympathies and hope remain one political State, one Nation, one Republic? or shall it be broken into two conflicting and probably hostile Nations or Republics?"[78]

Like all counterfactuals, these are suggestive, at best. The point is that mainstream Americans since 1865 have tended to see the American Creed the way that the Founders and Lincoln viewed it, as an Enlightenment doctrine in which liberty, equality, and democracy were mutually reinforcing. But partial versions of the American Creed like that of the leading

Confederates, versions that jettisoned or deemphasized the idea of universal natural equality, would have been compatible with the racist, hierarchical, conservative approach to world order of the British Empire and other European empires in the nineteenth and twentieth centuries. Lincoln's successors in the Republican Party, William McKinley and Theodore Roosevelt, engaged in European-style imperialism on a small scale in the Caribbean, Central America, and the Pacific, and expressed contempt for "inferior" races and nations, and Woodrow Wilson promoted racial segregation in the United States even as he called for self-determination abroad. Even so, the United States and the world might have been far worse if Lincoln, by the force of his eloquence before and during the Civil War, had not rejected racist and historicist theories of democracy.

IN INDEPENDENCE HALL in Philadelphia on February 22, 1861, where he stopped to speak as he traveled to his inauguration as President of the United States, Lincoln asserted that "the sentiment embodied in" the Declaration of Independence had made the American Revolution a source of "hope to the world for all future time." Lincoln asked: "Now, my friends, can this country be saved upon that basis? If it can, I will consider myself one of the happiest men in the world if I can help to save it. If it can't be saved upon that principle, it will be truly awful."[79]

Other presidents might have saved the American Union, and other movements might have produced forms of representative government in other countries. But Abraham Lincoln helped to ensure that "government of the people, by the people, for the people" as an ideal for all of humanity would "not perish from the earth." Lincoln preserved both the United States and its political creed: "The theory of our government is universal freedom."[80]

BIBLIOGRAPHICAL NOTE

Among the countless books on Lincoln are remarkably few studies of his public philosophy as a whole. One exception is Allen C. Guelzo, *Abraham Lincoln: Redeemer President* (Grand Rapids, MI: William B. Eerdmans Publishing, 1999). Guelzo's discussion of Lincoln's religious views is particularly strong.

Good introductions to the ideology of the Whig Party can be found in Daniel Walker Howe, *The Political Culture of the American Whigs* (Chicago: University of Chicago Press, 1984), and Michael J. Holt, *The Rise and Fall of the American Whig Party: Jacksonian Politics and the Onset of the Civil War* (New York: Oxford University Press, 2003). A valuable guide to the Republican Party of Lincoln is Heather Cox Richardson, *The Greatest Nation of the Earth: Republican Economic Policies during the Civil War* (Cambridge, MA: Harvard University Press, 1997). See also "A Whig in the White House," in David Herbert Donald, *Lincoln Reconsidered: Essays on the Civil War Era* (New York: Vintage Books, 2001).

For detailed studies of Lincoln's economic thought, see Gabor S. Borritt, *Lincoln and the Economics of the American Dream* (Chicago: University of Chicago Press, 1978), and Olivier Fraysee, *Lincoln, Land, and Labor, 1809–60* (Chicago: University of Illinois Press, 1988), translated by Sylvia Neely. For the Hamiltonian tradition in the United States to which Lincoln belonged, see Michael Lind, *Hamilton's Republic* (New York: The Free Press, 1997). For the worldwide influence of the American School of economic nationalism, see Roman Szporluk, *Communism and Nationalism: Karl Marx versus Friedrich List* (New York: Oxford University Press, 1988), and Ha-Joon Chang, *Kicking Away the Ladder: Development Strategy in Historical Perspective* (London: Anthem Press, 2002). As the high proportion of foreign and foreign-born scholars in this list demonstrates, American historians have been strangely incurious about Lincoln's views of political economy.

Despite its polemical tone, Lerone Bennett, Jr.'s *Forced into Glory: Abraham Lincoln's White Dream* (Chicago: Johnson Publishing, 2000) is a valuable examination of Lincoln's views on race and slavery. Detailed overviews of Lincoln's approach to constitutional issues during the Civil War can be found in Daniel Farber, *Lincoln's Constitution* (Chicago: University of Chicago Press, 2003), and Mark E. Neely, Jr., *The Fate of Liberty: Abraham Lincoln and Civil Liberties* (New York: Oxford University Press, 1991).

To changing perceptions of Lincoln, Merrill D. Peterson's *Lincoln in American Memory* (New York: Oxford University Press, 1994) is an indispensable guide. An excellent older study of the same topic is Roy P. Basler, *The Lincoln Legend: A Study in Changing Conceptions* (Boston: Houghton Mifflin, 1935). John Patrick Diggins provides an insightful critique of fashions in Lincoln scholarship in *On Hallowed Ground: Abraham Lincoln and the Foundations of American History* (New Haven: Yale University Press, 2000). Finally, students of Lincoln and the Civil War have much to learn from James M. McPherson's *Abraham Lincoln and the Second American Revolution* (New York: Oxford University Press, 1992), *For Cause and Comrades: Why Men Fought in the Civil War* (New York: Oxford University Press, 1998), and other books and articles.

NOTES

‒‒‒∞‒‒‒

CHAPTER ONE

1. Fareed Zakaria, *The Future of Freedom: Illiberal Democracy at Home and Abroad* (New York: W. W. Norton, 2003), p. 50.

2. Priscilla Robertson, *Revolutions of 1848: A Social History* (New York: Harper & Brothers, 1960), p. 417.

3. Roy P. Basler, ed., *The Collected Works of Abraham Lincoln* (New Brunswick, NJ: Rutgers University Press, 1953), cited hereinafter as CW, 7:18–19.

4. Merrill D. Peterson, *Lincoln in American Memory* (New York: Oxford University Press, 1994); Roy P. Basler, *The Lincoln Legend: A Study in Changing Conceptions* (Boston: Houghton Mifflin, 1935).

5. Quoted in Benjamin Schwarz, "Rail-Splitter," review of Douglas L. Wilson, *The Transformation of Abraham Lincoln,* in the *Los Angeles Times,* February 15, 1998.

6. Edmund Wilson, *Patriotic Gore: Studies in the Literature of the American Civil War* (New York: Oxford University Press, 1962), p. xvii.

7. Ibid., p. xvi.

8. George P. Forgie, *Patricide in the House Divided* (New York: W. W. Norton,

1981); Dwight C. Anderson, *Abraham Lincoln: Quest for Immortality* (New York: Random House, 1998).

9. Willilam H. Herndon and Jesse W. Weik, *Life of Lincoln* (New York: Da Capo Press, 1983), pp. 1–2.

10. Arthur M. Schlesinger, Jr., *The Age of Jackson* (Boston: Little, Brown, 1945).

11. Alfred Haworth Jones, *Roosevelt's Image Brokers: Poets, Playwrights, and the Use of the Lincoln Symbol* (Port Washington, NY: Kennikat Press, 1974), p. 67.

12. Ibid., p. 93.

13. Ibid., p. 110.

14. Ibid., p. 74.

15. Ibid., p. 68.

16. Ibid., p. 66.

17. Willmoore Kendall, *Willmoore Kendall Contra Mundum*, ed. Nellie D. Kendall (Lanham, MD: University Press of America, 1994), p. 69. See also Willmoore Kendall and George Carey, *The Basic Symbols of the American Political Tradition* (Baton Rouge: Louisiana State University Press, 1970).

18. Garry Wills, *Lincoln at Gettysburg: The Words that Remade America* (New York: Simon & Schuster, 1992), pp. 38–39.

19. George P. Fletcher, *Our Secret Constitution: How Lincoln Redefined American Democracy* (New York: Oxford University Press, 2001), p. 4.

20. Ibid., p. 231.

21. James M. Washington, ed., with foreword by Coretta Scott King, *I Have a Dream—40th Anniversary Edition: Writings and Speeches that Changed the World* (San Francisco: Harper SanFrancisco, 1992).

22. Lerone Bennett, Jr., *Forced into Glory: Abraham Lincoln's White Dream* (Chicago: Johnson Publishing, 2000).

23. CW 4:260.

24. Alexander K. McClure, *"Abe" Lincoln's Yarns and Stories* (Henry Neil, 1904), pp. 83–84.

25. CW 4:24.

26. John G. Nicolay and John Hay, *Abraham Lincoln: A History*, 10 vols. (New York: The Century Co., 1890), vol. 1, pp. 104–5.

27. Edmund Wilson, *Patriotic Gore: Studies in the Literature of the American Civil War* (New York: Oxford University Press, 1962), p. 99.

28. Alexander H. Stephens, *A Constitutional View of the Late War between the States*, vol. II (Philadelphia: National Publishing Co., 1868–70), p. 448.

29. Alexander H. Stephens, "Cornerstone Address March 21, 1861," in Frank Moore, ed., *The Rebellion Record; A Diary of American Events with Documents, Narratives, Illustrative Incidents, Poetry, etc.* (New York: O. P. Putnam, 1864), pp. 44–46.

30. CW 4:17.

31. Herndon and Weik, *Life of Lincoln*, pp. 140–41.

32. Don and Virginia Fehrenbacher, eds., *Recollected Words of Abraham Lincoln* (Stanford, CA: Stanford University Press, 1996).

33. CW 3:79.

34. Clay, address to American Colonization Society, 1827.

35. CW 2:131.

36. John Niven, *Gideon Welles: Lincoln's Secretary of the Navy* (New York: Oxford University Press, 1973), p. 222.

37. CW 2:126.

CHAPTER TWO

1. Allen C. Guelzo, *Abraham Lincoln: Redeemer President* (Grand Rapids, MI: William B. Eerdmans Publishing, 1999), p. 450.

2. William H. Herndon and Jesse W. Weik, *Herndon's Lincoln: The True Story of a Great Life* (Springfield, IL: Herndon's Publishing Co., 1889), vol. I, p. ix; Ward Hill Lamon, *The Life of Abraham Lincoln: From His Birth to His Inauguration as President* (Boston: James R. Osgood and Co., 1872), p. 18; cited in Barry Schwartz, *Abraham Lincoln and the Forge of National Memory* (Chicago: University of Chicago Press, 2000), p. 159.

3. Herndon, letter to T. H. Bartlett; quoted in Reinhard Luthin, *The Real Abraham Lincoln* (Englewood Cliffs, NJ: Prentice-Hall, 1960), p. 142.

4. Ibid.

5. Guelzo, *Abraham Lincoln*, p. 41.

6. Recollections of George Borrett in Charles M. Segal, ed., *Conversations with Lincoln* (New York: G. P. Putnam's, 1961); cited in Olivier Fraysee, *Lincoln, Land, and Labor, 1809–60*, trans. Sylvia Neely (Chicago: University of Chicago Press, 1994), p. 13.

7. Fraysee, *Lincoln, Land, and Labor*, p. 15.

8. John Locke Scripps, *Life of Lincoln*, ed. Roy P. Basler and Lloyd A. Dunlap (Bloomington: Indiana University Press, 1961), pp. 29–30; cited in Fraysee, *Lincoln, Land, and Labor*, p. 16.

9. CW 2:268.

10. CW 3:79.

11. CW 3:78.

12. Herndon and Weik, *Herndon's Lincoln*, p. 261.

13. Lamon, *Life of Abraham Lincoln*, p. 135.

14. Herndon and Weik, *Herndon's Lincoln*, p. 262.

15. Luthin, *The Real Abraham Lincoln*, p. 142.

16. "Dennis Hanks to WHH (interview) Chicago Ils-Sanitary fair June. 13th 1865,"

in Douglas L. Wilson and Rodney O. Davis, *Herndon's Informants: Letters, Interviews, and Statements about Abraham Lincoln* (Chicago: University of Chicago Press, 1998), p. 37.

17. CW 3:511.

18. Guelzo, *Abraham Lincoln,* p. 35.

19. Ibid.

20. Quoted in David Herbert Donald, *Lincoln Reconsidered: Essays on the Civil War Era,* 3d ed. (New York: Vintage, 2001), p. 67.

21. Recollection of Thomas Dowling, in Wallace B. Stevens, *A Reporter's Lincoln,* ed. Michael Burlingame (Lincoln: University of Nebraska Press, 1998), p. 159.

22. Alexander Hamilton, "Continentalist," July 4, 1782, in Harold C. Syrett, ed., *The Papers of Alexander Hamilton* (New York: Columbia University Press, 1961–79), vol. 3, p. 103.

23. See generally Carl J. Richard, *The Founders and the Classics: Greece, Rome, and the American Enlightenment* (Cambridge, MA: Harvard University Press, 1994).

24. See generally Robert A. Ferguson, *Law and Letters in American Culture* (Cambridge, MA: Harvard University Press, 1984).

25. Bruce A. Kimball, *Orators and Philosophers: A History of the Idea of Liberal Education* (New York: College Entrance Examination Board, 1995), p. 144.

26. "John L. Scripps to WHH, Chicago June 24th 1865," in Wilson and Davis, *Herndon's Informants,* p. 57.

27. Quoted in Donald, *Lincoln Reconsidered,* p. 73.

28. "Dennis Hanks (WHH interview) Charleston Ills Sept 8th 1865," in Wilson and Davis, *Herndon's Informants,* p. 105.

29. Caleb Bingham, *The Columbian Orator: Containing a Variety of Original and Selected Pieces Together with Rules, Which Are Calculated to Improve Youth and Others, in the Ornamental and Useful Art of Eloquence,* ed. David W. Blight (New York: New York University Press, 1998 [1797]), p. 5.

30. Ibid., pp. 5–23.

31. Ibid., pp. 29–30.

32. Ibid., pp. 246–47.

33. "Joshua F. Speed to WHH, Louisville 6 Decr 1866," in Wilson and Davis, *Herndon's Informants,* p. 500.

34. Ibid., pp. 498–99.

35. Herndon and Weik, *Herndon's Life of Lincoln,* p. 323.

36. Josiah G. Holland, *Life of Abraham Lincoln* (Springfield, MA: n.p., 1866), pp. 236–39; cited in Guelzo, *Abraham Lincoln,* p. 261.

37. Herndon and Weik, *Herndon's Life of Lincoln,* p. 356.

38. Ibid.

39. Ibid., p. 351.

40. Thomas Paine, *Collected Writings,* Library of America ed. (New York: Literary Classics of the United States, 1995), pp. 709–10.

41. C. F. Volney, *The Ruins, or, Meditation on the Revolutions of Empires: and the Law of Nature* (Baltimore: Black Classic Press, 1991), pp. 113–14.

42. Guelzo, *Abraham Lincoln,* p. 50.

43. "Dennis F. Hanks to WHH (interview) Chicago Ills—Sanitary fair June 13th 1865," in Wilson and Davis, *Herndon's Informants,* p. 37.

44. Guelzo, *Abraham Lincoln,* p. 38.

45. CW 1:382–83.

46. Herndon and Weik, *Herndon's Life of Lincoln,* p. 377.

47. CW 7:282.

48. CW 7:535.

49. CW 8:56.

50. Insightful discussions of the influence of Calvinism on Lincoln are found in Guelzo, *Abraham Lincoln,* and John Patrick Diggins, *On Hallowed Ground: Abraham Lincoln and the Foundations of American History* (New Haven, CT: Yale University Press, 2000).

51. Francis Bacon, *The Essays or Counsels, Civil and Moral, of Francis Ld. Verulam, Viscount St. Albans* (New York: Peter Pauper Press, n.d.), pp. 159–60.

52. Quoted in Guelzo, *Abraham Lincoln,* p. 152.

53. Browning to Isaac Arnold, November 25, 1872, in Arnold Papers, Chicago Historical Society; cited in Guelzo, *Abraham Lincoln,* p. 314.

54. CW 1:315.

55. Fred Somkin, "Scripture Notes To Lincoln's Second Inaugural," *Civil War History* 27, no. 2 (1981).

56. The sources may be 1 Corinthians 13:4: "Charity suffereth long, and is kind"; 1 Corinthians 16:14: "Let all your things be done with charity"; Colossians 3:14: "And above all these things put on charity, which is the bond of perfectness"; Ephesians 4:31: "Let all bitterness, and wrath, and anger, and clamor, and evil speaking, be put away from you, with all malice." Another possible influence is 1 Peter 2:1: "Wherefore laying aside all malice, and all guile, and hypocrisies, and envies, and all evil speakings." Herbert Edwards and John E. Hankins, *Lincoln the Writer: The Development of His Literary Style* (Orono: University of Maine Press, 1962), pp. 104–5.

57. Cited in Guelzo, *Abraham Lincoln,* p. 151.

58. Julia Taft Bayne, *Tad Lincoln's Father* (Boston: Little, Brown and Company, 1931), p. 184; quoted in Guelzo, *Abraham Lincoln Redeemer President,* p. 314.

59. Lincoln to Langdon Kaine, cited in Don and Virginia Fehrenbacher, *Recollected Words of Abraham Lincoln* (Stanford, CA: Stanford University Press, 1996), p. 273.

60. Herndon and Weik, *Herndon's Life of Lincoln,* p. 481.

61. Ibid., p. 354.

62. Ibid., pp. 477–78.

63. CW 3:476.

64. David Herbert Donald, *Lincoln* (New York: Simon & Schuster, 1995), p. 432.

65. Ibid., p. 431.

66. CW 6:151–52.

67. CW 3:362–63.

68. Ibid., p. 358.

69. Herndon and Weik, *Herndon's Life of Lincoln,* p. 478.

70. Charles H. Coleman, *Abraham Lincoln and Coles County, Illinois* (New Brunswick, NJ: Scarecrow Press, 1955), pp. 198–99; cited in Donald, *Lincoln,* p. 271.

71. CW 1:510.

72. CW 1:273.

73. CW 1:271–79.

74. CW 1:279.

75. CW 1:112.

76. Volney, *The Ruins,* p. 70.

77. Ibid., pp. 190–91.

78. Herndon and Weik, *Herndon's Life of Lincoln,* p. 416.

79. Ibid., p. 244.

80. Ibid., p. 113.

81. Cited in Luthin, *The Real Abraham Lincoln,* p. 91.

82. CW 1:384–85.

83. Herndon and Weik, *Herndon's Life of Lincoln,* p. 352.

84. Ward Hill Lamon, *Recollections of Abraham Lincoln, 1847–1865,* edited by Dorothy Hill Lamon (Washington, DC: published by the editor, 1911), p. 118.

85. Lamon, *Recollections of Abraham Lincoln,* pp. 111–12; Noah Brooks, *Harper's Monthly Magazine* (July 1865), pp. 224–25; cited in Nickell, "Paranormal Lincoln."

86. Nickell, "Paranormal Lincoln."

87. Lamon, *Recollections of Lincoln,* p. 120.

88. CW 1:8.

89. CW 1:378–79, 386–89.

90. Herndon and Weik, *Herndon's Life of Lincoln,* p. 421.

91. Ward H. Lamon, *The Life of Abraham Lincoln* (Lincoln: University of Nebraska Press, 1999), pp. 480–81.

CHAPTER THREE

1. CW 2:121–32.

2. Robert V. Remini, *Henry Clay: Statesman for the Union* (New York: W. W. Norton, 1991), p. 4.

3. Ibid., p. 227.

4. Edward G. Parker, *The Golden Age of American Oratory* (Boston: Whittemore, Niles and Hall, 1857), p. 36; quoted in Edgar DeWitt Jones, *The Influence of Henry Clay upon Abraham Lincoln* (Lexington, KY: Henry Clay Memorial Foundation, 1952), p. 13.

5. Alex Roberto Hybel, *Made by the USA: The International System* (New York: Palgrave, 2001), p. 15.

6. Ha-Joon Chang, *Kicking Away the Ladder: Development Strategy in Historical Perspective* (London: Anthem Press, 2002), p. 22.

7. Ibid.

8. Ibid., p. 52.

9. Ibid.

10. Edmund Burke, *The Works of the Right Honorable Edmund Burke,* vol. 1, p. 371, cited in Jonathan Haslam, *No Virtue Like Necessity: Realist Thought in International Relations since Machiavelli* (New Haven, CT: Yale University Press, 2002), p. 141.

11. Charles F. Adams, *Works of John Adams* (Boston: Little, Brown, 1850–56), vol. 10, 384; cited in Alfred E. Eckes, Jr., *Opening America's Market: U.S. Foreign Trade Policy Since 1776* (Chapel Hill: University of North Carolina Press, 1995), p. 19.

12. Because British law forebade skilled mechanics from emigrating, Samuel Slater, one of the founders of the U.S. textile industry, was forced to leave Britain for the United States in disguise in 1789. See E. H. Cameron, *Samuel Slater: Father of American Manufactures* (Bond Wheelwright Co., 1960).

13. Chang, *Kicking Away the Ladder,* p. 53.

14. Richard Cobden, *The Political Writings of Richard Cobden* (London: William Ridgeway, 1868), vol. 1, p. 150; cited in E. Reinert, "Raw Materials in the History of Economic Policy—Or why List (the protectionist) and Cobden (the free trader) both agreed on free trade in corn [wheat]," in G. Cook, ed., *The Economics and Politics of International Trade: Freedom and Trade* (London: Routledge, 1998), vol. 2, p. 292; and Chang, *Kicking Away the Ladder,* pp. 23 and 165n45.

15. Quoted in Robert Gilpin, *War and Change in World Politics* (Cambridge: Cambridge University Press, 1981), p. 137.

16. Adam Smith, *An Inquiry into the Nature and Causes of the Wealth of Nations* (New York: Random House, 1937 [1776]), pp. 347–48.

17. Thomas Jefferson to Gen. Thaddeus Kosciuszko, June 28, 1812, in Andrew A. Lipscomb and Albert E. Bergh, eds., *The Writings of Thomas Jefferson* (Washington, DC: Thomas Jefferson Memorial Association, 1905), vol. 13, p. 170.

18. Guelzo, *Abraham Lincoln,* p. 134.

19. Alexander Hamilton, "The Report on the Subject of Manufactures," 5 December 1791, in H. Syrett et al., eds., *The Papers of Alexander Hamilton* (New York: Columbia University Press, 1966), vol. 10, p. 263.

20. Chang, *Kicking Away the Ladder,* pp. 21–22.

21. See Jonathan Haslam, *No Virtue Like Necessity: Realist Thought in International Relations Since Machiavelli* (New Haven, CT: Yale University Press, 2002).

22. Haslam, *No Virtue Like Necessity*, p. 156.

23. W. Henderson, *Friedrich List—Economist and Visionary, 1789–1846* (London: Frank Cass, 1983).

24. Heather Cox Richardson, *The Greatest Nation on Earth: Republican Economic Policies during the Civil War* (Cambridge, MA: Harvard University Press, 1997), p. 19.

25. Rodney J. Morrison, *Henry C. Carey and American Economic Development* (Philadelphia: American Philosophical Society, 1986), p. 57.

26. Ibid., p. 81.

27. Henry C. Carey, *The Slave Trade: Foreign and Domestic* (1853), chapter 15, "How Can Slavery Be Extinguished?"

28. Henry C. Carey, letter to Schuyler Colfax, January 6, 1865.

29. Clay, speech of December 31, 1811, in Henry Clay, *The Works of Henry Clay Comprising His Life, Correspondence and Speeches,* ed. Calvin Colton, Federal edition, 10 vols. (New York and London: G. P. Putnam's Sons, 1904), vol. 6, pp. 40–41.

30. Ibid., vol. 6, p. 98.

31. Henry Clay, "On American Industry," Speech in the House of Representatives, March 30–31, 1824, in Calvin Colton, ed., *The Works of Henry Clay* (New York: A. S. Barnes and Burr, 1857), vol. V, pp. 255–94; quoted in Michael Lind, *Hamilton's Republic: Readings in the American Democratic Nationalist Tradition* (New York: The Free Press, 1995), p. 249.

32. Paul Bairoch, *Economics and World History: Myths and Paradoxes* (Chicago: University of Chicago Press, 1993), p. 34.

33. Ibid.

34. John Quincy Adams, letter to Charles W. Upham, February 2, 1837, in Walter LaFeber, ed., *John Quincy Adams and American Continental Expansion* (Chicago: Quadrangle Books, 1965), pp. 146–47.

35. Edward Everett, "A Discourse on the Importance to Practical Men of Scientific Knowledge, and on the Encouragement to its Pursuit," compiled by Everett in 1836 from speeches made in 1827, 1829, and 1830, in *Orations and Speeches, on Various Occasions,* ed. Edward Everett (Boston: American Stationers', 1836), p. 248; cited in Dean Hammer, *The Puritan Tradition in Revolutionary, Federalist, and Whig Political Theory* (New York: Peter Lang, 1998), p. 176.

36. Thomas Jefferson, *Notes on the State of Virginia,* ed. William Peden (Chapel Hill: University of North Carolina Press, 1955), pp. 138–43.

37. Thomas Jefferson. *The Letters of Thomas Jefferson: 1743–1826,* "To the Governor of Virginia, November 24, 1801" (New York: Funk and Wagnalls Company, 1900), p. 155.

38. Leon F. Litwack, *North of Slavery* (Chicago: University of Chicago Press, 1961), p. 25.

39. Clay to Thomas W. H. Moseley, November 4, 1845, Thomas J. Clay Papers, LC, quoted in Remini, *Henry Clay*, p. 670.

40. Clay to Conover, June 13, 1830, in Clay Papers, VIII, 222, quoted in Remini, *Henry Clay*, p. 362.

41. John Quincy Adams, *Memoirs of John Quincy Adams*, VII, pp. 89–90; cited in Reginald Horsman, *Race and Manifest Destiny* (Cambridge, MA: Harvard University Press, 1981), p. 198.

42. *National Intelligencer*, January 24, 1848; cited in Remini, *Henry Clay*, pp. 696–97.

43. Henry Clay, *An Address Delivered to the Colonization Society of Kentucky at Frankfort, December 17, 1829* (Frankfort, Kentucky: J. H. Holeman, 1830).

44. Henry Clay to Richard Pindell, February 17, 1849, in Calvin Colton, ed., *The Works of Henry Clay* (New York: A. S. Barnes and Burr, 1857), vol. III, pp. 346–52; quoted in Robert V. Remini, *Henry Clay: Statesman for the Union* (New York: W. W. Norton, 1991), p. 718.

45. Thomas Jefferson, *Writings*, edited by Merrill D. Peterson (New York: The Library of America, 1984), p. 1202.

46. Clay to Richard Pindell, February 17, 1849, in Clay, *Works*, III, pp. 346–52; cited in Remini, *Henry Clay*, p. 718.

47. Daniel Walker Howe, *The Political Culture of the American Whigs* (Chicago: University of Chicago Press, 1979), p. 136.

48. Ibid.

49. CW 3:29.

50. CW 2:282.

51. Don E. Fehrenbacher and Virginia Fehrenbacher, eds., *Recollected Words of Abraham Lincoln* (Stanford, CA: Stanford University Press, 1996), p. 37.

52. Quoted in Guelzo, *Abraham Lincoln*, p. 384.

53. Wilson and Davis, *Herndon's Informants*, p. 147n1.

54. George D. Prentice, *Biography of Henry Clay* (New York: John Jay Phelps, 1831), p. 280.

55. Ibid., p. 175.

56. Ibid.

57. Jones, *The Influence of Henry Clay*, p. 19.

58. Ibid.

59. Quoted in Kenneth J. Winkle, *The Young Eagle* (Dallas: Taylor Trade Publishing, 2001), p. 116.

60. John Nicolay and John Hay, *Abraham Lincoln*, 1:104–5.

61. Herndon and Weik, *Herndon's Life of Lincoln*, p. 343.

62. CW 1:439.

63. CW 2:127.

64. Jones, *The Influence of Henry Clay*, pp. 33–34.

65. Quoted in ibid., p. 36.

66. William D. Kelley, "The South—Its Resources and Its Wants," address at New Orleans, May 11, 1867, in *Speeches, Addresses and Letters on Industrial and Financial Questions* (Philadelphia, 1872).

67. George Winston Smith, *Henry C. Carey and the American Sectional Conflict* (Albuquerque: University of New Mexico Press, 1951), p. 85.

68. Quoted in Reinhard H. Luthin, "Abraham Lincoln and the Tariff," *American Historical Review* 49, issue 4 (July 1944): 614.

69. CW 3:487.

70. Quoted in Winkle, *Young Eagle*, p. 116.

71. William Herndon to Jesse Weik, January 1, 1886, in Emanuel Hertz, ed., *The Hidden Lincoln: From the Letters and Papers of William H. Herndon* (New York: Viking Press, 1938), p. 117.

72. M. R. Eiselen, *The Rise of Philadelphia Protectionism* (Philadelphia, 1932).

73. See, for example, CW 1:381–82.

74. CW 1:490.

75. CW 4:212.

76. CW 1:313.

77. CW 1:160.

78. CW 1:161.

79. Reinhard H. Luthin, *The Real Abraham Lincoln* (Englewood Cliffs, NJ: Prentice-Hall, 1960), pp. 56–57.

80. Olivier Fraysee, *Lincoln, Land, and Labor, 1809–60,* trans. Sylvia Neely (Chicago: University of Illinois Press, 1994), pp. 53–54.

81. *Springfield Sangamon Journal,* June 13, 1836; cited in Winkle, *Young Eagle,* p. 118.

82. Winkle, *Young Eagle,* p. 114.

83. Guelzo, *Abraham Lincoln,* p. 170.

84. Herndon and Weik, *Life of Lincoln,* pp. 141, 161.

85. Luthin, *The Real Abraham Lincoln,* p. 101.

86. CW 1:488.

87. Fraysee, *Lincoln, Land, and Labor,* p. 68.

88. Ibid., p. 78.

89. Ibid., pp. 127–28.

90. An alternate version of the reported remarks was this: "I think it worthy of consideration, and that the wild lands of the country should be distributed so that every man should have the means and opportunity of benefiting his own condition." CW 4:201–4.

91. CW 3:79.

92. CW 2:132.

93. Quoted in Remini, *Henry Clay,* p. 696.

94. Don and Virginia Fehrenbacher, *Recollected Words,* p. 446; Guelzo, *Abraham Lincoln,* p. 131.

95. Herndon to Lamon, March 3, 1870, in W. H. Lamon Papers, Library of Congress.

96. CW 4:11–12.

97. CW 5:48.

98. CW 4:240.

99. CW 3:541.

100. CW 1:114.

101. CW 2:221.

102. This point is emphasized by Lerone Bennett, *Forced into Glory: Abraham Lincoln's White Dream* (Chicago: Johnson Publishing Company, 2000).

103. Winkle, *Young Eagle,* p. 255.

104. Eugene H. Berwanger, *The Frontier against Slavery: Western Anti-Negro Prejudice and the Slavery Extension Controversy* (Chicago: University of Illinois Press, 1967, 2002), pp. 57–58.

105. Bennett, *Forced into Glory,* pp. 226–27.

106. Ibid., pp. 227–28.

107. Winkle, *Young Eagle,* p. 265.

108. Winthrop D. Jordan, *The White Man's Burden: Historical Origins of Racism in the United States* (New York: Oxford University Press, 1974), p. 218.

109. Winkle, *Young Eagle,* pp. 260–61.

110. Ibid., p. 261.

111. CW 3:78.

112. Herndon, p. 143.

113. Ibid., p. 251.

114. Don and Virginia Fehrenbacher, *Recollected Words,* pp. 455–56.

115. CW 1:113.

116. Bennett, *Forced into Glory,* p. 206.

117. CW 2:141, 157.

118. CW 3:145–46.

119. Berwanger, *The Frontier against Slavery,* p. 131.

120. CW 2:405.

121. CW 2:407–8.

122. CW 2:498.

123. CW 2:409.

124. Berwanger, *The Frontier against Slavery,* pp. 4–5, 228.

125. John Niven, *Gideon Welles: Lincoln's Secretary of the Navy* (New York: Oxford University Press, 1973), p. 222.

126. CW 2:520.

127. CW 7:243; 8:403.

128. Lawanda Cox, Akhil Amar.

129. Quoted in Bennett, *Forced into Glory,* p. 384.

130. CW 3:358.

131. CW 3:235.

132. James Mitchell, *Letter on the Relation of the White and African Races in the United States, Showing the Necessity of the Colonization of the Latter* (Washington, DC: U.S. Government Printing Office, May 18, 1862), quoted in Bennett, *Forced into Glory,* p. 455.

133. Quoted in Luthin, *The Real Abraham Lincoln,* p. 139.

CHAPTER FOUR

1. Brian D. Humes, "Estimating the Impact of the Three-Fifths Clause: Examining Speakership and Presidential Elections in the Ante-Bellum United States," delivered at the annual meeting of the American Political Science Association, San Francisco, August 30–September 2, 2001, p. 9.

2. Leonard L. Richards, *The Slave Power: The Free North and Southern Domination, 1780–1860* (Baton Rouge: Louisiana State University Press, 2000), p. 42.

3. Ibid., p. 10.

4. D. W. Meinig, *The Shaping of America: A Geographical Perspective on 500 Years of History,* vol. 2, *Continental America, 1800–1867* (New Haven, CT: Yale University Press, 1993), p. 460.

5. Barry R. Weingast, "Political Stability and Civil War: Institutions, Commitment, and American Democracy," in Robert H. Bates, Avner Greif, Margaret Levi, Jean-Laurent Rosenthal, and Barry R. Weingast, *Analytic Narratives* (Princeton, NJ: Princeton University Press, 1988), pp. 148–93, 166, and Table 4.3, p. 168; cited in Robert A. Dahl, *How Democratic Is the American Constitution?* (New Haven, CT: Yale University Press, 2001), pp. 53, 180.

6. William Earl Weeks, *Building the Continental Empire: American Expansion from the Revolution to the Civil War* (Chicago: Ivan R. Dee, 1996), p. 140.

7. W. E. B. DuBois, *Black Reconstruction in America* (New York: Russell & Russell, 1935), pp. 115–20.

8. CW 3:512.

9. Francis D. Adams and Barry Sanders, *Alienable Rights: The Exclusion of African Americans in a White Man's Land, 1619–2000* (New York: HarperCollins, 2003), p. 164.

10. CW 3:79.

11. CW 3:78.

12. CW 2:268.

13. CW 2:249.

14. CW 3:311.

15. Berwanger, *The Frontier against Slavery,* pp. 22–23.

16. CW 2:521.

17. *Congressional Globe,* 29th Cong., 2d sess., Appendix, p. 317; cited in Berwanger, *The Frontier against Slavery,* pp. 125–26.

18. *Congressional Globe,* 36th Cong., 1st sess., pp. 39–40, 58–59; cited in ibid., p. 134.

19. *New York Tribune,* December 17, 1860; cited in ibid., p. 130.

20. Blair (comp.), *Collection of Pamphlets,* "Shall the Territories Be Africanized?" delivered in the United States Senate, January 4, 1860, pp. 4–5, cited in ibid., p. 132.

21. George Baker, ed., *The Works of William H. Seward,* 5 vols. (Boston, 1884), IV, p. 317; cited in ibid., p. 123.

22. Quoted by James M. McPherson, *The Struggle for Equality: Abolitionists and the Negro in the Civil War and Reconstruction* (Princeton, Princeton University Press, 1964), p. 24.

23. Cited in Stephen Steinberg, *The Ethnic Myth: Race, Ethnicity, and Class in America* (Boston: Beacon Press, 1989), p. 178.

24. Willie Lee Rose, *Rehearsal for Reconstruction: The Port Royal Experiment* (New York: Vintage Books, 1967), p. 667.

25. Alexis de Tocqueville, *Democracy in America,* ed. J. P. Mayer, trans. George Lawrence, (1835; New York: Harper & Row, 1969), vol. 1, pp. 315–16.

26. Quoted by Herndon, p. 334.

27. CW 2:281.

28. CW 3:179.

29. CW 3:145–46.

30. CW 3:16.

31. *Congressional Globe,* 36th Cong., 1st sess., pp. 39–40, 58–59; cited in Berwanger, *The Frontier against Slavery,* p. 134.

32. CW 3:296.

33. Quoted in Reginald Horsman, *Race and Manifest Destiny: The Origins of American Racial Anglo-Saxonism* (Cambridge: Harvard University Press, 1981), p. 275.

34. *Dred Scott v. Sandford,* 60 U.S. 393 (1856).

35. Thomas Dew, *An Essay on Slavery* (Richmond, VA: J. W. Randolph, 1849), p. 24; cited in Gregg D. Crane, *Race, Citizenship, and Law in American Literature* (New York: Cambridge University Press, 2002), p. 34.

36. CW 3:79.

37. CW 3:234.

38. CW 3:177.

39. CW 3:220.

40. CW 2:404.

41. Thomas Jefferson, *The writings of Thomas Jefferson: being his autobiography, correspondence, reports, messages, addresses, and other writings, official and private* (New York, H. W. Derby, 1899), vol. 10, p. 157.

42. Peter Laslett, ed., introduction to Sir Robert Filmer, *Patriarcha and Other Political Works* (Oxford, Basil Blackwell Publishing, 1949), C. Vann Woodward, ed., introduction in *Cannibals All! Or, Slaves without Masters* (Cambridge, MA: Harvard University Press, 1960).

43. *Niles Weekly Register,* May 13, 1826, vol. 30, p. 1867; cited in David Leon Chandler, *The Natural Superiority of Southern Politicians: A Revisionist History* (Garden City, NY: Doubleday, 1977), pp. 28–29.

44. William H. Herndon, *The Hidden Lincoln*, ed. Emanuel Herz (New York, 1938), pp. 96–97; cited in Lawrence R. Tenzer, *The Forgotten Cause of the Civil War* (Manahawkin, NJ: Scholars Publishing House, 1997), p. 157.

45. CW 2:341.

46. CW 2:385.

47. Quoted in Lawrence R. Tenzer, *The Forgotten Cause of the Civil War: A New Look at the Slavery Issue* (Manahawkin, NJ: Scholars' Publishing House, 1997), p. 146.

48. Quoted in ibid., p. 215.

49. The *Muscogee (Alabama) Herald* and the *New York Day Book,* both quoted in the *National Anti-Slavery Standard,* October 11, 1856; cited in ibid., p. 127.

50. Quoted in Reinhard Luthin, *The Real Abraham Lincoln*, pp. 212–13.

51. CW 5:52.

52. CW 2:364.

53. CW 4:24–25.

54. *Belleville Weekly Advocate*, October 18, 1856 (Belleville, IL).

55. CW 2:323.

56. CW 3:312.

57. CW 1:338.

58. Tyler Anbinder, *Nativism and Slavery: The Northern Know Nothings and the Politics of the 1850s* (New York: Oxford University Press, 1992), p. 274.

59. Charles A. Dana to Henry C. Carey, November 27, 1856, Carey Papers, HSP; quoted in ibid., p. 278.

60. Quoted in Berwanger, *The Frontier against Slavery,* p. 93.

61. Walt Whitman, *Brooklyn Daily Eagle,* May 6, 1858; quoted in Alexander Saxton,

The Rise and Fall of the White Republic (New York: Verso, 1991), p. 153; cited in Michael Lind, *The Next American Nation* (New York: The Free Press, 1995), p. 74.

62. Justin Kaplan, *Walt Whitman: A Life* (New York: Simon & Schuster, 1980), p. 122.

63. Lorenzo D. Turner, "Walt Whitman and the Negro," *Chicago Jewish Forum* 15 (fall 1956).

64. Quoted in Luthin, *The Real Abraham Lincoln*, pp. 138–39.

65. Quoted in Thomas Keneally, *Abraham Lincoln* (Penguin, 2003), pp. 44–45.

66. CW 2:461.

67. Richard Franklin Bensel, *Yankee Leviathan: The Origins of Central State Authority in America, 1859–1877* (New York: Cambridge University Press, 1990), pp. 49–50.

68. *Philadelphia North American* and *United States Gazette*, May 19, 1860; quoted in Luthin, "Abraham Lincoln and the Tariff," *American Historical Review* 49, Issue 4 (July 1944): p. 618.

69. Greeley to Mrs. R. M. Whipple (probably in 1859), Horace Greeley Papers, Library of Congress, quoted in ibid., p. 615.

70. Giddings to Julian, May 21, 1860, Julian-Giddings Correspondence (Manuscript Division, Library of Congress), cited in Berwanger, *The Frontier against Slavery*, p. 136.

CHAPTER FIVE

1. James Buchanan, Fourth Annual Message, December 3, 1860, in Irving J. Sloan, ed., *James Buchanan, 1791–1868* (Dobbs Ferry, NY: Oceana Publications, 1968), pp. 70–80.

2. Appendix, *Congressional Globe*, 36th Cong., 2d sess., February 20, 1861, pp. 242–43; cited in D. W. Meinig, *The Shaping of America*, vol. 2 (New Haven, CT: Yale University Press, 1993), p. 490.

3. Meinig, *The Shaping of America*, vol. 2, p. 499. See also Howard Cecil Perkins, ed., *Northern Editorials on Secession*, 2 vols. (New York: D. Appleton-Century, 1942).

4. November 17, 1860, quoted in Nevins, *Emergence of Lincoln*, vol. 2, p. 338.

5. CW 2:355.

6. *Congressional Globe*, 31st Cong., 1st sess., pp. 399–405; Clay, *Works*, VI, pp. 394–409.

7. Clay, *Works*, VI, p. 567.

8. Eric Foner, *Free Soil, Free Labor, Free Men: The Ideology of the Republican Party before the Civil War* (New York: Oxford University Press, 1995), p. 224.

9. T. C. Pease and J. G. Randall, eds., *The Diary of Orville Hickman Browning* (Springfield, 1925–33), vol. 1, p. 453; cited in Allen C. Guelzo, *Abraham Lincoln, Redeemer President* (Grand Rapids, MI: Eerdmans, 1999), p. 255.

10. CW 4:172.

11. CW 4:149–50.

12. *New York Herald,* January 28, 1861; cited in David Herbert Donald, *Lincoln,* p. 269.

13. Pratt, *Concerning Mr. Lincoln,* p. 47; cited in Guelzo, *Abraham Lincoln,* p. 261.

14. Joseph Story, *Commentaries on the Constitution of the United States* (Union, NJ: Lawbook Exchange, 2001), pp. 154–61 (the American people as a whole declared independence), 251–72 (critique of compact theory).

15. John C. Calhoun, *A Disquisition on Government and a Discourse on the Constitution and Government of the United States* (1851), (New York: Macmillan Publishing Co., 1953), p. 156.

16. James Madison, letter to Daniel Webster, March 15, 1833, in Philip R Fendall, ed., *Letters and Other Writings of James Madison,* Published by Order of Congress (Philadelphia: Lippincott Publishing, 1865), p. 294.

17. William H. Herndon and Jesse W. Weik, *Herndon's Life of Lincoln* (New York: Da Capo Press, 1983), p. 494.

18. Ibid., p. 386.

19. CW 5:527.

20. CW 4:256.

21. CW 4:253.

22. Ibid.

23. Buchanan, Fourth Annual Message, in Morris, *Great Presidential Decisions,* p. 221.

24. CW 4:260.

25. Akhil Reed Amar cites as possible constitutional methods of providing for secession, in addition to constitutional amendments, "nonbinding national referenda, treaties, and congressional statutes," without providing evidence that Lincoln considered any method other than amending the Constitution. Akhil Reed Amar, *Abraham Lincoln and the American Union,* 2001 University of Illinois Law Review, 1109.

26. CW 4:264–65.

27. James Madison, in Fendall, *Letters and Other Writings,* supra note 16, p. 294.

28. CW 1:428.

29. Lincoln is quoted in James M. McPherson, *Abraham Lincoln and the Second American Revolution* (New York: Oxford University Press, 1991), p. 28.

30. *Texas v. White,* 74 U.S. 700 (1869).

31. William W. Freehling, *The South vs. the South: How Anti-Confederate Southerners Shaped the Course of the Civil War* (New York: Oxford University Press, 2001); statistics derived from Francis A. Walker, comp., *The Statistics of the Population of the United States* (Washington, DC, 1972), and the U.S. Bureau of the Census, *A Century of Population*

Growth: From the First Census of the United States to the Twelfth, 1790–1900 (Washington, DC, 1909).

32. *Illinois Daily State Journal,* January 22, 1861, p. 2, cc. 1–2, scrapbook, vol. 54, John Hay Papers, Library of Congress, cited in Michael Burlingame, *Lincoln's Journalist: John Hay's Anonymous Writings for the Press, 1860–1864* (Carbondale and Edwardsville: Southern Illinois University Press, 1998), pp. 350–51.

33. David Herbert Donald, *Lincoln Reconsidered: Essays on the Civil War Era,* 3d ed. (New York: Vintage, 2001), p. 302.

34. Ibid., p. 302.

35. James G. Randall, *Constitutional Problems under Lincoln* (Urbana: University of Illinois Press, 1964 [1926]), p. 459.

36. CW 4:429.

37. Carl Schurz, *Reminiscences of Carl Schurz* (New York, 1908), vol. 3, p. 104; cited in Guelzo, *Abraham Lincoln,* pp. 283, 486.

38. Quoted in Guelzo, *Abraham Lincoln,* p. 283.

39. Quoted in Donald, *Lincoln Reconsidered,* p. 144.

40. William Whiting, *The War Powers of the President,* p. 82, footnote.

41. Quoted in ibid., p. 35.

42. Ibid.

43. Ibid., p. 167.

44. CW 4:43.

45. Mark E. Neely, Jr., *The Fate of Liberty* (New York: Oxford University Press, 1991), pp. 69–72.

46. Whiting, *War Powers,* p. 171.

47. Mark E. Neely, Jr., *The Union Divided: Party Conflict in the Civil War* (Cambridge, MA: Harvard University Press, 2002), p. 185.

48. John Christopher Schwab, *Confederate States of America, 1861–1865: A Financial and Industrial History of the South during the Civil War* (Burt Franklin, 1968), pp. 186–92.

49. For a history of Confederate conscription policy, see Albert Moore, *Conscription and Conflict in the Confederacy* (Prometheus Books, 1963).

50. Randall, *Constitutional Problems under Lincoln,* pp. 161–63.

51. See generally Neely, *The Union Divided.*

52. CW 6: 260–69.

53. CW 6: 261.

54. CW 6: 265.

55. Herndon and Weik, *Herndon's Life of Lincoln,* p. 449.

56. *Ex parte Milligan,* 4 Wallace 2 (1866).

57. General Orders No. 100, Instructions for the Government of Armies of the

United States in the Field, prepared by Francis Lieber, LL.D (Washington, DC: Adjutant General's Office, 1863; Government Printing Office, 1898).

58. CW 4:532.

59. CW 6:78–79.

60. CW 8:100–101.

61. CW 8:101.

62. Frank J. Williams, *Judging Lincoln* (Carbondale: Southern Illinois University Press, 2002), p. 109.

63. Ibid.

64. Quoted in ibid., p. 120.

65. Ibid., p. 110.

66. George E. Baker, ed., *The Works of William H. Seward*, 5 vols. (Boston: Houghton Mifflin, 1883–84), V, p. 193; cited in Neely, *The Union Divided*, p. 198.

67. Joel H. Silbey, *A Respectable Minority: The Democratic Party in the Civil War Era* (Ithaca, NY: Cornell University Press, 1983).

68. Stephen W. Sears, ed., *The Civil War Papers of George McClellan: Selected Correspondence, 1860–1865* (New York: Ticknor and Fields, 1989), pp. 595–97; cited in Freehling, *The South vs. the South*, p. 185. My analysis is indebted to Freehling's discussion of McClellan and the Northern Democrats.

69. Robert W. Johansen, *Stephen A. Douglas* (New York: Oxford University Press, 1973), p. 860.

70. Neely, *The Union Divided*, p. 198.

71. Williams, *Judging Lincoln*, p. 116.

72. CW 8:333.

73. Ward Hill Lamon, *Recollections of Abraham Lincoln, 1847–1867*, edited by Dorothy Lamon Teillard (Washington, DC: published by the editor, 1911), pp. 247–48.

74. CW 4:426.

CHAPTER SIX

1. David Herbert Donald, *Charles Sumner and the Coming of the Civil War* (New York: Alfred A. Knopf, 1961), p. 269.

2. Quoted in David Herbert Donald, *Lincoln Reconsidered: Essays on the Civil War Era*, 3d ed. (New York: Vintage, 2001), pp. 145–46.

3. Quoted in William Whiting, *War Powers of the President*, p. 79.

4. Leonard Swett, letter to Herndon, January 17, 1866, in William H. Herndon and Jesse W. Weik, *Herndon's Life of Lincoln* (New York: Da Capo Press, 1983), p. 428.

5. CW 4:532.

6. CW 2:255.

7. Quoted in Roy M. Basler, *A Touchstone for Greatness*, p. 200.

8. CW 5:48–49.

9. CW 4:270.

10. CW 5:48.

11. U.S., "Statutes at Large, Treaties and Proclamations of the United States of America," vol. 12 (Boston, 1863), p. 617.

12. CW 5:192.

13. James Mitchell, *Letter on the Relation of the White and African Races of the United States, Showing the Necessity of the Colonization of the Latter: Addressed to the President of the U.S.* (Washington, DC: Government Printing Office, 1862), pp. 4–28.

14. Francis B. Carpenter, *Six Months at the White House with Abraham Lincoln* (New York: Hurd and Houghton, 1866), p. 22.

15. CW 4:156.

16. CW 5:373.

17. Quoted in Lerone Bennett, Jr., *Forced into Glory: Abraham Lincoln's White Dream* (Chicago: Johnson Publishing, 2000), p. 459.

18. Ibid., p. 460.

19. Ibid.

20. Gregg D. Crane, *Race, Citizenship, and Law in American Literature* (Cambridge University Press, 2002), pp. 141, 146–47.

21. Philip S. Foner, *The Life and Writings of Frederick Douglass,* vol. 3 (New York, 1955), p. 267.

22. CW 5:434.

23. This point is emphasized by Bennett, in *Forced into Glory.*

24. Gideon Welles, "The History of Emancipation," *Galaxy* (April 1872): 521–32; quoted in Bennett, *Forced into Glory,* pp. 509–10.

25. Gideon Welles, *Diary of Gideon Welles* (New York: Houghton Mifflin, 1911), vol. 1, p. 152, cited in Bennett, *Forced into Glory* (Chicago: Johnson Publishing Co., 2000), p. 509.

26. Carpenter, *Six Months at the White House,* p. 291; cited in Bennett, *Forced into Glory,* p. 510.

27. Welles, *Diary of Gideon Welles,* p. 152; cited in Bennett, *Forced into Glory,* p. 511.

28. Gideon Welles in Don and Virginia Fehrenbacher, eds., *Recollected Words of Abraham Lincoln* (Stanford, CA: Stanford University Press, 1996), p. 23; cited in Allen C. Guelzo, *Abraham Lincoln: Redeemer President* (Grand Rapids, MI: Eerdmans, 1999), p. 346.

29. John Niven, *Gideon Welles: Lincoln's Secretary of the Navy* (New York: Oxford University Press, 1973), p. 222.

30. Quoted in John Hope Franklin, *The Emancipation Proclamation* (Garden City, NY: Anchor Books, 1963), p. 85.

31. CW 5:535–36.

32. Edward A. Miller, Jr., *The Black Civil War Soldiers of Illinois* (Columbia: University of South Carolina Press, 1998), p. 12; Arthur Charles Cole, *Centennial History of Illinois: The Era of the Civil War, 1848–1870* (Springfield: Illinois Centennial Commission, 1919), p. 225.

33. Arthur Cole, *Centennial History of Illinois: The Era of the Civil War, 1848–1870,* (Springfield: Illinois Centennial Commission, 1919), p. 348.

34. Cole, *Centennial History of Illinois,* ibid.

35. CW 3:179.

36. CW 6:48–49.

37. CW 6:428–29.

38. CW 6:48–49.

39. Quoted in Bennett, *Forced into Glory,* p. 384.

40. Michael Burlingame and John R. Turner Ettlinger, *Inside Lincoln's White House: The Complete Civil War Diary of John Hay* (Carbondale and Edwardsville: Southern Illinois University Press, 1997), pp. 117–18.

41. William C. Harris, *With Charity for All: Lincoln and the Restoration of the Union* (Lexington: University Press of Kentucky, 1997), p. 133.

42. CW 7:51.

43. General Orders No. 14 (Richmond, Virginia: Adjutant and Inspector General's Office, March 23, 1865).

44. CW 5:520–21.

45. Paul J. Scheips, "Lincoln and the Chiriqui Colonization Project," *Journal of Negro History* 37, no. 4 (October 1952): p. 419; Nathaniel Weyl and William Marina, *American Statesmen on Slavery and the Negro* (New Rochelle, NY: Arlington House, 1971), pp. 228–29; citing L. E. Chittenden, *Recollections of Abraham Lincoln and His Administration* (New York: Harper & Brothers, 1901).

46. CW 8:403, 405.

47. *Cong. Globe,* 39th Cong., 1st Sess. 537 (1865), quoted in Andrew Kull, *The Color-Blind Constitution* (Cambridge, MA: Harvard University Press, 1992), p. 73.

48. *Cong. Globe* 1291, quoted in Kull, *The Color-Blind Constitution,* p. 78.

49. *Cong. Globe* 474, quoted in Kull, *The Color-Blind Constitution,* p. 76.

50. C. Vann Woodward, "The Political Legacy of Reconstruction," in *Reconstruction: An Anthology of Revisionist Writings,* ed. Kenneth M. Stampp and Leon F. Litwack (Baton Rouge: Louisiana State University Press, 1969), p. 518.

51. Cited in Kull, *Color-Blind Constitution,* p. 60.

52. Mark E. Neely, Jr., *The Union Divided: Party Conflict in the Civil War* (Cambridge, MA: Harvard University Press, 2002), p. 198.

53. Kevin Phillips, *The Cousins' Wars: Religion, Politics, and the Triumph of Anglo-America* (New York: Basic Books, 1999), p. 455.

54. Richard Franklin Bensel, *Yankee Leviathan: The Origins of Central State Authority in America, 1859–1877* (New York: Cambridge University Press, 1990), p. 380.

55. Cited in Eric Foner, *Free Soil, Free Labor, Free Men: The Ideology of the Republican Party before the Civil War* (New York: Oxford University Press, 1970), p. 294.

56. Chase to Beecher, December 26, 1863, Beecher Family Papers, Manuscripts and Archives, Yale University Library; cited in Kull, *Color-Blind Constitution,* p. 246.

57. See, for example, Lawanda Cox, *Lincoln and Black Freedom: A Study in Presidential Leadership* (University of South Carolina Press, 1982). Akhil Reed Amar claims that Lincoln had come "by the hour of his death to embrace a far more inclusive view of a multiracial Union of equal citizens, black and white, North and South, East and West." Akhil Reed Amar, *Abraham Lincoln and the American Union,* University of Illinois Law Review (2001), 1109.

58. CW 8:403 April 11, 1865.

59. Herndon and Weik, *Herndon's Life of Lincoln,* p. 134.

60. Tyler Dennett, ed., *Lincoln and the Civil War in the Diaries and Letters of John Hay* (New York: Dodd, Mead and Company, 1939), p. 203.

61. Bates to Lincoln, November 30, 1864, Lincoln Manuscripts, Library of Congress; cited in Bennett, *Forced into Glory,* p. 554.

62. Benjamin Butler, *Butler's Book* (Boston: Thayer, 1892), pp. 903–7; For a critique of Butler's veracity, see Mark E. Neely, Jr., "Abraham Lincoln and Black Colonization: Benjamin Butler's Spurious Testimony," *Civil War History,* XXV (March 1979), pp. 77–83. Among the scholars who find Butler's account credible are George M. Frederickson, "A Man but Not a Brother: Abraham Lincoln and Racial Equality," *Journal of Southern History* 41 (February 1975), p. 57, and Herman Belz, *Reconstructing the Union* (Ithaca, NY: Cornell University Press, 1969), p. 282, both of which are cited in Lerone Bennett, *Forced into Glory,* pp. 626–17.

63. Henry C. Whitney, *Life on the Circuit with Lincoln* (Union, NJ: The Lawbook Exchange, 2001; Boston, Estes and Lauriat, 1892), p. 4.

64. Quoted in Brooks D. Simpson, *The Reconstruction Presidents* (Lawrence: University Press of Kansas, 1998), pp. 145–46.

65. *American Federationist* 12 (September 1905): 636–37; vol. 4: 269–71; quoted in Michael Lind, *The Next American Nation* (New York: The Free Press, 1995), p. 72.

66. David Leon Chandler, *The Natural Superiority of Southern Politicians: A Revisionist History* (Garden City, NY: Doubleday, 1977), pp. 289–91.

67. Theodore Bilbo, *Take Your Choice: Separation or Mongrelization* (Poplarville, MS: Dream House Publishing Company, 1947).

68. D. W. Meinig, *The Shaping of America,* vol. 2 (New Haven, CT: Yale University Press, 1995), p. 495.

69. Foner, *Free Soil,* p. 53.

70. Ibid., p. 120.

71. Phillips, *The Cousins' Wars,* p. 444.

72. Quoted in W. Allen Salisbury, *The Civil War and the American System: America's Battle with Britain, 1860–1876* (ETR, 1992), p. 35.

73. CW 5:37.

74. CW 5:535.

75. Quoted in Foner, *Free Soil,* p. 54.

76. Quoted in Paul M. Angle, ed., *The Lincoln Reader* (New York: Da Capo Press, 1947), p. 65.

77. Bensel, *Yankee Leviathan,* p. 378.

78. CW 5:374.

79. Herndon and Weik, *Herndon's Life of Lincoln,* pp. 422–23.

80. CW 3:226.

81. CW 3:304.

82. Herndon and Weik, *Herndon's Life of Lincoln,* p. 483.

83. The Frederick Douglass Papers at the Library of Congress: "Oration by Frederick Douglass Delivered on the Occasion of the Unveiling of the Freedmen's Monument in Memory of Abraham Lincoln." (Washington, DC: Gibson Brothers Printers, 1876).

CHAPTER SEVEN

1. A number of authors have described American history in terms of a succession of "revolutions" and "republics." See, for example, James McPherson, *Abraham Lincoln and the Second American Revolution* (New York: Oxford University Press, 1992); Bruce Ackerman, *We the People: Foundations* (Cambridge, MA: Belknap Press, 1993); *The Next American Nation* (New York: The Free Press, 1995).

2. Fred M. Shelley, J. Clark Archer, Fiona M. Davidson, and Stanley D. Brunn, *Political Geography of the United States* (New York: Guilford Press, 1996), p. 79.

3. Cited in Heather Cox Richardson, *The Greatest Nation on the Earth: Republican Economic Policies during the Civil War* (Cambridge, MA: Harvard University Press, 1997), p. 94.

4. Herndon and Weik, *Herndon's Life of Lincoln,* p. 413.

5. Leonard P. Curry, *Blueprint for Modern America: Nonmilitary Legislation of the First Civil War Congress* (Nashville: Vanderbilt University Press, 1968), p. 116.

6. Leonard P. Curry, *Blueprint for Modern America: Nonmilitary Legislation of the First Civil War Congress* (Nashville: Vanderbilt University Press, 1968).

7. Phillips, *The Cousins' Wars,* p. 449.

8. Bensel, *Yankee Leviathan,* p. 252.

9. CW 3:486–87.

10. Gabor Borit, "Old Wine into New Bottles: Abraham Lincoln and the Tariff Reconsidered," *The Historian* 28, no. 2 (1966): 309.

11. Reinhard H. Luthin, "Abraham Lincoln and the Tariff," *American Historical Review* 49, issue 4 (July 1944): 619.

12. Letter to Noah Swayne, enclosed as copy in Swayne to Carey, February 4, 1865, Carey Papers, Box 78; cited in Luthin, "Abraham Lincoln and the Tariff," p. 629.

13. CW 4:212.

14. Paul Bairoch, *Economics and World History: Myths and Paradoxes* (Chicago: University of Chicago Press, 1993), p. 35.

15. Quoted in Alfred E. Eckes, *Opening America's Market: U.S. Foreign Trade Policy Since 1776* (Chapel Hill: University of North Carolina Press, 1995), p. 30.

16. J. Garraty and M. Carnes, *The American Nation: A History of the United States* (New York: Addison Wesley Longman, 2000), 10th ed.

17. Bruce D. Porter, *War and the Rise of the State* (New York: The Free Press, 1994), p. 259.

18. Paul Kennedy, *The Rise and Fall of the Great Powers: Economic Change and Millitary Conflict from 1500 to 2000* (New York: Random House, 1987), p. 202.

19. Bairoch, *Economics and World History,* pp. 166–67.

20. John J. Mearsheimer, *The Tragedy of Great Power Politics* (Chicago: W. W. Norton, 2001), p. 246.

21. Phillips, *The Cousins' Wars,* p. 458.

22. Ibid.

23. Ibid.

24. W. S. Woytinsky and E. S. Woytinsky, *World Population and Production: Trends and Outlook* (New York: Twentieth Century Fund, 1953), p. 83, table 40; p. 84, table 41.

25. Hinton Helper, *The Land of Gold* (1855); cited in Lind, *The Next American Nation,* p. 69.

26. H. B. Pasmore, "The Chinamen Must Go" (San Francisco, CA: J. W. Gibson, 1880), part of American 19th Century Sheet Music, copyright deposits, 1870–1885.

27. *United States v. Bhagat Singh Thind.,* 261 U.S. 204 (1923).

28. Proceedings of the Forty-third Annual Convention of the California State Federation of Labor, Long Beach, California, September 21–25, 1942, p. 225.

29. Paul Gordon Lauren, *Power and Prejudice: The Politics and Diplomacy of Racial Discrimination* (Boulder, CO: Westview Press, 1988), pp. 53–54.

30. John Morton Blum, *The Republican Roosevelt,* 2d ed. (Cambridge, MA: Harvard University Press, 1977), p. 34.

31. *American Federationist,* September 1905, vol. 12, pp. 636–37 and February 1898, vol. 4, pp. 269–71; cited in Michael Lind, *The Next American Nation* (New York: The Free Press, 1995), p. 72.

32. Quoted in C. Vann Woodward, *The Strange Career of Jim Crow* (New York: Oxford University Press, 1974), pp. 73–74.

33. Friedrich List, *National System of Political Economy*, trans. Sampston S. Lloyd, (New York: A. M. Kelley, 1966).

34. Stephen C. Neff, *Friends But No Allies: Economic Liberalism and the Law of Nations* (New York: Columbia University Press, 1990), p. 65.

35. For a comprehensive study of List's global influence in the nineteenth and twentieth centuries, see Roman Szporluk, *Communism and Nationalism: Karl Marx versus Friedrich List* (New York: Oxford University Press, 1988).

36. Richard J. Samuels, *"Rich Nation, Strong Army": National Security and the Technological Transformation of Japan* (New York: Cornell University Press, 1994).

37. Bairoch, *Economics and World History*, p. 90.

38. Ibid., p. 41.

39. Bureau of the Census, *Historical Statistics*, vol. 2, pp. 885–90; cited in Eckes, *Opening America's Market*, p. 302n1.

40. www.canadahistory.com/sections/documents/docmacdonaldnationalpolicy.htm

41. Bairoch, *Economics and World History*, p. 53.

42. John Macdonald, May 12, 1882, in *Canada, House of Commons, Official Debates, 1882* (Ottawa: Maclean, Roger, and Co., 1882), vol. 12, p. 1477; cited in Lind, *The Next American Nation*, p. 67.

43. Bairoch, *Economics and World History*, p. 39.

44. Ibid., p. 40.

45. Karl Marx and Friedrich Engels, *The Civil War in the United States* (New York: International Publishers, 1937), pp. 236–37.

46. Elting E. Morison, ed., *The Letters of Theodore Roosevelt* (Cambridge, MA: Harvard University Press, 1954 [1908]), vol. 5, p. 226.

47. Calvin Coolidge, "Whose Country Is This?" 72 *Good Housekeeping* (February 1921): 14.

48. "Franklin D. Roosevelt's Editorials for the *Macon Telegraph*, April 30, 1925," http://www.cviog.uga.edu.

49. Harry Truman, *Dear Bess: The Letters from Harry to Bess Truman, 1910–1959*, ed. Robert H. Farrell (New York: Norton, 1983), p. 63.

50. *Smith v. Allwright*, 321 U.S. 649 (1944).

51. Everett Carl Ladd, ed., *America at the Polls, 1998* (University of Connecticut: Roper Center for Public Opinion Research, 1999), p. 16.

52. Quoted in Eckes, *Opening America's Market*, p. 33.

53. Quoted in William Appleman Williams, *The Tragedy of American Diplomacy* (New York: Dell Publishing, 1972), p. 35.

54. Quoted in Walter LaFeber, *The American Age: United States Foreign Policy at Home and Abroad since 1750* (New York: W. W. Norton, 1989), p. 164.

55. Henry Clay Whitney, *Life on the Circuit with Lincoln* (Boston, Estes and Lauriat,

1892), pp. 64–67, 390–404, 601, quoted in Oliver Fraysse, *Lincoln, Land and Labor 1809–1860,* trans. Sylvia Neely (Urbana, IL: University of Illinois Press, 1994).

56. TR, Osawatomie speech, in Harbaugh, *Writings,* p. 319.

57. CW 4:201–3.

58. Timothy Egan, "As Others Abandon Plains, Indians and Bison Come Back," *New York Times,* May 27, 2001, section 1, page 1; Timothy Egan, "Vanishing Point: Amid Dying Towns of Rural Plains, One Makes a Stand," *New York Times,* December 1, 2003, section A, page 1; Peter T. Kilborn, "Vanishing Point: Bucking Trend, They Stay on Plains, Held by Family and Friends," *New York Times,* December 2, 2003, section A, page 1.

59. Willis Peterson and Yoav Kislev, *The Cotton Harvester in Retrospect: Labor Displacement or Replacement?* (St. Paul: University of Minnesota Press, 1991), pp. 1–2.

60. William Julius Wilson, *The Declining Significance of Race: Blacks and Changing American Institutions* (Chicago: University of Chicago Press, 1980), p. 65.

61. See generally Nicholas Lemann, *The Promised Land: The Great Black Migration and How It Changed America* (New York: Vintage Books, 1992).

62. Albert Votaw, "Hillbillies Invade Chicago," *Harper's,* February 1950, cited in Jim Goad, *The Redneck Manifesto* (New York: Simon & Schuster, 1997), p. 96.

63. Lewis M. Killian, *White Southerners* (New York: Random House, 1970), cited in Goad, *The Redneck Manifesto,* p. 96.

64. United States Senate Republican Policy Committee, "A Bad Law in Need of Repeal: The History & Economics of Davis-Bacon," September 18, 2002.

CHAPTER EIGHT

1. Jefferson Davis, *The Papers of Jefferson Davis,* "Second Inaugural Address" (Baton Rouge, Louisiana State University Press, 1971), vol. 8, p. 55.

2. Jefferson Davis, *The Papers of Jefferson Davis,* "Farewell Address to the U.S. Senate" (Baton Rouge, Louisiana State University Press, 1971), vol. 7, pages 18–23.

3. Carl Becker, *The Declaration of Independence: a study in the history of political ideas* (New York: Harcourt, Brace and Company, 1922), p. 147.

4. Alexander H. Stephens, "Cornerstone Address, March 21, 1861," in Frank Moore, ed., *The Rebellion Record; A Diary of American Events with Documents, Narratives, Illustrative Incidents, Poetry, etc.* (New York: O. P. Putnam, 1864), pp. 44.

5. Henry Clay, Address to the Colonization Society of Kentucky, December 17, 1829.

6. Stephens, "Cornerstone Address," supra note 4.

7. Quoted in Vivien Green Fryd, *Art and Empire: The Politics of Ethnicity in the United States Capitol, 1815–1860* (Athens: Ohio University Press, 2001), p. 206.

8. Quoted in ibid., p. 200.

9. Ibid., p. 188.

10. CW 4:438.

11. CW 4:439.

12. John Hay, diary.

13. CW 7:19–21.

14. Everett, in Svend Petersen, *The Gettysburg Addresses: The Story of Two Orations* (New York: Frederick Ungar Publishing Company, 1963), p. 137.

15. CW 5:388–389.

16. CW 6:409–10.

17. George Washington, June 8, 1783.

18. Alexander Hamilton, *The Federalist: A Commentary on the Constitution of the United States: A Collection of Essays* (Regnery Publishing, 1999), p. 49.

19. In Caleb Bingham, *The Columbian Orator,* ed. David W. Blight (New York: New York University Press, 1998 [1797]), pp. 234–35.

20. Andrew Jackson, "Farewell Address," cited in Robert Vincent Remini, *Andrew Jackson: The Course of American Democracy, 1833–1845.* (Baltimore: Johns Hopkins University Press, 1998), p. 414ff.

21. Robert L. Meriwether and W. Edwin Hemphill, eds., *The Papers of John C. Calhoun,* vol. 1 (Columbia: University of South Carolina Press, 1959–), pp. 329–30.

22. Robert T. McMahan, Diary, entry of September 13, 1863, State Historical Society of Missouri, Columbia; quoted in James M. McPherson, *For Cause and Comrades: Why Men Fought in the Civil War* (New York: Oxford University Press, 1997), pp. 113, 217n28.

23. Peter Welsh to Mary Welsh, February 3, 1863, Peter Welsh to Patrick Prendergast, June 1, 1863, in Laurence Frederick Kohl and Margaret Cosse Richard, eds., *Irish Green and Union Blue: The Civil War Letters of Peter Welsh* (New York, 1986), pp. 65–66, 102; cited in McPherson, *For Cause and Comrades,* pp. 113, 217n30.

24. CW Reply to Committee from Religious Denominations of Chicago, September 13, 1862.

25. CW 4:24.

26. CW 4:240.

27. CW 4:240.

28. See generally Gabor Borritt, *Lincoln and the Economics of the American Dream* (Chicago: University of Chicago Press, 1978).

29. Daniel Webster, *The Works of Daniel Webster* (Boston: Little, Brown, 1851), vol. 3, p. 70.

30. CW 2:364.

31. CW 5:51.

32. CW 3:315.

33. CW 1:452.

34. H. L. Mencken, "Gettysburg," *The Smart Set* (May 1920); quoted in Thomas J. DiLorenzo, *The Real Lincoln: A New Look at Abraham Lincoln, His Agenda, and an Unnecessary War* (Roseville, CA: Prima Publishing, 2002), pp. 114, 293n50.

35. Quoted in Samuel Flagg Bemis, *John Quincy Adams and the Foundations of American Foreign Policy* (New York: Alfred A. Knopf, 1965), p. 181.

36. Samuel Evans to father, September 13, 1863, Evans Family Papers, Ohio Historical Society, Columbus; cited in McPherson, *For Cause and Comrades,* pp. 112, 216n26.

37. Thomas Jefferson to John Taylor, *Writings,* vol. 7, pp. 263–66; cited in D. W. Meinig, *The Shaping of America: A Geographical Perspective on 500 Years of History,* vol. 2, *Continental America, 1800–1867* (New Haven, CT: Yale University Press, 1993), p. 462.

38. Edward Everett, *Orations and Speeches on Various Occasions* (Boston: Little, Brown, 1885), vol. 4, p. 624.

39. Quoted in William L. Vance, *America's Rome,* vol. 2, *Catholic & Contemporary Rome* (New Haven, CT: Yale University Press, 1989), p. 210.

40. William Ware, *Sketches of European Capitals* (Boston: Phillips, Sampson & Co., 1851), quoted in William L. Vance, *America's Rome,* vol. 2, *Catholic and Contemporary Rome* (New Haven: Yale University Press, 1989), p. 201.

41. Quoted in Michael Lind, *Hamilton's Republic* (New York: The Free Press, 1997), pp. 116–19.

42. Daniel Webster, "Discussion of the Greek Question, in the House of Representatives" (Boston: Printed at the Office of the Howard Gazette, No. 1 Dock Square); G. A. Gamage, publisher; Charles Crocker, printer, 1824.

43. CW 2:115–16.

44. CW 4:202.

45. CW 4:236.

46. CW 4:240.

47. First Inaugural.

48. CW 3:221–22.

49. CW 3:301.

50. CW 3:303.

51. Thomas Jefferson to John Adams, September 4, 1823, Library of Congress, http://www.loc.gov/exhibits/jefferson/202.html.

52. Thomas Jefferson to Joseph Priestly, November 1802, in Paul Leicester Ford, ed., *The Works of Thomas Jefferson,* 12 vols. (New York: G. P. Putnam's Sons, 1904–1905), vol. 8, p. 179; quoted in Martin Malia, *Russia under Western Eyes: From the Bronze Horseman to the Lenin Mausoleum* (Cambridge, MA: Belknap Press, 1999), p. 57.

53. Quoted in George Prentice Pierce, *Biography of Henry Clay* (New York: John Jay Phelps, 1831), pp. 133–34.

54. Clay to Hughes, March 19, 1848, copy CPP; cited in Remini, *Henry Clay,* p. 701.

55. Speech to Louis Kossuth, January 9, 1852, in Clay, *Works,* vol. 3, 221–24, cited in Remini, *Henry Clay,* p. 778.

56. CW 3:357.

57. CW 2:4.

58. Quoted in Tzetan Todorov, *On Human Diversity: Nationalism, Racism, and Exoticism in French Thought* (Cambridge, MA: Harvard University Press, 1993), p. 245; cited in Lind, *The Next American Nation,* p. 231.

59. Quoted in Louis Dumont, *German Ideology: From France to Germany and Back* (Chicago: University of Chicago Press, 1994), p. 230.

60. Cited in "Revolution: IV. World Impact," Houghton Mifflin, http://college.hmco.com/history

61. Volney, *Ruins of Empires,* p. 69.

62. Cited in Hugo Ball, *Flight Out of Time* (Berkeley: University of California Press, 1996), p. 118; and in Christoper Coker, *Twilight of the West* (Boulder, CO: Westview Press, 1998), p. 13.

63. D. P. Crook, *The North and South and the Powers* (New York: John Wiley, 1974), p. 10.

64. CW 6:64.

65. Quoted in Phillips, *The Cousins' Wars,* p. 474.

66. J. Rufus Fears, ed., *Selected Writings of Lord Acton,* vol. 1, *Essays in the History of Liberty* (Indianapolis: Liberty Fund, 1985), p. 363.

67. E. B. Washburne, *Recollections of a Minister to France, 1869–1877,* 2 vols. (London: Sampson Low, Marston, Searle & Rivington, 1887), vol. 1, pp. 137–38; cited in Graham Robb, *Victor Hugo* (New York: W. W. Norton, 1997), p. 448.

68. Harry Magdoff, *Imperialism: From the Colonial Age to the Present* (New York: Monthly Review, 1978), pp. 29, 35.

69. Robert A. Dahl, *How Democratic Is the American Constitution?* (New Haven, CT: Yale University Press, 2001), p. 127.

70. Herbert Mitgang, "Abraham Lincoln: Friend of a Free Press," *Sino-American Relations: An International Quarterly* 18 (spring 1992): 106.

71. Albert Gallatin, "Peace with Mexico" (1847), in Henry Adams, ed., *The Writings of Albert Gallatin,* 3 vols. (1879; reprint ed., New York: Antiquarian Press, 1960), vol. 3, pp. 581–86; quoted in Reginald Horsman, *Race and Manifest Destiny: The Origins of American Racial Anglo-Saxonism* (Cambridge, MA: Harvard University Press, 1981), pp. 269–70.

72. Kevin Phillips, *The Cousins' Wars: Religion, Politics, and the Triumph of Anglo-America* (New York: Basic Books, 1999), p. 445.

73. Quoted in John McCardell, *The Idea of a Southern Nation: The Southern Nationalists and Southern Nationalism, 1830–1860* (New York: W. W. Norton, 1979), p. 276.

74. John Fiske, "Manifest Destiny," *Harper's* (March 1885), quoted in H. W. Brands, *What America Owes the World: The Struggle for Foreign Policy* (Cambridge: Cambridge University Press, 1998), p. 16.

75. Quoted in John McCardell, *The Idea of a Southern Nation.*

76. George B. Baker, ed., *The Works of William H. Seward* (New York: AMS Press, 1972 [1884]), p. 575.

77. William H. Seward to the United States Senate, January 12, 1861; quoted in Richard Franklin Bensel, *Yankee Leviathan: The Origins of Central State Authority in America, 1859–1877* (New York: Cambridge University Press, 1990), p. 18.

78. Works of William H. Seward, 1:51–52, quoted in Gregg D. Crane, *Race, Citizenship, and Law in American Literature* (Cambridge: Cambridge University Press, 2002), p. 49.

79. CW 4:240.

80. CW 2:245.

INDEX

—◆◆◆—